Limited Classical Reprint Library

LECTURES

ON

THE BOOK OF PROVERBS

BY THE

REV. RALPH WARDLAW, D.D.

EDITED BY HIS SON,

THE REV. J. S. WARDLAW, A.M.

VOL. 1.

Foreword by
Dr. Cyril J. Barber

Klock & Klock Christian Publishers, Inc.
2527 GIRARD AVE. N.
MINNEAPOLIS, MINNESOTA 55411

Originally published by
A. Fullerton & Co.
London, 1861

4/915

ISBN: 0-86524-042-6

Printed by Klock & Klock in the U.S.A.
1981 Reprint

FOREWORD

Ralph Wardlaw (1779-1853) made an impact on Scottish congregationalism that survived long after his death. A descendant of Henry Wardlaw, bishop of St. Andrews and founder of the university in that city, Ralph was reared in Glasgow and following the completion of his studies for his baccalaureate degree, decided to enter the ministry. He chose to study in the theological school associated with those who had succeeded from the established church, where he had the good fortune to study under Dr. George Lawson, the famous expositor. Wardlaw so emulated his mentor that, in time, he even surpassed the greatness of Dr. Lawson in the comprehensiveness of his insights and the clarity of his expression.

Dr. William Lindsay Alexander, in his *Memoirs of the Life and Writings of Ralph Wardlaw, D.D.*, says:

> As the life of a great man is in the general composed of the history of his thoughts and actions, that of a great writer in particular is composed of the history of his thoughts.

Dr. Alexander then goes on to show how Ralph Wardlaw was both a great man and a great writer. He was also a gifted preacher and an able teacher, and while offered professorships in the universities of London, Birmingham and Manchester, chose to remain in Glasgow.

In 1818 Yale College (later to become Yale University) honored Ralph Wardlaw with a doctorate. Of this honor his biographer has the following comment:

> Mr. Wardlaw's reputation as a theologian and as a preacher was now such that his Alma Mater might have done herself credit, had she bestowed on him an appropriate mark of her approbation by conferring on him a theological degree. In the present day the University of Glasgow would not have overlooked the claims of so distinguished an alumnis; but in those days the spirit of ecclesiastical bigotry still predominated in the academic senate and forbade any recognition to be taken of the claims of one who had had the audacity to dissent from the [established] church . . . however eminent his talents and attainments, or however great his services to the common cause of Christianity. It was reserved, therefore, for a transatlantic college to do him the justice and itself the honour of conferring upon him the degree of Doctor of Divinity.

In a day when most pastorates last for only two-to-four years, the fact that Dr. Wardlaw held a single charge for fifty years is sufficient to command our attention. It proves that he was not only a capable administrator, but also a minister of the Gospel possessed of the ability to continuously feed and nourish the flock over whom God had made him an overseer.

After eight years as pastor of the North Albion Street Chruch (later compelled to build a larger sanctuary on West George Street), the congregation decided to establish the Glasgow Theological Academy in order to provide adequate training for those desiring to enter the ministry of the Congregational Church. In addition to his pastoral duties, Dr. Wardlaw was now appointed to the position of Professor of Systematic Theology. It is to Ralph Wardlaw's credit that he was able to discharge both areas of responsibility with the utmost grace and wisdom so that the church and school which it had founded were able to flourish.

An evangelical committed to upholding the truth of the Word, Ralph Wardlaw became in his day one of the best known preachers in Scotland. He also took a keen interest in missions and was frequently invited to address missionary conferences. While he authored only fifteen books during his lifetime, many of his expository and theological studies were prepared for publication after his death. Among these there stand his famous *Lectures on the Book of Proverbs* and *Gospel of John.*

In these volumes we find the thoroughness of preparation, keenness of logic, loyalty to the Scriptures as the inspired Word of God to man, and interest in the practical application of biblical truth to social issues, which made his messages relevant to those who first heard them. We are indeed privileged that his study of the *Book of Proverbs* is now available again.

Dr. Cyril J. Barber
Author, *The Minister's Library*

PREFACE.

Some years have now elapsed since my venerated Father's " Systematic Theology" made its appearance, under the editorial care of the Rev. J. R. Campbell, A. M., of Bradford; whose valuable services in carrying that work through the press, I would here, in my own name, and that of others, gratefully acknowledge.

It is a work for the *few* rather than the *many*—for the theologian rather than for the ordinary student of God's Word; and a desire has been repeatedly expressed, since my return from India, for the publication of some other portions of my father's writings, of a less elaborate character, and likely to prove of more general interest. Arrangements have, accordingly, been made, as already intimated, for the issue of a Series of Volumes, commencing with his Lectures on the Book of Proverbs.

These Lectures were delivered on the Lord's day morning, in the ordinary course of his ministry. Their delivery extended over a long period, numerous interruptions having been occasioned by absence from home, and various incidental circumstances. They were commenced in the close of 1838, and finished in January 1844.

By those privileged to hear them they were much admired; and the request was frequently and urgently made for their publication; but the continuous pressure of other engagements, numerous and varied, rendered compliance with it impracticable. Had he himself prepared the Lectures for the press, some portions would, in all probability, have been recast, and the whole, having received his finishing touch, would have appeared in a more perfect form.

The recent works of Arnot and Bridges, may tend to diminish the interest these Lectures might have awakened had they been given to the public immediately after their delivery. Still they have their peculiar characteristics, differing widely from either of the works referred to, both in style of thought and mode of illustration; and they may to some present attractions which the others fail to afford.

It is right to mention, that it has been found necessary to bring them within narrower limits than they would have occupied had they been printed entire. This has been accomplished chiefly by the omission, in whole or in part, of hortatory matter at the close of many of the Lectures, which it was thought unnecessary to retain; and by the further omission, to some extent, of passages in which the same sentiment is illustrated afresh, in very similar language. Of this there are frequent instances; for, in the Book of Proverbs, some subjects recur again and again, with at most but slight shades of difference; and as, in a course of Lectures extending over so long a period, they came up at considerable intervals of time, the Lecturer felt at liberty to enlarge upon them as they arose, and anew to press them home on the conscience and the heart. The propriety of avoiding, in some measure, the repetition of these passages in a printed volume, will be at once apparent. Should such repetition be occasionally noticed, it will be pardoned on the ground that the subject is, in every instançe, one of practical importance—that importance being indicated by the very frequency with which it appears on the sacred page.

Of *wisdom*, as it occurs in the eighth chapter and some other parts of this Book, a different view is adopted from that usually held, at which some will, no doubt, be surprised; though all acquainted with the Author's character will be ready to admit, that it was not adopted hastily, and still less from love of singularity. To the ordinary interpretation he long clung. " All my predilections," he writes, " were in favour of that interpretation; I was reluctant to abandon it, and would gladly have kept by it could I have done so consistently with sound principles of exegesis. Should others be disposed still to adhere to it I should not be inclined to argue the point keenly with them."

Two Lectures on *Temperance,* founded on the first verse of the 20th chapter, which appear in the Second Volume, have been given in full; and one on the close of the 23d chapter, has been introduced in connexion with them, having been delivered in that order. These Lectures created considerable excitement at the time, especially among the advocates of the *Total Abstinence* cause, many of whom attended on the occasion. Notes were taken by some, and the Lectures printed and circulated in a very garbled form, accompanied by strictures more bitter than hurtful. The principles laid down on the question were those of mature thought, and possess equal interest and importance still.

A considerable time has elapsed since the intended publication of these volumes was announced. The delay has arisen from causes over which neither editor nor publisher had any control, and will be pardoned.

For anything in the form of a note the editor must be held responsible.

J. S. WARDLAW.

MILLBURN HOUSE, RENFREW,
    December 1st, 1860.

LECTURE I.

Prov. i. 1.

"The Proverbs of Solomon, the son of David, king of Israel."

Here is the Title of the Book—"The Proverbs of Solomon." There is no necessity, however, from this title, for considering the collection, in the precise state in which we now have it, as the work of Solomon. The proverbs which the Book contains were all his; but the selection and arrangement of them appear, from the very statements of the Book itself, to have been made by different hands. In chap. xxv. 1, we read,—"These are also proverbs of Solomon, which the men of Hezekiah king of Judah copied out." "The men of Hezekiah" were, without question, "holy men of God," prophets, appointed by that eminently pious prince to the execution of the good work. By whom the previous and larger part of the collection was made, we cannot with certainty say— Agur, possibly, and Ezra, and others. But the proverbs forming the contents of the Book had been partly written by Solomon, and partly spoken and taken down from his lips.

Solomon was successor to his father David, and swayed the sceptre of Israel for forty years. He has obtained, by way of eminence, the designation of *The wise man;* and as this Book, had it been the only source of our judgment of him, is itself sufficient to vindicate his title to the distinction, we are naturally led to notice the origin and the recorded extent of his wisdom.

I.   A

Youth, and especially youth in high station,—born to
wealth and honour, and, above all, heir to a throne,—is in
proverbial hazard of being high-minded, self-sufficient, and
reckless of control.   Solomon was to the young, in the outset of his career, an eminent example of the contrary;—of
humility, and self-diffidence, and pious dependence upon
God.   How beautiful! how interesting and instructive the
manifestation of these lovely features of character, at the
commencement of his public life!   When God said, "Ask
what I shall give thee," his reply was, "O Lord my God,
thou hast made thy servant king instead of David my
father: and I am but a little child: I know not how to go
out or come in.   And thy servant is in the midst of thy
people which thou hast chosen, a great people, that cannot
be numbered nor counted for multitude.   Give therefore
thy servant an understanding heart to judge thy people, that
I may discern between good and bad: for who is able to
judge this thy so great a people?"*   Here we have the
origin of Solomon's unparalleled wisdom.   And yet, in
one sense, it preceded the answer to his request.   Was
not the request itself a proof of it?   Yes, my young
friends, in that request it was manifest that he had already
the best of wisdom—"the fear of the Lord,"—the principles
of early piety.   And these, too, we can trace to their origin,
not only as to the divine influence which inspired them, but
as to the human means by which that influence operated,
" Hear, ye children, the instruction of a father, and attend
to know understanding.   For I give you good doctrine, forsake ye not my law.   For I was my father's son, tender
and only beloved in the sight of my mother.   He taught
me also, and said unto me, Let thine heart retain my words:
keep my commandments, and live," Prov. iv. 1—4.   He
owed much, then, as many among us also do, to parental instruction.   When he was born, the pleasing intimation was
made, by a divine message to his father, that the special favour
of Jehovah rested upon him; the name being by the same

* Compare the whole passage, 1 Kings iii. 5—15.

authority given him of *Jedidiah*—the beloved of the Lord, (2 Sam. xii. 24.) And afterwards the expectations of David were raised high respecting him, although in the language there is a reference to a greater than Solomon, in whom it received its higher and more perfect fulfilment, (1 Chron. xxii. 9, 10.) This incident of his early choice was a fair commencement of the verification of all the hopes which intimations so remarkable had inspired. Let all, and especially the young, learn from his example, to whom they should apply, not only for the production and progress of those religious principles and affections of which the early exercise is the wisdom of youth, and the late exercise, amid the maturity of experience, the wisdom of age;—but also, for acuteness of discernment, enlargement of comprehension, and general illumination of mind, to fit them for the acquisition of all descriptions of knowledge, as well as to guide them successfully to its attainment. The powers by which all knowledge is acquired are, in all their variety of degrees, His gift. "There is a spirit in man ; and the inspiration of the Almighty giveth them understanding," Job xxxii. 8. All the mind in the universe is from Him. The human mind was His, when its powers were in all their original vigour and expansion, undebased and uncontracted by the power of evil. And still, in the inscrutable arrangements of his providence, according to the dictates of his sovereign will, it is He that makes the mind of the philosopher differ from that of the idiot,—conferring on the former faculties and means of their improvement, associated with an awful responsibility, of which the conscious possessor too often, in the plenitude of a lofty self-sufficiency, thinks not; but for the violation of which the solemn reckoning at last will make him envy the man whose destitution of them saves him from so fearful an account. The philosopher and the genius may forget to trace their powers to the true source; but it is He,—the omniscient God—that "teacheth man knowledge." Let the powers and the means be ever ascribed to Him, by which knowledge is obtained; and let the knowledge itself, when obtained, be consecrated to His glory.

The extent of the wisdom of Solomon is briefly sketched, 1 Kings iv. 29—34. The son of Sirach, in the apocryphal book of Ecclesiasticus, says of him, that "he was a flood filled with understanding; that his soul covered the whole earth; and that he filled it with parables." This is the language of hyperbole, and befits more an apocryphal than an inspired book; but it shows the height of estimation in which the wisdom of Solomon was held.

In the spirit of national partiality and vanity, which engender the disposition to exaggerate whatever contributes to our country's glory, the Jewish historian Josephus magnifies the three thousand proverbs of Solomon to three thousand *books* of proverbs; and it is not the only instance in which he is chargeable with the same fault,—a fault which, however the principle from which it springs may be natural and commendable, is a very serious one in a historian; and may, in some cases, be productive of no trivial evils.

The Bible is not given to teach us philosophy, but religion; not to show us the way to science, but the way to holiness and to heaven. Notwithstanding, therefore, the extent and variety of Solomon's knowledge in botany, in natural history, and other departments of science, we have in preservation none whatever of his discoveries or his speculations on such subjects.

We have only three productions of the wisdom of Solomon handed down to us; and they are all contained in the sacred canon of revelation, and are all in harmony, in their contents and their tendencies, with the other portions of the same blessed and holy Book. All that is preserved there is fitted to impart true spiritual wisdom, to change and sanctify the heart, and to regulate the life. Of the whole Old Testament canon, as it existed in his day, and as it exists in ours, the apostle Paul says:—"And that from a child thou hast known the holy scriptures, which are able to make thee wise unto salvation through faith which is in Christ Jesus. All scripture is given by inspiration of God, and is profitable for doctrine, for reproof, for correction, for instruction in righteousness; that the man of God may be perfect, throughly furnished unto all good works," 2 Tim. iii. 15—17. Of these "holy scriptures" the Book of Proverbs forms an integral and important part.

I do not think there is any reason that should lead us to conclude, that all has been preserved that ever was written by divine inspiration, any more than all that was spoken. From the mere fact of any dictate of the Spirit having been committed to writing, it does not follow that it was the divine purpose it should be preserved. A thing might be written for a temporary purpose, as well as spoken for a temporary purpose. Providence watched over, and preserved, and furnished with full evidence of authenticity and genuineness, all that divine wisdom saw needful to be transmitted to future generations, as containing the complete discovery of His mind and will, in regard to our own character, condition, and prospects.

The canon of the Old Testament appears to have been made up chiefly in the time of Ezra, and under his divinely directed superintendence. The Book of Proverbs, as forming a part of that canon, we regard as having been "given by inspiration of God," and as having, therefore, in all its contents, the sanction of Heaven. Our subjection to its dictates, therefore, is something quite different from mere deference to the judgment of a fellow-man, of extraordinary sagacity and eminent wisdom, and of unwonted extent of observation and experience. Such a man, how unparalleled soever his natural and acquired endowments, is still fallible. His authority imposes no obligation. But, considered as part of the divine oracles, the contents of this Book bind our consciences. They are from God; and not only *may* but *must* be received, and laid up in our hearts, and practised in our lives. It is not a book of which we may take or reject what we please. We must not presume to question the correctness of any of its maxims. Our only object must be to *understand* them rightly. When we do understand them, they are binding on us. We have simply to believe and obey.

This Book has, by frequent citation and allusion, the full sanction of the New Testament. Instances of quotation from it occur in Heb. xii. 5, 6, of Prov. iii. 11, 12; in James iv. 6, of chap. iii. 34; in 1 Peter iv. 8, of chap. x. 12; in Rom. xii. 20, of chap. xxv. 21, 22. I make these references the rather, for the purpose of showing you the identity, in their great principles and practical features, of the religion and the morality of the two great divisions of divine revelation,—the Old Testament and the New; between which there is frequently a disposition to make by much too wide a difference,—as if there were moral principles and practices tolerated and connived at, if not sanctioned, under the one, which are set aside and explicitly condemned under the other.

Such references in the New to the Old, at the same time show, that the Old and the New are mutually, in regard to authority, bound up in each other; so that they stand or fall together. And the entire evidence of the divine authority of the New is, by this means, brought to bear also in confirmation of the divine authority of the Old; so that we cannot consistently take the one and reject the other, but must receive or refuse both. There are, it is true, evidences of genuineness, authenticity, and inspiration peculiar to each; but from the reference of each to the other,—of the Old forward to the New, and of the New back to the Old,—the former being the introduction to the latter, and the latter the verification and completion of the former,—it is quite vain to attempt their separation, or to fancy the possibility of holding the New independently of the Old. They form together one consistent and perfect whole.

PROVERBS are short, weighty, authoritative sayings;—sententious maxims of practical wisdom. They are the condensations of human knowledge and observation, in a pithy and memorable form; resembling concentrated essences in chemistry, in which the strength of a large measure of a liquid is distilled into a few drops. The practice of expressing sentiments in this way, is very ancient; and it was common to the Jews with other oriental nations. The proverbs of the Old Testament are reckoned by eminent critics as belonging to the didactic poetry of the Hebrews. They are distinguished by the two characters of *brevity* and *elegance;* brevity being essential to their very nature, as well as necessary for aiding the memory in their retention; and their elegance giving them an attraction to taste, and contributing to fix them in the mind and promote their circulation. When I say these things, I speak of Eastern proverbs generally. Those of Holy Scripture stand on still higher ground. They are to be regarded, not as the mere recorded results of human wisdom, but as "the true sayings of God." The proverbs contained in this Book are not, by any means, to be regarded merely as ancient sayings which were in common use, and which Solomon only set himself to collect. This opinion has been adopted by some; but it is untenable. It is founded principally on the difficulty of imagining such a collection of wise sayings to be the work of one man. But this is weak ground. The difficulty arises from forgetting the passages quoted, in which the character and extent of Solomon's wisdom are described. To suppose him the mere gatherer of current sayings, is to assign him an occupation for which, surely, such wisdom as is ascribed to him was by no means necessary. Besides, there are many, very many of the sententious maxims of the Book, that could not by possibility be proverbs in the currency of other oriental nations. They are such as could be found nowhere but among a people possessing the knowledge of the true God.

The Book, throughout, bears all the marks in itself—*internal* evidence the most satisfactory, of being something infinitely superior to a mere collection of sayings in common use,—the gathered maxims of uninspired prudence. That some of them might be in currency, need not be denied. If any were, they have acquired by the place here assigned them, the full weight of divine authority.

The Book of Ecclesiastes, there can, in my opinion, be no doubt, was the production of Solomon's last days, after he had been recovered from his fearful apostasy. It contains the lessons he had learned by bitter experience in "the days of his vanity," when "his heart departed from the Lord;" and the solemn warnings which these lessons dictated to others, to keep them from the rocks on which he had well nigh irrecoverably foundered. That the Book of Proverbs was written in the same period, I am myself persuaded, from the whole style of the commencing chapters; which are strongly and affectionately monitory to youth, and are evidently dictated by a similar experience to that which dictated Ecclesiastes, of the misery arising from the evils against which he warns. His warnings are those of a man who had drunk deeply of the cup, against whose intoxicating qualities and bitter and deadly effects he lifts his monitory voice,—the voice of faithful and earnest dissuasion. The whole of the sayings are a record of his long observation of human nature, —of men and things.

That they were written in order before Ecclesiastes seems clear from chap. xii. 9, of that Book, "And, moreover, because the Preacher was wise, he still taught the people knowledge ; yea, he gave good heed, and sought out, and set in order many proverbs." This was one of the various methods which "the preacher" adopted in imparting instruction. He "gave good heed," applying himself to the object carefully ; investigating truth with deep deliberation ; not uttering hasty and crude sayings, but the results of meditation and prayer, and divine illumination. His "many proverbs" were "sought out"—not, as I have said, from other existing collections, but from wise and divinely directed observation of the circumstances, characters, and prospects of men ; and having been thus, with attentive care, sought out, they were committed to writing as they were successively framed, and then "set in order," as far as they were susceptible of arrangement, for public benefit. A wonderful book it is ! " What an inexhaustible treasure of admirable practical counsel! The more deeply it is searched into, the more will be discovered in it ; and the more attentive and close our observation of human life, and of human nature both in ourselves and others, the more of truth and accuracy will there be found in its various and valuable sayings."

The Book is usually divided into *five parts*. 1. The introductory—comprising *the first nine* chapters. This introduction is addressed principally to youth, and was, in all probability, prefixed, after the collection of proverbs, so far as made by Solomon, had been completed. 2. From chapter x. to the 16th verse of chap. xxii.: which part contains proverbs generally, though not always, unconnected. 3. From chap. xxii. 16. to the end of chap. xxiv. where the pupil is again addressed, somewhat more connectedly, as in the introduction. 4. From chap. xxv. to chap. xxix. inclusive,—which contain an additional collection of Solomon's proverbs, "copied out," by selection probably from a larger number, by such men as Eliakim, Joah, Shebnah, Isaiah, Hosea, and Micah, who lived in his reign:—and 5. Chapters xxx. and xxxi.;—the various opinions respecting whose authorship must be left till we shall arrive at that portion of the Book.

In entering on the exposition of the Book, I desire to apply—and do you, brethren, apply with me, to the source from which Solomon, its author, derived all his wisdom; that we may obtain, in answer to prayer, the Spirit's aid, so as rightly to understand its instructions; and receive that, in which we are all chiefly defective, the disposition to follow them, remembering the words of Jesus, "If ye know these things, happy are ye if ye do them."

May you, beloved brethren, enjoy the teaching of that Spirit, to give light to your minds and love to your hearts; and to prevent the indisposition to what is good, from engendering such prejudice as may come, like a film over your mental vision, and hinder your clear perception of the truth and the will of the Lord! And may the same teaching be imparted to your instructor, that he may thus be enabled, out of this treasure of "unsearchable riches," to bring forth, for your edification, and direction, your comfort and joy, your present spiritual improvement, and your final salvation, "things new and old!"

LECTURE II.

———◆———

Prov. i. 2—9.

" To know wisdom and instruction; to perceive the words of understanding; to receive the instruction of wisdom, justice, and judgment, and equity; to give subtilty to the simple, to the young man knowledge and discretion. A wise man will hear, and will increase learning; and a man of understanding shall attain unto wise counsels: to understand a proverb, and the interpretation; the words of the wise, and their dark sayings. The fear of the Lord is the beginning of knowledge; but fools despise wisdom and instruction. My son, hear the instruction of thy father, and forsake not the law of thy mother: for they shall be an ornament of grace unto thy head, and chains about thy neck."

In the Introductory Lecture I took some notice of the title and author, the general structure and arrangement of this Book, purposely avoiding all minute and elaborate discussion, my special object being the elucidation and enforcement of the important truths themselves contained in this interesting portion of the Sacred Volume.

For the same reason I should deem it an unprofitable expenditure of your time, were I to enter into critical disquisition as to the exact shades of meaning which attach to various terms of very similar import employed in this and other passages. Excepting when such distinctions become really necessary for some important practical end, it is not my intention to trouble you with them.

From verse second to verse sixth, we have a statement of the *general design* of the Book.

The *first* object here indicated, in regard to the readers of it, is that they may "*know*," that is, *understand aright* "wisdom and instruction"—the wisdom and instruction that

come from the highest source,—divine wisdom,—divine instruction.

The general idea of wisdom is, that it consists in the
choice of the best ends, and of the best means for their
attainment. This definition admits of application both in a
lower and in a higher department. In the first place, it
may be applied to the whole conduct of human life, in all
its daily intercourse and ordinary transactions, and amidst all
its varying circumstances. We stand in different relations;
we occupy different conditions; we are subjected to different
trials; we are exposed to different temptations; our lot is
characterized by different changes, difficulties, and perplexing incidents; one day, one hour, may shift our position,
and require an entire alteration of our course. To accommo-
date our conduct to these variations,—to suit to all of them
the application of the great general principles and precepts
of the divine law, and to "guide our affairs with discretion"
in them all—requires "*wisdom.*" And for enabling us to act
our part rightly, creditably, and usefully, from day to day,
there is, in this Book, an immense fund of admirable counsel,
and salutary direction.

And then, secondly, the knowledge of wisdom may be
taken in its higher application, to interests of a superior
order, to spiritual duties, to the well-being of the better
part, to all that regards true religion and the salvation of
the soul. Wisdom, in this Book, is generally understood in
this its highest application, as might indeed be expected in a
book of instructions from God. We would hardly imagine
a communication from Him, confined to the mere prudential
and successful regulation of our temporal affairs. How important soever this may be in a life, of which the personal
and the social enjoyment, so long as it lasts, is to so great
an extent made up of little things and dependent on their
due adjustment;—yet in a divine communication to man, as
an immortal creature, and occupying a position, in regard to
God and his everlasting destinies, so peculiar and so pregnant with interesting results,—we cannot conceive these to
be the only, or even the principal subjects. Nor are they.

They are in every way subordinate. We shall see, ere the close of the present lecture, wherein the " Oracles of God" place the true wisdom of man.

Of important "instruction," both as it relates to temporal and to spiritual concerns, there is a vast amount compressed in this Book into narrow bounds,—presented in a condensed form. The proverbial sayings, being very generally uncon- nected with each other, so that in many instances it is hardly possible to discern any link of association or of suggestion between them, are by no means easily committed to memory in a series—in the order in which they stand. But each maxim, by itself, when rightly understood, becomes "as a nail fastened in a sure place;" and, being thus fixed in the mind, is ready for application in the practical business of life. The Book is thus fitted to store the mind with true, and excel- lent, and useful principles,—principles, not of merely specu- lative abstraction, but of daily and hourly use.

"To perceive the words of understanding"—is a phrase which may be interpreted as meaning the discrimination of these from the dictates of folly, so as to entertain the one, as worthy of consideration, and to reject the other;—the power of justly distinguishing between good and evil counsel,—that which is right in its principle and salutary in its operation, and that which is unsound and pernicious:—and, as a con- sequence of such discriminative knowledge, the possession of the necessary qualifications for being a counsellor of others; for guiding them in "the way of understanding"—keeping them from evil and conducting them to good.

But it is not enough to possess the *mere knowledge*, or *speculative understanding*, of even the most profitable max- ims of wisdom. There must be the acceptance of them, as really good, with an approving purpose of application. We must "receive the instruction of wisdom, justice, and judgment, and equity." A disposition to "receive instruction," is the first and most important lesson for all, and specially for *youth;*—an humble, docile, self-diffident temper,—a mind open to the admission of sound advice, and desirous to apply it to practice. This disposition is the opposite of self-conceit, and self-will, which are amongst the greatest obstacles to improvement.

"Justice, judgment, and equity," are terms which have different shades of import; but they may all be considered as meaning a correct apprehension of the principles of rectitude, and their impartial and judicious application, in all the private and in all the more public concerns of life: in the regulation of our own conduct; in the arbitrative settlement of appealed differences; in giving direction in cases of difficult and doubtful casuistry; or in the official administration of government. The Book is full of important and discriminative maxims, as to all that is right and just, fair and equitable, in an endless variety of situations and circumstances.

In the fourth verse, we have an instance, or more instances than one, of the different senses in which the same word is used; and especially at different stages in the history of the same language.

The word *subtilty* is now generally understood in a bad sense, as meaning a cunning, artful deceitfulness — that is when it is applied to *character*. When used in reference to metaphysical or other recondite discussions, it has the sense of minuteness and refinement of discrimination in the process of investigation or of reasoning. It is obviously in a sense analogous to this that the term is employed here. I need not say that it does not, as used by our translators in their day, signify *cunning* or *artfulness*. This is a feature of character that is odious in all, wheresoever it may be found; and it is peculiarly distressing to witness it in the youthful mind. There, an open, frank, artless, generous disposition, is what we look for and delight to find. Even when such a temper leads to occasional imprudences, we greatly prefer it to a shrewd and guileful craftiness. "Subtilty" means here—*discriminative prudence*. It may be considered as explained by the admonition of our Lord to his apostles—"Be ye, therefore, wise as serpents." And this wisdom of the serpent, He at the same time teaches them, was to be associated with the harmlessness of the dove. (Matt. x. 16.)

It is contrasted with *simplicity*. Now simplicity is sometimes used in a good sense, in contrast with subtilty in its bad sense. Thus in Psalm cxvi. 6: "The Lord preserveth the simple;" and in 2 Cor. i. 12: "Our rejoicing is this, the testimony of our conscience, that in simplicity and godly sincerity, not with fleshly wisdom, but by the grace of God, we have had our conversation in the world." But in the passage before us, "the simple" are the *foolish* and *inexperienced;* those who lack wisdom, and are in constant danger of being misled.

"To give subtilty to the simple" is not, then, to make the artless cunning; but to make the inconsiderate prudent, —the short-sighted discerning, —the foolishly wayward wisely submissive to superior guidance.

True wisdom has for its companion, in the mind that possesses it, true lowliness and self-diffidence : "A wise man will hear, and will increase learning: and a man of understanding will attain unto wise counsels." Ignorance and folly are generally self-conceited and self-confident. They don't need direction—*not they*. They are not, therefore, disposed to "*hear*,"—to listen, that is, to the instructions and counsels of others. They think it would be more seemly that others should listen to *them*. But it is a mark of true wisdom to be ever ready to hear. It is ever conscious of its own deficiency, and desirous to gain new acquisitions to its stores of knowledge,—and to lay up hints for the regulation of its future course. The more a man knows, the more sensible will he become of his ignorance. As the circle of information widens before him, he sees the more of its unexplored extent. He becomes more and more convinced of the truth of the poet's answer to the question, "What is knowledge?"—"'Tis but to know, how little can be known."

And mark it, my friends :—this *hearing* is the only way to "increase learning." A vast deal of information is many a time lost, from the mere fear and shame of discovering our ignorance; but he who hears, acquires new ideas by the intercourse of mind with mind. It is incomparably better, surely, to obtain the knowledge at the expense of the detection of our previous ignorance, so as to become wiser to-day than we were yesterday, than to retain the ignorance and forfeit the knowledge, for the sake of the false credit of having what we have not. There are few descriptions of vanity more pernicious than this.

The proverbial sayings of this book afford numberless instances of what are called *parallelisms* in Hebrew composition. The structure of this verse is an example of parallelism; the second clause corresponding very nearly in meaning with the first:—"A wise man will hear, and will increase learning; and a man of understanding shall attain unto wise counsels." While he who hears increases knowledge, he who intelligently attends to direction and counsel, grows in a profitable acquaintance with the principles of human conduct; and, while he learns to regulate his own course of life aright, acquires the capability of being himself a judicious and useful adviser of others. He "attains unto wise counsels." His understanding is enlarged and sharpened under divine teaching.

"To understand a proverb, and the interpretation," signifies, to understand at once its true original import, and the proper and beneficial application of it to practice. The word rendered "dark sayings," occurs also Psalm lxxviii. 2; Psalm xlix. 4. It means, properly, *Enigmas* or *Riddles*. These were used of old, as one of the methods of conveying instruction. It was conceived, that by giving exercise to the understanding in finding out the solution of the enigma, it was calculated to deepen on the mind the impression of the lesson which was wrapt up in it. This was not done for mere amusement, but for imparting serious instruction;—although to the young, there might, in some instances, be the blending of an intellectual entertainment with the conveyance of useful information or salutary counsel. These enigmatical maxims of wisdom were sometimes rendered the more attractive, by being thrown into the form of verse, and even being set to music. A poetical taste, and a musical ear were thus made subservient to the communication and impression of truth. To this latter practice allusion is made in the second of the two passages just quoted, "I will open my dark saying *upon the harp.*"

We have, in verse seventh, an explicit declaration of what Solomon means by *wisdom:* "The fear of the LORD is the beginning of knowledge: but fools despise wisdom and instruction." *The fear of Jehovah,** is a phrase which may fairly be interpreted as meaning *true religion*—all the principles of godliness. The same sentiment is to be found in other parts of Scripture; as in Psalm cxi. 10; and in an inspired book of much greater antiquity, Job xxviii. 12—28; a passage marked by a sublimity worthy of the lesson with which it closes;—a lesson which should be "graven with an iron pen and lead in the rock for ever." Or rather, for that is of incomparably greater consequence, which ought to be written deeply and indelibly on the heart of every youth in this assembly. O that it were!—for if it be not written there,—on a heart softened to receive it by the Spirit of God, what would avail the permanent record of it on the flinty rock? It is preserved *here*—in this Book of God,—a Book under his own special keeping, and which, while the world lasts, can never be lost:—but if it be not transcribed from the book to the heart, what doth it profit?

This "fear of the Lord" is in invariable union with love, and in invariable proportion to it. You truly fear God just in proportion as you truly love him. It is founded in knowledge—in the knowledge of the divine character, especially as it is revealed in his word, and more especially still, in the gospel; where the lovely and blessed harmony of all the divine perfections is manifested in the work of man's salvation.—In Psalm xxxiv. 11, the Psalmist invites the young to him, and promises to "teach them the fear of the Lord"—to teach them, that is, the nature of true religion, in its principles and in its practice. And this is properly the *first* lesson for the young to learn. It is pronounced "*the beginning* of wisdom." All else is folly without it. All the previous part of life is spent in folly till this one lesson is

---

* It is Jehovah in the Hebrew, in all cases where Lord is printed in small capitals in the English version.

learned,—till this fear takes possession of the heart.   Every
day's observation shows us, that a vast amount of knowledge
may be accumulated in minds that are utter strangers to its
residence and power; that a man may be eminent for learning,
and science, and elegant literature, without religion—without
the indwelling principles of godliness.   Ah! how sadly true!
—and how sadly exemplified in the literary and scientific
history of our own day!   Have we not seen men—

> —— " thro' learning, and thro' fancy, take
> Their flight sublime, and on the loftiest top
> Of Fame's dread mountain sit "—

who have, at the same time, discovered a melancholy destitution of the first lesson of true wisdom—" the fear of the
Lord?"   O that I could impress the conviction on the mind
of every youth before me, that is engaged, and laudably engaged, in the pursuit of science and literature in all their departments, that valuable as their acquisitions may be, there is
one thing that is above them all in dignity, and better than
them all in real and permanent worth,—even this primary
lesson of the wisdom of Heaven.   Without this, I repeat,
all is comparatively folly; and the more ample the powers,
and the more abundant and various the learning they
enable their possessor to acquire — still the greater the
folly; because the more fearful the responsibility and the
final account of the man, who with such powers, by God
bestowed, has lived without God; who instead of inscrib-
ing on them, and on the attainments they enabled him to
make, "holiness to the Lord," has pursued his course with
a lofty independence of his Maker, and has consecrated all
to the idolatry of self; and, it may be, associated all the
light and sublimity of genius with the darkness and the
degradation of profligacy and vice.   He who pursues *any*
description of knowledge, however good and honourable in
itself, while he "forgets God," is, according to this book,
emphatically "a fool."   He may be admired by men, as a
very prodigy of science, or philosophy, or literature, and
may be adorned with all the titles of human honour, and

I.   B

send down his name to future ages with a halo of the light
of this world around it; but in the eye of God, he stands
the object of deep and merited condemnation; and, while
eulogized and extolled on earth, is pitied and deplored in
heaven. Far be it, that I should be understood as under-
valuing or disparaging human science. It is interesting and
useful to man; and its discoveries are glorifying to God.
But what I say is, in the language of a second poet—that
"an undevout astronomer is mad;" in other words, that the
man is beside himself who, while ever busied about the
works of God, disregards and forgets God himself; who lives
in disobedience to his will, and in the neglect or contumeli-
ous rejection of his revealed mercy,—providing an imaginary
immortality on earth and leaving unprovided for the real
immortality of the world to come! When I think on conduct like this, I cannot but say of those who thus "spend
the little wick of life's poor shallow lamp"—in the lofty
and devout language of a third poet—

> ——————— "When I see such games
> Play'd by the creatures of a power who swears
> That he will judge the earth and call the fool
> To a sharp reck'ning that has liv'd in vain;
> And when I weigh this seeming wisdom well,
> And prove it in th' infallible result,
> So hollow, and so false—I feel my heart
> Dissolve in pity, and account the learned,
> If this be learning, most of all deceived."

O let me recommend to you, first of all, the divine science
here and throughout this book inculcated. There can be no
infatuation more wretched than to "despise this wisdom
and instruction." Such contempt has been lamented in
tears of bitter anguish by many a one whom it has brought
ultimately to ruin. To this contempt and negligence there is,
alas! a sad tendency in the heart by nature, and it is strong
in youth. And the foolish are very often found, by the language of ridicule, tempting each other to the scorn and
mockery of religion as unmanly; as nursery prejudice and
antiquated restraint, to which no youth of spirit will submit;

or as at best befitting only the graver sobriety and dull decorum of a later stage of life. We shall have a full answer to every thing of this kind in the closing verses of this chapter. Should you hear it, as you often may, applied to the restraining and salutary lessons of parental education "in the nurture and admonition of the Lord,"—let me recommend to you, in preference, the counsel which follows—

Verse 8. "My son, hear the instruction of thy father, and forsake not the law of thy mother."

Mark, my young friends, the dark list of characters in which the *"disobedient to parents"* are placed by an inspired apostle. He ranks them with "backbiters, haters of God, despiteful, proud, boasters, inventors of evil things," and others of like stamp, Rom. i. 29—32. The command of God is, "Honour thy father and mother," Eph. vi. 2; and the judgment of God, couched in a beautiful figure, is—"The eye that mocketh at his father, and despiseth to obey his mother, the ravens of the valley shall pick it out, and the young eagles shall eat it," Prov. xxx. 17.

It is hardly necessary to say, that in all such counsels there is an implied restriction. It is implied that parental instructions, whether as to truth or duty, are in agreement with the mind and will of God made known in his word. Should they, in any case, be otherwise, no choice is left. The maxim with us all must be—"We ought to obey God rather than men," Acts v. 29. When He commands the young to obey their parents, He cannot mean to enjoin that, in obedience to *them*, they should do what involves disobedience to *Him*. Parents, on their part, should be careful that they give no orders that are out of harmony with God's word. Children, on their part, must be diffident of their own judgment, and very sure of their ground, ere they venture to decline obedience. But when any thing *is* taught, or any thing commanded, that is manifestly inconsistent with the truth or with the will of God, then comes in the solemn declaration, "He that loveth father or mother more than me, is not worthy of me!"

Youth is naturally fond—and truly the fondness is not

peculiar to youth——of what will recommend it to notice and regard. This is sought in a great variety of ways; sometimes by attention to external appearance; or by the cultivation of various attractive accomplishments. Solomon sets before you, young friends, the best of all recommendations——

Verse 9. " For they shall be an ornament of grace unto thy head, and chains about thy neck."

" The instruction of thy father" and " the law of thy mother" are to be regarded as the instruction and the law of true religion——the faith of its doctrines, and the practice of its precepts. And this is what Solomon here recommends, as the loveliest, the most beautiful, and the most precious ornament. The first question, with each one of you, ought surely to be, " On what does GOD set the highest value? What is it that is most attractive and estimable in His eyes?" He is infinite in wisdom. His judgment is infallibly right. And consider,——the judgment and taste of all whose opinion is worth having are in harmony with His;——all the wise, all the good. Would you set any value on what could recommend you only to fools? O! what avails *their* admiration and applause, how rapturously soever paid, if the eye of God loathes to look upon you; if the countenance of God frowns and turns away from you; if all holy and happy beings behold you with pity and aversion? Let me recommend to you, my youthful hearers, the beauty of early piety. O that I could so impress the conviction on your minds, that irreligion is degradation and deformity, the greatest that can attach to an intellectual and moral nature, and that of such a nature true piety is the only honour and the only loveliness, as that you might, with full purpose of heart, disown the one, and embrace the other! Alas! that in the eyes of fallen creatures, piety should so sadly have lost its charms!——They " savour not the things that be of God."

How affectingly was this perverted relish manifested, in regard to Jesus himself! His character was the perfection of sinless rectitude; yet what said the prophet of him——and how literally was it verified,——" He shall grow up before

him as a tender plant, and as a root out of a dry ground : he
hath no form nor comeliness; and when we shall see him,
there is no beauty that we should desire him," Isa. liii. 2.

His holy loveliness had no attractions for the worldly and
carnal mind.   But let *him*, my young friends, be your
pattern, who was indeed " fairer than the children of men,"
—" altogether lovely."   Seek to be like him, when, in his
early years, he showed his subjection to his heavenly Father
in his subjection to his parents on earth ; and when, as he
" grew in stature," he grew " in wisdom," " and in favour
with God and man."   The ornament of true religion is an
ornament that shall endure for ever;—that shall continue to
be your adorning where " ornaments of grace upon the
head, and chains about the neck" can be worn no more ; and
when the body which by these was decked, shall be humbled to the dust of the tomb, and be food for the loathsome
worms.   True religion is the ornament of the better, of the
immortal part—the ornament of the soul ; and shall continue
its ornament for ever in heaven.   You may read at times, on
festive days in the high places of the earth, of the elegance
and splendour of royal and courtly attire ; and your imaginations may be dazzled by the profusion of diamonds, and
pearls, and brilliants, and tasteful decorations, and costly
finery, indicating the anxiety felt and the pains expended, to
adorn this " painted piece of living clay."   Amidst all this
profusion of cost and care for such a purpose—for the passing pomp and pageantry of the hour,—ah ! how little thought
too generally is there about the adorning of the *inner man*—
" the hidden man of the heart !"—of those " ornaments of
grace," in a higher sense than that in which the word is used
here, " which are, in the sight of God, of great price," and
which shall last, in all their beauty and in all their worth,

> " When gems, and monuments, and crowns,
>   Shall moulder down to dust ! "

Let such be your adorning now, that it may be your
adorning for ever!   For you must not forget—or if you
do, it must not be by my ceasing to remind you—that the

ornaments of heaven must be put on on earth.   And in order to your putting them on here, remember where they are to be found.   Study the Bible.   Here is true religion. It is taught here, recommended here, exemplified here.   May God grant, as to every one of you, that you may rightly learn its lessons, imbibe its pure and sacred spirit, and exemplify its holy and consistent practice !

LECTURE III.

——◆——

PROV. I. 10—19.

" My son, if sinners entice thee, consent thou not. If they say, Come with us, let us lay wait for blood, let us lurk privily for the innocent without cause : let us swallow them up alive as the grave; and whole, as those that go down into the pit: we shall find all precious substance, we shall fill our houses with spoil : cast in thy lot among us; let us all have one purse. My son, walk not thou in the way with them ; refrain thy foot from their path : for their feet run to evil, and make haste to shed blood : (surely in vain the net is spread in the sight of any bird :) and they lay wait for their own blood; they lurk privily for their own lives. So are the ways of every one that is greedy of gain; which taketh away the life of the owners thereof."

WE have already considered what may be regarded as the primary and fundamental lesson of this Book ; and indeed of the whole Bible, so far as the practical counsels of it are concerned, and the ultimate design of all its discoveries :— " The fear of the Lord is the beginning of knowledge." It is in beautiful harmony with this great general lesson, that Solomon, in solicitude for the youth around him, and for the youth of all coming generations, makes his first solemn warning, a warning against the dangers of BAD COMPANY ; —" My son, if sinners entice thee—consent thou not." There is also an interesting connexion between this admonition and the previous exhortation to mind parental counsel. To such counsel the enticements of sinners are conceived to be in opposition, (the father and the mother of whom he speaks, being evidently understood to make " the fear of the Lord" the great principle and end of their tuition and training,) and to be, of course, in their tendency and result the

reverse;—so that instead of estimation and honour of the
truest and highest kind, they would infallibly bring to
shame all who hearkened to them and followed them.

"*Sinners*" is a designation sometimes used in Scripture
as the generic or universal designation of our race; to every
member of which, without exception, it is appropriate—for
" ALL have sinned and come short of the glory of God." But
it is also used, not unfrequently, of those who remain under
the power of their natural sinful lusts and passions, in dis
tinction from such as have been turned from the error of
their way, and are walking in newness of life. (See Psalm
i. 5. John ix. 31.)

Here it signifies those who do *not* fear God,—those who
hear not the instruction of their pious fathers, if they enjoy such instruction, but "forsake the law of their mother."
Against the enticements of such, the young are here affectionately admonished.—Youth is the season of ardent passions and of buoyant and sanguine hopes. Not having, as
yet, tried his strength, the young man is naturally self-confident; and, unexperienced as he is in the deceitfulness of the
world and the precariousness of temporal things, he is incredulous of the premonitions of coming evil. He smiles at
them as the gloomy presages of sombre and superstitious
minds, and exults in the lively anticipation of good. The
morning of life sparkles before his eyes in dewy freshness, and
promises, to his ardent spirit, a long day of sunshine and joy.
It is neither the purpose nor the tendency of the discoveries
of the Bible, to sadden the natural vivacity of early life; to
quench the gleam of light-hearted pleasure in the youthful
eye; to shroud the rising morn with dark clouds of melancholy. God is good. All his prohibitions are only prohibitions of what would be injurious to ourselves;—and all the
principles of which he orders the cultivation and exercise, are
inseparably associated with the attainment and enjoyment of
happiness.

But, alas! how small a proportion of mankind are under
the influence and guidance of these "great principles." And
in a world where the true fearers of God are so sadly in the

minority, those who are under their dominion cannot fail to
stand exposed to many temptations and to corresponding
hazards. They are surrounded, on all sides, by "sinners" of
every description and of every degree. They come in contact, at all points, with the infection of evil. They are in
danger, at every step, from the corrupting and deadening
power of all the varieties of irreligion,—that of the openly
profligate, and that of the creditably sober,—that of the
avowed infidel, and that of the inconsistent professor of the
faith. In a city like the one in which we dwell, such young
men as are at all inclined to the fear of God are environed
with innumerable perils. Their incipient piety, when not
yet confirmed into decided godliness, is like a spark of fire
hovering over the surface of the ocean. Allurements on the
one hand, and intimidations on the other, everywhere abound ;
and the Arch-Adversary plies all his wiles, to catch away
whatever seeds of truth and elements of goodness have been
sown in their hearts.

Of all the dangers to which the young can be exposed,
there is not one which experience pronounces more imminent
than the company and example of the ungodly. "Sinners"
are fond to have associates in their evil courses. Some of
these courses are such as cannot be pursued without associates. And in how many instances besides, is solitary vice,
—vice, of which the perpetrator has no companion but his
own conscience,—felt to be irksome and miserable ! How
often is it for the purpose of preventing the intrusions, and
silencing the annoying whispers or louder remonstrances of
this troublesome visitor, that company is courted ! "Hand
joins in hand." They keep one another in countenance.
They rally each other's spirits. They drown "dull care."
They unite in "making a mock at sin." They help each
other to "break God's bands asunder, and cast away his cords
from them," and, for the time at least, to give their foreboding fears to the winds. And, while the fearers of God, in
the exercise of a pure benevolence, rejoice with the angels of
heaven over a repenting sinner—over one who turns from
the "fatal paths of folly, sin, and death," into the paths of

wisdom, purity, and peace,—these children of the "Wicked
One" participate in his infernal pleasure, when they succeed
in seducing any from the right way, and thus obtaining an
accession to their numbers, and an encouragement to their
selfish indulgences, from the ranks of religion and virtue.

In the verses before us, Solomon evidently selects a particular case, in illustration of the counsel with which the
passage commences—"If sinners entice thee, consent thou
not." The particular case selected in exemplification, is
that of young men combining into parties for plundering
or marauding expeditions,—either against the caravans of
travellers in the desert, or into the territories of adjacent
tribes. You may, and not without reason, think that the
case is one that has very little application *to you.* And,
assuredly, I am under no serious apprehension of any of my
youthful auditors forming themselves into bands of free-
booters,—into gangs of thieves and robbers. But there are
involved in the particular exemplification, important principles, capable of general application. It shall be my aim to
bring out these principles; and in doing this, I shall avoid
dwelling on the *particular case* further than may be necessary for due illustration; conceiving that there is nothing
more unprofitable, than to spend time in dissuading from
courses which there is not the remotest likelihood of *one*
amongst my hearers following out. We have, in the first
portion of the passage, the ENTICEMENT OF SINNERS,—and
in the last, the DIVINE WARNING AGAINST IT.

The ENTICEMENT is contained in verses 11—14. "Come
with us, let us lay wait for blood, let us lurk privily for the
innocent without cause: let us swallow them up alive as the
grave; and whole, as those that go down into the pit: we
shall find all precious substance, we shall fill our houses with
spoil: cast in thy lot among us; let us all have one purse."

I wish your attention here to the style of artful temptation that is adopted,—the inducements that are held out
to compliance.

1. The first is—the *privacy and concealment* of their
villanies. "Come with us, let us lay wait for blood,

let us lurk privily for the innocent without cause."—
Even by minds that are little if at all under the influence
of the fear of God, a strong objection might be stated against
compliance with solicitation to evil because of the risk of discovery, and of consequent disgrace and punishment from
men. This very natural objection is here met and overruled.
"There is no danger," say those tempters; "we do nothing openly—we 'lay wait'—we 'lurk privily'—we take
good care not to expose ourselves—we have eluded detection
hitherto, and we shall elude it still." And they boast themselves in the very art and skill with which they have evaded
discovery, and cheated all their pursuers. And is not the
same objection many a time silenced in the same way, in
every department of wickedness?—in every description of
solicitation to evil? How often do the profligate, in coaxing
the inexperienced and unwary youth to become one of their
party, tell him, with insinuating address, how easily the
thing may be done without detection,—without father or
mother, or any one knowing at all about it! "It may be
kept perfectly secret, you know; you may depend upon our
secresy; no one of us, be assured, will ever betray you; and,
unless you choose to be such a fool as to blab it out yourself,
who is to know it? Come away. If no one finds it out—
where's the harm?"

Now, my young friends, there is only one thing which requires to be said in answer to such insinuating address.
These persons do not choose to remember, what, I fondly
trust, *you* will never allow yourselves to forget—that there
is an eye that never sleeps, always present, always wakeful,—
"Thou, God, seest me!" "There is no darkness nor shadow
of death, where the workers of iniquity may hide themselves." O beware. "Be sure your sin will find you out."
You cannot dig deep enough to hide it from the eyes of the
Lord. And if He sees it, what although it eludes the detection of every human eye! Should your sins never find a
place in any record on earth, forget not, they are recorded
in heaven, marked indelibly for judgment, in the book of
God's remembrance.

2. The second enticement is—the *courage and bold-ness* of their exploits: "Let us swallow them up alive as the grave; and whole, as those that go down into the pit."—This is the boastful language of determined bravoes. To many youthful spirits, there are few qualities so dazzling and captivating as *courage.* And some of the books which furnish lessons for early life, by presenting courage in attractive forms, and yet in association with qualities and actions far from justifiable, serve to take off from the opening mind the decided feeling of moral reprobation, which, but for such association, these qualities and actions would draw upon them. So strong, frequently, is this tendency to admire intrepid boldness, that we feel it difficult to help admiring it, even when the exploits in which it signalizes itself are in themselves unprincipled and wicked. And, as is the case in the passage before us, the imagination is artfully drawn away from the nature of the deed, of which, were it allowed to be duly contemplated, the atrocity might be startling, and is fixed on the heroism displayed in the doing of it.

Now, only change the term. For *courage,* substitute *spirit;* and we have immediately before us an every-day temptation to sin,—one in constant, hourly use,—extensively and ruinously prevalent. No charge is more dreaded by the young than that of *want of spirit*—the imputation of shrinking and dastardly timidity. A *lad of spirit* is the designation they are ambitious to attain. Now, here, too, my young friends, my warning is similar. I remind you, affectionately and seriously, how miserably perverted such terms as *courage,* and *spirit,* and others of like character, are, when the authority to be violated, and the displeasure to be incurred, and the sentence to be brought upon you, are the authority, the displeasure, and the sentence of the infinite God. Every sin is a direct defiance of omnipotence. O let not the name of *courage* be abused and desecrated by being so applied. It is *not* courage. It is insensibility. It is profanity. It is madness. (Job ix. 4. Isa. xlv. 9.)

3. The third enticement is, the *profit of crime:*—"We

shall find all precious substance, we shall fill our houses with spoil."

The allurement thus held out is that of *immediate riches;* —the acquisition at once, by a single bold adventure or two, of what it usually requires years of unrelaxing thought, and solicitude, and toil, and travail, to obtain. These seducers present the allurement of a *short cut* to wealth,—"Come with us; we shall soon make a man of you; you shall wallow in wealth immediately." And is *this* not capable of extended application? Are there no circles of companionship into which a youth may be drawn by circumstances or by solicitation, in which the old-fashioned every-day methods of making money are laughed at as spiritless and sickening; and shorter and easier ways to riches, or at least to what is necessary for the indulgence of vicious passions, are proposed and adopted? And when against particular startling practices, he ventures to raise objections on the ground of moral principle, he is coaxed, or ridiculed and bantered, out of them; or satisfied by unsound but specious arguments. He incurs the expenses I have alluded to. The funds for these must from time to time be recruited, for paying debts of vice or debts of honour; and the *how* becomes a question of agonizing perplexity and bitter disquietude. He is induced, by pressing but criminal necessity, to venture in thought on methods, or to listen to them when hinted or boldly proposed by others, from which, before, his conscience would have shrunk in horror. But that conscience has lost of its sensitiveness; and it is now to be soothed and drugged by the powerful though illegitimate pleadings of necessity. Objections are overruled and put down; and the moral obliquity of the action is as plausibly as possible covered from the arrows of self-reproach, by the force of the all-sufficient, irresistible plea—that *necessity has no law;* —the thing *must be done;* there is absolutely *no help for it.*

I hope I have not been describing a reality in the experience of any youth now hearing me. It is no mere fiction. It has many a time *been* a reality; and I warn you against whatever seductions, or enticements of sinners, might by possibility make it a reality with *you*.

4. The last consideration of an enticing nature here presented is—the *honourable union*, and the *frank and open-hearted generosity* of the fraternity by which the invitation is urged :—"Cast in thy lot among us ; let us all have one purse."

"The heart is deceitful above all things,"—and there are few ways in which its deceitfulness is more strikingly apparent than in the considerations by which even the worst, the most unprincipled of men, quiet their consciences, and get even beyond that,—plume themselves, and flatter one another with imaginary good qualities.   Confederates in the very worst of evils have valued themselves on their mutual good faith ;—their fidelity to the very engagements and oaths that constitute their chief guilt ;—their very honour and consistency in crime.

The tempters in the passage before us, are a kind of *gentlemen banditti.*   And the representation held forth of a generous, social brotherhood, pledged honour, joint stock, common risks and common profits, is not a little imposing and captivating to the youthful mind.

Is not this, too, or something akin to this, one of the enticements incessantly held out by dissipated associates in the merriment and the profligacy of vice, when they have marked out a victim of seduction, and court him to join their company? They are the *choice spirits.*   Theirs is the *good fellowship;* so open, so jovial, so kind-hearted ; so free of all the puling cant of sanctimonious grimace ; so generous and honourable to one another; so—every thing that can be wished for *enjoying life!*—But O my young friends, beware of the enticing illusion. That it *is* an illusion, let the dear-bought experience of thousands convince you, without your venturing to put it to the test of experiment for yourselves.   You would but add to the accumulation of proof and of practical warning.   It was the maxim even of a heathen moralist, that *there is no true friendship but amongst the good.*   Where there is not sound principle, union cannot be depended upon. It is but a name, an empty pretension, a deceitful lure, a snare of golden texture, for the feet of the inexperienced and thoughtless. May God deliver you from it! Again I say ―BEWARE!

Let me now request your attention to the DIVINE DISSUASION―*monitory* and *authoritative*, which follows in verses 15—19, "My son, walk not thou in the way with them; refrain thy foot from their path: for their feet run to evil, and make haste to shed blood. Surely in vain the net is spread in the sight of any bird. And they lay wait for their own blood; they lurk privily for their own lives. So are the ways of every one that is greedy of gain; which taketh away the life of the owners thereof."

1. The first thing to be noticed here is, the language of affectionate interest and trembling solicitude in which the admonition is couched;―"MY SON." Whether Solomon had any eye, as a father, to his own son, Rehoboam, we cannot with certainty say. It is more likely, that it is the language of affectionate concern for the young in general, expressing itself in *individual* address, for the sake of impression and effect―that so each youth who read the dissuasion might regard it as if he himself were personally spoken to. I call on each, therefore, now hearing me, to hear *for himself.* And if I know my own heart, I think I can adopt the address with a measure at least of the affection by which it was originally dictated―"*My son,* walk not thou in the way with them; refrain thy foot from their path." Every Christian minister, as well as every Christian parent, ought to feel for, and so to warn, the objects of his affection. How exquisite the delight of a godly parent, when he sees the child of his heart's love choosing the "fear of the Lord,"―walking in His ways, and departing from evil! How he "travails in birth" for those who are "bone of his bone, and flesh of his flesh," "until Christ be formed in them!"

And surely, to every benevolent and pious mind, there can be few sights more deeply moving than that of a young man — after a struggle, perhaps, with early impressions and the restraints and compunctions of conscience — giving way before temptation, yielding to the enticements, joining the company, and lending—at first a timid, but afterwards a more prompt and daring hand to the practices of the ungodly;—like the heedless insect, insensible of its danger, wheeling and fluttering, in sportive mazes, round the consuming flame;—like the gallant ship, that has come within the outermost slowly-circling eddies of the whirlpool, and is gradually, and with increasing celerity, sucked in to its destruction! When we behold such a youth, incredulous of warning because unconscious of his peril, thus going forward to irretrievable shame and ruin, it is not anger that is waked in our bosoms; it is pity; it is tender anxiety; it is compassionate and thrilling fear. Our heart swells; our eye fills; our hand is stretched out; our voice is lifted up in the accents of earnest and tender expostulation—"MY SON, walk not thou in the way with them; refrain thy foot from their path."

2. Mark, in the second place, the *extent to which the admonition goes.*—It is not to a gradual but an immediate; it is not to a partial but an entire, abandonment. It advises complete and instant separation; a renouncing of all intercourse; and a keeping cautiously and constantly aloof; —"Walk not thou in the way with them; refrain thy foot from their path."

This is the counsel of sound wisdom, not that of Solomon only, but of GOD. Half-measures will not do. There must be no tampering with temptation — no compromise — no partial adoption of the practices of sinners, in the hope, or with the resolution of stopping and retracing your steps when you have advanced a certain length. Would you swallow poison by degrees to try how much your constitution would bear,—how far you could go without actual suicide? No. You must not only *not comply,*—you must not *listen.* He who has listened, has half complied; and he who makes one step in compliance, wretchedly deludes himself, if he imagines he can recede at pleasure, or can tell confidently how far he is to go. O do not think of trying your own strength of principle and power of **self**-command. Rather, let the *first* exertion be, to resist **the** *first* solicitations to evil; or, if with these you have unhap-pily complied, to arrest your progress at the present **point**. To try your own strength is presumption; and God **helps** not the presumptuous. He "giveth grace unto *the lowly*."

3. In immediate connection with this, and partly indeed identical with it,—consider *to what extremes* the *commence-ments of evil ultimately lead :*—often to such extremes **as** the youth who is enticed into wicked company never antici-pated,—never dreamed of, or imagined it within the **range** **of** the possible that he should ever endure even to **witness**, far less to participate :—"For their feet run to evil, **and** make haste to shed blood."

There is a natural and fearful progress in sin. **Success** in it is a curse; for it is an encouragement to go on. **In** the course of advancement, the inclination onward **gains** strength, while the power of receding declines. **Beware** then, I pray you, of *first steps*. Smile not in self-confident scorn at the well-meant but needless warning. Many have scorned it before you, whose scorn has been turned into **the** bitterness of unavailing regret, when miserable **experience** has forced upon them the lesson of their folly. **Deem** nothing impossible for you, that it is within the **reach of** human power to do in the form of evil, if you have **once** given way to the violation of principle. You may **not only** go lengths that will ruin yourselves, you may contri**bute to** the shame and ruin of the companions and victims of **your** vices; you may ruin families and fortunes; you may **break** honest and sensitive hearts; you may bring down grey **hairs** with sorrow to the tomb,—the grey hairs of your own **loving** but disappointed and grief-stricken parents, or of the **fathers** and mothers of your associates in evil.

4. The objects of Solomon's affectionate solicitude are fur-ther reminded, that their folly and their guilt would be *the more aggravated and inexcusable,* if they should venture into the society of sinners *in despite of admonition :—* " Surely in vain the net is spread in the sight of any **bird**."

These words, it is true, might be interpreted of the artfulness and cautious secrecy, with which the seducers described
lay their snares.   They take care not to let their gins be
seen by the birds they are laid to catch, which might scare
them, and defeat their end.   They do not expose their designs all at once.   They deal subtley.   They show them at
first as little as possible; and the little that *must* be seen
they present in its least repulsive or most attractive form,—
keeping studiously out of view what might startle and shock
the uninitiated in the "mysteries of iniquity."   They lay
their schemes of seduction warily; and suit their decoys to
the various characters and circumstances of their victims.

I am disposed, however, to understand the words as rather
signifying the aggravation of the guilt which would be incurred in consequence of the warning thus given: as if he
had said—" Now you are put on your guard.   I have given
you faithful premonition.   I have set before your eyes the
gins of the seducer.   If you go into them, you go in with
your eyes open.   Let my warning have the effect upon you
which the sight of the fowler setting his nets has on the fowls
of heaven.   Flee from temptation. If your foot be taken now,
you will sin presumptuously—sin against light and knowledge.   The guilt will be entirely your own; and your blood
will be upon your own heads.   Let the snare, then, now you
are warned, be spread for you "in vain."   Show that you
are aware of your danger.   ' He that, being often reproved,
hardeneth his neck, shall suddenly be destroyed, and that
without remedy.' "

5. The last dissuasive consideration is—the *ruinous consequences* of yielding to the enticements of sinners :—" And
they lay wait for their own blood; they lurk privily for
their own lives.   So are the ways of every one that is
greedy of gain; which taketh away the life of the owners
thereof."   In the latter of these two verses, the pronoun
"*which*" is supplementary.   The meaning clearly is," So "—
that is, so deceitful, so ruinous—" are the ways of him who
is greedy of gain; it taketh away the life of its owners "—
or, "it taketh away the life of those who are under its

power." The verse will thus express—not the murderous conduct which the greed of gain produces in order to its gratification, but the mischievous and destructive effects of the base and criminal passion *to the person himself* by whom it is indulged,—exposing his bodily life to jeopardy and his soul to perdition. The sentiment of the two verses seems to be—that although the workers of iniquity might elude the vigilance of men, and the avenging visitation of human tribunals, or of the resentments of fellow-creatures, yet they were *their own very worst enemies*. The *certain effect*, or *inevitable consequence*, of any particular course of conduct is sometimes expressed by this figure of speech, and it is full of energy—as if it had been in the *intention* of the agent, the object he had in view. The idea is—that, *had it been so*, had he indeed intended it so, he could not have adopted means more appropriate for attaining his end. The expression in the 18th verse is evidently *borrowed* from the 11th. There the ungodly are represented as saying—" Come with us." But, says the wise man, they are bringing a surer and heavier destruction upon themselves, than any they can ever inflict upon others. They invite you to " lay wait," to " lurk privily," for the " blood" and the " life" of unoffending fellow-men; but in truth " they lay wait for *their own* blood,—they lurk privily for *their own* lives." They are themselves their surest and most pitiable victims. The vengeance of offended heaven pursues the evil-doer; secretly, silently, invisibly, but closely, constantly, unswervingly, tracking his steps. It is behind him in all the windings and doublings of iniquity; it finds him out in all the hidden haunts of vice. In a memory from which nothing escapes, it treasures up against him every act and word and thought of evil. It follows him all the downward road to perdition, and at last, shuts him up in the prison of hell, and there takes up its abode with him for ever. It may not be appointed to overtake him in this world. His schemes of evil may prosper to the end. But overtake him it inevitably will; if not here, hereafter. Will you seek, then, your own destruction? Will you, with frantic infatuation, try what amount of wrong and ruin you can bring upon yourselves? Will you foolishly and recklessly presume, in despite of the warnings both of men and of God? Will you, knowingly and wilfully, consign to damnation your never-dying souls? Will you be, in the very worst and most awful sense of the designation—a SELF-MURDERER?

I conclude with two observations.—*First,* Let not any imagine, from the nature of the case selected by Solomon, and of the course of illustration suggested by it—that there is no danger, excepting to the openly profligate—to adepts and bravoes in impiety, vice, and violence. That would be a sad mistake indeed. There is danger to all who are living without the fear of God—who are not thus " wise unto salvation." We require not to go to the dens and caves of robbers and assassins, to the cells of bridewells and jails, to the polluted and infernal haunts of abandoned licentiousness, in order to find those who are without this fear, and who are in danger of perishing,—who are perpetrating the fearful suicide just mentioned. They abound around you, even among the sober, plodding, money-making men of the world. All *ungodliness* exposes to death. You may ruin your souls by worldly-mindedness, as effectually as by profligacy. Whatever it be that keeps you from giving up your hearts to God,—whatever it be that keeps you from being in earnest about the salvation of your souls,—whatever it be that shuts the Saviour out of your hearts, and prevents you from taking up the cross and following him,—*that* will be the ruin of your souls.

2. We have in this passage associations for *evil.* We invite youth to ASSOCIATIONS FOR GOOD,—to the Church of the living God, the community of the faithful; and to those societies which Christian piety and Christian benevolence have instituted, for the promotion of religion, and for the diffusion of the knowledge of divine truth. Shall Satan have his combinations, and not Christ,—the god of this world, and not the God of heaven? Let Christians associate. Let Christian *youth* associate. Let them " consider one another, to provoke unto love, and unto good works." Let them " ex-

hort one another daily,"—strengthen each other's hands, and encourage each other's hearts in the way of the Lord.

Shall *Science* have its combinations, and not Religion? While Societies are formed for the advancement of general knowledge, or of particular departments of philosophy and the arts,—shall not the heads and hearts and hands of Christians be brought into united counsel and co-operation, for the promotion of knowledge still better, and blessings still more precious and enduring than those which all human discovery can ever confer? Shall not the experience of age and the energy of youth combine for ends, so glorifying to Christ, so salutary, so eternally salutary, to mankind?— O! if such associations of youth as those we have been contemplating be melancholy and revolting,—how delightful are Associations of youth for religious improvement,—for their own and one another's spritual benefit,—bands of young philanthropists, whose object it is, to make inroads on the kingdom of Satan,—to arrest the progress of vice and irreligion,—to do good to all as they have opportunity, —and in the terms in which their divine Master describes the end of his coming into the world—"not to destroy men's lives, but to save them?"—To the youth of all such Associations we say—Go on, and prosper! And if sinners entice you to quit your own for theirs, consent not. Be it your endeavour to allure them to yours, to win them over to the Lord's side, drawing them with the cords of love,—bearing in mind, that "he who converteth a sinner from the error of his way, shall save a soul from death, and shall hide a multitude of sins."

LECTURE IV.

———◆———

PROV. I. 20—33.

" Wisdom crieth without; she uttereth her voice in the streets: she crieth in
the chief place of concourse, in the openings of the gates: in the city she uttereth her words, saying, How long, ye simple ones, will ye love simplicity? and
the scorners delight in their scorning, and fools hate knowledge? Turn you at
my reproof: behold, I will pour out my Spirit unto you, I will make known my
words unto you. Because I have called, and ye refused; I have stretched out
my hand, and no man regarded; but ye have set at nought all my counsel, and
would none of my reproof: I also will laugh at your calamity; I will mock when
your fear cometh; when your fear cometh as desolation, and your destruction
cometh as a whirlwind; when distress and anguish cometh upon you. Then
shall they call upon me, but I will not answer; they shall seek me early, but
they shall not find me: for that they hated knowledge, and did not choose the
fear of the Lord: they would none of my counsel: they despised all my re   :
therefore shall they eat of the fruit of their own way, and be filled wit . cheir
own devices. For the turning away of the simple shall slay them, and the prosperity of fools shall destroy them. But whoso hearkeneth unto me shall dwell
safely, and shall be quiet from fear of evil."

IT has been a question with expositors, whether by WISDOM,
in this and subsequent passages, we are to understand a *person* under this designation—namely, the second Person of
the adorable Trinity, "the Word" and "Wisdom of God,"—
the medium of divine communications to men,—the "Light of
the world;" or simply the instruction of the word of God
personified as Wisdom, speaking to the children of men.

It is enough for the present to observe, what every sincere
believer in the inspiration of the Bible will at once admit—
that in this passage, the address is *divine.** The voice of

———

* For the discussion of the point see Lect. on ch. viii. 1—21.

WISDOM is the voice of GOD. The authority of WISDOM is the authority of GOD. The invitations and the warnings of WISDOM are the invitations and the warnings of GOD. The neglect and scorn of WISDOM are the neglect and scorn of GOD. The blessing of WISDOM is the blessing of GOD; and the vengeance of WISDOM is the vengeance of GOD. If it is a personification of *instruction*, it is not of human but divine instruction; it is not of instruction as coming from the wisdom of Solomon, but from the wisdom of GOD. And surely when the wisdom of God speaks, it is the wisdom of man to hear and obey. Indifference and scorn are impiety, infatuation, madness.

Divine Instruction addressed men of old by the Prophets. Those "holy men of God spake as they were moved by the Holy Ghost," (2 Peter i. 21;) in the name of Jehovah, "warning every man, and teaching every man in all wisdom," (Col. i. 28.) They informed, they invited, they reproved, they promised, they threatened;—all in the same name;—all with the same authority. There was the solemnity and the weight of Heaven's truth in every word they uttered. But "God, who at sundry times and in divers manners spake in time past unto the fathers by the prophets, hath in these last days spoken unto us by his Son, whom he hath appointed heir of all things, by whom also he made the worlds," (Heb. i. 1, 2.) Following his Son are his inspired "ambassadors," to whom he committed "the word of reconciliation," and who had in all things, whether regarding truth or duty, the "mind of Christ." Since the time when the "vision and the prophecy were sealed" in Patmos, there have been no new revelations, and no inspired teachers. Yet, all the servants of God still, who "speak according to this word"—(and it is very obvious, that no others *can be* his servants)—may be regarded as speaking with the voice of heavenly wisdom; and, however unworthy of notice or of deference in themselves, demanding audience for their message, as accredited by the Book from which they profess to take their instructions.

There are two things to be marked as characterizing the

address of Wisdom. The first is *publicity;*—Verses 20, 21.
"Wisdom crieth without; she uttereth her voice in the
streets: she crieth in the chief place of concourse, in the
openings of the gates: in the city she uttereth her words."

She thus chooses the most suitable places for giving her instructions all the publicity possible. Now, this has been, and
still may be, by the servants of God, done literally. Jesus
himself set the example. He uttered his voice in the syna-
gogues, in the courts of the temple, in the streets, in the fields,
on mountains, and in plains,—wherever human beings could
be assembled to listen. Pursuing, during his official life,
the great ends of his ministry, as "a teacher come from God,"
he acted as the occasions of that ministry required, seizing
on every opportunity of proclaiming truth, and publishing
the doctrines and admonitions of the Father that sent him.
And what the Master did, the servants need not surely be
ashamed to do. Street and field preaching have, in many
cases, been signally owned and honoured of God, for the
great end of all preaching—the bringing of sinners to Christ
—the turning of the disobedient unto the wisdom of the
just. It has sometimes been brought into disrepute by the
conduct of inferior, unworthy, and mercenary characters;
but there is the greater reason why it should be redeemed
from obloquy, by the countenance of right-principled and
right-hearted men; men who can truly say—"We seek not
yours but *you.*" And we rejoice that by ministers peculiarly
qualified for the work, it has, in our own day, been thus
redeemed. If there is a portion of the world's scorn, and
even of the so-called *christian* world's scorn, still attached to
it, what is that compared with saving souls from death?—
But the general idea of *publicity*—universal publicity—is
that which is intended to be conveyed; just as when our
Lord says—"What ye hear in the ear, that preach ye upon
the house-tops," (Matt. x. 27,) he simply means—make it
known openly and everywhere.

The second thing in the address of Wisdom is—*affectionate earnestness.*—The very publicity of her instructions
proves her earnestness. She does not wait in private, till

men may find her out, and come to her for her lessons. She
goes out to them. She not only embraces opportunities
when they present themselves; she seeks them, she makes
them. This must ever be the spirit and practice of Christians. The principle of regulating the supply by the demand, will never do in their department. The spirit of
Christianity must be the spirit of kind aggression. It must
seek men out, to tell them of the way of life. It must find
its way to the abodes of those who would never themselves
come to the house of God to hear of the things that " belong
unto their peace." It must carry the tidings of mercy to the
most distant and sequestered spots of our country, and make
" the dwellers in the mountains and the vales" hear its voice.
It must carry it " far hence unto the Heathen," bearing
thither " the unsearchable riches of Christ,"—the treasures
of that wisdom which " cannot be gotten for gold, nor can
silver be weighed for the price thereof." It must thus show
itself *in earnest* for the conversion of sinners, and the evan-
gelization of the world.—And in the earnestness of Wisdom,
there is *affection*, dictating all the force and tenderness of persuasive expostulation and entreaty. Such was the example of
the " great Teacher ;" of his prophets before him and of his
apostles after him. Theirs was not the style of cold, dry,
formal, didactic statement, but the urgency of persuasion, the
force of evidence, the exhibition and recommendation of their
lessons by motives addressed to all the hopes and fears and
longings of the human soul.* The language in the passage before us, is full of such tender and urgent solicitation :—verses 22, 23. " How long, ye simple ones, will ye
love simplicity? and the scorners delight in their scorning, and
fools hate knowledge? Turn you at my reproof: behold, I
will pour out my Spirit unto you, I will make known my
words unto you."

There are *three descriptions* of characters here addressed ;
—kindred characters, it is true, in their generic principles,
but different in the mode and measure of the development
of those principles.

* Luke xiii. 34; Mat. xi. 28—30; 2 Cor. v. 20.

" *Simple ones*," are evidently, as explained in Lecture second, the ignorant, thoughtless, inconsiderate, who, lightly regardless of admonition, "pass on and are punished."— " How long," it is said to such, " will ye *love simplicity ?*" —choose, that is, to persist in thoughtless levity and dissipation, loving ease, and not liking to be disturbed and troubled in their course of carelessness; disinclined to give heed to any thing that would at all interfere with the tranquillity or the indulgence of the passing hour.   The solemn import of the question, as intimating the duty and the necessity of immediate compliance with Wisdom's counsels, will appear from what comes after.

" *Scorners*" go beyond the " simple ones."   They are not merely indifferent and regardless : they scoff at the things of God; they ridicule or revile his lessons; they sneer at and mock his servants and people; they make his word their jest-book, and his day their holiday; they disdain alike the restraints of his precepts and the encouragements of his promises; they laugh at his threatenings, make sport of his terrors, and glory in their superiority to vulgar and superstitious fancies.   To them, in the same style of faithful and affectionate expostulation, it is said—" How long will you *delight in scorning ?*"   In so doing they took pleasure in what they should have hated; they made light of what ought to have made them serious; they gloried in their shame; they acted in opposition to all the plainest dictates of prudence; they were like " maniacs dancing in their chains;" their very delight and merriment were appalling; they joyed in what made all who loved them sorrowful; they courted death; they sported on the verge of hell.

" *Fools*" who " *hate knowledge*," may describe still another class :—those who are not ignorant of divine lessons,—the lessons of truth and of duty; to whom they have been imparted, and on whom they have been inculcated, by parental tuition, and during their attendance with their parents in the house of God.   But they have felt all this a restraint. It has been utterly distasteful to them; irksome to their inclinations, and troublesome to their consciences.   Determined on following their own ways, "walking after the sight of their eyes and the imagination of their hearts,"—they have hated the knowledge which has interfered with and thwarted their purposes, or made them unhappy in the prosecution of them. The career which such pursue is a career of sin against light,—in opposition to the convictions of their judgments, and the dictates and remonstrances of the inward monitor.*

All these are here addressed in the terms of heartfelt compassion and solicitude. The question is that of serious expostulation:—"How long, ye simple ones, will ye love simplicity? and the scorners delight in their scorning, and fools hate knowledge?" It is the address of one who clearly saw, in the conduct of all the three, in whatever diversity of measure, *folly*, and *guilt*, and *danger*. They were all acting unwisely, criminally, recklessly. The longer they persisted, the deeper was their guilt becoming, and the more imminent their danger. While they were thus "loving simplicity," "delighting in scorning," "hating knowledge," the moment might be at hand that should arrest their career and consign them to the woe from which there is no redemption! "How long" will ye act thus?—how long thus "forsake your own mercies?" how long thus provoke the slumbering vengeance of divine Justice? how long thus disregard or brave all that is fearful, and refuse and set at nought all that is exalted in honour and rich in happiness? The spirit of the address appears in the *exhortation* and the *encouragement* which are immediately added. The *exhortation* is—"Turn you at my reproof." The reproof was that of affectionate faithfulness; and the exhortation shows the temper of the reprover, as that of love: "*Turn you*"—to God, to truth, to holiness, to happiness. And we see from what follows, that the *motive* is a regard to their own well-being, urged upon them by the compassion of an all-merciful God;—as when he says, "Turn ye, turn ye, for why will ye die?" Ez. xxxiii. 11.

It is a call to repentance:—not to mere indolent regret—

* Comp. John iii. 19—21.

a repentance that needs "to be repented of"—the selfish sorrow of the world which "worketh death;" which for the moment admits the justness of the remonstrance, but still loves its old ways; and, carelessly alleging it is too late to think of changing now, resolves on going on as before:—but to a change of mind respecting their modes of thinking and living, feeling and acting; with the manifestation of the sincerity of both, by a decided turning to God and to the ways of faith and obedience.

And the most immediate and ample encouragement is held out to compliance. Every conceivable objection is anticipated. There is no obstacle in the way. God stands, with outstretched arms, waiting to receive them; and if they speak of their deficiencies, their own ignorance, their own weakness, their own inability, He takes every excuse out of their mouths, and silences all by the assurance, "*Behold, I will pour out my Spirit unto you, I will make known my words unto you.*"

The two things here mentioned are to be taken in connexion with each other. The latter is the result of the former—the former in order to the latter. There can be no plea, therefore, for continued ignorance. The word of God is in possession;—and the Spirit of God is in promise. What more can be required? What sinners are called to do, is to come to God's word, and to ask God's Spirit to enlighten them by means of it. Is there anything unreasonable and hard in this? If *unwilling* to do this, are they not to blame? Nothing,—nothing but unwillingness prevents them. God is all encouragement to them. It is not he that keeps aloof from *them*, but they that keep aloof from him. He offers instruction; but they will not have it. He promises his Spirit; but they will not so much as ask it. All the consequences lie with themselves. The promise here is—"I will not only make my words enter your ears, but will open your understandings to a discernment of their truth, and excellence, and suitableness, and glory; and will open your hearts to their gladdening and saving power." This is just what the natural man needs. "The natural man receiveth not the things of the Spirit of God: for they are foolishness unto him; neither can he know them, because they are spiritually discerned," 1 Cor. ii. 14. The inability to *know* them, in their real spiritual excellence, arises from no want of natural power of intellect, but from the blinding, perverting influence of a depraved heart and a vitiated will. And the Spirit of God "makes known God's word" unto the sinner, not in the mere meaning of its terms, but in the glory and worth of its great truths, their adaptation to His own character, and to the exigencies of the fallen creature for whose salvation they are designed.

These are "exceeding great and precious promises." If sinners are not sensible of their value, and are not induced by them to comply with the invitation which they are given to recommend and enforce, surely the fault is not His by whom they are made,—made in sincerity and kindness.

Such is the divine INVITATION. There is then a solemn interval or pause. Wisdom waits to see the result; to witness the reception it meets with from those to whom it is addressed. Alas! alas! Her hearers "make light of it." They go away, "one to his farm and another to his merchandise,"—each to his worldly and sinful pursuits. The simple ones still love simplicity; the scorners still delight in their scorning; the fools still hate knowledge. They persist in "going astray." Then Wisdom, with awful majesty, proclaims:—verses 24—27. "Because I have called, and ye refused; I have stretched out my hand, and no man regarded; but ye have set at nought all my counsel, and would none of my reproof: I also will laugh at your calamity; I will mock when your fear cometh; when your fear cometh as desolation, and your destruction cometh as a whirlwind; when distress and anguish cometh upon you."

The season of forbearance is gone. The time of expostulation, and warning, and entreaty, could not always last. The voice of invitation is exchanged for the voice of judgment. The God of mercy having waited, and in many instances waited long, to be gracious, in the exercise of his "goodness and forbearance and long-suffering" — the God of righteousness summons to his bar, and pronounces sentence. The sentence is from the throne of justice, against those who refused, when invited, to come to the throne of grace. The description is in harmony with what goes before. The appeal to themselves as to the past is founded in truth. Wisdom appears in it tender, urgent, importunate, calling, and continuing to call even when sinners refuse; "stretching forth her hands, and all day long stretching them forth, to a disobedient and gainsaying people." Her language had been—"Ho, every one that thirsteth, come ye to the waters, and he that hath no money; come ye, buy, and eat; yea, come, buy wine and milk without money and without price. Wherefore do ye spend money for that which is not bread? and your labour for that which satisfieth not? hearken diligently unto me, and eat ye that which is good, and let your soul delight itself in fatness. Incline your ear, and come unto me: hear, and your soul shall live; and I will make an everlasting covenant with you, even the sure mercies of David," Isa. lv. 1—3. Importunate repetition had been employed; and she had tried it in every possible form, of tenderness and of terror; of drawing with the cords of love, and of awakening by salutary alarm; of "counsel," and of "reproof." But all had been in vain. The heart would neither break nor melt. The ear was closed alike to the voice of mercy and of judgment, of persuasion and of threatening. Then comes the terrific CLOSE:—"I also will laugh at your calamity; I will mock when your fear cometh; when your fear cometh as desolation, and your destruction cometh as a whirlwind; when distress and anguish cometh upon you." This is indeed dreadful! Calamity, fear, desolation, whirlwind, destruction; and NO REFUGE!—"no ear to pity, no hand to help!"—the only ear to which they could appeal, finally closed; the only hand that had power to save, inflicting the ruin! They prospered in sin; they forgot providence; they laughed at the forewarning of danger, and banished from their hearts and from before their eyes "the fear of the Lord." But now, their day of grace is ended. Their "judgment lingereth not, their damnation slumbereth not."—"Be not deceived; God is not mocked;—for whatsoever a man soweth, that shall he also reap." "He that soweth the wind, shall reap the whirl-wind." *Here it is*—the whirlwind of divine wrath, the impetuous, sweeping, desolating storm, driving all before it; scattering all their hopes like chaff and stubble; annihilating everything from which they had looked for happiness, and overwhelming themselves in irretrievable ruin! Even as the hurricane and the flood carry devastation and overthrow along the cultured fields, laying prostrate the habitations of men and the replenished stores of wealth, and leave the wretched proprietors, houseless and penniless, to poverty and starvation:—such, (only as much more fearful as eternal des-titution of all that can contribute to the happiness of an im-mortal being is more tremendous than the loss of all that pertains to sense alone, and is limited by the span of human life in the present world), *such* destitution may well warrant the employment of the strongest terms to express the woe occasioned by it—*"distress and anguish."* O! who can form any imagination of the agony of a soul that *feels it-self lost*,—and has, at the same moment, the deep and sure conviction that the loss is *irretrievable*,—all opportunities of escape gone—gone for ever! What a change from the proud derision of the scorner, and the thoughtless dissipation of the simple!

And the bitterest ingredient of their cup—the most en-venomed sting of the anguish, yet remains. The God whom they have despised,—to whom they said "Depart from us, for we desire not the knowledge of thy ways," will disregard their sufferings and their terrors,—"I also will laugh at your calamity; I will mock when your fear cometh." These are terms of awful import. If sinners feel the thought rising within them, that such expressions present a harsh and re-pulsive view of God,—a view of him very unlike a Being who says of himself that he "delighteth in mercy,"—I ask them, What would they have? God *does* delight in mercy. Is it no sufficient evidence of this that he spares them, and warns them, and invites them, and beseeches them, and stretches out his arms and opens his heart to them, and importunes them to come to him, and assures them—adding his oath to his word—that he "will in nowise cast them out?" Is it not enough, that in order to make way for them to his favour, and to form a ground on which he may receive them to the arms of his love, he "has not spared his own Son," but given HIM up to humiliation and expiatory tears and woes and death for them? Are these things not enough, but they must be allowed also, as a proof of his mercy, to break his laws, scorn his invitations, brave his judgments, and, insulting the agonies of a bleeding and dying Saviour, reject with disdain the grace and pardon that are offered them in his name? If they will not be satisfied that God is merciful, unless they are permitted to do all this and more with impunity—woe unto them! We can give them no countenance and no encouragement in such a posture of mind, without compromising the glory of God, and sacrificing the insulted majesty of Heaven to the misconceptions, the pride, the passion, of a worm of the dust! The government of God must be maintained. And impenitent sinners forget, that mercy to the *individual* might be the very reverse of mercy to *the great community of the intelligent creation.* They require to be assured, that the time is coming when, as *they* disregarded *God's* voice, *He* will disregard *theirs.* The address in these verses is *to them;* and it amounts to—"Where is now your bravado courage? where now your haughty scorning? where now your foolhardy confidence? where now your impious and incredulous taunts and jests, when, 'walking after your own lusts,' you scoffed at my people, and turned to ridicule both their hopes for themselves and their fears for you?"

In what follows, there is a remarkable change in the person; and it is singularly impressive. Ceasing her address *to them,* Wisdom turns to *us,* and speaks *of* them—pointing to their awful end, and converting it into a warning to others to beware of encouraging it:—verses 28—31. "Then shall they call upon me, but I will not answer; they shall seek me early, but they shall not find me: for that they hated knowledge, and did not choose the fear of the Lord:

they would none of my counsel: they despised all my re
proof: therefore shall they eat of the fruit of their own way,
and be filled with their own devices."

Such a scene as that here depicted is sometimes witnessed
on a dying bed:—the heart unsubdued, remaining in all its
stubborn alienation, but the conscience awakened, and speaking to the agitated and foreboding spirit "terrible things in
righteousness;"—and the wretched sinner crying to God, not
as the object of love or of hope, but of mere terror,—feeling his irresistible superiority—his "arrows" already "stick-
ing fast within him," and "the poison of them drinking up
his spirit:"—yet God still hated; his vengeance only dreaded; all within hard as the nether millstone, abandoned to
judicial obduracy; and HELL opening to the vision of the
conscience-stricken and terrified culprit! My friends, there
is not to be seen under heaven a scene more horrible than
such a deathbed!

But perhaps "the day of wrath and revelation of the
righteous judgment of God," may itself be more especially
intended; which will produce a striking correspondence between this passage and several in the New Testament.—
See, for instance, Luke xiii. 23—28, and Matt. xxv. 10—12.
All cries for mercy will then be too late,—all unavailing.
The door is shut. The ear of God is shut. The lips of divine Wisdom are shut. There are no more accents of love;
no more pressing invitations; no sweet sounds of mercy;
no "Ho, every one that thirsteth;" no "Come unto me, and
I will give you rest;" no "Turn ye, turn ye, why will ye die?"
but—"Depart from me, ye cursed, into everlasting fire."

Is not the sentence *just*—"Therefore shall they eat of
the fruit of their own way, and be filled with their own devices?" Their miserable end is the fruit—not of God's way,
but of their own. Had they hearkened to *Him*—had they
obeyed *His* voice, very different had been the issue. *His* plan,
His device for them, was a plan of salvation. It is by "their
own devices" they are ruined. Had they, when they might,
complied with the gracious counsels of Heaven, they should
have had "their fruit unto holiness and the end everlasting

I. D

life;"—and, instead of the sentence of banishment and curse, they should still have heard the language of invitation, associated with that of welcome and blessing—"Come, ye blessed of my Father, inherit the kingdom prepared for you."

Let me impress upon the mind and conscience of every one the reason, and the *only* reason, of the issue so fearfully described. There is not a word here of *inability;* it is all *unwillingness.* And point me out one passage of the Bible, where it is otherwise; where sinners are represented as condemned for *inability,*—for not doing what they *could not* do. The blessèd God is no such tantalizer. It is never, "Ye *could* not"—but "ye *would* not:"—and when, at any time, inability *is* spoken of, it is inability all of a *moral* nature, and resolves itself into *unwillingness.* And this alone leaves the blameworthiness where it ought to lie—not with God, but with the sinner. It is of infinite importance thus to justify God. Every sinner to whom the voice of heavenly Wisdom is addressed—if he perishes, perishes as the consequence of his own unwillingness to hear and obey that voice. Every such sinner who thus perishes, perishes as one who *might* have been saved; and whom nothing whatever kept from salvation, but his own want of liking to its nature or to its terms. He *would not.* Every term here is of this description—"would not"—"refused"—"set at nought"—"hated"—"did not choose"—"despised." "They eat of the fruit of their own way, and are filled with their own devices."

And the same is the doctrine in the language which follows:—verse 32. "For the turning away of the simple shall slay them, and the prosperity of fools shall destroy them."

It is the *turning away* from the warnings and invitations of wisdom, that slays them. And this turning of the ear from divine instruction and from all that relates to the soul and salvation, is many a time the result of this world's prosperity—"*the prosperity of fools shall destroy them.*" (Luke xii. 16—21.) The temptation is represented in Scripture as peculiarly strong; and the representation is in harmony with fact. But *he* is emphatically *a fool* who allows the prosperity of this world to "destroy" him, for—"What is a man profited, if he shall gain the whole world, and lose his own soul? or what shall a man give in exchange for his soul?"

How simple, but how beautiful and striking, the contrast:—verse 33. " But whosoever hearkeneth unto me shall dwell safely, and shall be quiet from fear of evil."

He who listens to, and complies with, the counsels of Wisdom —the believer in divine truth—the CHRISTIAN—shall possess genuine security. " Resting on the Lord," on the wisdom, faithfulness, love, and power of a covenant God and Saviour, his mind will enjoy unmoved tranquillity, amidst all the turmoils and all the vicissitudes of this life. (Phil. iv.. 6, 7.) And, infinitely more than that, he shall be quiet from the fear of ultimate and final evil—the evil of which the wicked and the careless, the "simple ones," the "scorners," and the "fools," become the victims—the terrors of death and hell. The season of the impenitent sinner's last alarm shall be to him the season of peace and hope and joy. He shall stand unappalled in the judgment—"quiet from fear of evil" even at the bar of the Eternal—quiet from the fear of a sentence of condemnation and banishment, such as shall drive away God's enemies. " Accepted in the Beloved," and safe from all evil in virtue of his union to Him, he shall "enter into His joy." And there—in the residence of the redeemed, no "fear of evil" shall ever find admission. There shall be in the very fullest sense of the words, "quietness and assurance for ever." How delightful the representations of the serene tranquillity, the perfect peace and joy—of the everlasting habitations:— " These are they which came out of great tribulation, and have washed their robes, and made them white in the blood of the Lamb: therefore are they before the throne of God, and serve him day and night in his temple: and he that sitteth on the throne shall dwell among them. They shall hunger no more, neither thirst any more; neither shall the sun light on them, nor any heat: for the Lamb, which is in the midst of the throne, shall feed them, and shall lead them unto living fountains of waters: and God shall wipe away all tears from their eyes," Rev. vii. 14—17.

LECTURE V.

———◆———

PROV. II. 1—9.

" My son, if thou wilt receive my words, and hide my commandments with thee; so that thou incline thine ear unto wisdom, and apply thine heart to understanding; yea, if thou criest after knowledge, and liftest up thy voice for understanding; if thou seekest her as silver, and searchest for her as for hid treasures; then shalt thou understand the fear of the Lord, and find the knowledge of God. For the Lord giveth wisdom: out of his mouth cometh knowledge and understanding. He layeth up sound wisdom for the righteous: he is a buckler to them that walk uprightly. He keepeth the paths of judgment, and preserveth the way of his saints. Then shalt thou understand righteousness, and judgment, and equity, yea, every good path."

Is WISDOM here to be considered as the speaker, or SOLOMON? If Wisdom, she must be understood as addressing herself to *her own children;* that is, those who receive her counsels and place themselves under her tuition and guidance, her instruction and authority; as she had just finished her solemn admonition of danger and of their final doom to those by whom her words are unheeded and disobeyed. If Solomon, he may be understood as addressing himself either to Rehoboam, or to youth in general, under the designation of paternal affection, as one that felt all a father's interest in their well-being.

In the passage, (verses 1—4,) there is an EXERCISE recommended, or rather, a DUTY enjoined, of the first importance and the most imperative obligation; and it is enforced by the happy results which are represented as arising from it.

The exercise—the duty, is a *candid, earnest, persevering* inquiry after Divine truth.

1. The inquiry must first be candid—sincere. It is said of "fools," that they "despise wisdom and instruction." But the children of Wisdom "receive" her words. They do not shut their ears against them. They do not slight them. They do not hastily and thoughtlessly disregard them. They give them, what they are entitled to,·a serious and deliberate attention. They listen, they remember, they meditate, they examine, they accept, they lay up for use.—The words of divine wisdom are now *in the Bible.* There the voice of Wisdom, or of God, addresses you. In reading the Bible, you should consider yourselves as listening to GOD. And it is a blessed privilege, to have this Word in your possession,—to have God addressing you in it. It is the most valuable of all deposits that can be committed to you. But it is one of those deposits of which the value to you depends, not on the possession but on the *use.* It will prove, through neglect and misimprovement, a curse, instead of a blessing. O! how few are duly impressed with the preciousness of a communication from GOD,—of a record of the mind and will of the INFINITE BEING "with whom they have to do!"

If you feel the value of this privilege, you will attend to the instructions and counsels, the admonitions, the encouragements, the commands, which in the Bible are set before you. It will be your sincere and cherished desire, as the children of Wisdom, to comprehend her lessons. You will "apply your heart to understanding."—There are some who refuse to hear at all. This is unreasonable, uncandid, unmanly, and most infatuated: for if the claims of the Bible be well-founded, what can be imagined more important than the knowledge of its contents? There are some who *do* hear, or rather it should be said, *seem* to hear. They profess to be all attention; but it is all pretence, — the mere result of politeness and courtesy to the speaker,—the spirit of assentation in which there is no sincerity, no *heart:*—like the temper of the son in the parable, who said, "I go, Sir; and went not." This is worse than not hearing at all; inasmuch as it is the reality of neglect, with the guilt of hypocrisy superadded to it. You must "apply your *hearts* to understanding,"—cherishing a true and sincere desire for its attainment. And when there is this sincerity, you will "*hide with you*" the divine counsels and commands: not hiding *the book* that contains them, laying *it* aside and allowing it to lie in safe and secluded custody, under the guardianship of lock and key; but hiding its contents in the memory, in the understanding, in the conscience, in the heart. The father of Solomon expresses in few words what Solomon means—when he says, "Thy word have I hid *in my heart*, that I might not sin against thee," Psal. cxix. 11.

2. The inquiry that is thus sincere, will be an *earnest* inquiry—an inquiry determined on gratification, and that spares no pains for its attainment. This is the spirit of verse third.

Divine Wisdom, as we have seen, is herself in earnest in imparting and recommending her salutary counsels. And while the instructress is thus in earnest, so should the pupil be in *seeking* her instructions. That about which we really are in earnest, we cannot satisfy ourselves with asking in a careless and scarcely audible whisper, as if indifferent whether we were heard or not—ah no! Thus will not the awakened soul do with God. "Crying," and "lifting up the voice," are frequently in Scripture the indications of *earnestness;* and he who is in earnest for the right understanding of the lessons of Wisdom, will "cry mightily to God" for that illumination which he needs, and which it is God's to bestow. The man who has lost his way, and is wandering in the dark, knowing not which way to turn him, unable to find the right path, will seek a guide. He will *cry out* for one, exerting all his powers of voice, if, peradventure, he may be within the hearing of any one who can come to his relief, and conduct him to safety. So he who is sensible of his inability to guide himself in the perplexing paths of life, while he feels "pleasures tempting from without, and passions warring within," will be all solicitude for a conductor—a divine guide, who may bring him into the right way, and keep him

in it.   Nor will he rest till he has secured what he so earnestly seeks.   Hence,

3. With earnestness is united importunate *perseverance.*
This is implied in the variety of expressions used in
succession to each other.   It is implied specially in the
repetition of the same thing in different terms in the third
verse; where it is not *one* cry succeeded by silence, but evidently *importunate* crying that is meant—" If thou *criest,*
and if thou *liftest up thy voice*"—not ceasing to cry, but
crying with augmented vehemence.   And the idea of perseverance united with earnestness is strongly brought out in
the figure employed in verse fourth,—" If thou seekest her as
silver, and searchest for her as for hid treasures."   Men
discover the value they set on the treasures of this world,
by their unrelaxing diligence in seeking them.   They do
not give up the search immediately, because they do not
immediately succeed.   So long as any hope remains in one
direction, they persist in the search; and if, at length, they
find that in that direction it is vain, they try in another ,
and try, and try again, till they discover the way to what
they are in quest of.   If any expectation exists of a mine of
silver or of gold, or of aught the working of which may
yield silver or gold by its merchandise, what earnestness is
discovered ! what "drilling and boring of the solid earth !"
what excavating toils in all directions, perpendicularly here,
and horizontally there ! what searching, and washing, and
breaking, and testing !—And then, when a vein of precious
ore has been discovered, with what patient perseverance and
care it is traced and worked, in its main trunk and in all its
ramifications ; and never relinquished, till the last fibre of
it has been explored and exhausted.   The application of
this appropriate figure is, in every view, obvious.   Divine
knowledge is fitly compared to treasure, to treasures of gold
and silver,—the articles which are held by men in highest
estimation.   The comparison is natural and common.   It
occurs repeatedly in the introductory part of this book ; and
in many other parts of the Scriptures.   David says—"The
law of thy mouth is better unto me than thousands of gold

and silver," Psalm cxix. 72. Job says of the excellence of wisdom, "It cannot be gotten for gold, neither shall silver be weighed for the price thereof. It cannot be valued with the gold of Ophir, with the precious onyx or the sapphire. The gold and the crystal cannot equal it; and the exchange of it shall not be for jewels of fine gold. No mention shall be made of coral, or of pearls; for the price of wisdom is above rubies. The topaz of Ethiopia shall not equal it, neither shall it be valued with pure gold," Job xxviii. 15—19. Thus, were the mines of all that is precious in the bowels of the earth emptied of their treasures, there would be a treasure still remaining, not only surpassing each, but surpassing all;—the accumulation of the whole, in all their weight, and worth, and lustre, and beauty, and variety, being nothing compared with the treasures of the divine word—the "excellency of the knowledge" which it contains. Paul speaks of "all the treasures of wisdom and knowledge," and of the "unsearchable riches of Christ;" divine knowledge being a mine of precious ore, which we shall be exploring through eternity, without ever exhausting it. Alas! how little of a disposition appears in the world to form, or to act upon, this estimate! How few are thus earnest in the pursuit of divine knowledge—the lessons of heavenly wisdom! How few who "count all things but loss" compared with it; and who would sacrifice all the treasures of earth, rather than not find it, or, having found it, rather than part with it!—How few even of the people of God, who profess to have learned the value of this wisdom and knowledge by a happy experience, discover the longing, the thirsting, the vehement and persevering research, for the attainment of a larger and larger amount of it which might be expected of them! It is the admonition of an inspired apostle—"Let the word of Christ dwell in you richly"—laid up in the understanding and in the heart. Now there is no way in which that word can *be* in us richly without an eager seeking after it; or *dwell* in us richly, without a careful and jealous keeping of it—"giving the more earnest heed to the things which we have heard, lest at any time we should let them slip," Heb. ii. 1.   Do Christians show anything like the anxious, persevering ardour in seeking such knowledge, which the men of the world discover in seeking wealth?   Nay, is it not sadly true of some Christians, and of Christians who have no excuse from poverty, and small wages, and the necessity of unceasing toil for themselves and their families, that such is the eagerness with which they allow themselves to be absorbed in the pursuit of the riches of the world, that they can hardly redeem daily time for the reading and the study of the divine word, and for making daily additions, even however small, to their stock of spiritual wealth?   It ought not so to be.   Among the richest, and among the poorest, if there but exist in the soul such feelings towards the word of God as are in this passage described,—feelings arising from, and maintained by, a right estimate, and settled impression, of its incomparable excellence, there will be the *practical result* of such feelings— the determined redemption of time for keeping up and increasing the knowledge of that word.   And Christians may be assured, that in proportion as they act on this principle, and, while they are "not slothful in business," are, at the same time, "fervent in spirit, serving the Lord,"—that Lord will bless them, not in their spiritual state alone, but even in their temporal affairs.   Whatever else there may be included in our Lord's words, surely *this* is, when he says to his disciples, "Seek ye first the kingdom of God, and his righteousness ; and all these things shall be added unto you," Matt. vi. 33.   Remember, there is no *converse* of the promise.   God will "add" what is good of the blessings of this life to those who place his kingdom first in their desires and pursuit ;—but there is no promise that he will add the blessings of the kingdom to those who place the world first.

But there are, in the passage before us, powerful spiritual inducements presented to the course which has thus been recommended:—verse 5. "Then shalt thou understand the fear of the Lord, and find the knowledge of God."

The nature of *true religion* is expressed in similar terms in the preceding chapter.   "The fear of the Lord" is *the religious* principle, and may, without impropriety, or unnatural straining, be regarded as comprehensive of all the variety of holy affections, which are appropriate to the various views and attributes of the divine character, revealed in the divine word. "The fear of the Lord," taken thus comprehensively, is founded, of course, in the "*knowledge of God.*"

This knowledge of God is the first lesson of heavenly wisdom. On the right apprehension of this lesson all the rest necessarily depends:—

> "You cannot be right in the rest,
>   Unless you think rightly of HIM."

Wrong views of God will vitiate every other department of your knowledge. Without right views of God, you can have no right views of his law. Without right views of his law, you can have no right views of sin, either in its guilt or in its amount. Without right views of sin, you can have no right views of your own character, and condition, and prospects as sinners. Without right views of these, you can have no right views of your need of a Saviour, or of the person, and righteousness, and atonement of that Saviour. Without right views of these, you can have no right views of your obligations to divine grace, and can be under the influence of no right principles of obedience, and must be insensible to all those impressive appeals on God's behalf, that are founded on the wonders of his mercy in the gift of his Son, or of the grace of the Son in the gift of himself. Thus fundamental, in the lessons of Wisdom,—thus fundamental amongst the principles of all religion,—is the "KNOWLEDGE OF GOD." And, beyond all question and comparison, this is the noblest and most valuable of *all* knowledge.

The "fear of the Lord," founded in the knowledge of Him, is something, to the right understanding of which *experience* is indispensable. To a man who had never tasted anything sweet, you would attempt in vain to convey, by description, a right conception of the sensation of sweetness. And what is true of the sensations, is true also of the emotions. To a creature that had never felt *fear*, you would hardly convey, by description, an idea of its nature; and equally in vain would be the attempt to make *love* intelligible to one that had never experienced that affection. It is thus to a depraved creature with regard to spiritual and holy affections. "The fear of the Lord"—a fear springing from love, and proportioned to it, such a creature cannot "understand" but by being brought to experience it. He may talk about it, but it will, in general, be very injudiciously and incorrectly; and while he does not live under its influence, the very absence of that influence shows that he does not understand it in one of its most important characteristics *as a practical principle.* But blessed are they who have the experimental understanding of the principles of true religion! They know the value of the promise contained in this verse. It may be undervalued and slighted—alas! it is, by multitudes; but this only shows that they understand it not. And none are more to be pitied than they who have no relish for the best of all knowledge, and no experience of the best and most divinely blessed of all principles!

We have then the source from which true wisdom is to be obtained:—verse 6. "For the Lord giveth wisdom: out of his mouth cometh knowledge and understanding."

"The Lord giveth," or, "*will give*—wisdom." From the connexion we are naturally led to remark, that God giveth wisdom—"to them that ask him." The admonition is to seek it; and the encouragement to seek is the assurance of finding.* He "giveth wisdom" in two ways; by his *Word,* and by his *Spirit:*—or rather these two should be conjoined, and considered as *one:* for he neither gives wisdom by his word without his Spirit, nor by his Spirit without his word. He has given wisdom *in* his word. He has given it through those "holy men of God" that wrote "as they were moved by the Holy Spirit." It is *from* that Word that all true knowledge and wisdom in the things of God must be derived. But it is got thence under the illuminating influence of the same Spirit by whom it was supernaturally dictated.†

* Comp. James i. 5—7.   † 1 Cor. ii. 14.

We might take the words more comprehensively. "The Lord giveth wisdom," is a declaration of very general import. Of this, Solomon himself was a remarkable exemplification. When he asked of God "a wise and understanding heart," God gave it him; and it was, in consequence, that he not only knew the fear of the Lord, but had so extensive and scientific an acquaintance with all the kingdoms of nature. But without doubt, Solomon's chief reference here is to the *best* knowledge and the *best* wisdom,—that which is contained in those oracles which were "given by inspiration of God," and which he imparts thence to sinners of mankind, when by his Spirit he "opens their understandings that they may understand the scriptures."

The assurance is further expanded in verse seventh:— "He layeth up sound wisdom for the righteous: he is a buckler to them that walk uprightly."

The word rendered "*sound wisdom*" is one of general import, signifying anything real, solid, substantial. It might be understood as meaning in general—*substance;* and this would suit well with the verb—"he *layeth up* substance for the righteous." It is rendered in the same way as in this verse, in chap. iii. 21: and chap. viii. 14. And in these passages it seems to be the rendering most in harmony with the context. Considering this as its meaning here, the words will signify two things: that for "the righteous"—for those who are justified through the righteousness provided for them in the work of the Redeemer's mediation—*then* promised, *now* come; and who are brought, at' the same time, by his regenerating Spirit, under the dominion of the principles of personal righteousness, and are living "soberly, righteously, and godly"—that for them the Lord has stores of wisdom laid up for their present use, to be imparted according to their need, and according to the sense of need, and the measure of faith with which they ask it; so that He will give them larger and larger, clearer and clearer manifestations of himself, of his truths, of his ways, and of his will, out of these inexhaustible stores. And then further, that beyond all that is attainable in the present life, there is still

a treasure of this invaluable wisdom and knowledge, in reserve for his people in a future and better world; where all
that they had come to know while here will appear to them
but as the simplest elements of information in the mind of
an infant, compared with the most extensive and varied ac-
quirements of the perfect man.   They have here but gone
to school; their full instruction is above.   This accords well
with the view given by Paul—1 Cor. xiii. 9—12.   It is
"sound wisdom" that God bestows and keeps in store.
There is a great deal that passes under the name that is *not*
sound—a "science falsely so called."   There is a knowledge
of the works of God, unassociated with the knowledge of
God himself.   There is a knowledge that is mere speculation, exerting no influence on the heart and life, inspiring
no devotion, no fear, no love, no spirit of dependence and
of obedience.   There is no "sound wisdom" but that which,
coming *from* God, leads *to* God;—none, but that which tells
upon character, engendering moral and spiritual principles
and affections, fitting the man for the "chief end" of his
being—"to glorify God, and to enjoy him for ever."

Another blessing to the righteous is—*safety*.   This had
been specified in the way of promise before, at the close
of the first chapter.   Here is the same promise under another form—"He is a buckler to them that walk uprightly."
Mark again the *character*.   This is essential, to prevent
self-delusion.   To "walk uprightly," is to maintain a course
of life regulated by right principles, and directed to right
ends.   He "walks uprightly" who lives with the fear of
God as his principle, and the word of God as his rule, and
the glory of God as his end; whose "eye is single;" whose
"heart is right with God;" whose constant study it is to
have a "conscience void of offence toward God and toward
men;" to have his conversation in the world in simplicity
and godly sincerity, not with fleshly wisdom, but by the
grace of God;"—who thus "walks not after the flesh, but
after the Spirit;" and "in whose spirit," as "an Israelite
indeed," "there is no guile."   To such, Jehovah is "*a buckler*."   He is their security amidst all the assaults of their

enemies, and especially amidst the "fiery darts of the Wicked One," which, when the shield of Jehovah's power is interposed, cannot touch him, but fall, quenched and pointless, to the ground.*

The same idea is amplified in verse eighth:—" He keepeth the paths of judgment, and preserveth the way of his saints."

"He *keepeth* the paths of judgment"—or of righteousness, means that He is there, watching over all that walk in them; superintending, guiding, and guarding them.   He is not the guardian of the broad way,—the way of the world and of sin. *That* way Satan superintends,—"the god of this world,"—doing everything in his power, by all his varied acts of enticement and intimidation, to keep his wretched subjects and victims from leaving it.   But the saints, in "the way of holiness,"—the way of wisdom,—"the paths of judgment," are ever under the gracious eye of Jehovah; ever under his watchful care and mighty protection.   Of the way—the "highway" of holiness, in which they walk, it is said—"No lion shall be there, nor any ravenous beast shall go up thereon, it shall not be found there; but the redeemed shall walk there.   And the ransomed of the Lord shall return, and come to Zion with songs, and everlasting joy upon their heads: they shall obtain joy and gladness, and sorrow and sighing shall flee away," Isa. xxxv. 9, 10.

Those whose "way" Jehovah thus "preserveth," are "*His saints.*"   It is a term of reproach in the world, but of high honour and endeared affection with God;—those whom He hath "renewed in the spirit of their minds"—implanting in their hearts the principles of sanctity, and destining them to the perfection of holy conformity to himself.   The *practical character* of their religion is further expressed in next verse, "Then shalt thou understand righteousness, and judgment, and equity; yea, every good path."   It is needless to state the import of each of the particular terms here used.   We only observe, that they include, as a part of the "sound wisdom" which the Lord giveth,—acquaintance with the

---

* Comp. Ps. lxxxiv. 11: cxliv. 2.

great principles of holy living, and with the peculiar duties
of the various relations and conditions of life,—the right
way in all these in which God would have us to walk.
This very Book of Proverbs is itself eminently fitted to supply a means of verifying this promise. And if you, in
childlike ingenuousness of spirit, yield yourselves up unreservedly to the dictates of the word of God, you will seldom
be at a loss, in any circumstances, for the "right path"—
the "good path"—the way of rectitude and of peace.

To "understand" must here, as in verse fifth, mean to
understand *experimentally;* to have experience of the tendency of those ways to true happiness;—to know them "as
ways of pleasantness" and "peace"—not *right* only but
good. The ways which the Lord keeps cannot fail to be
ways in which a blessing is to be found; "the way of
truth;" "the way of peace;" "the way of holiness;" "the
way of life."

Sinners!—forget not, O forget not, that the way of *sin* is
the way of DEATH. Turn from it! Flee from it. God is
not there. Peace is not there. Safety is not there. Life
is not there. Heaven is not there. Neither happiness for
time nor for eternity is there.

LECTURE VI.

Prov. ii. 10—22.

"When wisdom entereth into thine heart, and knowledge is pleasant unto thy soul; discretion shall preserve thee, understanding shall keep thee: to deliver thee from the way of the evil man, from the man that speaketh froward things; who leave the paths of uprightness, to walk in the ways of darkness; who rejoice to do evil, and delight in the frowardness of the wicked; whose ways are crooked, and they froward in their paths: to deliver thee from the strange woman, even from the stranger which flattereth with her words; which forsaketh the guide of her youth, and forgetteth the covenant of her God. For her house inclineth unto death, and her paths unto the dead. None that go unto her return again, neither take they hold of the paths of life: that thou mayest walk in the way of good men, and keep the paths of the righteous. For the upright shall dwell in the land, and the perfect shall remain in it. But the wicked shall be cut off from the earth, and the transgressors shall be rooted out of it."

SOLOMON here proceeds to show, that true religion,—the wisdom of which he celebrates the excellence and recommends the cultivation,—not only has a positively, but also a negatively beneficial influence; inasmuch as, while it conducts in every "good path," it at the same time is a preservative from paths that are evil:—verses 10, 11. "When wisdom entereth into thine heart, and knowledge is pleasant unto thy soul; discretion shall preserve thee, understanding shall keep thee."

You can never be too frequently reminded of the distinction between the understanding of the meaning of divine discoveries, and the perception of their excellence and truth. The knowledge spoken of in Scripture, with which salvation is connected, must be considered as including the latter.

This proceeds upon a sufficiently simple principle. The knowledge of anything means the knowledge of *its real and distinctive properties.* Thus the knowledge of the natural historian, is the knowledge of the properties of different animals, by which they are distinguished from each other. The knowledge of the botanist, is the knowledge of the properties of the various plants in the vegetable kingdom. The knowledge of the chemist, is the knowledge of the properties of the materials with which he is conversant, considered in their elementary composition and relative affinities. The knowledge of the mental philosopher or metaphysician, is the knowledge of the properties and powers of mind, with their several appropriate uses and functions. None of these could with propriety be said to know the objects of their respective departments of inquiry, if they knew only their *existence* while they had no acquaintance with their qualities; if they knew only the fact of their *being*, without knowing *what* they were, in their distinguishing attributes. The same thing is true with regard to any proposition. You cannot be said to know it, if you merely hear it announced, and understand the meaning of its terms, while you know nothing of its properties, whether it be true or false, whether it has any important relations to other propositions, or any real use and capability of application to any purpose in moral or intellectual science. If a proposition is true, if truth be one of its properties, then to know it is to know it *as true.* If a proposition is of real value and excellence, and capability of useful application in the system of truth, to know it is to know it *as thus excellent and valuable and suited to important ends.* On such principles we at once explain such texts as 1 Cor. ii. 14—" But the natural man receiveth not the things of the Spirit of God: for they are foolishness unto him: neither can he know them, because they are spiritually discerned." It is plain that in order to the "things of the Spirit of God" even appearing "foolishness to the natural man,"—in order to his scorning and rejecting them, he must have some understanding of their meaning. No man can disbelieve or despise a state-

ment, without *knowing* it, in *this* sense.   But to *know* the
" things of the Spirit," evidently, from the very position
which the word holds in the verse, signifies, *so* knowing
them as that they shall *no longer appear "foolishness;"* it
is to know them, that is, as possessing the divine attributes
of truth and excellence, and appropriateness to the character
of God and to the condition and exigencies of man.   This
is what the apostle calls *spiritual discernment.*   It includes
a spiritual taste for moral and spiritual beauties, just as the
mere sight of a rich and varied landscape, or the mere hearing of the most perfect combination of sounds, can impart
little or no pleasure, unless there be a taste for the beauties
of scenery, and an ear for the charms of harmony.   The
man who has this taste and the man who lacks it, may
both, with equal clearness and precision, so far as the mere
picture on the retina of their respective eyes is concerned,
see the very same objects, in the very same relative positions
and combinations;—and the very same sounds may strike
on the tympanum or drum of their respective ears; and
the one be entranced in ecstasy, while the other is vacant
and unmoved.   Thus to the carnal eye—the eye of the
" natural man," who is destitute of *spiritual discernment*, or
spiritual taste, the Saviour appears " as a root out of a dry
ground, having no form or comeliness, no beauty that he
should be desired;" while to the eye of the spiritually enlightened, He stands forth " fairer than the children of men,"
" the chiefest among ten thousand," the " altogether lovely."
The same things may be said of Him in the ears of the one
and of the other.   In the mind of the one the description
awakens no sentiment but one of contempt and aversion,
while it draws forth, in the bosom of the other, all the combined and delightfully blending emotions of admiration, reverence, and love.   And thus it is with regard to divine
truth generally.   I need not say that there is much more
meant than the mere speculative understanding of divine
doctrines in the tenth verse.   "Wisdom entering into the
heart," is accordingly to be explained from previous statements—chap. i. 7 : chap. ii. 5.   It clearly implies the spir-

itual illumination of the mind, and renovation of the heart by divine influence accompanying divine truth. This is the only way in which true wisdom ever finds entrance into the naturally foolish heart of man. And then it is, that "knowledge becomes pleasant unto the soul"—the knowledge before spoken of—the knowledge of God, and of the things of God, as revealed in his word. There are many kinds of knowledge which may be " pleasant unto the soul," while the understanding is darkened as to these things, and the heart enmity against them. What delight the man of science, in whichsoever of its various departments, derives from the knowledge acquired of any additional fact or additional principle, while yet he is stone-blind to the beauties of divine truth, and has no relish for the light and the love of the Godhead, or for the wonders of that gospel, — that scheme of redemption by grace and by blood, which is emphatically " the wisdom of God"—the most truly marvellous of all its displays! But when, by divine illumination, " the eyes of the understanding" are opened to the discernment of divine excellence in the discoveries of God's word, that word becomes "sweet unto the taste," "sweeter also than honey to the mouth." Such is the recorded experience—recorded in terms full of emphasis—of all God's people.*

Verse 11. " Discretion shall preserve thee, understanding shall keep thee."

" Discretion" and "understanding," may well be regarded, in such a connection, as meaning especially *self-jealousy* arising from *self-knowledge.* The knowledge of ourselves includes the knowledge, theoretical and experimental, of the unlimited deceitfulness of our own hearts. And this, connected with a right knowledge of the sources of temptation as they exist in such abundance and variety around us, will inspire and maintain "*discretion.*" The man whom God has enlightened knows his own remaining corruption, and is deeply conscious of his own weakness to withstand its ten-

* Ps. i. 1, 2: cxix. 72, 97, 111, 127, 129—131: xix. 7—11. 1 Pet. ii. 1—3.

dencies. With these impressions he will be ever vigilant. He will "watch unto prayer;" "keep his heart with all diligence, out of which are the issues of life;" and "ponder the path of his feet," in every single step of his walk through life. Nor will he trust to *his own* discretion; but, while he keeps all the powers and energies of his mind, all his foresight, all his resources of observation and caution, ever on the alert, will still look upward and say—" O Lord, I know that the way of man is not in himself: it is not in man that walketh to direct his steps," Jer. x. 23. Diffidence of himself and confidence in God may be considered, in combination, as constituting the "discretion" of the spiritual man. It is a part of his prudence to take the best counsel, to have it always at hand, to be ever asking it—"in all his ways acknowledging God, that he may direct his paths."

From the twelfth to the nineteenth verse, the wise man dwells, specifically, on *two* sources of temptation. And he may be considered as addressing himself, with a peculiarity of interest and of emphasis, to YOUTH. These two sources of temptation are—*wicked men*, and *wicked women:*—

Verses 12—17. " To deliver thee from the way of the evil man, from the man that speaketh froward things; who leave the paths of uprightness, to walk in the ways of darkness; who rejoice to do evil, and delight in the frowardness of the wicked; whose ways are crooked, and they froward in their paths: to deliver thee from the strange woman, even from the stranger which flattereth with her words; which forsaketh the guide of her youth, and forgetteth the covenant of her God."

Against "the way of the evil man," with the temptations and dangers attending it, he had already affectionately and strongly warned the young—chap. i. 10—15. The paths of irreligion, vanity, and vice, while they are all devious and downward, are at the same time exceedingly various; and they have all their peculiar enticements, by which those who themselves walk in them, endeavour to allure others into them. And he who has the "discretion" spoken of in the eleventh verse will, amongst other exercises of it, seek to be

duly aware of his own most easily-besetting sin—of the evil
desire which he is most prone to indulge, or the evil temper
to which he is most apt to give way; and will keep a double
guard over that particular point of assault and temptation.

The *"evil man"* is here described as "the man that speaketh froward things:" that is, the words of perverse rebellion,
—of a spirit stubborn, refractory, scornful, self-willed.*
And such "froward things," having the sound and appearance of freedom and independence, are apt to work with a
most seductive and perilous influence on youthful minds of
a particular temperament. O the fondness of poor fallen
humanity for *independence!* It extends it even to GOD,
and vainly says of Jehovah and his Anointed—"Let us
break their bands asunder, and cast away their cords from
us." From the influence of such vain boastings, let "discretion preserve thee;" let "understanding keep thee!"

Minute analyses of the different parts of the description
are unnecessary, especially after the illustration of former
passages.—We may remark on the thirteenth verse, "Who
leave the paths of *uprightness*, to walk in the ways of *darkness*,"—that darkness, as thus set in contrast with uprightness, may be interpreted as descriptive both of the nature of
the ways, and of their tendency and end. The man who
walks in "uprightness," walks in light. His eye is "single."
There is "none occasion of stumbling in him." He has but
one principle;—his "eyes look right on, his eyelids look
straight before him." He is not always looking this way and
that, for devious paths that may suit a present purpose; but
presses onward ever in the same course; and thus all is light,
all plain, all safe. "The ways of darkness," are the ways of
concealment, evasion, cunning, tortuous policy, and deceit.
He who walks in them is ever groping; hiding himself
among the subtleties of "fleshly wisdom:" and being ways
of false principle and sin, they are ways of danger, and
shame, and ruin. They are dark; and they lead to darkness—"the blackness of darkness for ever."

* Comp. Ps. xii. 1—4.

What a wretched kind of "delight" and "joy" is that in verse fourteenth! The happiness of God is his perfect holiness. He "rejoices to do good." He "delights" in true virtue—the virtue that has its basis in godliness—in the fear and love of himself; "and that which *He* delights in must be happy." What a fearful account, then, of any moral and accountable agents, that they "rejoice to do evil,"—rejoice in that which is the very opposite of all that God is, and of all that God approves and loves!

There is a correspondence between their ways and themselves—"Whose ways are crooked, and they froward in their paths."—"*Crooked ways*," is a designation, not unusual in Scripture, for the ways of sin and the world; and it is very appropriate.* The ways of sin are not like "the way of holiness." *It* is a straight and direct way—an even, uniform, unbending course. God has marked it out; and his people have but to follow it, never swerving to the right hand or to the left. The ways of evil are the reverse— "crooked ways," in which sinners, in their frowardness, are ever winding about; turning in every direction; and changing from purpose to purpose, as wayward caprice or shifting inclination, the alternations of evil propensity, happen to dictate. O forget not that these ways all terminate at the gates of the eternal prison! "Avoid them; pass not by them; turn from them, and pass away."

The same admonition applies, with special emphasis, to the way of "the *strange woman*," with her seductive wiles. This was one of the principal occasions of Solomon's own awful departure from God; by which he brought his soul into such jeopardy of perdition. No wonder he dwells upon it so often and so earnestly as he does. He knew the danger of youth, not only from his own experience,—an experience recorded by himself with shame, but from extensive observation, in regard to the prevalence and the fatal results of this sin;—a sin which, I am verily persuaded, if there be another that slays its thousands, may with truth be affirmed

* See Ps. cxxv. 5.

to slay its *ten* thousands.   I must not, by a false and over-fastidious delicacy, be prevented from faithfully, affection-ately, and vehemently warning youth against its awfully seductive blandishments.   Of these Solomon here speaks as if they were chiefly on one side,—on the part of the un-principled female seducer, with her fair and flattering words, her endless arts of allurement, and silken toils of fascination. But they are on both sides.   We are not to forget that that accomplished seducer has herself perhaps been seduced.   By " studied, sly, ensnaring art" it may have been, that she has been tempted to " forsake the guide of her youth, and forget the covenant of her God."—The " guide of her youth" may either mean God himself—who by Jeremiah says to his wandering people, "Wilt thou not from this time cry unto me, My Father, thou art *the guide of my youth;*"—or her earthly father or mother, the natural guardians and guides of their youthful offspring; or, according to the more gen-eral, although I am far from sure of its being the more rea-sonable interpretation, her *husband,* whom it was incumbent on her to hear, and love, and obey, as the " guide" assigned her in her youth by a gracious Providence.

" Forgetting the *covenant of her God,*" may either have reference to the marriage compact, made in God's name ; or, more generally, to the law and commandments of God : accord-ing to a very common phraseology in the Old Testament Scriptures—as in Psalm ciii. 17, 18.   The circumstance of the case subsequently detailed by Solomon in its particulars of seduction, being that of a faithless and perfidious wife, gives the greater likelihood, it is admitted, to this interpre-tation.   No matter.   It is the general lesson and the general warning we are anxious to impress.   Many a time had this wise observer of mankind had occasion to see the havoc wrought among the principles and characters, the rising in-terests, and the prospects for time and eternity, of the young and the unstable, by this particular sin.   " Many strong men "—strong to all appearance in moral and even religious principle—he had seen "cast down by it."   From a " heart that had known its own bitterness," he admonishes youth to

beware. O let me, young friends, reiterate and urge the
admonition. Mark the rocks on which vessels like your
own, full of promise, have struck and gone to pieces, and
avoid them. Take the warning. Guard against first steps
in this path of imminent hazard—nay, according to Solomon
of almost inevitable ruin:—verses 18, 19. "For her house
inclineth unto death, and her paths unto the dead. None
that go unto her return again, neither take they hold of the
paths of life.

"*Death*"—to which her paths "incline"—is the death both
of body and soul, but especially "the second death;" and
"the *dead*" are the miserable victims of that never-dying
death. Ah! how many a poor infatuated deluded youth
has been led on, step by step, the downward road to "the
chambers of death!"—led on, by soft and silken bonds,
—amidst "the pleasures of sin for a season,"—to "adaman-
tine chains and penal fire!" To every youth, then, now
hearing me, I say, with all the earnestness of affection,—
the earnestness of a father to his children,—Shut thine ear
to the syren voice of pleasure! Escape for thy life!

Opposed to the way of *evil* men is the way in which
Solomon was desirous those with whom he pleads should
walk:—verse 20. "That thou mayest walk in the way of
good men, and keep the paths of the righteous."

The "way of good men" is the way of God's commandments,—of faith and love and active obedience;—and "the
paths of the righteous" may mean all the varieties of that
obedience, in the different departments of life and service.

The chapter closes with encouragement on the one hand
and repeated warning on the other:—verses 21, 22. "For
the upright shall dwell in the land, and the perfect shall
remain in it. But the wicked shall be cut off from the
earth, and the transgressors shall be rooted out of it."

The continued possession of the land of promise was often
by Moses connected with obedience, as in Deut. iv. 40.
And so also was it by the prophets, Isa. i. 19, 20. This
obedience was the obedience of faith. Such obedience was
always what Jehovah required of his people; and the pro-

mise expressed his delight in it.   It was on account of the
true Israelites—the spiritual seed of Abraham—by whom
this obedience of faith was rendered, that the land continued
to be possessed by the nation at large : but abounding unbelief, and the wickedness produced by, and indicating it,
were ultimately to be the cause of entire dispossession:—
"Else if ye do in any wise go back, and cleave unto the
remnant of these nations, even these that remain among
you, and shall make marriages with them, and go in unto
them, and they to you: know for a certainty that the Lord
your God will no more drive out any of these nations from
before you; but they shall be snares and traps unto you,
and scourges in your sides, and thorns in your eyes, until
you perish from off this good land which the Lord your
God hath given you.   When ye have transgressed the
covenant of the Lord your God, which he commanded you,
and have gone and served other gods, and bowed yourselves
to them; then shall the anger of the Lord be kindled
against you, and ye shall perish quickly from off the good
land which he hath given unto you," Josh. xxiii. 12, 13, 16.

By such assurances the Israelites were reminded of the
original terms of God's covenant with them ; of his unceasing, unabating, uncompromising, and universal detestation
of all sin, by whomsoever committed, especially by those
who called themselves his people, and of his determination
to visit it with merited vengeance.   He ever, from the beginning, made a difference between the righteous and the
wicked.   He could not *but* make this difference.   The saying has always been, and must always be, a truth—"The
ungodly shall not stand in the judgment, nor sinners in the
congregation of the righteous.   For the Lord knoweth the
way of the righteous: but the way of the ungodly shall
perish," Psalm i. 5, 6.

Even in this world, the good man, with the love of God,
the pardon of sin, a new heart, and a good hope for eternity
—has the best of it,—a goodly heritage.   And when he
leaves this world, he has the animating anticipation of a
better country—"a land of pure delight"—the heavenly

Canaan—"the inheritance incorruptible, and undefiled, and that fadeth not away." Whereas, when the wicked are removed from the earth, instead of being *taken* they are *driven*—not *to* God, but *from* God,—"driven away in their wickedness." They are "rooted out," finally and for ever. The wheat is gathered safely into the barn, while the tares, bundled together, are cast into the "unquenchable fire."

Would you escape this fearful end? There is but one way—the way of FAITH and HOLINESS: faith to unite you with CHRIST; and holiness to prove its reality.

LECTURE VII.

———◆———

PROV. III. 1—10.

"My son, forget not my law; but let thine heart keep my commandments: for length of days, and long life, and peace, shall they add to thee. Let not mercy and truth forsake thee: bind them about thy neck; write them upon the table of thine heart: so shalt thou find favour and good understanding in the sight of God and man. Trust in the Lord with all thine heart; and lean not unto thine own understanding. In all thy ways acknowledge him, and he shall direct thy paths. Be not wise in thine own eyes: fear the Lord, and depart from evil. It shall be health to thy navel, and marrow to thy bones. Honour the Lord with thy substance, and with the first-fruits of thine increase: so shall thy barns be filled with plenty, and thy presses shall burst out with new wine."

THE admonition in the first verse, "My son, forget not my law; but let thine heart keep my commandments," is substantially the same as that in the eighth verse of the first chapter. The terms, however, are not identical, and there is a shade of corresponding difference in the meaning. *Three things* may be considered as implied in this verse— REMEMBRANCE, ATTACHMENT, and OBEDIENCE. First, then, it is an admonition to *remembrance:—"forget not* my law." Some there are—not a few indeed—who almost put away from themselves every admonition that relates to the exercise of *memory.* They say they have *no* memory. It too often happens, however, that the failure in memory is confined to subjects of this nature; that in other matters it is sufficiently ready and sufficiently retentive. Allow me, then, to remark, that the mental faculties have a close relation and a mutual dependence on each other. There are, without doubt, original diversities in the power of memory. But memory

depends greatly on *attention ;* and attention depends not less
upon the *interest* which the mind feels in the subject.   He
who feels no interest will not attend ; and he who does not
attend will not remember.   The admonition *not to forget*
involves, therefore, an admonition to attention—to the giving of "earnest heed"—that so the divine laws and truths
might be fixed in the mind.—The words include, secondly,
affectionate attachment,—"Let *thine heart* keep my commandments."   It is not enough that we merely remember
as we might the laws of the twelve tables, or any other code,
in which we feel no farther interest than that which arises
from historical curiosity.   We must feel our interest in them,
as commandments binding on ourselves.   They must have
more than even the approbation of the conscience; they
must have the concurrent affections of the heart, as the commandments of One to whom the love and devotion of our
whole souls is supremely due.   And wherever there is this
consent of heart, there will be the *third* thing involved in
the words, *spiritual obedience.*   The "heart keeping the commandments," must surely be considered as meaning, not external conformity merely to their requirements, but agreement with them in the inward principles, desires, and motives.   God's laws are, in this respect as in others, like himself : they search the heart.   They require *it* to be right
with God.   "If we regard iniquity in our hearts, the Lord
will not hear us."   "The thought of wickedness is sin."
"The Lord weigheth the spirits."   "The law is spiritual."
The HEART is what he requires ; and it is his, just in proportion as, under the influence of his *love,* it is conformed
to his *law.*

A motive is held out in the second verse to compliance
with the admonition of the first :—"For length of days, and
long life, and peace shall they add to thee."

Such declarations are frequent.   They certainly are not
to be interpreted as a promise of long life in this world, in
every instance, as the result of obedience to God's laws.
Had this been a promise even *then,* there would never have
been a case of death among "Israelites indeed," except in

old age.   But assuredly, in point of fact, it was not so.
There are promises to Israel, of their days being prolonged
in the land which the Lord their God had given them,
which are greatly mistaken when interpreted of the
life of individuals; and as pledging in every case its prolongation to all the good.   Such passages relate to the *continued possession of the land of promise by the people,* if
they, in their successive generations, *continued to serve God
in the obedience of faith.*—But there is a *general tendency*
in the keeping of the divine precepts to the preservation of
health and the prolongation of life, which is all that was
then meant, or can now be meant, when the declaration is
applied to *individuals.*   The virtues of sobriety, of temperance, and chastity, and industry, and contentment, and
control of the tempers and passions, and regularity, and
integrity, and kindness,—and others that are included in
subjection to the law of God, have all, in various ways, a
manifest tendency to such a result.   They conduce, eminently, in the ordinary course of things, to the enjoyment of
health and long life—to the prevention of the tear and wear
of the constitution, and to general prosperity and well-being;
for here, as in many other places, *"peace"* may be understood as meaning more than *quietness* merely—even general
prosperity.   Such a tendency forms a quite sufficient ground
for general declarations such as that before us.

In verse third is a specification of certain of the virtues
to be cultivated and practised:—"Let not mercy and truth
forsake thee: bind them about thy neck; write them upon
the table of thine heart."

"Mercy and *truth"* are to be maintained in the whole of
our intercourse and transactions with our fellow-men.

"Mercy" has two departments of exercise.   There is
mercy to *offenders,* and mercy to *sufferers.*   The first is the
spirit of gentleness, conciliation, and forgiveness;—a temper
often and strongly inculcated on *us* in the New Testament
Scriptures, (Eph. iv. 32; Col. iii. 12, 13.)   The second is
the spirit of humanity, and sympathy, and compassionate
and active tenderness and kindness.   This is associated with

the other in the passages already quoted, and often urged as indispensable to the Christian character, as it was of old to that of the true Israelite, (1 John iii. 16—18.) It was this spirit which the Saviour so beautifully inculcated, even towards enemies, in the parable of the good Samaritan; and of which, in his whole life, he gave so interesting and perfect an exemplification.

Added to this must be "truth"—in all our *words*—in all our *conduct*,—for we may lie in look and in act, as well as with the lips. Truth implies that universal and unswerving veracity and integrity which secure the unhesitating confidence of all,—guileless simplicity and godly sincerity in all our ways.

Respecting "mercy and truth," three things are here enjoined: 1. "*Let them not forsake thee:*"—that is, let the practice of them be steadfastly and invariably adhered to by thee in all thy course—in all circumstances however trying, how strong soever the temptation to different feelings and an opposite course:—never in any case let them leave thee; keep them by thee constantly and perseveringly, that in no situation in which thou mayest be placed, they may ever fail to prompt and counsel thee.—Then 2. "*Bind them about thy neck:*"—that is, let them be at all times the grace and ornament of thy character. That this is the idea appears from chap. i. 9, "For they shall be an ornament of grace unto thy head, and chains about the neck." And then the command to "bind them about thy neck," seems to imply the wearing of them constantly, as the permanent adorning;—not to be put on at one time and put off at another, like certain ornamental articles of dress that are worn only on special occasions and in particular companies. These are ornaments fit for all times and for all descriptions of society. All will admire "mercy and truth."—And 3. "*Write them upon the table of thy heart.*" Inscribe them deeply there. Let them not be the *ornament* of thy character merely, but thy *treasure* too. Let all thy heart's affections and desires be under their control. Be not satisfied with knowing them as what was "written on tables of stone;" but let thy desire be, to have them incorporated with all the dispositions of the inner man,—to possess a heart in entire unison with their dictates,—to have, through prayer, the promise of the new covenant fulfilled in thee.*

Here too a motive is subjoined—verse 4. "So shalt thou find favour and good understanding in the sight of God and man."

I have already said, that the ground of divine favour to *sinners* is nothing of theirs. The entire tenor of God's word, and many most explicit passages in it, bear testimony to the grace of his covenant, and to the "redemption that is in Christ Jesus," as the ground of reconciliation and forgiveness. But the enjoyment of the favour of God stands in inseparable association with the possession and manifestation of a certain character.† There is no enjoying the smile and blessing of God in any other way than the way of holy obedience. They who would walk with God must walk *there;* for nowhere else can God be found.

And as to *men:*—they are of two descriptions—the *good* and the *bad.* It is very obvious, that by the character recommended the favour of all the *good* will be secured. They are of one mind with God. They love what God loves, and hate what God hates. They that "love the Lord hate evil." "Mercy and truth" are the recommendations of all human character; for they are the recommendations of the divine.—But even as to *bad* men—to mankind in general, favour will be shown to "mercy and truth." The men of the world may hate the *principles* of the man of God, but the latter will have a testimony in their conscience; and if he maintains a steadfast consistency, will command their respect and good-will. This is the only legitimate way of finding favour with men. Their favour must be foregone, if it cannot be gotten but by conduct inconsistent with right principle. It is but a false and selfish and temporary favour at the best that can thus be obtained; and it is obtained at the expense of what is infinitely more precious, the favour of God.

* Jer. xxx. 33. 2 Cor. iii. 3.
† See Psal. v. 4—6, 12: xi. 7: xxxiv. 15, 16.

But the Scriptures teach us that "the way of man is not
in himself: it is not in man that walketh to direct his
steps." How, then, is steadfast consistency to be maintained?—how is the favour of the Lord to be thus steadfastly
enjoyed? The answer is—verses 5—8. "Trust in the
Lord with all thine heart; and lean not unto thine own
understanding."

Self-sufficiency and self-dependence, ever since man gave
credit to the lie of the tempter, and violated God's law, in
the vain hope of thereby exalting himself to the possession of knowledge like his Maker's—has been one of the
characteristics of his fallen nature. Instead of "trusting in
Jehovah," with the becoming lowliness of a dependent creature, he has all along, from that time, shown an infatuated
proneness to rely on himself—on his own might, his own
wisdom, his own resources. "Leaning to our own understanding" is, as far as it prevails, a kind of practical atheism.
To form and prosecute our plans in this spirit of self-confidence, entirely forgetting Him "in whose hand our breath
is, and whose are all our ways," is to act as if there were *no*
God—as if the fool's *thought* or the fool's *wish* were true.

Remember, however, that "trusting in the Lord"—does
not mean that we are not to *use* our "own understanding"—
forming our plans with discretion, and with all possible foresight and precaution,—and in pursuing our ends employing
all suitable and legitimate means. No. There is a legitimate
using of the understanding that is not chargeable with "leaning to it." While we use it, we are to depend on God for
success, trust in the promises of his word, and trust in the
care and overruling direction of his providence. Many a
time has he shown by what trivial circumstances he can dis-
concert the most carefully arranged and apparently promising
human devices. But still—as dependence upon God for
strength to resist temptation does not preclude our applying
all the energy of our own minds, so dependence upon him
for *direction* in our ways does not set aside the employment
of our own prudence and sagacity. It is our duty to acknowledge Him as *Sovereign*—" doing according to his will—

none staying his hand;" as our Creator and Preserver, without whom we cannot draw a breath,—cannot live a moment for the effectuation of our purposes;* as the Supreme Director of all events, whose concurrent will is essential to the success of every measure, and without it all the thoughts of men are vain, turning out subversive of their own designs and subservient to God's.†

Verse 6. "In all thy ways acknowledge him, and he shall direct thy paths."

Such acknowledgment of God, implies the careful consultation of God's word for guidance, with a spirit that is disposed to bow implicitly to its authority in regard to the *lawfulness* or *propriety* of our ways—undertaking nothing till we have first ascertained this—that there is nothing in what we project and purpose to do that is out of harmony with God's moral precepts. This must always be first. And, in doing this, unless we come to God's word with the spirit mentioned—the spirit of sincere determination to follow the dictates of the oracle—to relinquish whatever we may have designed the moment we perceive any inconsistency between it and his will,—we are not "*acknowledging*" him. We are mocking him,—seeking to know *his* will with the secret resolution of following *our own;*—coming to his directory only in the expectation of finding our will supported by his,—and when we find it otherwise, spurning or compromising his counsel. Then, when we have ascertained our purpose to be *lawful,* we must look for direction and illumination, in considering its *prudence* and *expediency* and *probable results,* expecting God's counsel and blessing, owning his authority, aiming at his glory, exercising submission to his sovereign pleasure; taking him as friend and counsellor in all our concerns, and leaving no means untried to discover what will be well-pleasing in his sight. He who, in lowly reliance, and in earnest, acts this part, will not often fall into very erroneous or hurtful measures. God, by his word, and Spirit, and providence, will lead him in a right way,—will "make darkness light before him and crooked things straight."

* See James iv. 13—15.   † See Isa. x. 5—16.

In "acknowledging" God, we are not to trust enthusiastically to impressions, to dreams, to fancied voices and inward suggestions. Far less are we to make a lottery of the Bible—opening it at random, and taking the text that first meets our eye as *given us* by God, and putting our own meaning upon it. We are to apply our understandings to the blessed volume of inspiration, that we may find its principles and precepts that bear upon our case, and give our hearts to prayer, for that influence of the Holy Spirit, which is necessary to deliver us from all undue prepossessions and prejudices in examining it. We are not now warranted to look for immediate inspiration,—for any direct intimations of the Spirit in regard to the course which at any time we ought to follow. The Spirit guides by the word—imparting that childlike simplicity—the simplicity and sincere submissiveness of " babes in Christ"—which will seldom leave those who are influenced by it long in the dark.

The seventh verse is a continuation of the same admonition :—" Be not wise in thine own eyes: fear the Lord and depart from evil."

A woe is pronounced by Jehovah against the spirit of self-sufficiency—"Woe unto them that are wise in their own eyes, and prudent in their own sight!" Isa. v. 21. And the injunction of the Lord to Christians is—" Be not wise in your own conceits," Rom. xii. 16. Such a conceit of our own wisdom as produces the prohibited self-dependence and forgetfulness of God is inconsistent with the proper *fear of God.* Hence the connexion—" Be not wise in thine own eyes—*fear the Lord.*" Cherish that reverential awe which will induce the constant acknowledgment of Him ; and beware of provoking his jealousy of his own glory, for " the proud he knoweth afar off;" and it is " the *meek* he guides in judgment, to the meek he teaches his way."

We may remark another connexion. Where there is this self-conceit and self-reliance, there is danger of too little regard being paid to the first and highest of all questions, the question of the divine will,—of too little discrimination as to the morality of either *end* or *means.* Hence, in connexion with the condemnation of trust in our own wisdom, the wise man says, "Fear the Lord, *and depart from evil*"— into which, as if he had said, trust in yourselves and *distrust* of God will ever be apt to lead you. There is no true "fear of the Lord" unless there is departure from evil; and a genuine, humble, deep-felt fear of God—the constant, steadfast, self-diffident operation of the religious principle—will keep all right. It is a posture of mind that is beneficial alike to *body* and *soul*. This is the sentiment of the eighth verse: "It shall be health to thy navel, and marrow to thy bones." By the influence of this principle the mind is preserved in a state of cheerful tranquillity and peace—as the prophet says —"Thou wilt keep him in perfect peace whose mind is stayed on thee," Isa. xxvi. 3. Now this tranquil and cheerful evenness of temper is in a high degree conducive to the health and comfort and vigour of the bodily frame. Every one knows how a state of anxiety and care, by chasing sleep from the eyes, and depriving of appetite, and otherwise affecting the functions of the animal nature, injures the health; and, when long continued and pressing heavily, may waste the vital energies, and even bring to the grave. And while health is thus promoted, the spirit of humble dependence and firm confidence in God contributes eminently to the prosperous growth of all the other graces and virtues of the Christian character. "Faith in God" is the germ of all spiritual growth;—and "the joy of the Lord," springing from the exercise of an undoubting and unceasing dependence upon him in temporal and in spiritual things, "is the strength" of God's children in all the activity of the divine life.

There was never a grosser slander than that which is thrown on religion when it is represented as tending to injure the body and the mind, by preying upon the spirit and sinking it to the earth. False *views* of religion may prey upon both mind and body—engendering distress and despondency; but true religion never can. It is cheering as the light of heaven, and healthful and bracing as the mountain breezes. The state of mind from which true religion is designed and fitted to deliver, is sometimes mistaken for religion itself—I mean a state of conviction, alarm, and fear. But this is not religion:—it is that from which religion delivers. The knowledge and faith of God as his own word reveals him,—confidence in him as he is there made known, —produces peace, and hope, and joy,—expels the fear which hath torment, and settles the soul in the sunshine of divine love.

As a large proportion of the speculations, and projects, and plans, and labours of men are directed to the acquisition of wealth, Solomon counsels, in the two following verses, how to use it when it has been obtained:—verses 9, 10. "Honour the Lord with thy substance, and with the first-fruits of all thine increase: so shall thy barns be filled with plenty, and thy presses shall burst out with new wine."

If, under the influence of the fear of the Lord, we consider all as *his gift*—got under his providential direction, and smile, and blessing—the same spirit will prompt us to consecrate *to Him*, what *through Him* has been acquired. Moses admonishes the Israelites of the danger of forgetting God as the author of all their prosperity. (Deut. viii. 10—18.) It was in proportion as they kept in mind their obligations to Jehovah for all the blessings of the land of promise, that they consecrated the substance which was his gift to his worship and to his glory; and in proportion as they fell into the sin of self-sufficiency and forgetfulness of him, they alienated his gifts from him, and gave his glory to another. So will it be with *us*. The more humbly and devoutly we remember God as the *author* of our prosperity, will we practically honour God in the *use* of our prosperity.

The Israelites "honoured the Lord with their substance," when, at the erection of the tabernacle in the wilderness, so willing and abundant was the contribution, that a proclamation of excess was required to restrain it. And similar had been the disposition manifested in the preparation for the erection of the first temple. They "honoured the Lord with their substance," when they devoted the due proportions of

it to the ends of piety and charity which he had enjoined it
on them to mind.

The law of the first-fruits you find in Deut. xxvi. 1—3;
12—15. They "honoured the Lord," when they followed
his law—first, because the act itself was an act of obedience,
which is always honouring to him; second, because it was
accompanied with a confession of God's covenant faithfulness
in the fulfilment of his promises, and a thank-offering for
that faithful accomplishment of his word; and third, because
the offering was designed for the support of his worship,
and thus for securing the glory of his name.

The spirit of the law referred to is here inculcated; and
neither in the terms of the duty nor of the motive, on
principles at all *peculiar to Israel.* The duty is a duty
still. The motive is a motive still. The injunction before us stands opposed to the *selfish use* of God's temporal
gifts,—of what we are ever too prone to think and call
our own. God's language to his people now is the same
as it was of old — "The silver is mine, and the gold is
mine, saith the Lord of hosts," Hag. ii. 8.

In the language before us works both of piety and charity are evidently included. By both God is honoured; because both are enjoined by him as parts of the true use of
worldly substance. They do not "honour the Lord with their
substance" who use it for the gratification of vanity, or pride,
or ambition, or covetousness; who squander it *on* self, or
hoard it *for* self. They honour him with it, who employ it
in ways consistent with his will, and calculated to promote
his glory—*indirectly* by the manifestation of the influence
of his religion, and *directly* by promoting the diffusion of
the knowledge and influence of its principles. The law of
the *first-fruits* teaches us the important principle, that God,
instead of the last place, should have the first in his people's
generous calculations and bestowments. The arrangement
of the petitions in the Lord's prayer teach us the same lesson: those which relate to God, his name, and his kingdom,
preceding those which relate to ourselves. The injunction
of the Saviour justly interpreted, is in spirit and letter the

same—" Seek ye first the kingdom of God."—Do we then
honour the Lord with our substance, when, after bestowing
lavishly on self all that self can wish,—not withholding our
heart from any joy,—we give a little driblet of our surplus
for him, for his poor, for his cause and kingdom? Does *he*
honour the Lord who, without a grudge, expends ten, twen-
ty, fifty, or a hundred guineas on some article of ornamental
elegance, or mere convenience, or at any rate of very questionable necessity, while the smallest pittance can with difficulty be wrung from him for the great interests of the
Redeemer's kingdom?—sums after sums, large and small,
for worldly accommodations and enjoyments,—and a pound
a-year for the salvation of the world!

Various are the motives held out to encourage the duty of
liberality. In the verses before us, you may be tempted to
regard the motive as a somewhat selfish and questionable
one :—"So shall thy barns be filled with plenty, and thy
presses shall burst out with new wine." But second
thoughts may give you another view of it. It is *a trial of
faith.* And it is a trial than which few are found more
difficult. It is hard to persuade a man that *giving away*
will make him rich. We look with more confidence to
bank interest, or the still better interest of a vested loan,
than to a return of profit from what is *given wholly away.*
It is difficult to convince a man that *scattering* will increase
his store.

While, therefore, the motive in itself looks worldly and
selfish, he who comes to feel it so as to act liberally upon it,
exercises a *faith in God* that is rare and of the highest order.
He walks by faith, not by sight. He who gives to the
poor, because God hath said—"He that hath pity on the
poor, lendeth to the Lord"—gives *in faith.* He who bestows of his substance for the cause of God, because God
hath said, "Honour the Lord with thy substance, and with
the first-fruits of all thine increase : so shall thy barns be
filled with plenty, and thy presses shall burst out with new
wine"—bestows *in faith.* The promise is that the blessing
of God shall be upon the substance and upon the industry

of the liberal,—of those whose godliness overcomes their selfishness, and who show their faith and love by their liberality especially to God's own cause.*

My brethren, there is too little of *proving God* in this matter. We can only discover God's faithfulness by trying it; and without a doubt, if there were more of trial on our part, there would be proportionally more of the manifestation of faithfulness on his.

And there is a higher motive, even as it respects the results to ourselves, than earthly prosperity. Compliance with this injunction is not only a means of increasing our temporal good, but of augmenting our blessedness for eternity. For, while all the happiness of the world to come, shall be bestowed and enjoyed on the ground of *grace*, yet there shall be degrees of blessedness and glory corresponding to the measure in which the principles of faith and love have been practically manifested—a correspondence between the one and the other, as the apostle expresses it, like that between the seed sown and the crop reaped; the reaping corresponding in amount to the sowing. The right use of worldly substance is one of the ways in which the Lord exhorts his disciples to " provide themselves bags that wax not old, a treasure in the heavens that faileth not." But He whom we serve *knows the motives* by which we are influenced : —so that, if one is giving either in the spirit of self-righteousness, or of ostentation, or of any other unwarranted principle—" Let not that man think that he shall obtain anything of the Lord."

* Look at a striking and edifying exemplification of the principle: Hag. i. 3—11: ii. 15—19. Mal. iii. 10.—And in the New Testament see Phil. iv. 14—19. 2 Cor. ix. 6—8.

LECTURE VIII.

———◆———

Prov. iii. 11, 12.

" My son, despise not the chastening of the Lord; neither be weary of his correction: for whom the Lord loveth he correcteth; even as a father the son in whom he delighteth."

" Ye have forgotten," says the inspired writer to the He- brews, " the exhortation which speaketh unto you as unto children, My son, despise not thou the chastening of the Lord, nor faint when thou art rebuked of him: for whom the Lord loveth, he chasteneth, and scourgeth every son whom he receiveth," Heb. xii. 5, 6. We have thus the highest authority for regarding the address in this passage, as *divine*—as the address of *God* to his own children.

Is the address, then, to *all men?* No.—There is a sense indeed, and a very natural one, in which we are God's children, as being the *creatures of his hand.* We are his children by creation. He gives us being; and by him our being is constantly sustained, and its wants all supplied.— In tracing the genealogy of Jesus, Luke terminates it with " Adam, who was the *son of God.*" All the rest in the enumeration, had their birth by successive parentages; but Adam had no father but God. And in this sense, as having all alike our being from God, it may truly be said, in the terms of the prophet—" Have we not all one Father? hath not one God begotten us?"

But there was a higher sense in which Adam, when created, was a child of God: I mean, *by character.* In the phraseology of Scripture, one is called the *son* of another, who bears remarkable resemblance to him in this respect. And indeed we are not unaccustomed to the figure ourselves. We are wont to say of a youth who bears, in various features of his character, a striking likeness to his father, that he is *quite his father's son.* It is in this sense that our Lord says to the Jews, in reply to their indignant allegation—"Abraham is our father"—"*if ye were Abraham's children, ye would do the works of Abraham.*" This is a very important sense of the designation. And in this sense, Adam ceased to be a child of God, when he fell into sin. He lost the divine image—the moral likeness of his Maker. He was made after that image, but sin effaced it. And in this sense, all his race have ceased to sustain the spiritual relation. As sinners, they are not the children of God, but "children of the *Wicked One,*" the great enemy of God, by whose temptation the seduction and apostasy were effected.

And the grand design of God by the scheme of mediation, is to bring men back to this holy and happy relation,—to restore apostate men to the honour and the blessedness of sonship to God. In this reconciliation—this transference from their relation to Satan to the family of God—there are two things essentially implied—they must be *pardoned*, and they must be *purified.* A state of sonship is a state of *favour;* and this necessarily includes forgiveness. No unforgiven sinner is a child of God. He is not in a state of reconciliation and acceptance; and not, therefore, one of his *children;* paternity involving and being the very image of love. This is effected by the *atonement*—by the work of Christ in expiating human guilt by the sacrifice of himself. Sinners who believe in that atonement, as the ground of pardon, are forgiven. God's "anger is turned away" from them. He "receives them graciously," "loves them freely;" and gives them "a name and a place in his house," even that of "sons and of daughters."

The other requisite to this relation is *resemblance.* They must be *renewed* and *purified.* No sinner continuing under the *power* any more than in the guilt of his sins, can be a child of God. When God created man, he made him "*after his likeness."* When God *adopts* a sinner—he re-instamps this image on his soul: and this new assimilation constitutes him a *son.* The Scripture expresses the sum of human depravity by the phrase, "the carnal mind is enmity against God." When a sinner becomes a child of God—there is a transition from enmity to love. God loves the renewed sinner; the renewed sinner loves God. This mutual love, paternal and filial, enters into the very essence of the relation. This saving change is effected by the agency of the Holy Spirit:—and it is effected by means of the gospel. The pardon is *on the ground* of the atonement. The renewal is *by means* of the atonement—the truth, that reveals the love of God in the provision of the ground of pardon, subduing the alienated heart to surrender itself to God. The very doctrine of pardon is the means of regeneration. There is forgiveness with God, *that he may be feared.*

Believers, then, are *God's children:* such is invariably the statement of his word.* And this is the gift of God's grace, and the work of God's Spirit.† And this, brethren, is no mere empty title—not a title of which the only accompaniment is the honour of it. It is a real relation, with which stand associated the most unspeakably precious privileges—privileges in time and eternity.

One of these privileges is brought before us in the text. It is one of no trivial value. The world in which we live is a place of trial. Many and various are the sufferings to which men in general, and the people of God among the rest, are subjected. The text speaks of the aspect which all these trials and sufferings bear, to those who have been brought into this new relation. The aspect is widely different from that which the same dispensations bear to the men of the world, the children of "the Wicked One." It is very plain, that the same description of events may be viewed in different lights, and may be designed by Him who sends them for different purposes, according to the character of the parties affected by them. To the one they may be *judicial,*

* See John i 11—13. Gal. iii. 26.
† See 1 John iii. 1. Rom. viii. 14—17. Gal. iv. 4—7.

to the other *gracious;* to the one a fruit and a part of the
curse, to the other, though not in themselves yet in their end,
a blessing—the curse being extracted from them, and the
paternal love of God turning them all to purposes of salutary
correction. There is a beautiful amplification of the sentiment in the words of the Apostle, "And ye have forgotten
the exhortation which speaketh unto you as unto children,
My son, despise not thou the chastening of the Lord, nor
faint when thou art rebuked of him: for whom the Lord
loveth he chasteneth, and scourgeth every son whom he receiveth. If ye endure chastening, God dealeth with you as
with sons; for what son is he whom the father chasteneth
not? But if ye be without chastisement, whereof all are
partakers, then are ye bastards, and not sons. Furthermore
we have had fathers of our flesh which corrected us, and we
gave them reverence: shall we not much rather be in subjection unto the Father of spirits, and live? For they verily
for a few days chastened us after their own pleasure; but
he for our profit, that we might be partakers of his holiness.
Now no chastening for the present seemeth to be joyous, but
grievous: nevertheless afterward it yieldeth the peaceable
fruit of righteousness unto them which are exercised thereby,"
Heb. xii. 5—11.

We shall consider—

I. THE ADMONITION. It consists of two parts. The one
is an admonition against *insensibility;* the other against
despondency. And both admonitions are founded in the
view of the trials of life, as divine visitations or chastisements
—paternal corrections. Every one of them is a stroke of
the Father's rod:—and the twofold admonition warns us
against the *two extremes* into which we are ever prone to fall.

1. When may we be said to *despise* the chastening of the
Lord? In the following cases. i. When it is not *felt;*—
when there is a want of natural sensibility to the particular
stroke of the rod. This is but rare. Men in general are
quite sufficiently alive to the value of temporal things. But
the value is comparative. There are cherished and favourite
possessions, and others less highly thought of, less fondly

held. The Lord, it may be, deals gently. He spares the "gourd." He does not take what is most highly set by. And, instead of humbly owning the kindness,—being lowly and submissive, and seeking a blessing on the gentle stroke that the heavier one may be withheld,—the preservation and safety of the greater produces insensibility to the privation of the less: and the correction is thus disregarded, and proves inefficient.—ii. When it is not duly felt *as from God;* when God's hand, in the correction, is not duly considered, acknowledged, and submitted to. How much soever an event may be felt in itself; how much soever the feelings of nature may be wounded to the quick, and the heart ready to break under the sad calamity, be what it may, —unless it is felt as coming *from God*, it is "despised." Every thing depends on this. A child may smart under the rod, or his punishment may vex and distress him greatly, but he may not feel it *as from his father.* It is not the sense of *his displeasure* that grieves him. And so with the child of God. If while smarting under his suffering he fails to own his heavenly Father's hand; if it is considered as a mere chance that has befallen him,—as something that forms a part of the common lot of men, the *fortune* of others as well as his,—it is "despised." That which should be most seen and most regarded, and give most concern, is overlooked or little thought of.—iii. When, although God is seen in it, and his hand is felt, it is not felt *humbly and submissively; not bowed to but resisted;*—when, in the expressive phrase of the wise man elsewhere, "the heart fretteth against the Lord;" or when the chastisement has the effect that restraint and coercion have, in the expressive figure of the prophet, on the "bullock unaccustomed to the yoke," rendering him stubborn, wayward, refractory. This is the reverse of the admonition of James—"Humble yourselves under the mighty hand of God." It is the very opposite of all that correction is intended to effect. Job exemplified the proper state of mind under correction. He felt God's hand; he owned it; he bowed to it: "The Lord gave, and the Lord hath taken away; blessed be the name of the Lord."—

"Shall we receive good at the hand of God, and shall we not receive evil?" Job i. 21; ii. 10. The spirit of Jonah was a mournful exemplification of the opposite, when he fretted impatiently and selfishly at the loss of his gourd, and said, in the heat of a discontented and rebellious heart—"I do well to be angry." Never surely could there be more unseemly and sinful irreverence. It was "doing despite" to the correcting hand of the Lord—treating contemptuously the procedure of Him whose chastisement should have laid him low. All unsubmissiveness is contempt.—iv. When the *design* or *end* of correction is not duly laid to heart; is not seriously thought of and sought after. We never treat a fellow-creature with due consideration, when we show no concern about the *objects* he has in view; and especially when we ourselves are the subjects of his solicitude and his schemes. A child shows no respect for his parents, when, on being corrected by them for a fault, instead of seeking to shun the fault in future, he repeats it. This is practical contempt. So when the Lord tells his children the design of his corrections, and they show no anxiety after the attainment of that design, they "despise" his "chastening." The design may be. more general, or more particular. The *general* design of all affliction is—"to take away sin." He who receives correction, but discovers no solicitude about being made by it a "partaker of God's holiness," "despises" it. The *particular* design may be involved in the nature of the correction. If there is worldly ambition—a commencing or growing prevalence of the "lust of the eyes and the pride of life"—it may be particularly aimed at by the infliction of sweeping losses in earthly substance; the frustration of sanguine hopes, and of painfully concerted schemes of gain and of worldly advancement. If there is the idolatry of the natural affections—any fondly cherished object of these drawing the heart away from God, and absorbing its interest, its solicitude, and its love—*that* may be rebuked and repressed by the smiting of the husband, or the wife, or the favourite and idolized child. Now if in either case, instead of the heart being weaned from the world and the excesses of its earthly affections—neither is its ambition cured in the one, nor its idolatry in the other; if it continues set, in all its desires, on the objects of which it has been deprived, so that it cannot let go its hold of them, but hankers after them, wastes itself in regrets and lamentations, unreconciled to the divine will, and forgetting the *purpose* of the privations, in sighing over the privations themselves, —we are then "despising the chastening;" for we are not seeking in earnest the accomplishment in us of the divine intention. We are not of one mind with God. We are treating despitefully his judgment,—for while he considers the *end* of affliction as well worth the sacrifice involved in the affliction itself—as more really valuable than the objects of earthly attachment and sources of earthly enjoyment which, for the sake of it, he takes away,—*we* judge otherwise; and mourn over our losses, and would have the objects of our attachment and the sources of our enjoyment back again,—instead of being humbly thankful for our intended benefit, and seeking with anxiety to obtain it.

2. The *second* of the two extremes against which we are admonished is—"being weary of his correction;" or, as the apostle has it, "fainting when we are rebuked of him." We are chargeable with this—i. When we cherish a spirit similar to that just noticed—*dwelling* on, and brooding over, the trial itself; indulging fond memory in hanging and weeping over the recollection of it,—the spirit sinking to faintness, or wearying itself to exhaustion, by incessant bemoaning. This is wrong; and it arises, like the last mentioned, from forgetting, in the trial itself, the *end* for which it has been sent. It is remarkable how precisely opposite to "fainting" and "wearying" is the use which the apostle exhorts the Hebrews to make of their trials— "Wherefore lift up the hands which hang down, and the feeble knees; and make straight paths for your feet, lest that which is lame be turned out of the way; but let it rather be healed," Heb. xii. 12, 13.—ii. This "wearying" and "fainting" may arise from unbelief of the divine promises on *two* points—as to the *design* of the trial,

and as to *strength* or *grace* duly to bear and to improve it. There is nothing so bracing to the spirit, which might otherwise be ready to give way to feebleness and fainting, as the firm conviction of the two important Bible truths—*first*, that "all things are of God;" and *second*, that "all things work together for good to them that love God." If the mind loses sight, or loses hold, of such assurances, the spirit will droop and languish. And so too is it, when the suffering saint forgets God's "precious promises"* to the afflicted, and neglects to plead them at the throne of grace." —iii. "Fainting" and "wearying" may take place in two ways. The heart may be overwhelmed by *sudden* trials—suddenness and heaviness united, giving an effect so stunning and over-powering, that the spirit sinks into a temporary stupefaction, its energies giving way—as the nervous and circulatory systems in the bodily frame are apt to be affected by any very sudden mental shock—going sometimes, with momentary intervals of revival, from one faint to another, each interval only giving time for the mind to receive a fresh impression of the stunning calamity, ere it has leisure for invigorating reflection. Or, it may become wearied out and exhausted by the long continuance of the same trial, or by the rapid succession of different strokes of the rod—another and another coming, ere the wound of the former has had time to heal. There are cases of both kinds to be met with, which have a strong claim on the sympathy of fellow-christians. But how long soever the chastening hand of the Lord may be allowed to lie on the subject of his correction, and how numerous and frequent soever may be the successive strokes, there ought to be no "fainting" and no "wearying." One thing alone—the assurance that *"It is the Lord"*—should be enough to prevent both the one and the other. This naturally leads to—

II. The CONSIDERATION ENFORCING THE ADMONITION—" For whom the Lord loveth he correcteth; even as a father the son in whom he delighteth."

* As 2 Cor. xii. 9.   Is. xl. 28—30.

There is in the words a beautiful and most touching appeal to the very strongest and tenderest of nature's affections.
There is in this much of divine condescension and kindness.
Had the infinite God addressed us in terms of divine loftiness, such as befitted only GODHEAD, expressing what be-
longed to himself exclusively, and to which there was nothing
in our own nature and our own experience to which it bore
even a distant analogy—we could not have understood, and
therefore we could not have *felt* it. We might have mar-
velled at the incomprehensible grandeur of the communication—of which possibly we might, by the straining of our
faculties, grasp as much as to make us wish for the mind of
an angel, that we might comprehend more. But it would
have awed us by its sublimity, more than it could have
melted and cheered us by its kindness. But when "the
high and lofty One who inhabiteth eternity," deigns to speak
to us "after the manner of men;" to enter into our own
hearts, and draw his figures and illustrations thence,—exhibiting himself under relations which we bear to one another,—assuring us of the affections on the one part of that
relation, as borne and exercised by himself towards us, and
claiming from us in return those which appropriately pertain
to the other,—we understand this; we feel this; we have a
commentary on its meaning, written on our hearts with the
very finger of God. He addresses us in terms of which we
have the interpreter within. When we try to form to ourselves the conception of a Being without passions, without
emotions, without variableness, — an ocean-depth, whose
surface no storm can ruffle, whose unfathomed abysses nothing
can agitate,—we are lost in veneration and awe. We can
form no conception of what the state of such a mind can be
towards any other existing being. "It is high; we cannot
attain unto it." But when that infinite Being breaks the
dread silence; and his voice comes upon our ear in accents like
these—"As a father pitieth his children, so the LORD pitieth
them that fear him;"—"I will be a Father to you, and ye
shall be my sons and daughters, saith the Lord Almighty;"
—our bosoms thrill with new and unutterable delight:

the smile of ecstasy plays upon our lips; and the starting tear of grateful joy gushes to our eye; and through that tear we look up with the reverential but confiding love and gladness of children. And when, amidst the trials of the world, He reminds us of his paternal relation to us, and assures us that they are of his appointment,—the dictate of his fatherly affection and wisdom; when through the clouds that shroud our sky his eye beams upon us, and his voice, not in thunder but in the whisper of peace, comes upon our ear—"My son, despise not thou the chastening of the LORD, nor faint when thou art rebuked of him: for whom the Lord loveth he chasteneth, and scourgeth every son whom he receiveth,"—what a comfort in our deepest distresses—what a light of joy in our gloomiest day!

Let us not fail to observe, in order that we may not lose the benefit of our trials, that they *are* tokens of disapprobation and displeasure. God hates sin. He hates it in all. And if there be any in whom he regards it with special detestation, it is in his own children. He never "afflicts willingly." He has no *pleasure* in correcting. But in proportion as his children are the objects of his love, sin in his children is the object of his hatred. It mars their character, and interferes with that complacency with which he contemplates his own image in them.

We must beware of allowing our minds to be so absorbed in contemplating the divine *love* in trials, as to overlook the divine *displeasure* in them. All are *for sin*. There is no suffering in the universe but what is the fruit of sin—all its righteous desert. His children, even the best of them, have ever abundant reason to acknowledge that he corrects them less than their iniquities deserve. But still he corrects. The correction partakes of the nature of punishment; and punishments are expressions of the righteous displeasure of him by whom they are inflicted. And we should seek with all earnestness, that we may be "of one mind with God" in regard to the faults for which he chastens us. If his chastisements produce *this* effect;—if they transfuse into our minds a portion of the hatred with which he regards the

G

evil corrected—all is well. And this cannot be the case if
we omit to reflect on the *displeasure* that is in them; if we
smile at the thought of God's unchanging love, so as to fail to
mark the frown that darkens his brow. O that frown! How
should the thought of it go to our hearts! To have offended
our kind and gracious Father! To have deserved his displeasure! To have rendered it necessary for him to assume
the rod! If we think thus, and are led by the thought to
inquire into the causes of the displeasure, as they exist in our
hearts or in our lives,—then may we profit by the stroke;
not otherwise.

But still, the displeasure is the displeasure of love. The
frown is the frown of love. The correction is the correction
of love. And a conviction of this also is necessary to its
proving salutary, and to the prevention of the two extremes
against which the text warns us. We shall not "despise"
it, when we are convinced of its being in love; nor, on the
other hand, shall we "faint" and be "weary."

Correction, when required, is represented as an essential
part of an affectionate and faithful parent's trust; so that
God would relinquish his love, and violate the promises of
his faithful covenant, if he did not administer needful chastisement—if he "spared the rod." Thus the apostle represents the case, "For whom the Lord loveth he chasteneth,
and scourgeth every son whom he receiveth. If ye endure
chastening, God dealeth with you as with sons; for what son
is he whom the father chasteneth not?" Heb. xii. 6, 7. This
corresponds with the terms used by Solomon, "even as a
father the son *in whom he delighteth.*" The language implies his delighting in him *at the very time* when necessity
is laid upon him to "visit his transgression with the rod,
and his iniquity with stripes." The bowels of the fond father yearn over his son—never more tenderly than when
thus constrained by affection to put him to pain.

On the part of God, there is love in the gracious *end* of
every trial. What is it? It is expressed under no fewer
than three forms in the same chapter of Hebrews, verses 9
—12. "Furthermore, we have had fathers of our flesh which

corrected us, and we gave them reverence: shall we not much rather be in subjection unto the Father of spirits, and live? For they verily for a few days chastened us after their own pleasure; but he for our profit, that we might be partakers of his holiness. Now, no chastening for the present seemeth to be joyous, but grievous: nevertheless, afterward it yieldeth the peaceable fruit of righteousness unto them which are exercised thereby." There is the general idea of *profit*. And this profit is expressed first in the emphatic phrase—"*and live.*" The end is to maintain and promote the spiritual life in the soul, and thus to "keep it unto life eternal." The spiritual life is in imminent danger from the world and the things of the world; and even from the overweening excess of affections that are in themselves not only lawful but right and incumbent—

> Our dearest joys and nearest friends,
> The partners of our blood—
> How they divide our wandering minds
> And leave but half for God!

It may be necessary to wound these affections by removing their objects, in order to quicken anew the affections that are due to God, and which the excess of the others was in danger of *deadening:*—that we may *live!* It is further expressed in being "made *partakers of his holiness.*" This is much the same thing in other terms. The spiritual life consists essentially in holiness; and the eternal life in which it ends, or rather, which is its maturity, is just the perfection of holiness. *He* has the life in perfection, who has the holiness in perfection. (Comp. Isa. xxvii. 7—9.) There is no end the love of God can pursue—there is nothing whatever the love of God can possibly effect, in behalf of its objects, more precious than making them PARTAKERS OF HIS HOLINESS. O! there is nothing which his children should not—and, if they are right-minded, *will* not cheerfully endure, for the attainment of such a good! What is there that can be taken away, that does not, if *this* is substituted, make the loss an unspeakable gain?—We have it again in "*the peaceable fruits of righteousness.*" We are all sensible of the truth,

that "no affliction for the present seemeth joyous but grievous:"—and it is a comfort that we are not commanded to
be in any such state of mind, as that it should seem to us
other than we feel it to be:—but oh! what a harvest to
reap from the seeds of bitterness and death! if they "yield
the peaceable fruits of righteousness!"

And while the *end* is in love, love *times* and *measures*
every correction.   It comes in its proper season—just when
He who is infinitely wise and kind sees it to be needed, and
when it will be most salutary.   And He corrects in measure
—never inflicting one stroke beyond the requisite number;
never infusing one drop of bitter beyond what, as the Great
Physician, he sees will be salutary.

In addition to all this, God has, in love, given promise
of those influences of the Spirit that are necessary to render his discipline efficacious.   And he makes the very same
appeal to paternal feeling and sensibility that he does in the
text, to give us the full assurance of his readiness to grant
them, "If ye then, being evil, know how to give good gifts
unto your children, how much more shall your heavenly
Father give the Holy Spirit to them that ask him?" Luke
xi. 13.   What an encouragement!   And if, by the influence that comes from our heavenly Father, such are the
happy results of the afflictions of life, we may realize the
words of Paul, "We glory in tribulations also: knowing
that tribulation worketh patience; and patience, experience;
and experience, hope; and hope maketh not ashamed; because the love of God is shed abroad in our hearts by the
Holy Ghost which is given unto us," Rom. v. 3—5.   Such
is the blessed influence on earth; and this ultimately rises
still higher; it tells on heaven—"For our light affliction,
which is but for a moment, worketh for us *a far more exceeding and eternal weight of glory!*" 2 Cor. iv. 17.

LECTURE IX.

Prov. iii. 13—20.

"Happy is the man that findeth wisdom, and the man that getteth under-standing. For the merchandise of it is better than the merchandise of silver, and the gain thereof than fine gold. She is more precious than rubies: and all the things thou canst desire are not to be compared unto her. Length of days is in her right hand; and in her left hand riches and honour. Her ways are ways of pleasantness, and all her paths are peace. She is a tree of life to them that lay hold upon her: and happy is every one that retaineth her. The Lord by wisdom hath founded the earth; by understanding hath he established the heavens. By his knowledge the depths are broken up, and the clouds drop down the dew."

"There be many that say, Who will show us good?" This indeed is the universal inquiry. Wherever men are found, they are found making and pressing it. All the world is astir in seeking an answer to it. In all the conditions of human society, from the lowest to the highest—from the most barbarous to the most civilized, there is one principle in operation—varying in its manifestations, according to the conceptions of good which, in the different stages of human progression, prevail. That principle is the desire of enjoy-ment—a desire expressed in this question, "Who will show us good?" The pursuit is the same. The modes and directions in which the object is sought are infinitely diver-sified. In civilized countries like our own, where the truth of Solomon's words elsewhere—"Money answereth all things" —is so universally experienced, the acquisition of wealth be-comes one of the most general and engrossing of aims and occupations. It fixes more than anything else, the earnestness and constancy of desire and pursuit. *He* is the happy man who proves most successful in this chase; whose speculations are most prosperous, and yield the highest return; who strikes the best bargains, and hits the luckiest chances; who accumulates the largest amount in the shortest time, and with the least trouble. That man is called emphatically *fortunate*, and becomes the object of envy or of ardent emulation to the less successful. And yet—I now speak especially to Christians, to the people of God, whose proper character is, that they are "not of this world," but "renewed in the spirit of their mind"—terms of very opposite import may many a time be applied to such prosperity, when considered in its influence on spiritual character and state. How often has the prosperity of the present world, been the date of commencing declension in prosperity of a far higher and more valuable kind—the prosperity of the soul in the divine life! How often has the gain thus been loss!—and, as the treasure has augmented on earth, has it diminished in heaven! So that, in the highest and best sense, the acquisition has been *anything but* fortunate—a curse, rather than a blessing. What is the lesson of the Book of God?—verse 13. "Happy is the man that findeth wisdom, and the man that getteth understanding."

"The mind's the standard of the man." Even in the sense of mere *mental cultivation*, this is true. A well-informed, well-stored mind, is an acquirement greatly superior in real excellence to aught that is merely external,—to wealth, or to all the outward distinction that wealth can procure. It is a source of more rational and richer enjoyment to the person's self, and a far worthier ground of respectability and honour. There are few objects really more pitiable than an ignorant, senseless rich man,—a man whose mind, in its unfurnished poverty and emptiness, presents a perpetual contrast, which it is impossible not to mark, with his outward pomp and plenitude. Such a man is far from being so truly respectable or happy, as the poorer man who is in possession of a trained and cultivated understanding, and some portion of the treasures of useful knowledge.

But in stating the matter thus, we have taken but the lowest ground. The meaning of the words before us is far higher. The wisdom spoken of is not the mere acquaintance with science and literature, with men and things:—it is of a loftier order, and a richer preciousness. It is the knowledge of GOD—but not knowledge that "plays round the head" without "reaching to the heart." It is the knowledge of God inspiring the *fear* of God;—the fear that is associated with and proportioned to *love*. This is heavenly wisdom; and of this alone could such things be affirmed as in the passage before us.

The connexion with the eleventh and twelfth verses, justifies the observation here, that this divine wisdom is often effectually learned *in adversity.* Indeed it is the one grand design of all God's corrective discipline, to teach wisdom. To this correspond the words of the psalmist—"Blessed is the man whom thou chastenest, O Lord, and teachest him out of thy law," Ps. xciv. 12. The *chastening* is evidently connected here with the *teaching;* the former as contributing to the efficacious accomplishment of the latter.

With the possession of wisdom, or of true religion, there stands connected what silver and gold, and all the jewels of earth can never possibly procure to their possessor—no, nor "all the things that can be desired," belonging to earth and time. Suppose all the objects of earthly desire and pursuit in the one scale,—riches, with all that riches can command, in the largest variety and abundance,—and true wisdom in the other; the former would "fly up and kick the beam"—lighter than vanity in the comparison. Put everything a luxuriating imagination can suggest on the one side, with the exception only of this wisdom; and put this wisdom by itself on the other, stripping the possessor of all else that heart can wish—the latter is, beyond expression, the more eligible. But, in forming such an estimate, it must never be forgotten of what sort of being we speak, when we speak of *man.* Speak we of a creature whose breath is in his nostrils—a creature whose existence is bounded, at the longest, by a few years, and who then sinks into annihi-

lation, and is as if he never had been? No. We speak
of an *immortal* being; of a being destined by the Author of
his existence, to live *for ever*—to live as long as Himself—
through a vast, a boundless eternity; possessing an existence
which neither his own nor any created power can terminate,
and which, when cycles of unimagined extent shall have
passed away, will be no nearer than now to a close, no
length of time diminishing eternity! Were the former supposition true, the ground assumed by Solomon might be more
than debateable. Reduce man to a child of earth and time,
and you render what belongs to earth and time, the only
things of real consequence to him:—for what *to him* are
matters that relate to a futurity he is never to reach, but in
which he is to have ceased to be? But if man is to exist
for ever—O into what comparative nothingness does every
thing bounded by the span of his life on earth immediately
dwindle! Whatever secures the happiness of his immortal
being, it must be an abandonment of reason not to prefer.
And yet this preference of eternity to time, is one of the
great and distinctive principles of true religion. "We look
not at the things which are seen, but at the things which are
not seen: *for* the things which are seen are temporal; but
the things which are not seen are eternal," 2 Cor. iv. 18. Is
there any enthusiasm in this? Is it not rather obvious com-
mon-sense reckoning?—Whenever you admit man's eternity,
and regard true religion as providing for the happiness of
that eternity, the truth of Solomon's comparison *must* be
felt. The mind cannot be sound that does not feel it—
verses 14, 15, "For the merchandise of it is better than the
merchandise of silver, and the gain thereof than fine gold.
She is more precious than rubies: and all the things thou
canst desire are not to be compared unto her."

And that true religion—the "wisdom that cometh from
above"—*does* so provide for man's eternity, appears to me to
be the lesson of the verse which follows—"Length of days
is in her right hand; and in her left hand riches and honour."

I am aware that respectable commentators interpret this as
meaning simply long life, and all desirable prosperity and

comfort in it. But I am of opinion, that both parts of the verse refer to something higher and better; and for this reason especially—that in the verses preceding, Solomon affirms the incomparable superiority of wisdom to silver, and gold, and rubies, and all things that can be desired of a similar transitory kind. Now it certainly appears far from likely, that Solomon should bring prominently forward as a *reason* for this superiority, the tendency of wisdom to procure *these very things*—the long life, and the riches and honours of the present world. "Length of days," therefore, and "riches and honour," I cannot but regard as meant in the way of contrast to the same things as they are "highly esteemed amongst men." It is true, I freely allow, that wisdom does possess a most favourable tendency as to this life; but still its chief recommendation goes far beyond time and the things of time. The "length of days" is the same with that promised to the Redeemer in reward of his work—"He asked life of thee, and thou gavest it him, even length of days for ever and ever," Ps. xxi. 4.—It is eternity itself. And the "riches and honour" conferred by divine Wisdom, are riches and honour incomparably more excellent and more lasting than those which the world or which man can bestow. If you compare the verse with chap. viii. 18, you will be satisfied of this. The *epithet* here applied to the riches— "*durable* riches," is evidently intended to make an emphatic distinction between them and the riches of earth. *These* are ever described in God's word as the very reverse of durable. The riches meant here, then, are such riches as are spoken of elsewhere, as bestowed by the Saviour on all who come to him—the glories and enjoyments of heaven, or rather of the spiritual life begun on earth and consummated in heaven—being represented under the figure of those things which are most highly prized amongst men.* And as to the *honour*, it is not "the honour that cometh from man," the eager aspiration after which the Saviour represents

* See Rev. ii. 9: iii. 18. 2 Cor. viii. 9: vi. 10. James ii. 5. Matt. vi. 20.

as one of the greatest obstacles to men's submission to the wisdom of God—"How can ye believe, which receive honour one of another, and seek not the honour that cometh from God only?" John v. 44.—But God hath said—"Them that honour me I will honour, and they that despise me shall be lightly esteemed," 1 Sam. ii. 30.—And the Saviour hath said—"If any man serve me, let him follow me; and where I am, there shall also my servant be: if any man serve me, him will my Father honour," John xii. 26.—What an honour is this—bestowed by God himself—a participation in the glory of his exalted Son! And that Son declares—"To him that overcometh, will I grant to sit with me in my throne, even as I also overcame, and am set down with my Father in his throne," Rev. iii. 21.

How complete the two things in this verse, when put together! With one hand Wisdom bestows length of days; with the other provides for the enjoyment of the life thus bestowed:—or, inverting the order,—with one hand she bestows riches and honour, and with the other eternity to possess and enjoy them! Then follows—verse 17. "Her ways are ways of pleasantness, and all her paths are peace." The *ways* of Wisdom are the ways of practical piety—of faith, and love, and holy obedience. All the variety of obedience is comprehended in the phrase *her ways*. These are the ways she marks out. And these ways are "ways of pleasantness, and her paths are paths of peace."

Such has been, and such is the experience of every true child of God. I speak not of him who has "a name to live"—profession without principle—form without power,—whose religion is the dictate more of the *conscience* than of the heart. I speak of him who has really experienced the renovating power of the gospel, and who "delights in the law of God after the inward man." True religion yields its joys only to the heart that is unreservedly surrendered to its sway. While the heart continues to be parted between God and the world,—while, amidst outward conformity to the claims of religion, the love of the world is still retained and cherished,—it cannot be to the disparagement of religion,

that the happiness promised by it to its votaries is not enjoyed. Even in consistency with his own happiness, "no
man can serve two masters." Their opposing characters and
demands must ever render the attempt irksome and unhappy. But in true religion itself—in the ways and paths
—the more open and the more private walks—of heavenly
wisdom—there is true blessedness. What, O what is there
in true religion to engender *gloom?* It is light; and it is
the property and office of light, not to gather mists, but to
dispel them. It turns the shades of night into the morning.—Is a sense of God's love gloomy?—the thought of
having our sins forgiven, and being the objects of the divine
favour, the paternal affection of our heavenly Father? Is
this melancholy? Is it saddening to have the hope of
eternal life? Is it an unhappy thing to have the mind
tranquil and serene amid all the trying vicissitudes of life,
through firm faith in the wisdom, the faithfulness, and the
love of a covenant God? Is it fitted to make a man miserable, to have his appetites, passions, and desires under
subordination and control, their restless turbulence and contending demands repressed, and their murmurs and agitations
and frettings quieted? Is it an overpowering cause of dejection, to be made like God, and to have the presence,
and smile, and aid, and guidance, and blessing of God, as
our God, in every season of darkness and distress, and in the
valley itself of the shadow of death? Is the anticipation a
disheartening one, of being with God for ever, in fulness
of joy?

Is this a picture of gloom and wretchedness?—a picture
from which the mind should shrink with aversion or turn
with disdain? Must not the mind be in a strangely unnatural and unreasonable state that thinks so, or feels so?
And yet this is *true religion.* These are its native accompani-
ments and results! There is not, indeed, here the "laughter
of the fool"—the intemperate merriment which is so often
but a poor cover to a spirit that is ill at ease; but there is
true joy,—substantial delight—the steady sunshine of the
soul—" pleasantness and peace."

The same train of thought is pursued in verse 18. " She
is a tree of life to them that lay hold upon her: and
happy is every one that retaineth her." Whatever is productive of true happiness—or rather, perhaps, whatever
has a salutary and life-giving influence on the spiritual
condition—is called by Solomon " *a tree of life.*" * The
allusion is obvious; and in the words before us, it must
be understood in the highest amount of import of which
it is susceptible. The tree of life, the sacred symbol
and pledge of immortal blessedness to continued obedience,
had its place in the centre of the original Eden; and the
import of it, as a symbol *now*, may appear from such passages as these:—"To him that overcometh will I give to
eat of the tree of life, which is in the midst of the paradise of God."—"In the midst of the street of it, and on
either side of the river, was there the tree of life, which
bare twelve manner of fruits, and yielded her fruit every
month : and the leaves of the tree were for the healing of
the nations."—"Blessed are they that do his commandments,
that they may have right to the tree of life, and may enter
in through the gates into the city," Rev. ii. 7 : xxii. 2, 14.

Observe the two clauses of the verse—" She is a tree of
life to them that *lay hold* on her; and happy is every one
that *retaineth* her." There is a necessity for *retaining* as
well as *laying hold*. If we retain the instruction of Wisdom, hidden in our hearts—the principle of steadfast practical godliness,—it will then be in us a fountain of perennial
joy—a "well of water springing up unto everlasting life."
Or, to keep by the figure in the passage—the "tree of life"
will continue to yield its pleasant and salutary fruits, not
through the present time of sojourning on earth merely, but
for ever, in the paradise above.

" *Happy* is every one that retaineth her." We spoke of
man as immortal—destined to an interminable existence.
This is one view of his true dignity. There is another. It
arises from the amount of his susceptibilities, of enjoyment on

---

* Comp. chap. xi. 30: xiii. 12: xv. 4.

the one hand, and of suffering on the other. Think of what
man was, of what he is, and of what he is capable of again
becoming. His capabilities are such, that nothing beneath
God himself can satisfy them. To make man truly and per-
manently happy, he must be " filled with all the fulness of
God." God himself must be "the portion of his inheritance
and cup." His soul can be filled from no created fountain.
And Wisdom provides for him a portion adequate to his
most unbounded desires, to his most expanded capacities.
GOD will be the fulness of his joy!

The excellence of wisdom is further recommended from
its source. It is divine. It comes from Him whose possession of it is infinite, and who, in all his works, has given
displays so wonderful of its infinitude :—verses 19, 20. " The
Lord by wisdom hath founded the earth; by understanding
hath he established the heavens. By his knowledge the
depths are broken up, and the clouds drop down the dew."

The entire plan of creation—the mental model of this wonderful universe—in all its vastness and all its variety—was the
product of wisdom—of divine wisdom—of Him from whom
we must learn *our* wisdom. There are some who take Wisdom here to be a personal designation and to have the same
import as THE WORD. The ancient Jewish interpreters give
not a little countenance to this principle of interpretation,—
explaining it of *the Messiah.* It is sufficiently evident, however, from the variety of terms in these two verses—" *wisdom,*" " *understanding,*" " *his knowledge,*"—that it cannot be
personally taken here. Wisdom, understanding, knowledge,
are all recommended—by *this* consideration, that they are
divine attributes, and were exercised and manifested by their
divine possessor in the contrivance and formation of the universe. The spirit of the recommendation seems to be, that,
as it is " *the Lord* that giveth wisdom"—the wisdom which
Solomon eulogizes and recommends—that which comes from
such a source must be excellent—well worthy the desire and
the solicitation. Think of what wisdom, as it exists in
Deity, has done—the wonders it has wrought! This will
recommend God's lessons. *He* is able to *give* wisdom, who

has thus displayed it: "The LORD by wisdom hath founded the earth."

The *founding* of the earth seems designed simply to convey the idea of the stability of this well-ordered world,—a world still "clothed with beauty," even for rebellious man. And what must it have been in its original perfection, ere marred and blighted by the curse? The earth, in the sublime phrase of another scripture writer, is "hung upon nothing;" yet is it used as the very emblem of stability—"the firm foundations of the earth"—"the earth abideth for ever." The foundation of every part of the earth's surface is its centre; because by a force whose nature we do not understand, and which may be considered as but another name for the might of the ever-present Creator, all the parts gravitate towards the centre, and by this power are all held together, as steadfastly as if they rested on an immoveable basis; and by the same power, the earth, with unalterable constancy, retains its position in the system—pressed by it equally on every side, as firmly as by the most solid material, never shifting one hand's-breadth from the place assigned it.

The "establishing of the heavens," is explained by the account of their creation. (Gen. i. 6—8.) Or by "the heavens" we may understand something more extensive than the firmament of our globe—that atmosphere of superincumbent air that gives its blueness to the concave over our heads. "The heavens" may be interpreted of the visible regions of space—the starry heavens with all their hosts.

The reference, in the *first* clause of the 20th verse—"By his knowledge the depths were broken up" seems to be, not to the breaking up of "the fountains of the great deep" at the deluge, but to the account of the first separation of sea and land at the creation. The continuous fluid mass was then broken up and dissevered, being separated thenceforward by the intervening barriers of land—a work to which no less sublime allusion is made in the Book of Job:—"Who shut up the sea with doors, when it brake forth, as if it had issued out of the womb? When I made the cloud the garment thereof, and thick darkness a swaddling-band for it, and brake up for it my decreed place, and set bars and doors, and said, Hitherto shalt thou come, but no further: and here shall thy proud waves be stayed?" chap. xxxviii. 8—11.

In the latter part of the verse, we have a beautiful exemplification of the resources of God's "manifold wisdom"—"by his knowledge—*the clouds drop down the dew.*" From the entire surface of the earth, and more especially from that of seas, and lakes, and brooks, and rivers, there is insensibly effected, by the warmth of the solar rays, a perpetual exhalation of vapours. In the higher and colder regions of the atmosphere, these vapours condense into clouds, and are poured down in return upon the earth in the form of rain,—or distil insensibly, in the coolness of the evening and the night, in refreshing and fructifying dews. There is thus a constant reciprocation of supplies between the earth and the atmosphere—giving and receiving with common benefit,—a kind of circulation of fluids, the water being the life in the vegetable world, as the blood is in the animal. The waters which are above the firmament are supplied from the waters which are beneath the firmament. They again descend, to supply the springs, and streams, and rivers and seas, so as to "water the earth, that it may bring forth and bud, to give seed to the sower, and bread to the eater;" and to clothe it with all the untold variety, and exuberant profusion of vegetable life and loveliness.

To this "only wise God," then, his creatures are to come for wisdom. Let them "ask of God, who giveth to all liberally, and upbraideth not."—And those whom God makes truly wise, he makes like himself. Mark the character of true wisdom, as it appears in Him. *His* wisdom is not mere speculative, or even mere practical skill—skill of contrivance, skill of execution;—it is skill directed to *good ends;* skill appropriately and beneficially applied; applied for ends in which are united the glory of his own name and the happiness of his creatures. The entire system of nature demonstrates this. In the same manner, the wisdom that "cometh from above"—that cometh from God—is like his own. It is not mere knowledge. It is knowledge, with the disposition and ability rightly to apply and improve it,—agreeably to the ends of our creation — the glory of God, our own happiness, and the benefit of fellow-creatures. And knowledge —the knowledge which God by his word and Spirit imparts —thus improved, is substantially TRUE RELIGION.

In inviting you from the ways of the world to the ways of wisdom, we invite you to true happiness, to happiness which will never either pall in the enjoyment, or prove bitterness in the recollection, or terminate in disappointment and eternal loss. We invite you to the best, the purest, the highest, the richest enjoyment of which your ethereal and immortal nature is susceptible; to the enjoyment of the divine favour, the divine image, the divine presence, the divine intercourse!

LECTURE X.

———◆———

Prov. iii. 21—35.

" My son, let not them depart from thine eyes: keep sound wisdom and discretion: so shall they be life unto thy soul, and grace to thy neck. Then shalt thou walk in thy way safely, and thy foot shall not stumble. When thou liest down, thou shalt not be afraid: yea, thou shalt lie down, and thy sleep shall be sweet. Be not afraid of sudden fear, neither of the desolation of the wicked, when it cometh. For the Lord shall be thy confidence, and shall keep thy foot from being taken. Withhold not good from them to whom it is due, when it is in the power of thine hand to do it. Say not unto thy neighbour, Go, and come again, and to-morrow I will give; when thou hast it by thee. Devise not evil against thy neighbour, seeing he dwelleth securely by thee. Strive not with a man without cause, if he have done thee no harm. Envy thou not the oppressor, and choose none of his ways. For the froward is abomination to the Lord: but his secret is with the righteous. The curse of the Lord is in the house of the wicked: but he blesseth the habitation of the just. Surely he scorneth the scorners: but he giveth grace unto the lowly. The wise shall inherit glory; but shame shall be the promotion of fools."

" Sound wisdom," which in the first of these verses we are enjoined to "keep"—to retain in our hearts, and follow in our lives, is the wisdom taught by the word and Spirit of God. It has been already considered; as also the true *benefit* and *honour* which it secures; and to which allusion is again made in the words which follow—"They shall be life unto thy soul, and grace to thy neck." And as it is the part of "sound wisdom and discretion" to renounce confidence in self, and to trust in the Lord, the assurance follows—"*Then shalt thou walk in thy way safely*, and thy foot shall not stumble."

The following verses very beautifully describe the serenity of spirit, the undaunted fortitude, the equanimity, the tran-

quil satisfaction, which spring from this constant, steadfast
reliance on the providence and promises of God; when accompanied by "the testimony of a good conscience"——a
conscience unscared by the remembrance of wilful sins, and
that enjoys peace through the blood of atonement:——verses
24—26. "When thou liest down, thou shalt not be afraid:
yea, thou shalt lie down, and thy sleep shall be sweet.
Be not," rather, *thou shalt not be*, "afraid of sudden fear,
neither of the desolation of the wicked, when it cometh.
For the Lord shall be thy confidence, and shall keep thy
foot from being taken."

We have the truth of these verses finely exemplified in
the experience of the pious father of Solomon, in those
times when he was encompassed with enemies, on the alert
for his apprehension and his life—"I laid me down and
slept; I awaked; for the Lord sustained me. I will not be
afraid of ten thousands of people, that have set themselves
against me round about," Psalm iii. 5, 6. And in the form
of assurance to others, founded upon his own experience,
and amounting to a divine engagement, he says, "Jehovah
is thy keeper: Jehovah is thy shade upon thy right hand.
The sun shall not smite thee by day, nor the moon by night.
Jehovah shall preserve thee from all evil: he shall preserve
thy soul. Jehovah shall preserve thy going out and thy
coming in from this time forth, and even for evermore,"
Psalm cxxi. 5—8.*

"The desolation of the wicked," (verse 25), may be
taken in one or other of *two* senses:——the *desolation made
by the violence of the wicked;* or the *fearful and desolating
vengeance executed upon them*, whether in temporal judgments, or in the infliction of their final sentence.

From the terms before used, respecting the final destruction of the wicked, it is most likely that to it the reference is
in this verse.† *Then* the people of God shall be undismayed.
When "the heavens being on fire are dissolved, and the elements melt with fervent heat," they shall smile over the ruins

---

* See Psalm xlvi. 1—3; xci. 1—5.   † See chap. i. 27.

of a burning world; for in that last dread day, "the Lord shall be their confidence;" so that they shall say with triumph, "Lo! this is our God; we have waited for him, and he will save us: this is Jehovah; we have waited for him, we will be glad and rejoice in his salvation," Isaiah xxv. 9.

In the verses which follow, we have some of the *practical maxims* of sound wisdom:—verses 27, 28. "Withhold not good from them to whom it is due, when it is in the power of thine hand to do it. Say not unto thy neighbour, Go, and come again, and to-morrow I will give; when thou hast it by thee." This practical injunction may be applied—

1. To all lawful *debts*—for *articles purchased*, or for *work performed:*—2. It is strongly applied to the *wages* of labourers and servants; they being inferiors, and therefore in the greater danger of being treated in the manner described. Their case, accordingly, is carefully guarded.*—3. To Government *taxes*, which ought to be regarded as debts due to the community; due by every member of it, for value received; namely, for the protection of person, and property, and liberty, and for all the benefits of good government. They should be paid with the same readiness and cheerfulness as other lawful debts.†—4. To *debts of charity and benevolence*. For such debts there are. They cannot indeed be claimed; they cannot be made good in law. But they are *due*—due on the principle of the great rule or principle of right as laid down in this book—the "royal law," (Matth. vii. 12.) Wherever the obligation of this law is felt, it will effectually prevent the conduct reprobated in these verses. The conduct, alas! is too common. It may arise from various sources; as—

1. From an *avaricious reluctance* to part with the money; —a reluctance which discovers itself even although it is known that the thing *must* be done, that the payment must be made. The avaricious man is so loath to part with the object of his idolatry, that even a day's delay pleases him. *To-morrow* is his day when he has to *give; to-day*, when he

---

* See Lev. xix. 13.   Deut. xxiv. 14, 15.   Jam. v. 3, 4.
† See Rom. xiii. 6, 7.

has to *receive*. In either case he has the pleasure of a day's longer possession, and a day's more interest. It may be little, but still it is *something*.—2. From *indolent listlessness;* careless, sluggish indifference. The man "has it by him;" but he is not in a mood to be troubled. He is occupied about something else, or he is not disposed to be occupied at all; and if the creditor be an inferior, very slight reasons or excuses will suffice. The man does not think either of the trouble, or the more serious inconvenience, to which he may be putting the claimant; while from mere inertness, mere indolent inconsiderate self-indulgence, he puts him off; and that, it may be, for successive times. This selfish thoughtlessness is very reprehensible. — 3. From *insolent superciliousness*. This is often discovered towards inferiors, or towards persons against whom there exists a grudge. It arises from a pitiful and despicable desire to show superiority, and make its opposite be felt; to make it appear that the rule of payment to *them* is, not when *they want*, but when *we choose!* It is the vice of little minds—ungenerous, unjust, unchristian, unmanly.

It is a very common case in matters of *charity*. Great backwardness is frequently shown. There is an inward struggle between the dictates of avarice on the one side, and those of conscience or politeness on the other—"I dare say," exclaims your money-loving professor, "the case is a very deserving one; but really I have not thought of it, and have not time to think now; *do please call again* in a few days, when I shall have considered it a little." You *do* call: but in the midst of so many other matters, he really has quite forgotten the matter; he is sorry, truly sorry for it— but could *not* help it. And again you are put off; and all in the hope, the real but hypocritically dissembled hope, that you surely will not take the trouble of coming a third time. If, trusting to the sincerity of his assurances, you do venture the third call, ten to one but your importunate dunning affords a good apology for a passion, and a con- sequent flat and hasty refusal—to which his mind had been made up from the beginning!

With regard to debts, which we are aware are to fall due at certain times, the precept clearly involves the duty of "having it by us" when those times come round. That it *is not* in our power at the time, may be a truth; but it forms no sufficient excuse, when we might have had it in our power had we been duly provident. Every debtor is bound to exert himself to the utmost, in every practicable way, to make provision for meeting the just demands of his creditors at the date of his engagements. This is what we ourselves *expect* when we are the creditors; and it is what we are bound to *do* when we are the debtors.

The next precept is one against the *abuse of confidence:*—verse 29. "Devise not evil against thy neighbour, seeing he dwelleth securely by thee."

The conduct here condemned is one of the basest of possible crimes. He "dwelleth securely by thee," means he has full confidence in thee, depends on thee, is altogether unsuspicious of thee. How odious, then, the idea of imposing on that unsuspecting confidence. Specially odious must it be, if pains have been previously taken to inspire confidence, by the assumed appearances of friendship and good-will, for the very purpose of leading into a snare—thus laying the train, studying and devising evil, betraying and disappointing the trust purposely inspired and cherished!

In such cases, some *selfish end* must of course be supposed in view. And the evil may be practised in a very great variety of ways. As for instance:—A man in business does what he can to obtain another's confidence; or, whether he acts with a view to this end or not, he knows he has that confidence; and he takes advantage of it to obtain large quantities of goods from him, when quite aware that his own affairs are precarious and his credit sinking, and that neither the goods nor the money for which he applies can retrieve them! This is treachery, and treachery of no ordinary turpitude.

Servants too may advance their selfish interests by practising upon the confidence of their masters or mistresses; and by a winning and artful address may insinuate themselves into that confidence, for the very purpose of abusing it. This has been done. It is signally base. On the other hand, there is not a more honourable or a more really valuable character than a trustworthy, faithful servant,—one who fully merits confidence, who never betrays or abuses it, but makes it in every way subservient to his or her employer's interest. Such a servant is *a treasure;* and such servants ought all Christians in that station of life to be.

Such, alas! is the depravity of human nature, that there are not wanting cases in which the most nefarious crimes have been perpetrated through the medium of unsuspecting confidence, previously and studiedly inspired. The wife of a man's bosom, or the child of his fond paternal love, has been seduced, and his heart wrung with incurable agony, and his family comfort, and happiness, and honour destroyed, by the unwitting confidence he has reposed in a seeming friend, to whom he has given up the fulness of an unsuspicious heart. And the assassin himself has plunged his dagger into the bosom which he had previously succeeded in divesting of all apprehension, and even while the smile of security and unsurmising trust has played upon the lips, and sparkled in the eyes, of the betrayed and murdered friend! Far—O far from all who call themselves by the Christian name, be everything of the nature of falsehood and treachery! It is, in all circumstances, wrong to "devise evil" against others; but to devise it under the cover of confidence, inspired by us and reposed in us, is infamous—is *Satanic.* It is the very sin by which "the devil beguiled Eve through his subtilty." The very first thing he did was to insinuate himself into her good graces—to gain her confidence—to inspire a feeling of security. And having brought her mind to this position, he tempted her to the deed by which a world was involved in misery and death. All, therefore, who act such a part as is here condemned, "are of their father the devil."

The same spirit that will avoid this evil, will avoid also the next:—verse 30. "Strive not with a man without cause, if he have done thee no harm."

The spirit here condemned is not seldom discovered

when any spite or jealous grudge, on whatever ground, is
entertained towards one who is known to be a man of
quietness and peace, averse to every thing like contention.
There is a special pleasure in vexing and annoying such a
person; forcing him into ill-humour and strife,—a most malignant pleasure!—compelling him, by dint of annoyance, to say
and do things, which are then converted into charges and
grounds of difference and quarrel! There are men of so
strange a temper of mind, that they will not allow others
to live in peace. Their delight is in teazing, vexing, and
plaguing their neighbours. They seem to make a study of
the art of strife. They have no rest, but when disturbing
the rest of all about them. With such men of contention
David had to do, when he said, "My soul hath long dwelt
with him that hateth peace. I am for peace: but when I
speak, they are for war," Psal. cxx. 6, 7.

Under this particular must be included a *litigious* spirit.
You find men loud in their protestations against *law*—the
folly and the evil of *going to law*, who yet, somehow, are
ever belying their professions. They can't help it, they say,
it is their neighbour's fault, not theirs; but they are seldom
out of court—ever after some plea or other. They magnify
to importance the merest trifles; and suppose, or make, and
prosecute injuries, where none were ever either intended or
committed.

The language before us does not mean that we may indulge a spirit of strife, even when there *is* cause—even when
harm has been done. The man of God will ever be the opposite of a man of strife. He will rather take wrong, than
foment discord; he will bear much rather than come to any
rupture. Instead of *making* quarrels, he is ever anxious to
compose and to heal them. This is the spirit inculcated by
the Lord of Christians, and exemplified in his own character. He did not "strive nor cry." When "he was reviled,
he reviled not again; when he suffered he threatened not."
And all his laws inculcate the spirit of amity and peace.*

---

* See Matth. v. 39—41. Rom. xii. 18—21. 1 Cor. vi. 6—8.

The spirit of strife is allied to the spirit of *oppression*, or a proud and overbearing spirit. This comes next in order:— verse 31. "Envy thou not the oppressor, and choose none of his ways."

"The *oppressor*," whether public or private, the man who "grinds the faces of the poor" by severity and extortion, may succeed, may prosper; may, by this means, amass a fortune, and rise to still higher honour. Suppose this the case. Still, he is not to be envied; not only because envy is in itself wrong, but because there is really nothing in his character and career to produce it. His prosperity is not to be envied even by the poorest and most suffering victim of his oppression. And while he is not to be envied, far less are his ways to be imitated, for the sake of obtaining the envied results—the same wealth, the same greatness, the same power; "*Choose none of his ways.*" The reason is assigned in the next verse, "For the froward is abomination to the Lord: but his secret is with the righteous."

"The *froward*" is a *general* denomination, under which the oppressor is evidently here included. It means one who is self-willed; bent on the gratification of his own propensities, the indulgence of his own passions, in spite of the restraints imposed by either divine or human authority. Men of this description are "*abomination to the Lord.*" This is a certain truth, and ought to be held as a firm and fixed conviction, all their success and prosperity notwithstanding. It may seem as if God smiled upon them; but temporal prosperity is a very fallacious measure of divine favour. So the psalmist Asaph was convinced, after being recovered from his temptation, arising from the observation of the troubles of God's people, in contrast with the abundance and the ease of the wicked. They were still wicked, and the more the objects of God's wrath that they were the enjoyers and the abusers of his goodness.*

In contrast with these being an "abomination" to the Lord, it is added—"but *his secret is with the righteous.*"

---

* See Psal. lxxiii. 18—20. So also Psal. xxxvii. 1, 7—9.

This, then, must be understood as an expression of special favour—of approbation, delight, and love.* It seems to mean, that the Lord will freely reveal to the righteous what he keeps from others—the truths and promises, the blessings and joys of His covenant of peace—secret to the soul that possesses them, intransferable, "passing all understanding," "unspeakable and full of glory." The secret of the Lord— "the secret of His covenant," had then perhaps a special reference to what was at a future time to be more fully and clearly revealed; that which, to use Paul's expression, "from the beginning of the world, was *hid in God.*" Thus God did to Abraham his friend, imparting to him, and to some others, in special favour, clearer discoveries than to the generality of believers, of the coming glories of his salvation. Speaking, however, simply after the manner of men, those with whom our "secret" is, are clearly our most intimate and confidential friends. The expression, therefore, may be interpreted of *the friendship of God.* Our blessed Lord throws light upon it, when he says to his disciples, "Ye are my friends, if ye do whatsoever I command you. Henceforth I call you not servants; for the servant knoweth not what his lord doeth: but I have called you friends; for all things that I have heard of my Father I have made known unto you," John xv. 14, 15. And this may be compared with the assurances of intimate fellowship expressed in the preceding chapter, verses 21, 23. "He that hath my commandments, and keepeth them, he it is that loveth me; and he that loveth me shall be loved of my Father, and I will love him, and will manifest myself to him. If a man love me, he will keep my words: and my Father will love him, and we will come unto him, and make our abode with him."

Instead of choosing the oppressor's ways, then, choose the ways of God's people—of those with whom "his secret" is; in whom He delights; whom He admits to his confidential intimacy, and blesses with the secret intimations of his love. Cast in thy lot with *them.*

---

* See Psal. xxv. 14.

The same idea is expanded in verse 33. " The curse of the
Lord is in the house of the wicked: but he blesseth the
habitation of the just."

The expression is an affecting and fearful one. There may
be in it an allusion to the terms in which the denunciation
was delivered to the disobedient and rebellious in Israel,
Deut. xxviii. 15—19. Upon the man who departs from
God—from his truth and from his ways—" his wrath abideth." His curse rests on him in the house and by the way.
It remains in his dwelling-place. It mingles with all his
domestic enjoyments; and his family, following his footsteps,
entail upon themselves his guilt and his punishment, become
inheritors of this curse of Heaven. It is the melancholy
portion of the households that " call not upon the name of the
Lord;" in which no domestic altar is erected to God's worship,
and no incense is offered of morning and evening devotion;
where, instead of being trained in " the nurture and admonition of the Lord," the rising inmates are suffered to grow up
with " no fear of God before their eyes." How delightful the
opposite side of the alternative, *"But he blesseth the habitation of the just!"* This is exactly the reverse—as in Deut.
xxviii. 2—6. The Lord loved of old, and loves still " the
dwellings of Jacob." These are among the places where
" Jehovah records his name," and where He fulfils the promise
—" I will come unto thee, and I will bless thee." He is " the
God of the families of Israel."—His blessing the habitations
of his people, does not imply that affliction shall never be permitted to enter them. It may; it does. Death itself finds
his victims there as well as elsewhere. But *trials* are not
curses. Even when they come in heaviest accumulation, the
blessing of the Lord is still there. It is not withdrawn. It
is many a time bestowed more richly than before. He himself, with the hand of a Father, mingles the cup; and he in-
fuses blessing into it:—

> " 'Tis mix'd with his unchanging love,
>   And not a drop of wrath is there."

And, through divine influence on instruction and example,

in answer to believing prayer, the children of God's people succeed to the grace and the blessing of their parents. Grace, indeed, does not "run in the *blood;*" but it runs in the *promise,* and in the current of faithful parental tuition.*

The same strain of sentiment continues in the following verse—·"Surely he scorneth the scorners; but he giveth grace unto the lowly." "The scorners" are here set in contrast with "the lowly." They are, therefore, *the proud;* whom the Lord "knoweth afar off." They are those who, in the spirit of lofty self-consequence and arrogance, treat with scoffing disregard the truths and precepts of God; who will not submit themselves to God's humbling terms of reconciliation and favour; who disdain being, as all sinners must be, "debtors to grace;" who refuse to be taught, and to submit their minds to divine dictation, or their consciences to divine authority, or their lives to divine guidance and control.—"The *lowly*" are those who have learned their true character and situation as sinners, and have taken the position assigned to them and appropriately theirs, as suppliants for mercy. Their representative is before us, in the character and behaviour of the publican in the parable— who, in contrast with the high-minded Pharisee, the prototype of the scorners,—"stood afar off, and would not so much as lift up his eyes unto heaven, but smote on his breast, saying, God be merciful to me a sinner." They are sensible of guilt, and willing debtors to mercy. They are sensible of weakness, and dependent on God for promised strength. They are sensible of ignorance, and look upward for divine light, instruction and guidance. They are humble learners —"the meek," whom the Lord "guides in judgment, and to whom he teaches his way." They are gentle and forgiving to men, as they are abased and lowly before God.

Verse 35. "The wise shall inherit glory; but shame shall be the promotion of fools."

"The *wise*" are the same description of persons as the "*lowly.*" This is indicated by the words (chap. xi. 2.)

* See Psal. ciii. 13—18.

"When pride cometh, then cometh shame: but with the lowly is wisdom." Nothing indeed is more foolish *in a creature* than pride; unless it be pride *in a sinner:* and it is *only there* that pride is to be found. The wise are those who "fear God;" and all who fear God must be "lowly." They shall "inherit *glory.*" The glory meant can be no mere earthly honour—that which "cometh from man." It is the "glory of God"—the glory of which his people are *heirs,* which is the object of their steadfast and joyful hope (Rom. v. 1, 2.); and of which the saints under the old as well as those under the new dispensation were the blessed partakers. They "*inherit* glory." It is prepared for them from before the foundation of the world. *Heirship* presupposes *sonship.* They are God's re-deemed and adopted children, and in this relation are heirs, (Rom. viii. 14—17.) "But shame shall be the promotion of fools." They shall find in the end the very opposite of all that they sought and anticipated. They looked for "*pro-motion.*" On "the honour that cometh from man" they set their hearts. And "fools," in Solomon's sense of the term, may succeed in obtaining what they seek. But how great soever the amount of honour the forgetters of God acquire; how high soever their worldly exaltation, how splendid soever their establishments, how vast soever their authority and how eagerly soever courted their favour,—they are "*fools*" after all; fools in the estimate of all holy beings; fools in the estimate of Heaven. And the final result of all their worldly occupations and worldly attainments will be —"shame and everlasting contempt." This shall be their final "promotion;" and the remembrance, and the irretriev-ableness of their folly shall be their everlasting torment.

There are one or two closing reflections which the pas-sage naturally suggests—

1. If it is wrong to delay fulfilling the just claims of men, how much more criminal must it be to put off the duty we owe to GOD. But many, alas! who are the very patterns of scrupulous punctuality in the discharge of their obligations to fellow-creatures, never pass a thought on the deep debt

of obligation under which they lie to their Maker, Preserver, and Benefactor! They plume themselves on their honest and conscientious regularity in meeting every just demand upon them,—yet never give themselves the slightest concern about the undischarged, nay the unacknowledged obligations to HIM, which every day and every hour brings with it. These obligations, indeed, are such as we never can repay; but both in words and in practice it becomes us devoutly to own and to express them.

2. Surely the maxims of the Bible, were they but followed out, are fitted in their operation to make a happy world! The grand end of the discoveries of the Bible is, SALVATION. But it has a most important influence on the personal and the social happiness of mankind. Were its dictates obeyed —there would be no avarice, no injustice, no devising of evil, no envy, no strife, no oppression, no frowardness, no scorning, no pride, no evil passions; but the universal prevalence of "whatsoever things are true, just, pure, lovely, and of good report."

3. On both these grounds there rests on every Christian the weighty and solemn obligation to spread the knowledge of God's word—the knowledge of "the glorious gospel." O! if there be one thing more than another to which the injunction "Withhold not good from them to whom it is due, when it is in the power of thy hand to do it," is applicable with special force—it is the spiritual and eternal welfare of our fellow-men!

4. Again we say—"Blessed is the people whose God is the Lord!" A man "without God in the world" may amass its wealth, may rise to its honours, may revel in its pleasures, may have "more than heart can wish;" but the saying of the Lord to the Church in Smyrna may as to him be inverted—"I know thy riches—but thou art poor." The mud-walled cottage of the humble peasant, with the blessing of a Father in heaven resting upon it, surpasses infinitely in desirableness the most gorgeous palace of an ungodly prince. The pomp and vanity of the world is but a passing pageant —the gaudy glitter of a day ending in perpetual night!

LECTURE XI.

—◆—

"Hear, ye children, the instruction of a father, and attend to know understanding. For I give you good doctrine, forsake ye not my law. For I was my father's son, tender and only beloved in the sight of my mother. He taught me also, and said unto me, Let thine heart retain my words: keep my commandments and live. Get wisdom, get understanding; forget it not: neither decline from the words of my mouth. Forsake her not, and she shall preserve thee: love her, and she shall keep thee. Wisdom is the principal thing; therefore get wisdom: and with all thy getting get understanding. Exalt her, and she shall promote thee; she shall bring thee to honour, when thou dost embrace her. She shall give to thine head an ornament of grace: a crown of glory shall she deliver to thee. Hear, O my son, and receive my sayings; and the years of thy life shall be many. I have taught thee in the way of wisdom; I have led thee in right paths. When thou goest, thy steps shall not be straitened; and when thou runnest, thou shalt not stumble. Take fast hold of instruction; let her not go: keep her; for she is thy life."

SOLOMON, in the introductory portion of this Book, is especially addressing *the young;* and youth he knew to be naturally volatile, and listless as to the topics to which he was most solicitous to secure their attention. Hence, like a speaker who sees attention drooping—the interest of his hearers becoming languid—the eyelids heavy—the countenance vacant, and indicating an absent and wandering mind—he often rouses by a fresh appeal, in the language of affectionate concern:—Verse 1. "Hear, ye children, the instruction of a father, and attend to know understanding."

"*Attention*" is necessary to the acquisition of *all* knowledge, and not least the knowledge of divine truth. And

when the instruction is imparted by a parent's lips, earnest
and thoughtful attention is specially incumbent on children.
The obligation is reciprocal. It lies on parents to *teach;*
it lies on children to *learn.* Of all knowledge, pious parents
will ever be most solicitous to impart to their children the
knowledge of God's will. Whatever be second, this must
be first. And while it should be that which parents are
most anxious to impart, it should be that which children are
most eager to gain. Remember, my young friends, Solomon
here speaks of the "instruction of *a father.*" And for children to disregard paternal instruction, is *ungrateful, cruel,
wicked, and infatuated.*

It is *ungrateful.* The obligations under which children
lie to parents, are of a nature never to be fully discharged.
My young hearers, your fathers and mothers wept for joy at
your birth, and many a time wept for sorrow at the sufferings of your helpless infancy and childhood. In that period
of your entire dependence, they protected and cherished you;
they fed and clothed you; they fervently prayed for you;
they hung over your sickbed with the tenderness of unwearied
anxiety—trembling between hope and fear; watching each
moment every symptom, and rejoicing in the turn of the
ebbing tide, and your restoration to health and life. O!
your bosoms are yet strangers to the indescribable tenderness
and force of parental love. To be rightly known, it must be
experienced. How ungrateful, then, not to hear the instruction of a father or a mother, (for the obligation applies alike
to both) when, from solicitude about your bodies, they are
taking thought for your souls; when, from care for your
temporal, they are rising to care for your eternal interests.
As this is the department of *their* highest obligation, so is
it of *yours.* Sad evidence is it of your gratitude for the
one, that you disregard and reject the other!

It is *cruel.* If you but knew it, there is nothing more
agonizing to a godly parent's heart. It is incomparably
worse than that inspired by your severest bodily ailments.
O! were you but aware of the secret anguish that wrings the
bosom—that gnaws and consumes the spirit—of a pious

father or mother, when instruction is contemned, and carelessly or stubbornly refused, you would not act thus.

It is *wicked*. It is a violation of God's law. He has made it the duty of parents to instruct their families; and he has enjoined it as the corresponding duty of children, to hear their instructions. In refusing parental counsel, you are disobeying GOD.

It is *infatuated*. The young are always in danger of self-sufficiency. They will have their own way, refusing the dictates of superior wisdom and age. But "this their way is their folly." They are their own enemies. They are treasuring up regrets for the close of life, and for eternity.

In all that I have thus said, one thing has been assumed. Solomon states it in the second verse:—"For I give you *good* doctrine, forsake ye not my law." I am speaking of the instructions of godly parents, and supposing them to be in harmony with the lessons of God. Children and youth are prone to question the goodness of them. Their hearts naturally dislike them. They are too strict, too spiritual, too holy, for their taste. Ever prone to worldly and sinful pleasures, they fret at the rein that holds them in. Even though that rein is of silk, and held by the hand of the kindest affection, they would rather be free. Their deceitful heart blinds and perverts their better judgments, so that they " call good evil, and evil good." The doctrine of God, taught in the Bible, and instilled into the opening mind by godly parents, is, in every sense, "*good* doctrine." It is good in its own nature—coming as it does from the very mind of God, by the illumination of his Holy Spirit; and it is good in its results, on the present and everlasting happiness of all who receive it. When temptations allure the young to "forsake the law," which God gives them, they will find in their sad experience that it is *good* they are forsaking, and *misery* they are pursuing.

Solomon recommends his instructions to *his own* children, —as having been, not his only, but those of their venerable grandfather to himself. And he herein sets before us at once a *filial* and a *paternal* example:—verses 3, 4. " For I was my father's son, tender and only beloved in the sight of my mother. He taught me also, and said unto me, Let thine heart retain my words: keep my commandments, and live." Solomon, like Isaac, was a child of promise. He was the appointed heir of his father's throne, and type of an infinitely greater successor than himself, (2 Sam. vii. 12, 13.) He had a name given him, as formerly noticed,* significant of the divine affection and favour towards him. He discovered symptoms of early wisdom and piety, which could not fail greatly to endear him to the heart of his father, and of his mother also. He here shows how he felt the affection of both, and returned it.

Solomon was born to a kingdom. Too often has the education of the heirs of thrones been neglected—especially in that department which is incomparably the most important, both for their own sakes, and for the sake of their future subjects. It is of unutterable consequence, that those who are to be intrusted with *power*—so very dangerous a commission, and one which the temptations to abuse are so strong—should have principle to use it aright; that they to whom the interests of so many others are to be intrusted should be qualified to consult and promote those interests to the most advantage. David manifested his paternal affection for Solomon, in union with patriotic affection for his people, in the instructions he imparted to him, and the counsels and admonitions he addressed to him, in his early years. This example of David as a father, is here recommended to parents; while that of Solomon is recommended to youth.

Ye fathers and mothers, if you love your children, as David did Solomon, you will teach and admonish them as David did Solomon. You will "say unto them,"—and that with all tenderness and importunity, and the tears of solicitude for their well-being, "Let thine heart retain my words: keep my commandments, and live." You will be anxious for the *life* of your offspring;—for the true happiness of their life on earth,—of which you know by your own expe-

* Lecture i. p. 3.

I.   I

rience, if you are God's people, true religion is the very zest and relish; and more especially for their *future* life,—their meetness for heaven, and their final attainment of "life everlasting." Nothing short of this will satisfy you. Were you to be assured that all wealth and honour, and every variety of earthly good, in the richest abundance, were to be the lot of your children in the world, your hearts would still ache for them; you would feel that all was nothing, less than nothing, if the assurance was unaccompanied with any intimation of the safety of their souls. You would feel it an infinite relief to you,—a burden lifted off your spirits,— a joy unspeakable infused into your hearts, were all that variety and abundance of earthly good swept away, and the life of the soul and the hope of heaven substituted in its room.

And, my young friends, look at the example of Solomon. See here, how he goes back in recollection to the days of his childhood, with pious thankfulness—thankfulness both to his earthly and his heavenly Father—verse 4. "He taught me also, and said unto me, Let thine heart retain my words: keep my commandments, and live." He thus records it with filial reverence and love, to his father's honour. I can conceive his heart, when he wrote these words, swelling in the remembrance of the days of his youth, and his eyes filling with the tears of tenderness.

And are there none of *us* who have cause for similar grateful remembrances? I for one must record mine; and many there are who can look back with delight and gratitude on the same scenes. Well I remember the family group, on the evenings of the "Lord's day," with our Bibles and our catechisms, storing our memories, and receiving, in simple explanations, and comparisons of one scripture with another, the early rudiments of saving knowledge—mingled with affectionate warnings, coming from the very bottom of a fond and devout heart, against "the ways of the destroyer," and all the errors and sins and temptations of the world. The whole circle is before my eye—the eye now of memory and imagination alone, for all who constituted that circle are now gone but he who addresses you. To the Christian faithfulness of

a long-departed father I rejoice to bear my renewed testimony, in the very words of Solomon—verse 4. "He taught me
also, and said unto me, Let thine heart retain my words:
keep my commandments, and live." I speak to many who
have, through the grace of God, reaped the blessed fruits of
such early lessons. Are there any hearing me who can remember scenes of a similar description, but not with sweetness, not with satisfaction?—none by whom, to this day,
both the instructions and the recollection of them have been
fruitless of saving benefit? O let such, how far soever advanced in life, yet remember, and yet improve the remembrance. Hear, with the ear of memory, "the instructions of
a father," or of a mother, or of both. If your secret convictions tell you that they "gave you *good* counsel," it will
even yet be for your good to improve it, that you may have
their happiness in life, their hope in death, and a participation in the blessedness to which they are gone, and the
choice of which they were so anxious to induce you to make.
Make it *yet*—make it *now*. Ere you leave this house to-
day, make it, and keep to it!

In the whole passage, from verse fifth to verse thirteenth,
there is much that is similar to what has already been under
our review.

Mark the urgency of the exhortation to the *acquisition* of
wisdom—verses 5 and 7. "Get wisdom, get understanding;
forget it not: neither decline from the words of my mouth.
Wisdom is the principal thing; therefore get wisdom: and
with all thy getting get understanding."

If you look at what keeps the world astir, you will at once
conclude, that most men around you are under the actuating
influence of a very different maxim from that presented in
the latter of these verses. You might, without being at all
chargeable with a libel, read—"*Money* is the principal thing;
therefore get money; and with all thy getting get *a fortune.*" This, alas! is the world's "one thing needful." All
else is postponed to this. The world's advice to the young
is, Get money first. Secure a *competency* (a word of which
the limit is never defined); and when that has been done

you will have leisure to think about what good folks
call "better things." Mind you the main chance. This
world is the one with which we have first to do, as we are
placed first in it. *This world*, then, *first, and then the next!*
Ah! what a delusion! How many thousand times has it
been found that, instead of leisure afterwards presenting itself for acquiring a better portion, the attachment of the
heart to the world becomes stronger and stronger, and its
seductive power the more and the more fascinating, as it is
progressively acquired! The meshes of the net become the
tougher and the more entangling, and the escape increasingly difficult, every hour. Its miserable victim comes to be
held faster and faster in the toils, from which he flattered
himself he would at any time set himself free. He is caught,
and kept, and ruined, in the very net which he laid, unwittingly it may be, for himself. O! when true wisdom is
neglected for this—how pitiable! *That* preferred, which
may never be got ; and if got, may not be kept even for a
day!—and that foregone for its sake, which cannot fail to
be got, if in earnest desired and sought, which is the richest
and sweetest relish of everything else, and which itself en-
dures for ever—the portion of the soul, sure as eternity!

The urgency to "*get wisdom*," is fully justified by the
benefits here enumerated :—verse 6. "Forsake her not, and
she shall preserve thee: love her, and she shall keep thee."

The "preservation" is from the ways of sin, of folly,
of the world, of death. From these true religion is the
only safety.*

And true religion is the only way to true honour and
joy—to ultimate and permanent *good :*—verse 8. "Exalt her,
and she shall promote thee: she shall bring thee to honour
when thou dost embrace her." This may be connected with
the previous verse ; the one being just a carrying out of the
conviction of the truth of the other. To "exalt wisdom,"—
when we recollect that "the fear of the Lord is wisdom"—
is to honour God. It implies the choice of true religion as

---

* See chap. ii. 10—12.

the chief good—giving it the first and highest place among the objects of desire and pursuit—enthroning it in our hearts, or rather enthroning there *Him* who is the object of it.—"She shall *promote* thee; she shall *bring thee to honour*," might be interpreted, as before, of the *esteem* which really consistent religion is fitted to inspire. It may, by its admirable practical effects, produce confidence, and obtain elevation to offices of trust and consequence and honour amongst men. But something more, something higher and better is intended. This appears from the ninth verse—"She shall give to thine head an ornament of grace: a crown of glory shall she deliver to thee."* The meaning of the two parts of this verse, when taken together, may be—She shall give thee true dignity here, and confer upon thee glory for ever hereafter. It is impossible, consistently with the ordinary import of the language of the Bible, to interpret the phrase "a crown of glory" of any thing else than the everlasting honours of heaven.†

The blessing mentioned in the tenth verse—"The years of thy life shall be many," has been more than once before us.‡ I dwell not on it now.

The repetition of the same thoughts, in nearly the same words, inclines me to interpret the whole passage as the strain of David's lessons to Solomon. And then we see the pattern after which, under the influence of the same Spirit which rested so abundantly upon his father, Solomon framed his own lessons. The likelihood of this is strengthened by the eleventh verse—"I have taught thee in the way of wisdom; I have led thee in right paths." This, we say, is probably, though not certainly, the appeal of David to Solomon. If we may regard the language, 1 Chron. xxviii. 9, "And thou, Solomon my son, know thou the God of thy father, and serve him with a perfect heart and with a willing mind: for the Lord searcheth all hearts, and understandeth all the imaginations of the thoughts: if thou seek him, he will be

---

* See on chap. i. 9; iii. 22.
† Comp. Heb. ii. 9.   2 Tim. iv. 8.   1 Pet. v. 4.   Rev. ii. 10.
‡ Comp. chap. iii. 1, 2; iii. 16.

found of thee; but if thou forsake him, he will cast thee off for ever,"—as the sum of the many previous lessons and admonitions of David, we shall have a favourable, and, from what Solomon himself here tells us, a just impression of the tenor of the parental training, of which he had been the subject. Happy, enviably happy the parent who can, with a clear conscience, make this appeal!

We have here set forth the *two branches* which constitute the sum of parental tuition—*instruction* and *direction;* teaching truth and guiding to duty. The one part relates to *knowledge*—the other to *practice.* In all rightly-conducted education, the two should never be disjoined. To teach *duty* without *truth*, is to teach *action* without *motive*—virtue without its principle. To teach *truth* without *duty* is to teach motive without the practice to which it should lead. They are both partial—and if kept asunder, both worthless. To act without the only right motive, and to understand the motive, without following it out and realizing it in action—must be alike unacceptable to " Him with whom we have to do."

The happy practical results of attention to parental counsel, and imbibing the principles and spirit of true wisdom, are expressed in verse twelfth. "When thou goest"—that is, in thy daily walk—thy course of conduct, "thou shalt not be *straitened.*" The word seems to express the case of one in difficulty and perplexity—contradictory impulses and obstacles pressing and hindering on every side—perpetually producing embarrassment and hesitation, and uneasy apprehension—hedging up the way, and hemming us in, and destroying the freedom and the confidence of advancement. Such is the case of the man who walks according to the maxims of a worldly and carnal policy. He is ever at a loss. As circumstances are ever shifting, he is ever shifting his principles and plans to suit them,—ever teazing and fretting himself with devices for this and the other end. But the "wisdom that is from above" inspires a simplicity and unity of principle, by which a vast amount of this agitating and painful perplexity is taken away, and liberty, delightful liberty, imparted to the steps. This wisdom has one point alone to ascertain—*what the will of the Lord is.* That point discovered, the mind is instantly at rest. The path is clear; the step free, bold, fearless.—Then, "when thou *runnest,* thou shalt not stumble." May not this refer to cases of urgency, cases calling for instant decision and prompt action? He whose mind is implicitly subject to the divine authority and direction; who is well-informed in God's word, and familiar with its contents; whose eye is single; whose principle is one; who looks not to the dictates of a crooked policy, but simply to *God's will* and *God's glory*—will not be often at a loss, or in great danger of making false steps, even when taken suddenly, and at unawares. He will be ready at all times and in all emergencies for action; and his duty will be done, while another is hesitating and considering, looking to results, and balancing probabilities; and, if necessitated to act on the instant, will be in great danger of stumbling—of hitting on some wrong, and far from advisable expedient. In the character of the former—of the man of principle, there is a firmness, a steadiness, a consistent uniformity of conduct, which appears in all circumstances, however different and opposite. His course does not shift with the wind. He is under no necessity of tacking from side to side, and accommodating to every changing current of air, like the vessel that must reach her point by the dexterous and ever-varying management of sails and rudder; but like the ship that is impelled by the marvellous might of steam—goes forward, direct to his destination, against wind, and tide, and current.

The urgency of Solomon's admonitions, implies the existence of temptation and consequent danger—danger, as we have said before, of "letting slip the things which we have heard." Hence the style of the next verse, "Take fast hold of instruction; let her not go: keep her; for she is thy life." The natural giddiness and levity of youth; the allurements, in all their variety and force, of the world and of vice; the seductive enticements of evil company; the power of inward corruption, and the "wiles of the wicked one"—

all draw one way—all against the impulse of heavenly principle, of divine wisdom; and they are all aided by the natural resistance to control of pride and self-will.

That on which we feel that we depend for safety, or for the attainment and continued enjoyment of something on which our hearts are set, and which is essential to our present or our future well-being or both, we "take fast hold of;" we will not let go; having seized it with avidity, we cling to it with tenacious grasp. Thus is it with a shipwrecked and drowning man within reach of a floating plank. With what eagerness he seizes it!—with what a desperate embrace he maintains his hold of it!—he will not "let it go"—he "keeps it, for it is his life." Thus must it be with the sinner and heavenly wisdom. Thus must you feel your need of it. Thus must you lay hold on it. Thus must you cling to it:—"*it is* your LIFE." You are lost without it. Let no buffeting wave of temptation drive you from it. Let nothing that seems to offer greater security induce you to quit your hold. It is your *only life.* You must lay hold of true religion, even as the trembling and sinking Peter caught at the out-stretched hand of his gracious and omnipotent Lord. Laying hold on CHRIST is laying hold on wisdom. In conclusion,—

1. If it be an evil to spurn at the instructions of an earthly father, how much greater an evil must it be to slight the paternal counsels and entreaties of the divine FATHER OF ALL! How ungrateful, how wicked, how infatuated! *cruel* we cannot with propriety call it; for all the suffering in which such neglect or refusal results must be *your own.* It cannot affect the blessedness of DEITY.

2. The sentiment respecting wisdom in the seventh verse is the same in substance with that of a greater than Solomon, when he says—"One thing is needful," Luke x. 42. SALVATION and the means of its attainment must be the "*one thing needful*" for a sinful creature. He is wise who seeks and finds this. He is emphatically the "fool" who neglects it. This is the pearl of great price, which is "not to be gotten for gold," and which he is an infinite gainer

who parts with all else to find, as his everlasting treasure.
How poor and miserable are those who get their desires as
to this world, in the gratification of avarice, of ambition, of
literary and scientific reputation, of personal and social
pleasures, and get them to the full, if they live and die
without *wisdom*—without fitness for the life to come—
without Christ, without God, without hope!

3. *Christian* parents, let no infatuated wish to get your
children forward in the world—to put them in the way of
wealth or honour—to introduce them to what is reckoned
genteel society and good connexions, or any earthly consideration whatever, tempt you to neglect their souls or to expose
them to jeopardy.   Proceed on the principle, that you are
making the best provision for their *temporal* happiness by
securing, in the first instance, that which is eternal.   If you
do otherwise you may rue it with tears of bitterness in the
latter end.

LECTURE XII.

———◆———

PROV. IV. 14—27

" Enter not into the path of the wicked, and go not in the way of evil men. Avoid it, pass not by it, turn from it, and pass away. For they sleep not, except they have done mischief; and their sleep is taken away, unless they cause some to fall. For they eat the bread of wickedness, and drink the wine of violence. But the path of the just is as the shining light, that shineth more and more unto the perfect day. The way of the wicked is as darkness: they know not at what they stumble. My son, attend to my words; incline thine ear unto my sayings. Let them not depart from thine eyes; keep them in the midst of thine heart. For they are life unto those that find them, and health to all their flesh. Keep thy heart with all diligence; for out of it are the issues of life. Put away from thee a froward mouth, and perverse lips put far from thee. Let thine eyes look right on, and let thine eyelids look straight before thee. Ponder the path of thy feet, and let all thy ways be established. Turn not to the right hand nor to the left: remove thy foot from evil."

THE connexion of the fourteenth verse with the thirteenth is obvious and important. In the latter, youth are admonished in these terms—" Take fast hold of instruction." But one of the principal sources of temptation to " let instruction go," arises from the influence of evil company and example. Solomon was strongly impressed with this, knowing well the strength of corruption, and of the natural propensity to imitate evil rather than good. All who have, or ever have had, the charge of the young, must be aware of the natural predisposition to evil. Account for it as you will, the *fact* is beyond question, established by the recorded experience of all the thousands of years of the world's history. Were the original bent of our nature *to good*, the difficulty would be to persuade to evil. It would require the arts of tempta-

tion to insinuate an evil thought, to suggest an evil wish, to
induce to the speaking of an evil word, or to the doing of an
evil act.   But the difficulty lies all on the other side.   How
very easy to teach a child to sin!   It may be questioned, indeed, if it require teaching at all to lie, to steal, to cheat, to
swear; to be proud, and selfish, and vindictive; to pursue
the world, and to disregard and forget God.   How difficult
the reverse!   What unremitting vigilance is demanded, in
instructing, admonishing, persuading, expostulating, correcting, plying all the arts of fear and love, in "training a
child in the way wherein he should go!"   Sin is a conta-
gious distemper, of which there is a predisposition in the
moral constitution of our fallen nature to catch the infection.   Parents are solicitous, and dutifully solicitous, to keep
their children from exposure to the contact of bodily disease.
O how much more anxiously should they dread their exposure to the contagion of sin, and worldliness, and folly!
They may well adopt, with affectionate earnestness, the terms
of dissuasive expostulation in these verses—"Enter not into
the path of the wicked, and go not in the way of evil men.
Avoid it, pass not by it, turn from it, and pass away."*   The
language is strong; but to none who know the amount of the
danger, will it appear at all stronger than the case warrants.
It implies an intense propensity in youth to be self-confident
—to see no danger—to flatter itself with its possessing sufficient powers of resistance—to resolve on showing this, and
to please itself with the thought of cheating the grave prog-
nostications, and mortifying the timid wisdom, of its grey-
beard counsellors.   Many a youth has lived to repent his
adventurous self-ignorance and fool-hardiness.   Sin is like a
whirlpool.   He who once ventures within the circle of its
eddying waters, in the self-sufficient assurance that he may
go a certain length, and then turn, at his pleasure, and stem
the current back, may feel the fancied strength of the sinews
of his moral resolution but weakness in the moment of need,
and may—nay almost certainly will, be borne on further and

* Comp. chap. i. 10, 15: chap. ii. 10—12.

further, till, all power of resistance failing, he is carried round
and round with increasing celerity, and sucked into the
central gulf of irrecoverable perdition!

The reason of the previous caution is assigned in verses
16, 17—"For they sleep not, except they have done mischief; and their sleep is taken away, unless they cause some
to fall. For they eat the bread of wickedness, and drink
the wine of violence."

What a contrast between the good man and the evil!
When a good man *falls into sin*, overcome by temptation,
his mind is wretched. He cannot bear himself. His crime
continues to haunt him by day, and to give him a wakeful
and restless couch by night. And when he forms and ma-
tures a benevolent plan for the welfare of others, and fails
in it, his wishes being frustrated by the slighting of his
counsels and the refusal of his aid, he cannot sleep for regret
and vexation. He sighs over the folly and infatuation which
"forsakes its own mercies." What a shocking and odious
character the converse of this, here brought before us! of the
bad man—the man who desires and watches for opportunities of evil, who prefers them to the very repose of his weary
nature, and even to its necessary sustenance!—who forms
schemes of mischief for his fellows, seeks their execution
with restless impatience, and, when these schemes are frustrated, can "find no sleep to his eyes nor slumber to his
eyelids!"—mortified pride, disappointed avarice, unappeased
resentment, unsatisfied ambition, and the fretfulness of dis
tracted and conflicting passions, scaring away from them
"tired nature's sweet restorer," and depriving them of their
appetite for their daily food! The meaning of the latter of
these two verses evidently is, that the bread these "evil
men" eat is the product of their wicked practices, and the
wine they drink, of their injustice and rapacity. "They
make their violence and deceit bear the expenses of their
voluptuousness." It is not that the wine produces the violence, any more than that the bread produces the wickedness; but that they *live by wrong*, getting what they eat and
what they drink by wicked and violent dealing. Surely

these words teach us the correctness of the psalmist's estimate, "A little that a righteous man hath is better than
the riches of many wicked."

Solomon proceeds to place in contrast the present condition and the end of both:—verses 18, 19. " But the path
of the just is as the shining light, that shineth more and
more unto the perfect day. The way of the wicked is as
darkness: they know not at what they stumble."

The image in the former verse is a very beautiful one.
We have before us the feeble glimmerings of the morning
dawn, gradually brightening, dispelling the lingering shadows, tinging the eastern clouds and the mountain tops, till
at length the risen sun pours the fulness of his gladdening
light upon the earth, and thence mounts the heavens with
increasing intensity of brilliance, till he reaches the meridian
of his glory. Such is "the path of the just"—the progress
of " the good man," from the time of his conversion to the
close of his life and his entrance on eternity. *Light* is em-
blematic of *knowledge, holiness,* and *joy.* The three bear
invariable proportion to each other,—holiness springing from
knowledge, and joy from both—joy spiritual and endless.
" The entrance of God's word giveth light." The entrance
of this light into the mind is often, like the early dawn,
feeble, glimmering, uncertain. But when it is the real "light
of life" from the Spirit of God, it does not abide so; it increases gradually from the moment of its entrance. He who
is "enlightened from above" is eager for more of the blessed
light. He thirsts for knowledge, and is on the alert to obtain it. He derives growing information from the works
and ways, but most especially from the word of God; and
reads all these volumes of divine discovery with new eyes.

Then, with growth in knowledge there is growth in *holiness.* At the first dawn of spiritual light, some faint desires
are felt after God and sanctity. These progressively increase,
as the experience increases of the peace of them who love
God's law; and they show their influence in the increase
of practical godliness. The renewed sinner receives his
light from the "Sun of righteousness," and he reflects the light

with a growing purity and brilliance. The "beauty of holiness" thus expands and brightens in the character, "shining more and more." *Perfection* itself remains as the attainment of a future and higher state of being. *There* is the zenith of the believer's glory, of the advancing light of his holy conformity to Him who "is light, and in whom there is no darkness at all." From that highest point in his heavenly course he shall never go down, never lose one ray of his splendour.

With the progress of knowledge and holiness *happiness* keeps pace. Every gladdening and delightful association is connected with the image before us—"the shining light, that shineth more and more unto the perfect day." The sun emerging from the east, is likened to a "bridegroom coming out of his chamber," and to a "strong man rejoicing to run a race."—*Joy* is both the *duty* and the *privilege* of the believer. It is the natural attendant of spiritual illumination and inward purity. This joy too is progressive. Like the sun in every stage of his diurnal course, it may be subject to the overcasting of occasional clouds. But as the sun appears the brighter on his emerging from behind the cloudy veil, so the trials of the just, the darkening shadows that come over them, serve to give lustre to their virtues. They promote their experimental knowledge of God and of themselves, of temporal and spiritual things; and thus they promote their real happiness even on earth. And when they reach their meridian altitude, no cloud shall ever intercept their light. No shadow shall ever for a moment obscure the radiance of their joy. Their felicity shall be perfect, undisturbed, and unending.

On the contrary—verse 19. "The way of the wicked is as darkness: they know not at what they stumble." Darkness is, as an image, the opposite of light. It represents *ignorance, unholiness, and misery*. An awful compound! Yet such is the way of "the wicked," in the eye of God, and of all holy creatures. All is darkness—behind them, around them, before them. There is no light on which they can look back with pleasure; none to which they can look

forward with hope.   There is a sense, indeed, in which they
are lights.   But they are false lights—lights that "lead to
bewilder"—meteors, that, when pursued, sink in darkness,
and add to the gloom in which those who follow them are
enveloped, when they have wandered still further astray in
the pursuit.   And this darkness increases, till, shadow after
shadow deepening and accumulating upon it, it terminates
at length in "the blackness of darkness for ever!"   Thus
there is a progress downward as well as upward—a progress
to perfect night as well as to perfect day.

The way of the wicked being "as darkness," implies at
once its cheerlessness and its danger.   They " know not at
what they stumble."   There are obstacles and perils in their
path at every step.   The very next movement may throw
them over a stone or into a pit; and, as every step in life
may be the last, they are at every step in peril of sinking
into the pit of woe itself, where "their worm dieth not, and
the fire is not quenched."

Such considerations may well enforce attention to what
follows in verses 20—22.   " My son, attend to my words;
incline thine ear unto my sayings.   Let them not depart
from thine eyes; keep them in the midst of thine heart.
For they are life unto those that find them, and health to all
their flesh."

The terms of the twenty-first verse may be compared, for
illustration, with those in Deut. vi. 6, 8—" And these words,
which I command thee this day, shall be in thine heart.
And thou shalt bind them for a sign upon thine hand, and
they shall be as frontlets between thine eyes."   Amongst
the Jews, there was a sad propensity to take the latter injunction *literally* and *externally*.   Hypocrites and formalists
satisfied themselves with having little scraps of the law written on parchment, and actually worn as frontlets upon the
forehead.   But this was a delusion.   The laws of God are
never rightly " before the eyes," unless they are "in the
heart."   The meaning of the former clause of the verse is,
that the commandments of God should be kept *constantly in
view,* as the guides of the whole conduct.   And this will be

the case, when they are "kept in the midst of the heart."
The expression implies the cherishing towards them of a cordial attachment—loving them, delighting in them, and ever
cultivating a sincere and earnest desire after conformity to
them.

The *motive* to compliance with the injunction, in verse
22, we have had repeatedly before us:—"For they are life
unto those that find them, and health to all their flesh."

"Health" in the Hebrew means *medicine:* and beyond
question, the tendency of sobriety, temperance, and regularity
of behaviour, is to the possession of health in the best definition of it—*a sound mind in a sound body.* But the
phrase seems intended to convey the idea of general prosperity and blessing; comfort and enjoyment.*

The next verse contains a most important admonition—
"Keep thy heart with all diligence; for out of it are the
issues of life."

In the animal system, the heart is the fountain of life to
the whole body. Thence the vital fluid, the red arterial
blood, is propelled to the remotest extremities and the minut-
est parts. In the physical economy, therefore, a great deal
must and does depend on the healthy state, and regular and
efficient action, of this central organ.—In the moral system,
the heart is the term employed for the affections, of which it
is regarded, from whatever cause, as the seat. And there is
an analogy between the action of the heart in the physical,
and the exercise of the affections in the moral economy. As the
healthy action of the former affects the vitality and vigour of
the entire corporeal frame, so does the well-regulated exercise of the latter, influence the entire character of the moral
agent. To the heart, accordingly, all the good or evil in the
deportment of the life is ever traced—as to the fountain,
whether of sweet waters or bitter—as to the tree, whether bearing
good fruit or bad.† The natural character of the heart is
given in few but emphatic terms—"Enmity against God,"
Rom. viii. 7. This being its character, it needs to be *renewed.*

---

* Comp. chap. iii. 8: xii. 18: Jer. xxxiii. 6.
† Mark vii. 21—23. See Luke vi. 43—45.

Its leading and comprehensive principles of action must be reversed. Enmity must be changed into love. This is conversion. This is being "born again." It is the work of God's quickening Spirit.

Even the renewed heart requires the exercise of an unceasingly jealous vigilance. Hence the injunction, verse 24— "Put away from thee a froward mouth, and perverse lips put far from thee."

In counteracting the power of the "law of sin in the members," we need the constant aid of the Holy Spirit. But the influence of the Spirit is never to be understood as superseding our own watchfulness and diligence; any more than our "living and moving and having our being in God," renders unnecessary our taking the requisite aliment, and attending to the care of our health. In the animal system, the heart would soon cease its action, and the body decay and die, unless food were supplied to the organs of digestion, and vital air inhaled into the lungs;—by the former of which the means of secreting the blood are furnished, while by the latter its purity is successively restored as it returns from its nutritive circuit to the fountain whence it issued. So, if we would keep the moral affections in healthy action, we must feed on "the bread of life," and breathe the air of heaven. We must avoid error, and live upon truth. It is thus that the affections are to be kept vigorous and pure. It is thus that the spiritual life is to be maintained in its active vitality—its efficient and influential energy. But the language implies the exercise of an unremitting jealousy over every propensity to sin, and especially the "sin that may most easily beset us." It implies also a close attention to the *motives* of all our words and actions. The reason assigned for vigilance over the heart is, that "out of it are the issues of life." As the fountain is, so will be the streams. But this is not the *only* reason. While the issues of the life indicate the state of the spring from which they proceed, the state of the spring itself is that which constitutes the character, and that to which God looks. As the *heart* is, so in God's estimate is *the man*. It is the state of the heart that with Him decides the charactor. The true character indeed of every word and every action—of all that is external, depends on the inward impulse; on the principle, the motive, the disposition in the heart.

One description of " the issues of life" is then specified in verse 24. " Put away from thee a froward mouth, and perverse lips put far from thee."

It is true that vigilance over the heart is vigilance over the tongue, inasmuch as " out of the abundance of the heart the mouth speaketh." But there is need for particular specification of evils to be sedulously shunned; and of none have we, in general, more need to be reminded than the evils of the tongue. " A froward mouth," is a mouth not subject to control; a mouth that gives utterance, with proud self-will and scorn of restraint, to the dictates of a rebellious spirit—an unsubdued, unsanctified mind.* Beware of imagining that there is little evil in mere words. There is no surer index of the state of the " inner man." As is the conversation so is the heart.†

The admonition that follows is one of first-rate importance—verse 25. " Let thine eyes look right on, and let thine eyelids look straight before thee."

What is in these terms specially inculcated is, simplicity of principle and aim; singleness of motive; an upright unswerving regard to *duty*. The path of duty is *one*. It is narrow and straight. On it the eye should constantly and steadily be set—looking " right on;" not to any seducing objects that present themselves on the one hand or on the other. Many things may allure—may hold out tempting seductions from the onward path. Many other paths may appear more smooth, more easy, and, in all respects, for the time more desirable; but the one and only question must ever be, *What is duty?*

Verse 26. To "*ponder* the path of the feet," means to consider it well. It should be " pondered," by the word of God — whether it is in accordance with its directions;

---

* See Psal. xii. 3, 4; and compare it with Eph. iv. 29; Jam. i. 26; iii. 2—10.   † See Matt. xii. 34—37.

whether it be in harmony with our obligations to God and to our fellow-creatures.   The latter part of the verse may be regarded as expressing the *result* of the pondering, " All thy ways *shall be* established;" " all thy ways shall be ordered aright."   And such regard implies discretion, inquiry, examination, and prayer.*

The path "*pondered,*" there must be a subsequent resolute practical adherence to it:—verse 27. " Turn not to the right hand nor to the left: remove thy foot from evil."

Nothing must be allowed either to draw or to drive you from the good way; neither prosperity nor adversity, riches nor poverty, love of friends nor fear of enemies, hope of good nor apprehension of evil; or in the terms of the apostle, " neither tribulation, nor distress, nor persecution, nor famine, nor nakedness, nor peril, nor sword,"—" neither life nor death, nor angels, nor principalities nor powers, nor things present, nor things to come, nor height nor depth, nor any other creature"—any thing else in the universe that may be imagined to possess any power of temptation.

The proper improvement of the whole passage is, in the simple but significant words of the Redeemer, " If ye know these things, happy are ye if ye do them."

* See chap. iii. 5, 6.

LECTURE XIII.

PROV. v. 1—23.

" My son, attend unto my wisdom, and bow thine ear to my understanding, that thou mayest regard discretion, and that thy lips may keep knowledge. For the lips of a strange woman drop as an honey-comb, and her mouth is smoother than oil: but her end is bitter as wormwood, sharp as a two-edged sword. Her feet go down to death; her steps take hold on hell. Lest thou shouldest ponder the path of life, her ways are moveable, that thou canst not know them. Hear me now therefore, O ye children, and depart not from the words of my mouth. Remove thy way far from her, and come not nigh the door of her house: lest thou give thine honour unto others, and thy years unto the cruel: lest strangers be filled with thy wealth; and thy labours be in the house of a stranger; and thou mourn at the last, when thy flesh and thy body are consumed, and say, How have I hated instruction, and my heart despised reproof; and have not obeyed the voice of my teachers, nor inclined mine ear to them that instructed me! I was almost in all evil in the midst of the congregation and assembly. Drink waters out of thine own cistern, and running waters out of thine own well. Let thy fountains be dispersed abroad, and rivers of waters in the streets. Let them be only thine own, and not strangers' with thee. Let thy fountain be blessed: and rejoice with the wife of thy youth. Let her be as the loving hind and pleasant roe; let her breasts satisfy thee at all times; and be thou ravished always with her love. And why wilt thou, my son, be ravished with a strange woman, and embrace the bosom of a stranger? For the ways of man are before the eyes of the Lord, and he pondereth all his goings. His own iniquities shall take the wicked himself, and he shall be holden with the cords of his sins. He shall die without instruction; and in the greatness of his folly he shall go astray."

THE whole of this chapter, the latter half of the sixth, and all the seventh, relate to one subject; a subject on which Solomon had before merely touched in general terms. It is a subject which admits not, in a public assembly, of minute illustration, and to which frequent recurrence is not desirable.

It is, at the same time, a subject, from which, when I think of the frequency and earnestness of Solomon's warnings respecting it, and the amount of real peril to souls which it involves, I should feel myself chargeable with a criminal abandonment of duty, were I for a moment to shrink.

I take the entire subject at once, as presented in the passages to which I have referred—passages which it is impossible to read without sentiments of deep abhorrence of the sins that are there portrayed in their native deformity and mournful results; and without melting compassion for the wretched victims of profligacy and licentious indulgence.

And this, I may here remark in general, is the character of all those passages in the divine word which relate to similar subjects. Were such topics altogether unnoticed, there would be an unaccountable defect of faithfulness in a professed communication from God, and a communication of which the main design is *to save souls from death.* How strange would it have been—how contrary to every conception we can form of divine fidelity and kindness—had warning been withheld where most it was needed; had the rocks which exposed to the most imminent hazard in the voyage of life been left without a beacon-light; and the eternal destinies of immortal beings sacrificed to any principle of false and misnamed *delicacy!*

"Thy word is *very pure,*" says the Psalmist, "therefore thy servant loveth it." That word is like the God from whom it comes. It is light of Light. In itself pure, it is the detecter and exposer of all impurity; and, while detecting and exposing it, it condemns it by its authority, and by its influence cleanses it away. I am aware that infidels have attempted to fasten on this blessed book—the Bible, a charge of a very contrary tendency. They have selected particular portions of it, and, with light-hearted sportiveness or with sarcastic bitterness, have made them the grounds of this most calumnious charge. I call it so without the slightest hesitation. First of all, who are the men who thus object? If they are in earnest, they ought to be persons of singularly pure and holy character; evidently and deeply concerned for the interests of religion and virtue; shrinking with sensitive dread from all that is immoral, and solicitous to preserve all others from the taint. And is the reason why they do not come to the Bible really an apprehension of having their moral principles contaminated, and their spiritual sensibilities impaired? Their consciences tell them the contrary. The passages, moreover, which they are fond of selecting, are all of them, as every one must be sensible, of a complexion totally different from that of voluptuous writing, with its sly inuendoes, its covert insinuations, its artfully studied refinements, its enticing and passion-stirring scenes. And their *effect* is the very opposite. They are, throughout, so manifestly and strongly marked with the very contrary design—to set forth impressively the evil and the danger of all sin; with the divine abhorrence of it, and the revealed and threatened indignation of God against it;—or, it may be, from the chaste and cheerful endearments of connubial life, to unfold the happiness of communion with God, and His condescension and kindness in admitting his sinful creatures to the enjoyment of it. Who, O who ever had recourse to the Bible for the stimulation of sinful passion, or the encouragement of licentious indulgence? Is it not the book from which the licentious ever shrink? which they cannot bear? which opposes, and thwarts, and condemns, and torments them? which they are glad to keep out of their thoughts, and which they are fain to laugh at because they feel it wounds them, and are too proud and bent on their vices to acknowledge the wound? If the contrary were true—if the charge of infidelity were well-founded, we might expect to find the Bible on the table of the man of pleasure,—the favourite *vade-mecum* of the gay and voluptuous libertine. But the very hatred with which bad men regard it; the very care with which they shun it, shows that it is not really to their mind; that it bears witness against them, shows them no countenance, but consigns them and their ways to reprobation and destruction. And while they pretend to speak against it, their conduct belies their words. If they spoke the truth, they would say—what, after all, most of them *do* say—that it is too pure for them, too strict, too damnatory of all evil. Were it *not* pure, the *im*pure would like it. Were it not the uncompromising enemy of sin, it would not find an enemy, as it does, in the sinner. And when, as has sometimes happened, a youth who has had a Bible education, who has been trained in the knowledge of its contents, and has, for a time, conformed to its instructions, imbibes the principles of scepticism, lays it by, and betakes himself, instead of the apostles of the Lamb, to the apostles of infidelity—what is the result? Is it a sterner virtue? Is it a more pious deportment? Is it a purer chastity? Is it a more uncompromising integrity—a more home-loving sobriety—a more consistent and self-denying devotedness to God? Alas! is not the answer written in the bitter tears of many a parent and of many a friend—of many a brother, and of many a " wife of youth?"

Beware, my young friends, of all those flimsy reasonings by which the deceitful heart so often imposes on the judgment, and, though it cannot satisfy, silences the conscience. And beware of all that might tempt you to think lightly of the sins here denounced. They may not, nay, they *do* not, exclude from what is called the best society. You may hear them without their being directly named, spoken of as *juvenile indiscretions and irregularities.* You may hear many a time, with an affected compassion, but with very gentle terms of condemnation, of good-natured, good-hearted, good-dispositioned, fine, honest, open fellows, that are *nobody's enemies but their own:* and from the tone of leniency and indulgence in which their vices are spoken of, it seems as if it were scarcely believed that they were *even their own!* But indeed they *are* their own; and they are more—they are the very worst enemies of all about them. They are only the more dangerous on account of the very qualities for which they are commended, and which produce the palliation of their vices. Let me warn you against such palliation, and every thing that tends to it. Take, I pray you, the *Bible account* of these vices. It will, in the end, be found the true one. Conscience even now more than whispers that it will. O let not the truth be left to be discovered when it is too late!

What was said of evil company in general in chap. iv. 14, 15, is here applied to this kind of company in particular, verses 5—8. " Her feet go down to death; her steps take hold on hell. Lest thou shouldest ponder the path of life, her ways are moveable, that thou canst not know them. Hear me now therefore, O ye children, and depart not from the words of my mouth. Remove thy way far from her, and come not nigh the door of her house." The meaning, as before, is—Flee temptation. He that "trusteth to his own heart," and fancies he may go certain lengths with evil-doers, and retreat with safety, "is a fool." He has yet to learn the heaven-taught lesson, " KNOW THYSELF." Thoughts are the germs of actions : "guard well your thoughts." Words cherish thoughts and quicken evil desires. Speak them not. Hear them not. Stop your ear like the deaf adder. Listen not to the "voice of the charmer." To open your ear is to have your memory, your imagination, your heart polluted, and thus your stability undermined.

In the passages before us, the consequences of sinful indulgence—of a course of libertinism, are very vividly depicted. Thus, verses 9, 10. " Lest thou give thine honour unto others, and thy years unto the cruel : lest strangers be filled with thy wealth; and thy labours be in the house of a stranger." These are some of the temporal consequences. A life of profligacy exposes him who enters upon it, to merciless unrelenting avarice ; makes him the pitiable dupe of those whose sole object it is to *fleece* him,—to make the most of him, and then, with a sneer, to abandon him. It transfers his substance to the vilest, the most odious and worthless of human beings ; to the most indifferent, selfish, hard-hearted strangers; who are all friendship while *profit* can be made, but are alienated the moment it ceases.

The temporal effects are still more fearful, when the wicked voluptuary is himself the head of a family—a husband and a father; or when the wretched partner of his guilt is such—a wife and a mother. Oh! of what unutterable domestic misery has this sin been the prolific parent! How many hearts has it broken—of wives, and husbands, and children! What anguish, and resentment, and alienation, and discord, and blood, has it caused! What scorpions has it thrown into the family circle!—what infuriated and vengeful pride, or what heart-sinking melancholy that refuses to be comforted and hastens to the grave! And to what poverty, and desolation, and squalid wretchedness has it reduced its victims! "For by means of a whorish woman a man is brought to a piece of bread: and the adulteress will hunt for the precious life," chap. vi. 26.

The manner in which this crime is treated by the laws of our country is a disgrace to our jurisprudence. Solomon says—" Men do not despise a thief, if he steal to satisfy his soul when he is hungry," chap. vi. 30. Yet this thief may be tried, convicted, imprisoned, transported; and, till the recent happy improvements in our sanguinary criminal code, I might have said *executed*. And what is done to the wretch who has torn the hearts, ruined the reputation, and annihilated the peace, and comfort, and joy of individuals and of families, in a way where to talk of reparation is only to add insult to injury! The wretch escapes with a pecuniary mulct under the execrable designation of *damages!* Can there any thing be imagined more base and sordid?—any thing more fitted to hold out temptations to worthless husbands to set a price on female honour; to encourage the wealthy profligate; and—by converting a crime of the most atrocious moral turpitude into a mere civil offence, for which compensation may be made in a certain amount of pounds, shillings, and pence—to pervert all the moral feelings of the community? Such a mode of viewing and treating the crime has, beyond question, contributed to diminish its turpitude, to augment its melancholy frequency among the higher circles of society, and in a great degree to obliterate its infamy: so that cases of this nature come to be read and spoken of, not with the feelings of indignant and unutterable loathing, as they ever ought to be, but with the coolness of commercial calculation, and the inquiry, What damages?—

what laid, and what granted? It is disgusting and sickening to think of it!

Further, dissipation tends to the ruin of both body and soul:—verses 11—14. "And thou mourn at the last, when thy flesh and thy body are consumed, and say, How have I hated instruction, and my heart despised reproof; and have not obeyed the voice of my teachers, nor inclined mine ear to them that instructed me! I was almost in all evil in the midst of the congregation and assembly." The apostle Paul says, "Flee fornication. Every sin that a man doeth is without the body: but he that committeth fornication sinneth against his own body," 1 Cor. vi. 18. This is one of those evils to which a just God, in his righteous providence, has affixed, in its temporal consequences, the brand of his reprobation and abhorrence. How many a healthy and robust frame has a life of profligacy and dissipation wasted away and brought to a premature grave!

How inexpressibly pitiable the scene here described— "Lest thou mourn *at the last!*" It is a scene that has many a time been realized on the deathbed of the wasted debauchee. The fixed and sunken eye, the parched, pale, and quivering lip, the cold and dewy brow, the livid countenance, and all the ghastly appearances of death—O! these are nothing, compared with the torture of an awakened conscience, with the anguish of a "wounded spirit" preying upon his vitals! Often is this agony of regret experienced, when there is no repentance—no true sorrow for sin, or wish to forsake it; when there is mere concern that the time of indulgence is past, and that the time of recompense is come. Then the poor sinner curses his irreparable folly, and amidst the present pangs of dissolution, anticipates, with a tortured and desperate spirit, the future and the worse torments of hell!—-for the SOUL is the ruined victim of such a life, as well as the body. It ruins both. "Her end is bitter as wormwood, sharp as a two-edged sword. Her feet go down to death; her steps take hold on hell." "Whoso committeth adultery with a woman lacketh understanding: he that doeth it destroyeth his own soul." "He goeth

after her straightway, as an ox goeth to the slaughter, or
as a fool to the correction of the stocks; till a dart strike
through his liver; as a bird hasteth to the snare, and knoweth not that it is for his life."—Chap. v. 4, 5: vi. 32: vii.
22, 23.

From this ruin there is no escape. Sin may have been
committed *in secresy*. No human eye may have seen it. But
there is an eye from which it cannot be concealed—" For the
ways of man are before the eyes of the Lord, and he pondereth all his goings." "There is no darkness, nor shadow of
death, where the workers of iniquity may hide themselves."
" All things are naked and open unto the eyes of Him with
whom we have to do." God is no inattentive or uncon-
cerned spectator of your actions. "He *pondereth* all your
goings." He weighs every word, every deed, every thought
of the mind, every imagination and every desire of the heart,
in the balance of that law which is "holy, and just, and
good." The Lord will "bring every work into judgment,
with every secret thing." The sinner is as certain of being
brought to trial and to punishment, as if his sins themselves
were cords and chains, that reserved him in awful safe-keep-
ing to the day of wrath—the "day of the revelation of the
righteous judgment of God:" "His own iniquities shall take
the wicked himself, and he shall be holden with the cords
of his sins. He shall die without instruction; and in the
greatness of his folly he shall go astray," verses 22, 23.

The *certainty* of a result *corresponding* to the course of
sin, is strongly expressed by the figures in chap. vi. 27, 28:
"Can a man take fire in his bosom, and his clothes not be
burnt? Can one go upon hot coals, and his feet not be
burnt?" This is fearfully true in regard to divine retribution. He who persists in sin, and expects impunity, acts as
unreasonably as the man who should expose his body to the
scorching flame, or walk over burning fire, and expect to
escape uninjured!

It is an affecting and alarming fact, that despisers of the
counsels of heavenly wisdom *most generally*, after persisting
for a length of time, die as they have lived. This is the

sentiment in verse twenty-third—"They die *without instruc-tion.*" Mistake me not. I say not that there is any season when repentance toward God is impossible, or when, if gen-uine, it can come too late. No; blessed be God—

> " While the lamp holds on to burn,
> The vilest sinner may return."

I speak of *matter of fact.* Generally, such persons go on in sin, refuse instruction, and put away from them to the end, whether in scorn or in sad despair, all the invitations, assur-ances, and promises of the gospel. This sounds an awful warning to dissipated youth. Some of them (for there are not many so hardened and daring as to determine they will never repent and never change) may be flattering themselves, that at some future day they will *take thought* and amend. But alas! for the infatuated anticipation. By persistence in sin they are every day fastening its cords about them with increasing firmness, and rendering change the more unlikely. The indisposition to good grows. The conscience hardens. The heart becomes more and more callous; and they go astray *to the last* in " the greatness of their folly;"—a folly, of which the *end* shows the amount. The lesson is read—the tremendous lesson—by the flames of HELL! *There* the regret, so vividly depicted, in the verses already under re-view, as characterizing the close of even this life, shall be experienced in its most agonizing form; and shall constitute no small portion of the torture inflicted by " the worm that never dies!"

O then, my hearers—my youthful hearers in a special manner—listen, and beware. I have spoken to young men. But on both sides, the ruin is equal: and the number of those wretched corrupters of the morals of our youth who live by the wages of iniquity is, in great cities and towns, unspeakably deplorable. He must have the heart of a mon-ster; he must be one from whose heart the obduracy of vice has wrung out the very last warm drops of humanity, who can contemplate the evil in all the extent of its consequences, without horror and self-loathing at the part he may himself have had in producing it.   And such considerations should recommend to liberal support every legitimate means of mitigating its amount, and of rescuing any of its miserable victims from the fatal effects of sin in time and eternity— "plucking them as brands from the burning!"

As a preventive of evil, and as a means of true happiness, Solomon recommends early marriage, and the experience of the comforts and joys of connubial and domestic life:— verses 15—18. " Drink waters out of thine own cistern, and running waters out of thine own well.   Let thy fountains be dispersed abroad, and rivers of waters in the streets.   Let them be only thine own, and not strangers' with thee.   Let thy fountain be blessed: and rejoice with the wife of thy youth."

It is evident, that this must be understood with reservation.   It requires the application of prudence, and the prospective consideration of the question, how a family is to be supported.   Much unhappiness often arises from overlooking and disregarding this.   The most virtuous and ardent affection must not be encouraged to set at nought entirely the dictates of discretion.   But in general, and with a proper degree of attention to this, early unions are, in many respects, of eminent advantage.   Virtuous love operates with a most salutary restraint on the vicious principles of our fallen nature.   The marriage union, formed and maintained on right principles, has ever been found a fountain of the purest and richest joy on this side the grave—joy unmingled with guilty shame, and that leaves behind it no tormenting sting.   There are few things more pleasing than to see youth joined to youth in virtuous and honourable and hallowed union,—living together in all the faithfulness and all the tenderness of a first love.   O! with what delight does the eye rest on such a scene, when disgusted with the loathsomeness, and distressed by the misery of vice!

It is a circumstance deserving notice, that, although Solomon himself had fearfully trespassed against the original law of marriage—the constitution authoritatively fixed when God made a male and a female, and said, " For this cause shall a man leave father and mother, and shall cleave to his wife,"—he here proceeds, in his admonitions and counsels, according to the provisions of that constitution. It was the law from the first, and is the law under the Christian economy, that "every man should have his own wife, and every woman her own husband." Solomon had himself reaped the bitter fruits of departure from that law; and so, though not to the same degree, had many before him.

I conclude by reminding every one that *all* sin tends to ruin. The indulgence of one sin cannot be compensated by abstinence from another. There is no such principle of compensation in the Bible. And yet, nothing is more frequent in regard to sinful indulgences, than for men to—

> " Compound for those they are inclined to,
> By cursing those they have no mind to."

Such is the delusion which men, in this respect, are accustomed to practise on themselves, that, even in regard to propensities that are absolutely opposites, in the nature of things incapable of being indulged together, they may be found, while giving themselves up to the one, pluming themselves on the absence of the other!

Again: mere external sobriety and chastity and general decency of character, is not enough. There is still remaining the all-important question—*What is the principle of it?* The only sound principle is—*"the fear of God."* In all schemes that have for their object the outward reformation of men—their restoration from the habits of outward vicious indulgence—it were well that this be kept in mind; for if you succeed in making men externally sober, while they do not become internally godly, and if they are encouraged to rely upon their outward reformation and to make a righteousness of it, you may essentially benefit them in their corporeal and temporal well-being, but you fail of saving their souls. They may have a far reputation amongst their fellow-men; but in God's balance they must be found wanting.

LECTURE XIV.

———◆———

" My son, if thou be surety for thy friend, if thou hast stricken thy hand with a stranger, thou art snared with the words of thy mouth, thou art taken with the words of thy mouth. Do this now, my son, and deliver thyself, when thou art come into the hand of thy friend; go, humble thyself, and make sure thy friend. Give not sleep to thine eyes, nor slumber to thine eyelids. Deliver thyself as a roe from the hand of the hunter, and as a bird from the hand of the fowler. Go to the ant, thou sluggard; consider her ways, and be wise: which having no guide, overseer, or ruler, provideth her meat in the summer, and gathereth her food in the harvest. How long wilt thou sleep, O sluggard ? when wilt thou arise out of thy sleep? Yet a little sleep, a little slumber, a little folding of the hands to sleep : so shall thy poverty come as one that travelleth, and thy want as an armed man."

A surety is one who becomes security for a debt due by another, in case of the insolvency of the original debtor. In different countries, the customary or legal forms have been different, by which such suretiships are undertaken, and are rendered valid. In the first verse, allusion is made to the practice of the surety confirming his engagement by giving his hand to the creditor, in presence of witnesses—" My son, if thou be surety for thy friend, if thou hast *stricken thy hand* with a stranger.'

Solomon, on different occasions, condemns the practice of suretiship.* The condemnation is general. It does not follow, however, that what he says is to be taken as an absolute unqualified prohibition, to which there are no circum-

* See chap. xi. 15. and xxii. 26.

stances that can constitute an exception.   There are cases in
which it is unavoidable; and there are cases in which the
law requires it; and there are cases in which it is not only
in consistency with law, but required by all the claims of
prudence, and justice, and charity.   These, however, are
rare.   And it may be laid down as a maxim regarding the
transactions of business, and all the mutual dealings of man
with man, that *the less of it the better*.   In such cases as the
following, it is manifestly inadmissible, and may even, in
some instances, involve a large amount of moral turpitude :—

1. It is wrong for a man to come under engagements that
are *beyond his actually existing means*—beyond his ability
to pay, in case of need.   Such a course is not one merely of
imprudence.   There is in it a *threefold injustice*.   First, to
the *creditor* for whom he becomes surety; inasmuch as the
security is fallacious, not covering the extent of the risk.
Secondly, to his family, if he has one, to whom, in case of
the security being required, and the payment called for, the
requisition must bring distress and ruin.   And thirdly, to
those who give him credit in his own transactions, with the
risks of his own trade: for in thus undertaking suretiships,
he involves himself, without their knowledge, in the risks
of *other* trades besides his own, and thus exposes them to
hazards of which, in the outset, they were not aware.

It may be thought that a person may always be justified
in becoming a surety, provided he retains as much clear as
is sufficient for the payment of his own obligations, and, at
the same time, do justice to his family.   But it ought not to
be forgotten amidst what uncertainties we live—the incessant liability to fluctuations and reverses.   We "know not
what shall be on the morrow."   In trusting to what we now
have, we may be "setting our eyes on that which *is not*."
All may be quite square, and to every appearance prosperous,
to-day; and to-morrow all may be ruin.   So that, if in giving his security, a man *goes to the limit* of his means, without taking into account the risks of his own business, he
does wrong; and his own calamity, and that of others associated with him, may come speedily.

2. The same observations are applicable to the making of engagements *with inconsideration and rashness.* The case here supposed, is evidently that of suretiship *for* a friend *to* a stranger. And the rashness and haste may be viewed in relation either to the *person* or to the *case.*

First, as to the *person.* The partiality and warmth of friendship, may be a temptation to agree precipitately and without reflection to what both prudence and equity forbid: and especially when the friend presents and presses his suit on the very ground of friendship. That is very trying. How can we refuse an old, attached, and valued friend, or one, it may be, to whose kindness we have been more than once indebted! If a man stands alone, out of business, and without a dependent family, and has, at the same time, abundance of which to dispose, he may be quite at liberty to make such sacrifices to friendship as he pleases. But suppose the reverse of all this—then the claims of justice to others must take precedence of the claims of kindness to the friend. The friend, in such cases, must be regarded, not merely in his capacity as a friend, but in his capacity as a man of business. If, for example, he is known to us as a man who is indolent and careless, incorrect and improvident, profuse and extravagant; then, whatever may be our *feelings,* they must on no account be allowed to supersede, in the slightest, the demands of justice. These demands lie against their indulgence, on the part of family and of creditors; whose rights, in such a case, would be clearly and egregiously violated. In such circumstances, it is very wrong in your friend to urge you; but, let the urgency be ever so great, and the pain to which you are put ever so excruciating, *right* ought to prevail, even if the forfeiture of friendship should be the penalty. Men, when they feel the generous impulse of friendly emotion, and say at once while under it, " I'll be his surety," are exceedingly apt to think at the moment only of themselves, as if the risk were *all their own;* and to forget, that in thus hastily "striking hands," they are making creditors and family securities, without asking their consent, or making them aware of their risks.

I. L

In the case of the person in whose behalf we bring ourselves under the obligation being "a stranger," the culpability is indefinitely augmented. The young, naturally warm, inexperienced, unsuspecting, and credulous, are very apt to allow themselves to be drawn away by their juvenile ardour, and to commit themselves fast and fondly to new and open-hearted companions. Suretiships "for strangers" are accordingly laid under special condemnation:—"He that is surety for a stranger shall smart for it: and he that hateth suretiship is sure." "Take his garment that is surety for a stranger: and take a pledge of him for a strange woman," chap. xi. 15. and xx. 16. The force of the latter passage is, "If he is your debtor who has come under suretiship for a stranger, you had better see sharply to payment. 'Take his garment' for your debt. He will soon come to it; will soon have nothing more to pay; take in pledge whatever you can get." In the verses before us the case is different. It is the case of becoming surety, not *for* a stranger, but, as was formerly noticed, *to* a stranger *for* a friend.

In regard to all such cases, it should be recollected, that, although we may have a confidence in our friend that is in the main well-founded, we can never be sure in what speculations he may be tempted to embark, or what new courses in business he may be induced to pursue. The practice is elsewhere condemned as that of indiscretion and folly:—"A man void of understanding striketh hands, and becometh surety in the presence of his friend," chap. xvii. 18. The words, "in the presence of his friend," may mean, being swayed and overcome by the influence of friendship—his friend being before him in distress, needing and seeking his aid: a situation which every man of sensibility will feel it very difficult to withstand. Or, it may mean, complying with the request *hastily*, on the instant, ere the friend who pleads for the favour has left his presence.

It is very far wrong in any man to avail himself of the claims of friendship to bring another into a situation which, his conscience tells him, is one into which he would not like himself to be drawn; or to induce the friend to do what he knows is either in principle faulty, or in tendency and possible results injurious. This is the very opposite of friendship. It is selfishness betraying friendship, and making it available for its own ends. He who, in business, makes such a use of friendship, exposes himself to just suspicion that all is not right; that he is trying unwarrantable means to prop up a false credit, and to gratify a haste to be rich. It is very natural for us, no doubt, to wish to make our own bargains as secure as possible. But does any man like to be security for the bargains of others? If this is what none like, should any tempt others to do it? Should any one, for the sake of making all sure for himself, seek to place others in circumstances by which *their* security may be affected? Here, as in every case, comes in the golden rule, "All things whatsoever ye would that men should do to you, do ye even so to them." If we cannot trust a man ourselves, so as to transact business with him, would it not be better to forego our bargain, even though it may seem a tempting one, and to decline dealings with him, than to accomplish our purpose by bringing others into a situation we ourselves dislike?

I may further ask, whether, in the spirit, and to no small extent in the letter of it, what has just been said does not bear application to the whole system of what is known, in modern business, under the term ACCOMMODATION. Is not that a system which, on the principles stated, ought to be denounced and put down? Some say it is impossible to transact business without it. It may be well, however, to inquire how far this alleged impossibility does not arise from the very modes of transacting business which modern usage has introduced? I allude to the unrighteous, lying, ruinous method of speculation without capital; of extensive risks on a baseless credit; of what may be called the *lottery* plan of business, where wealth to ourselves, or ruin both to ourselves and others, are put upon the cast of a die. If the credit is *baseless*, the business is *base*. All are, in theory, of one mind, that *the accommodation system*, as it has been carried on, is a false, treacherous, hollow, ruinous system; a system of utter delusion, stamped throughout with lies. Christian men of business should set their faces decidedly against it, doing what they can to fix on it the stigma of dishonour, and to *oust* it from the mercantile world.

But while Solomon condemns suretiship, he at the same time intimates that when an engagement has once been made, it is *binding*. Such seems the import of the second verse—"Thou art snared with the words of thy mouth, thou art taken with the words of thy mouth."

This is one of the very considerations by which previous caution and forethought are rendered necessary. You may wish, after the thing has been done, that it had not been done, or that it could be undone. But truth and honour may now tie you down to your promise. The case may come under that feature of the acceptable worshipper in God's courts—"He that sweareth to his own hurt, and changeth not." You have brought yourself into a snare, and by your own word, in speech or in writing, have placed yourself in the power of others. What, then, is to be done? Solomon's counsel is—*Extricate yourself, if you can;* that is, if by any means consistent with the principles of truth and honour, it is at all in your power. He exhorts you to the very humblest concessions:—verse 3. "Do this now, my son, and deliver thyself, when thou art come into the hand of thy friend; go, humble thyself, and make sure thy friend."

The closing words seem to mean, as in the margin, "Humble thyself that thou *mayest prevail* with thy friend." The object is, to induce him, by all equitable and self-denying concessions, to pay the money himself, or to prevail with the creditor to dispense with the security,—to discharge your obligation. There is a *pride* sometimes which, after a man has committed himself, even how strongly soever he may see and feel afterwards his error, both as it affects himself and others, will not allow him to stoop to any means whatever of disentangling himself. The principle, to a certain extent, is one which we cannot but admire. But it may be carried too far; especially when we find that we have been implicating others as well as ourselves. What will it profit to add pride and pertinacity to folly and wrong?

Solomon, observe, treats it as a matter of most urgent exigency:—verses 4, 5. "Give not sleep to thine eyes, nor slumber to thine eyelids. Deliver thyself as a roe from the hand of the hunter, and as a bird from the hand of the fowler."

The urgency of the case will of course correspond in degree with the extent of the obligation and the risk. It is here supposed to be one of magnitude and importance. But the *principle* comprehends all cases, though applicable with various measures of force. There is a correspondence between the figure in these verses and that which had been used in the *second:* "Thou art snared with the words of thy mouth,"—"Deliver thyself as a roe from the hand of the hunter, and as a bird from the hand of the fowler." The hunter and the fowler catch their prey for their own purposes, not for the benefit of the roe or the bird. So you have suffered yourself to be snared and caught by others, not for your profit, but for theirs. If they, then, have caught you for theirs, for your own you should seek escape.

It is evident, however, that the language implies, If, with all your efforts, you are unsuccessful in obtaining your discharge, you must *stand to your engagement.* Treachery would be a much greater loss in character, than would be compensated by evading, or attempting to evade, the loss of property; and, even were you able to keep your money, while you would lose caste in the world, you would lose "peace with God" and "the answer of a good conscience."

This, then, is *one* of the ways in which a man may bring himself into straits, and even reduce himself to beggary. It is not the first nor the second time that a man has beggared himself by suretiships. We may commend his generous and accommodating kindness; but we cannot praise the prudence with which it has been exercised: and if others are connected with him, and involved in his downfall, the error has been one of *principle* as well as of prudence.

In the verses which follow, Solomon brings before us another way in which straits and poverty may be induced. It is SLOTH. "Go to the ant, thou sluggard; consider her ways, and be wise: which having no guide, overseer, or ruler, provideth her meat in the summer, and gathereth her food in the harvest."

The indolent and improvident are addressed; and they are sent to the inferior creation for a lesson: and not to the greatest and the noblest of animals, but to one of the least and most insignificant of insects. Of the ANT there are various species even in the same country; and some that are peculiar to their respective climates and regions of the earth. They differ in size, in colour, and in some particulars both of their structure and of their instinctive habits. All are remarkable for their *industry*. It is indeed astonishing; and the results of their united labours are no less so, when the diminutiveness of the agents is considered. Of some of the species the abodes—the *ant-hills* as they are usually termed —are of great size, exceeding the height of a man; and they are constructed with wonderful regularity and skill, the result of labours that would seem incredible were they not thus ascertained in their effects. They are in the form of a conical mount, with roads winding through every part of the settlement; and all their granaries for food, and their depositories for their young (in their care of which they are most singularly assiduous and exemplary) are arranged in suitable positions, and in due order. Their travels and exertions in procuring provisions are not less amazing than their habitations, and the order of their community. These expeditions in quest of food are sometimes made solitarily, and sometimes in bands; and it would appear as if individuals, when they fall in with any article of public utility, but too bulky for their unaided efforts to remove, have methods of communicating the intelligence, and leading off swarms of assistants, to accomplish by numbers what could not be done by strength. They go in these troops to very considerable distances, and repeat their journeys till they have got all secured. Ants may be seen pushing on before them grains of corn which they are unable to carry. It is further said (and it is previously likely, and seems to be sufficiently authenticated) that, to prevent the grain in their deposits from growing,

they instinctively gnaw off the germ from the extremity.
The little white substances, resembling very small peas,
which appear in such numbers at times on the surface or
when the surface is at all displaced, are not their food; nor
are they their eggs, but their young at a particular stage of
their progress. These are the first objects of their attention;
and when the settlement is disturbed and thrown into alarm
by any foreign invasion, whether from the foot of man or
otherwise, the eagerness, the toil, and the rapidity with which
all instantly set about and effect their removal, are not less
instructive than they are surprising.

On the subject of the other particular, the *providence* of
the ant, it has, by some naturalists, been questioned. It
has been alleged that during winter they are, like some other
insects, in a state of torpidity, and therefore need not the
precaution ascribed to them in the eighth verse, of " providing their meat in the summer, and gathering their food in the
harvest." On this we may observe—

1. If the *fact* of their laying up provisions be ascertained,
all analogy more than warrants the conclusion that it is
for some end. We do not find these extraordinary instincts
operating to no purpose. Nature, or more properly, the God
of nature, does nothing of this kind in vain.

2. Whereas it has been said, the stock thus laid up is not
for winter, but for the sustenance and nourishment of the
community, at a period when the young come to need the
almost undivided attention of the whole, and when, consequently, they have not leisure for their predatory excursions;
—I need not say that, as a proof of providence, even were it
admitted, this comes to the very same thing. But observe—

3. The assertion that the laying up of provisions is a
mistake, is, even by those who make it, confined to the ants
with which we are acquainted in England or in Europe,
while it does not extend with certainty even to all of *them.*
It is granted by these sceptical naturalists themselves, to be
more than probable in regard to the ants of other and
warmer climates. "What has been said *with exaggeration,*"
says one of them, " of the European ant, *is, however, true* if

asserted of those of the tropical climates. They build an
ant-hill with great contrivance and regularity; they *lay up
provisions;* and, as they probably live the whole year, they
submit themselves to regulations entirely unknown among
the ants of Europe." * There is often no little amount of
uncertainty respecting the instinctive customs of these minute creatures. Such uncertainty is apparent even in the
terms used in this extract—"*exaggeration*" and "*probably.*"
But the admission it contains is itself quite enough. If
there were ants of the kind described, known in the time and
country of Solomon, we need not carry our inquiries further.
Not a few fabulous extravagances, as might be expected,
have been asserted, both respecting this and other creatures
of a similar description; but when all that is fabulous has
been deducted, there remains enough, in the well-ascertained
facts, to excite our astonishment and call forth our praise.

But the lesson for which these little wonders of sensitive
creation are *here* introduced is of a different kind. It is a
lesson of reproof and shame to the slothful, "Go to the ant,
thou sluggard."

The language of the seventh verse is far from being intended to convey the idea that these creatures have no regular subordination among themselves in their little settlements.
For although here, in a special manner,—under the influence
of a fancy enamoured of the subject, and addicted to the
marvellous, fond itself of wondering and making others
wonder,—fabulous things have been imagined to have been
observed, and have been recorded among the facts of their
natural history; yet, as in the case of the *Bee* and other insects, there is no reason to doubt, but good ground for believing, that they have a government—a regular system of
subdivision into *castes*, or peculiar occupations, and of rule
and subjection and social operation. But the ants, as a
community, are here spoken of; and the meaning is, that
they have no creature of superior intelligence to teach them
what to do and how to do it; to inform them of their future

* Buffon.

necessities, and direct them in what way to provide against them. It is in their nature,—impressed there in a way that is full indeed of mystery, yet full of the wisdom of Him, all whose works are perfect.

The lesson is, that INDUSTRY is the *duty* of man, as it is the *practice* of the ant. Even in paradise, man was *not to be idle*, though his occupation was to have nothing in it of toil, fatigue, or disappointment. He was placed in the garden "to dress it and to keep it." And on men now, numerous are the inculcations of this duty in the Word of God.*

We may mention *three grounds* of the duty, as indicated in Scripture. The first is, that persons may not be a burden on society, or on the church. On this point, indeed, the apostle's language is strong even to seeming harshness; but it is the language of God's Spirit, and shows the light of severe reprehension in which He regards the idle. He interdicts support to them—*prohibits charity*, "If any *will* not work, neither should he eat." A further reason is, that they may be out of the way of temptation; there being many temptations in idle habits, and in the want to which they lead, from which the industrious are free; temptations to dishonesty, and pilfering, and extorting by false pretexts, *living* by *lying*.† The third is, that they may have wherewith to assist others, whose need, from unavoidable causes, may be greater than their own. This motive is strongly inculcated by the apostle, "Let him that stole steal no more: but rather let him labour, working with his hands the thing which is good, *that he may have to give to him that needeth*," Eph. iv. 28.

It is characteristic of *sloth*, as of some other dispositions, that it is *ever growing*. Give it any measure of indulgence, and it demands more. The indolent man is ever seeking apologies for keeping his bed or his easy chair. When these fail, he still pleads for *a little*—were it but ever so little—just another half-hour—just *one minute* more! Solomon in

---

* See, for example, Rom. xii. 11. 1 Tim. v. 8. 1 Thess. iv. 11, 12. 2 Thess. iii. 6—14.

† Comp. 1 Thess. iv. 12.

the next verses sounds the alarm, "How long wilt thou sleep, O sluggard? when wilt thou arise out of thy sleep? Yet a little sleep, a little slumber, a little folding of the hands to sleep: so shall thy poverty come as one that travelleth, and thy want as an armed man." How graphically descriptive of the yawning sloth; the useless piece of lazy lumber in society!—

> " Like the door on its hinges, so he on his bed,
> Moves his sides and his shoulders, and his heavy head."

And how forcibly is he warned of the natural tendency, and the inevitable consequence! Poverty may make slow, but they are sure, advances. "It comes as *a traveller.*" And when it arrives, the habit of inaction has become so powerful and inveterate, that it proves "as an *armed man.*" All resistance is vain. The very effort of prevention, if it can be called such, is that of indolence, and proves fruitless; and the poor sluggard, thoroughly mastered by arms which himself has furnished, becomes a prey to all the wretchedness of pinching penury; and is doomed to endure it without any portion of that soothing sympathy which is ever extended to the diligent but unfortunate—or let us rather say *providentially unsuccessful* labourer; who will always find a place in the compassion and the practical charity of others.

The passage suggests the following among other important reflections:—

1. The great importance of *Christians* exemplifying in all their transactions with the world, what may be denominated *business virtues,*—integrity, prudence, and diligence. Remember, fellow-christians, the men of the world, while they may scorn, or affect to scorn, your piety,—in regard to the business of life, and the principles by which it ought to be reciprocally regulated, are, in many respects, acute and discriminating judges. Yes; and they have the eyes of lynxes upon Christian professors, to detect whatever is inconsistent with uprightness and honour, and even with industry and discretion. Oh! it is a sad thing when those who "name the name of Christ,"—who profess the faith of his truth

and subjection to his will, and from whom all that is exemplary is naturally and justly expected, are found failing in
these palpable and every-day duties of life; when they not
only give occasion to the world to say of them, What do ye
more than others?—but even to point to them as falling
short of the world's standard! The Christian does not look
for spirituality and devotion in the man of the world; but
the man of the world looks, and justly looks, for uprightness
and diligence and honour in the Christian. It is melancholy
when *devotion* is divorced from *practical righteousness;* when
a man appears affecting unwonted sanctity; makes long
prayers and long faces; talks much about religion, and takes
a prominent part in all Bible, and Missionary, and Tract, and
Sabbath-School Societies; and by his transactions in business, by his hardness, by his chicanery, by his false credit
and mean shifts, gives the world reason for its favourite
nicknames, the utterance at once of contempt and indignation, of a *canting, psalm-singing hypocrite!*

2. Let Christian parents in every station train their
children to habits of *industry* as well as of incorruptible
honesty. It is said to have been the rule and practice of
the Jews to teach all their children some handicraft employment, to which they might be able to have recourse in all
circumstances. The principle of the rule was excellent.
Idleness not only tends to "clothe a man with rags," but as
before noticed, is the inlet to numberless temptations. It
is one of the HIGHWAYS TO VICE. Young friends, if you
would be *virtuous,* be *busy.* If you would be *vicious,* be *idle.*

3. *Spiritual service,*—all that regards religion and the
divine life in the soul, no less than the interests of the present world, requires, in order to prosperity, "*all diligence.*"
Without it there can be no spiritual acquisitions any more
than temporal; no riches in the things of God, any more
than in the things of the world.

Thus we apply the admonition to the cultivation of *personal godliness.* We apply it also to the duties of parents
in the instruction of their families. We apply it to the
labours of pastors and deacons in the church. We apply it

to the whole course of Christian duty, in zeal for God, and benevolence to men. In regard to *all*, "whatsoever thine hand findeth to do, do it with thy might."

The first thing to which the ungodly are called is *faith in Christ*. If you are expecting or attempting to get pardon and heaven in any other way—never was there a more hopeless undertaking. Many an airy speculation has been gone into in this world's business, and gone into with a confidence in the direct ratio of its unsubstantiality and unsoundness. But never was there a speculation surer of failure than this. You are trading without a capital. You are trying to force credit, where you have none, and where you never can get it. You are not merely bankrupt. Bankrupts may make a composition, paying a smaller or a larger proportion of their debts. But yours is a case—as is that of every sinner on earth—of *absolute destitution*. You have *nothing* to pay. The question—"What shall a man give in exchange for his soul?" is a question which admits but of one answer, *what can he give who has nothing?* O my friends, there is but ONE SURETY who, in this exigency, can stand between you and ruin. Jesus will answer for you; and none else in heaven or earth can. If you come to Him, with a sense of your own destitution, He *will* undertake for you. If you believe in Him, you will find the full amount of your debt to God paid in the ransom of his precious blood. Whatever you have owed, it will be frankly and for ever cancelled. And then you will set out anew, "working the works of God," on a new principle and new credit; with a stock, not of fancied merit, but of real grace. Receiving from Christ's fulness, while you rely upon his mercy, you will trade with the talents committed to you for the interests of his kingdom and the glory of his name, and he will say to you at last with the smile of approving love—"Well done, good and faithful servant: thou hast been faithful over a few things, I will make thee ruler over many things: enter thou into the joy of thy Lord!"

LECTURE XV.

Prov. vi. 12—19.

" A naughty person, a wicked man, walketh with a froward mouth. He winketh with his eyes, he speaketh with his feet, he teacheth with his fingers; frowardness is in his heart, he deviseth mischief continually, he soweth discord. Therefore shall his calamity come suddenly; suddenly shall he be broken without remedy. These six things doth the Lord hate: yea, seven are an abomination unto him: a proud look, a lying tongue, and hands that shed innocent blood, an heart that deviseth wicked imaginations, feet that be swift in running to mischief, a false witness that speaketh lies, and he that soweth discord among brethren."

The description with which this passage commences, of the character and end of unprincipled men, might possibly be suggested by what had just been said, of the tendency of idleness to lead into their society, and thus to vice, profligacy, and ruin; and it is introduced for the obvious purpose of warning all against such, and especially the young.

Of the " naughty person," " the wicked man," it is here said first, in general terms—he " walketh with a froward mouth." *Walking* is the Bible word for a man's daily course of conduct. A *froward mouth* is, as already noticed, a mouth under the influence of a froward, that is, a self-willed, rebellious spirit. It is a mouth that gives fearless and unrestrained utterance to the suggestions of such a spirit; that speaks its own words without regard to God or man.

In human nature, as in every other, there is an innate *love of freedom*. But alas! in human nature, as fallen, this principle, good in itself, has taken a sadly perverse direc-

tion.   It is too often the mere love of following, without restraint, our own inclinations.   And while aversion to restraint is common to all, it is peculiarly strong in the bosoms
of youth.   They spurn at it.   They wince and fret; are
restive and turbulent; feel, when the rein of authority is
imposed upon them, as if their proper liberty were abridged,
and are envious of those who can indulge themselves in
all they set their hearts upon, without coercion and without
fear.   They cherish a secret wish that the precepts of God's
word were somewhat less rigid, or its denunciations against
evil less awful, that so they might gratify their sinful
inclinations in a similar way.   There is, in the fearless indulgence of the libertine, an appearance of spirit and independence, of *their* want of which, when laughed at for their
stiffness and precision, they are ashamed, and sigh impatiently for the breaking of the yoke.   Ah! young friends,
this is a mournful kind of shame.   The freedom, not the
want of it, is that for which the shame ought to be felt.
It is that fearful liberty of which the Apostle speaks, when
he says—"When ye were the servants of sin, ye were *free
from righteousness!*"   Rom. vi. 20.

Allow me to remind you, that the *mouth* is by no
means always a true index of the *heart*.   It *is* such an index
indeed, as to the wickedness that is in it; but it is far from
being so in regard to its happiness and peace.   Ah! no.   The
mouth is many a time the *cover*, rather than the index, of
what is in the heart.   While the mouth pours out its arro-
gant and boastful impiety, as if the spirit were a stranger to
fear and foreboding, let but some sudden accident, or disease, or danger, bring death and judgment and eternity near,
and you may see the countenance of the braggadocio assume
an ashy paleness, his lips quiver, and his fearless vauntings
give way to silent trembling, or to the stifled groans or the
loud exclamations of agony.   The greatest boasters have
often proved the greatest dastards.   Look to *Belshazzar.**
Wherefore all his perturbation?   He knew not the meaning of the mysterious writing.   For aught he knew, it
might be an intimation of *good*.   It was conscience, that

sternly though silently, told him the contrary. It was conscience that made the mirthful and heaven-daring reveller a quaking coward,—turning in a moment his jovial festivity to consternation, and the laughter of profanity to the awe-struck silence of amazement and dread. It was *this* that made his eyes start from their sockets, and his knees to smite together. Was he *then* to be envied?—Ah! it is a dreadful liberty—the liberty to sin. It is a desperate, an ill-named and ill-omened courage that sets at defiance the God of heaven—that turns to scorn His restraints and His intimations of vengeance!

The next verse adds to the description of the " naughty person," the " wicked man:"—verse 13. " He winketh with his eyes, he speaketh with his feet, he teacheth with his fingers."

Different interpretations may be put upon these words— which are all allied to each other, and may be all found in real existence *together*. They may refer, first, to the clubs and cabals of the ungodly—with their slang language, and their secret signs, or, secondly, to the fact of all the members and all the powers of such men being made, jointly and severally, the instruments of evil, and *that* in every form and mode of their exercise, or, thirdly, to the multiform artfulness and duplicity—the " cunning craftiness whereby they lie in wait to deceive." This last is probably the true purport of the verse:—that they convey their meanings, and carry on their schemes, and promote their ends, in every sly, covert, unsuspected way. If at any time there is a risk in committing themselves *by words*, they keep to signs; "they wink with their eyes, they speak with their feet, they teach with their fingers." What an amount of evil may be thus *communicated*, and thus *effected!* Who can tell what mischief may be done by a *wink of the eye!* In that simplest and least perceived of motions, accompanied by a certain expression of the countenance, there may lurk falsehood, treachery, slander, suspicion, jealousy, alienation, revenge,

---

* Dan. v. 5, 6.

murder, covetousness, lasciviousness, and a host more of the
worst passions and purposes of the human heart. And there
may fairly be included in the description all the signs and attitudes of hypocritical devotion; of sanctity assumed for selfish
and secular ends—the bended knee, the lifted hand, the
closed or the turned-up eye, the sanctimoniously shaken
head, the ejaculated *Amen!*—with all the affected grimace
of ostentatious and worldly-minded pharisaism.

The source of this evil is *in the heart:*—verse 14. "Frowardness is in his heart, he deviseth mischief continually;
he soweth discord." *Frowardness,* as explained, is the
spirit of scornful insubordination, and a pride in expressing
and showing it. The *devising of mischief* may be against
various descriptions of persons, and may be modified accordingly, in regard to the principles or passions by which it is
dictated. It may be against the *pious and the good,* and
may spring from malignity—from the innate hatred of God
and holiness, dictating the wish to injure their reputation;
to make them ridiculous; or otherwise to gratify, at their
expense, the spirit of impiety. It may be against *the prosperous,* and may be dictated by *envy.* It may be against
their *enemies,* real or imagined, and may be the effect of
pique, resentment, avarice, or possibly mere *sport;* for, as
the wise man elsewhere says, "It is a sport to a fool to do
mischief." *Devising* mischief is a step beyond the doing of
it, as opportunities may present themselves. It implies the
setting of the wits to work in inventing and studying plans
of evil, and the means of carrying them into effect. Of
similar characters it is said by the Psalmist, "He deviseth
mischief *upon his bed*"—devises by night, and executes by
day.

The last of the particulars in this verse is that of having
pleasure in the Satanic employment of fomenting alienation
and strife: "He soweth discord." He delights in the horrid
success of his artful insinuations, in the miserable harvest
springing from his busy and often unsuspected seed-time: for he
is "sowing discord" even when the seed he is scattering seems,
to the credulous and ignorant, the seed of "righteousness and

peace." It is not unlikely that to the arts of such mischief-makers there may be an allusion in the thirteenth verse. And while by such means their envy is gratified, that is not always the limit of their aim. They sometimes have purposes of more substantial benefit to their selfish spirits. They fish in troubled waters:—first troubling them themselves, and then taking advantage of the disagreements they have stirred up from the muddy bottom of the heart's corruptions, to promote their own profit. But these disturbers of peace; these subverters of the delights and blessings of mutual love; these distillers of venom for the darts of the Wicked One; these froward inventors and workers of mischief—these "naughty persons," these "wicked men," are ultimately the authors of their own ruin—

Verse 15. "Therefore shall his calamity come suddenly; suddenly shall he be broken without remedy." Their calamity often comes, and comes suddenly, *from men.* When those who have unsuspiciously listened to their poisonous insinuations, and by means of them, have been led to suspect, and have come to be suspected by, their former associates and friends, happen to discover the malignity that has severed intimacy, and robbed them of mutual enjoyment, when they have got a clue by which to trace the mischief to its origin in the centre of the labyrinth of the intricate mazes of malice, —indignation is roused, and the author of the evils justly suffers by abandonment, or even by merited infliction of punishment, the due desert of his odious acts. And even should the mischiefs never be mended, and the source of them never be discovered so as to suffer at the hand of man, *God's* displeasure is awake against him; and he shall experience the sudden lighting-down of the arm of divine vengeance. God may bear long with the wicked. But though the transgressor be tempted by His very forbearance to take encouragement in what is wrong—in the end, " suddenly shall he be broken, and that without remedy "—reaping from the seed he has sown a harvest of irremediable misery to his own soul.*

* Comp. 1 Thess. v. 3. Ps. lxxiii. 18—20. Eccl. viii. 11—13.

I. M

The "*seven things*" enumerated in the following verses as the special objects of divine abhorrence, are naturally introduced in connexion with the *general character* of such men, in its leading features:—verses 16—19. "These six things doth the Lord hate; yea, seven are an abomination unto him: a proud look, a lying tongue, and hands that shed innocent blood, an heart that deviseth wicked imaginations, feet that be swift in running to mischief, a false witness that speaketh lies, and he that soweth discord among brethren."

The language of the first of these verses is strong. The reduplication of the assertion is intended to impress the fearfulness of the evils. Let all lay the terms of reprobation to heart. There cannot but be unspeakable danger in indulging in aught that is "abomination to the Lord."

1. The first of the seven is *pride*—"*a proud look.*" I have said *pride*. You must at once be sensible, that it is not the look merely that is meant, but the temper of mind which the look expresses—not the mere indication of the principle, but the principle itself. There may be much pride in the heart, that is *not* indicated by haughtiness in the look, but *covered* from observation by the assumed air of humility and lowliness of spirit. In this case, the *look* is absent, but the *thing* is there; and is there in a doubly odious form. The "proud look" is to be interpreted as including pride *of all kinds*. There is, first of all, if I may use an expression that is really, in its terms, contradictory, *religious pride*. I have called it contradictory; because there never has been, never is, never can be, any pride in religion. Its very essence is humility. The pride of religion is of all things the most *ir*religious. You know what I mean—the pride of the Pharisee, when he stood in God's sanctuary before the very "beauty of holiness" and prayed, "God, I thank thee that I am not as other men are." That this pride of self-righteousness is an abomination in God's sight, his whole word tells us; and the verdict of Jesus, in the parable referred to, testifies in the plainest terms. There is the pride of *high station and wealth*, with its look of lofty supercilious disdain upon its inferiors. There is the pride of *high spirit* and

false honour, of quick touchy resentment, that cannot brook
an injurious act, word, or even glance, however passing and
slight; whose eye of kindling and impetuous fire flashes on
the offender, and whose revenge sighs for his prostration,
and even, it may be, thirsts for his blood.

The face of God is set against this high-mindedness. He
"resisteth the proud." He "knoweth them afar off." He
"hath respect unto the lowly." And the lowliness which
He respects must begin with Himself—with the acceptance
of mercy, in the spirit of self-renunciation. There is no
true humility in a sinner's spirit, till it is brought to this.

2. We have next in order, "*a lying tongue.*" God is
the God of truth. He "desireth truth in the inward
parts." As in the former case, so here, a "lying tongue"
must be understood as comprehensive of all the modes of
wilfully conveying a false impression. This is the essence
of a lie; and it may be done in many ways. There are lying looks, and lying motions, as well as lying words. The
"naughty person" who "winketh with his eyes, speaketh with
his feet, teacheth with his fingers," may by the eye, by the
feet, by the fingers, *tell lies*—tell them as really, as effectually, as guiltily, as if he uttered them with his tongue. The
declarations of the divine displeasure against this sin are
specially frequent and strong;* and in the outset of the
Christian church, there was read to both believers and the
world, a solemn and awful lesson of God's opposition to all
deception and lying, in His judicially visiting Ananias and
Sapphira with death for their selfish dissembling—a dissembling in which they sought the gratification of covetousness, and the desire of *eclat* for their liberality, by the
sin of falsehood.

3. Then we have—"*hands that shed innocent blood.*"
The first innocent blood shed on earth was the blood of a
brother. At the second commencement of the human race,
Jehovah, with obvious reference to this first murder, set a

---

* See Ps. v. 6: cxx. 3, 4: Hos. iv. 1—3: John viii. 44: Rev.
xxi. 8, 27.

guard of threatened vengeance around the life of man. (Gen. ix. 5, 6.)

Life may be taken—"innocent blood shed"—otherwise than directly by the armed hand. It is not the assassin alone, with his murderous knife, that is intended. The *judge* is guilty who gives sentence against the innocent. The executioner whose hands *actually* shed the blood, is not, in that case, the culprit, but he by whom the sentence was pronounced. The promoters of *persecution* are guilty, whether acting *with* legal form or *without* it:—if *with* it, only so much the worse. He who, *by cruel treatment, breaks another's heart*, is guilty. When the broken heart brings its victim, by pining atrophy, to the grave, there can be no question to whose account that "innocent blood" must be placed. Remember, the Lord is the righteous "avenger of blood." He "maketh inquisition" for it. He will allow no blood-guiltiness to escape. The murderer was even to be dragged from His altar unto death.

4. The fourth in order, is one in which divine omniscience is implied for its detection—"*a heart that deviseth wicked imaginations.*" "The thought of wickedness is sin." You may form, and even cherish, desires which it is not in your power to execute. Or even those which are in your power, so far as ability is concerned, you may, by uncontrollable circumstances, be prevented from executing. But God knows them all; and He will judge and avenge them, as if actually done.

This leads to the general reflection, that "the law is spiritual." The reflection applies to the immediately preceding particular, and indeed to them all.*

5. The fifth is "*feet that are swift in running to mischief.*" "Running to mischief" may mean, either running to *do* it, or running to *see* it. In either case we are supposed to *enjoy* it. "Feet that are *swift*" in carrying us to do it, are supposed to be the agents of a heart that has a relish for it. The one will be proportioned to the other. And

---

* Compare Matt. v. 21, 22: 1 John iii. 15.

the feet that are swift in "running to mischief," will be slow to works of benevolence, slow to the abodes of distress, slow to the house of God, slow to whatever is good.

6. "*A false witness that speaketh lies*," may be considered as having been already included in a former particular—the "*lying tongue.*" But there is a peculiarity of guilt in falsehood when it is committed in *witness-bearing*—when it assumes the form of *perjury.* The cause of others is thus injuriously affected: it leads to a false decision; and therefore adds *injustice* to untruth: the judges, or the arbiters are deceived, troubled, wronged, by being frustrated in their solicitude to give a fair and equitable verdict. And, when an *oath* has actually been taken, there is the superadded guilt of blasphemy—the "taking of God's name," in the most heinous sense, "in vain."

There is a species of witness-bearing, in which a deep criminality is involved, that is too often little thought of—being "found false witnesses of God," 1 Cor. xv. 15. O! this is a fearful description of false-witnessing!—setting the seal of the God of truth to falsehood!—forging upon heaven! God keep from such guilt all his professed servants! It is at once the guilt of blood, and the guilt of making God a liar.

7. The last in this enumeration is, "*he that soweth discord among brethren.*" There is here an emphatic addition to the language of verse fourteenth—"*among brethren.*" In proportion to the loveliness of any scene, even in external nature, and the degree in which we are captivated by its beauties, are we offended by the man who defaces it—despoils it of its chief attractions, and spreads disorder and desolation where before every sense found its richest and sweetest gratification. So is it in the moral world. There is not on the face of the earth a scene of more engaging interest and delight, than a family all united in the bonds of nature's love, making each other's joys and sorrows their own; every heart beating in unison; every eye and every hand eager to anticipate each other's wants and wishes. And what is beautiful as a specimen of the affections of na-

ture, is no less beautiful when the bond of union is " the love of the Spirit," the spiritual love by which the children of God are bound together in "the household of faith." The disturber of the harmony of a united family, or of a united church, is incomparably worse than the man who desolates the face of any earthly paradise. God is the God of love and peace. He delighteth in them. The prevalence of them among his people is honourable to his truth in the eyes of the world; and his eye rests on the scene with divine satisfaction.* Hateful, then, diabolical the man who seeks to introduce discord into such a scene of harmony—to embitter its joys, to destroy its benefits!

There are cases in which we cannot be responsible for the discord to which we give rise;—in which we are only its *innocent occasion*, not its *guilty cause*. The Saviour himself anticipates such discord, (Matt. x. 34—36.) But neither he nor his truth is answerable for it. It arises from the opposition of the carnal minds of men to the principles of his kingdom. For this, these principles are not to blame. It is not the end Jesus or his servants had in view. What they teach is fitted, when received, to knit all mankind in one blessed bond of peace, and purity, and joy. The GOSPEL alone can extirpate the evils here enumerated, and other evils of kindred nature. It produces humility, sincerity, regard for human life and happiness, holiness of heart, reverence for God's name, and that love which is " the bond of perfectness."

* Comp. Ps. cxxxiii.

LECTURE XVI.

Prov. viii. 1—21.

"Doth not wisdom cry? and understanding put forth her voice? She standeth in the top of high places, by the way in the places of the paths: she crieth
at the gates, at the entry of the city, at the coming in at the doors: Unto you,
O men, I call; and my voice is to the sons of man. O ye simple, understand
wisdom: and, ye fools, be ye of an understanding heart. Hear; for I will speak
of excellent things; and the opening of my lips shall be right things. For my
mouth shall speak truth; and wickedness is an abomination to my lips. All the
words of my mouth are in righteousness; there is nothing froward or perverse
in them. They are all plain to him that understandeth, and right to them that
find knowledge. Receive my instruction, and not silver; and knowledge rather
than choice gold. For wisdom is better than rubies; and all the things that
may be desired are not to be compared to it. I wisdom dwell with prudence,
and find out knowledge of witty inventions. The fear of the Lord is to hate
evil: pride, and arrogancy, and the evil way, and the froward mouth, do I hate.
Counsel is mine, and sound wisdom: I am understanding; I have strength. By
me kings reign, and princes decree justice. By me princes rule, and nobles, even
all the judges of the earth. I love them that love me; and those that seek me
early shall find me. Riches and honour are with me; yea, durable riches and
righteousness. My fruit is better than gold, yea, than fine gold; and my revenue than choice silver. I lead in the way of righteousness, in the midst of
the paths of judgment: that I may cause those that love me to inherit substance; and I will fill their treasures."

THE majority, if I mistake not, of those regarded as evangelical expositors, interpret what is said in this chapter by Wisdom as the words of the Second Person of the ever-blessed
Trinity; by whom, in his character of Mediator, all divine
communications have, from the beginning, been made to mankind,—THE ETERNAL UNCREATED WORD, ordained to his mediatorial office "before the foundation of the world." In this

view, indeed, the passage has even been adduced in evidence
of the pre-existence and eternity of the Son of God. One
highly venerates the piety that seeks to find Christ everywhere; and would bear more readily with the mistake that
finds him where he is not, than with the indifference, or the
learned apathy, that finds him not where he is. At the
same time, the only correct principle for guiding us in our
exposition of the word of God, is the principle of being satisfied with no view of any part of it but that which there is
reason to regard as the *mind of the Spirit;* by which I mean,
not merely what is consistent with the general and pervading
doctrine of the inspired volume, but what the Spirit intended
to express in the particular passage. An interpretation may
be quite in accordance with what is usually called " the analogy of faith," and may even, in the spirit and substance and
terms of it, be fitted to excite the emotions of piety, and
yet may not be the true one. Nay, persons, by long-con-
tinued associations and habits of thought, may have a certain
sense so attached to a particular passage, as to be in the
habit of referring to it in proof of some important doctrine; and, every time they quote it, they may experience
the excitement of devout affections, of a kind and in a
degree such as to afford the sweetest satisfaction to their
minds; and thus they may have become greatly disinclined
to listen to any interpretation at all fitted to disturb those
associations, and deprive them of their spiritual feast. But
if the doctrines from which their holy *pleasure* has arisen,
are to be found in other parts of the sacred volume, the
source of that pleasure remains in reality untouched. And,
at all events, we cannot relinquish the position, that the
only emotions which are legitimate, when excited by any
particular portion of God's word, are those excited *by its
true sense*—that is, by the sentiment in it which the *Holy
Spirit intended to convey.*

Whatever, therefore, may have been the satisfaction experienced by many devout minds in reading this chapter,
especially the latter part of it, as if it contained the words of
Christ and evidence of his pre-existent divinity, and of his

love from eternity, and his eternal purposes of mercy towards our fallen world, I dare not, on this account, withhold what I believe to be the true principle of interpretation. The objections to its meaning Christ, or the Word, ere he became flesh, when " in the beginning he was with God and was God," are to my mind quite insuperable. For example :—

1. It should be noticed that the passage is not so applied in any part of the New Testament. You will misunderstand me, if you imagine that I adduce this consideration as any *direct objection* to the interpretation in question. It certainly does not follow, from the circumstance of a passage not being actually explained of Christ in the New Testament that it *must not* be so explained. What I mean is no more than this—that from its not being so explained there, we are relieved from any *necessity* of so explaining it. Had any New Testament writer expressly applied any part of the chapter to the Son of God, this would have been *a key* which we could not have been at liberty to refuse. Such necessity, then, being thus precluded, the direct objections may be allowed to have their full force. Observe, then—

2. Wisdom here is a *female personage.* All along this is the case.* Now under such a view the Scriptures nowhere else, in any of their figurative representations of "the Christ," ever thus describe or introduce Him. The application, on this account, appears to me exceedingly unnatural.

3. Wisdom does not appear intended as a *personal* designation, inasmuch as it is associated with various other terms, of synonymous, or at least of corresponding import.† Were it meant for a personal designation, like the Logos or Word in the beginning of John's Gospel, this would hardly have been admissible.

4. That the whole is a bold and striking *personification* of the attribute of wisdom, as subsisting in Deity, appears further from what she is represented as saying in verse twelfth—"I wisdom dwell with prudence, and find out knowledge of witty inventions." Here wisdom is associated

* Chap. i. 20, 21: viii. 1—3: ix. 1—3.   † Verse 1: ch. iii. 19, 20.

with prudence; and the import of the association is, that *wisdom* "directs to the best ends, and to the choice of the best means for their attainment;" and *prudence*, or *discretion*, teaches to shun whatever might, in any way or degree, interfere with and impede or mar their accomplishment. This is precisely what wisdom, as an attribute or quality, does. And it is worthy of remark, that this association of wisdom with prudence, is introduced by the Apostle as characterizing the greatest of the divine inventions and works,—that of our redemption. Wisdom was associated with prudence in framing and perfecting that wonderful scheme.*

5. It is very true, that there are many things here, especially in the latter part of the chapter—indeed through the whole—that are, in a very interesting and striking manner, applicable to the divine Messiah. But this is no more than might have been anticipated—that things which are true of a *divine attribute* should be susceptible of application to a *divine person*. This is not at all wonderful. And the question is, not whether particular expressions and representations are capable of being applied, and applied naturally and emphatically to the Eternal Word; but simply,—since they *also* admit of equally easy interpretation when applied to Wisdom as a personified attribute of Deity,—which, on other grounds, appears to have the strongest claims to preference? And in settling the question, we must be determined by such considerations as have been mentioned, and by the general scope of the passage and style of the Book.

Instead, however, of showing the application of this principle to the contents of the entire chapter, in which there are various things that stand in the predicament mentioned, —capable of application either in the one way or the other, —we shall rather leave these parts of the chapter to be explained on the principle of *personification*, when we come to them.

Verses 1—5. "Doth not wisdom cry? and understand-

* Eph. i. 7, 8.

ing put forth her voice? She standeth in the top of high places, by the way in the places of the paths: she crieth at the gates, at the entry of the city, at the coming in at the doors: Unto you, O men, I call; and my voice is to the sons of man. O ye simple, understand wisdom; and, ye fools, be ye of an understanding heart."

The words correspond with those of chapter first, verses 20—22. Wisdom's address here, as there, is universal,— "Unto you, O men, I call." Her counsels are suited to men of all nations, ranks, and characters. By ALL alike are they needed; and to ALL alike are they addressed. And her language is urgent, importunate, tender, persuasive; full of deep and anxious concern about the best interests of those to whom she speaks,—embracing every opportunity to warn, instruct, and entreat, with a pitying heart and a tearful eye. And by whomsoever divine Wisdom addresses men, this is the style and spirit of her address: whether it be in the person of Jehovah himself, of his Son, or of his servants.*

The characters of the *simple* and the *foolish*, we have before had occasion to describe:—the former meaning the inconsiderate, the thoughtless; the latter, (since folly is the reverse of wisdom) those who do not choose "the fear of the Lord,"—that fear which is here, and throughout the Bible, pronounced true wisdom. Remember, it is not *mental incapacity* that prevents men from receiving the instructions of heavenly wisdom. That, as a natural obstacle, constituting a natural inability, would stand as a valid excuse, and acquit them of guilt. This was the sentiment of Jesus to the Pharisees, when he said, "If ye were blind, ye should have no sin." And in the great day, many will there be by whom the veriest idiot, from whom it pleased God to withhold the capacity of understanding, will be envied. The guilt of men lies in their *indisposition of heart* to attend to divine counsels. It is *this* that warps, and prejudices, and blinds, and dupes the understanding.

* Ps. xlix. 1, 2: Rom. i. 14, 15: Col. iii. 11: Ezek. xxxiii. 11: Matt. xxiii. 37: Jer. xxv. 4—6: 2 Cor. v. 20.

The *heart*, as I have had occasion before to notice, is frequently used simply for the mind or seat of intellect, as well
as for the affections; so that "an understanding heart" might
mean nothing different from an *intelligent mind*.   At the
same time, since the state of the heart affects, to such a degree. the exercise of the judgment, "an understanding heart"
may signify a heart freed from the influence of those corrupt
affections and passions, by which the understanding is perverted and its vision marred and destroyed.

This "understanding heart" you must have.   Let not
pride; let not worldliness; let not corrupt affections blind
and mislead you to your ruin.   That is "folly" to which
there is no other comparable.

Readily, and with all attention will men listen, on any
subject that has relation to their interests in the present
world.   And even as to the merest trifles, unworthy of a
moment's consideration, their ear and their interest may
be gained, and gained without difficulty.   But oh! the
difficulty of obtaining any thing like a really earnest attention in regard to matters of everlasting and infinite
moment!

To *such* things Divine Wisdom bespeaks attention:—
verses 6, 7. "Hear, for I will speak of excellent things; and
the opening of my lips shall be right things.   For my mouth
shall speak truth; and wickedness is an abomination to my
lips."

The discoveries of Wisdom relate to things of the highest
possible *excellence;* such as the existence, character, works,
and ways of God; the soul; eternity; the way of salvation
—the means of eternal life.   And they are, on all subjects,
"*right.*"   They could not, indeed, be excellent themselves,
how excellent soever in dignity and importance the subjects
to which they related, unless they were "right."   But all
her instructions are so.   They are *true* in what regards
doctrine; and "holy, just, and good," in what regards *conduct* or *duty*.   There is truth without any mixture of error,
and rectitude without any alloy of evil.   The *seventh* and
eighth verses are an amplification of the more general posi-

tion in the *sixth*.   They contain the same general sentiment;
and are fitted and designed to impress it the more strongly,
—the truth, the purity, the righteousness, the beneficial
tendency, of *all* without exception that comes from the lips
of Divine Wisdom.   And the terms may be applied, in all
their emphasis and amount of meaning, to this blessed Book
—the Bible.   Here it is that Wisdom speaks; speaks in
every part; and in every part with the same authority.
And her words, coming as they do from the INFINITE REA-
SON, the MIND of the UNIVERSE, have nothing "froward or
perverse in them."

We have hinted at what keeps men from the clear apprehension of divine truths.   The wise man says in verse 9.
"They are all plain to him that understandeth, and right to
them that find knowledge."

The first part of this verse wears very much the aspect of
a *truism*.   But it is not said, "They are all plain to him
that understandeth *them;*" but simply to him that "*understandeth.*"   It seems to signify, who has the understanding
necessary to the apprehension of divine truth—*spiritual
discernment*.   "He who is spiritual *discerneth all things.*"
"They are all plain" to him who *thus* understandeth.

It may further be observed, how very much depends, in
the prosecution of any science, for correct and easy apprehension of its progressive development to the mind, on the
clear comprehension of its *elementary principles*.   The very
clearest and plainest demonstrations, in any department of
philosophy, will fail to be followed and to carry conviction,
—will leave the mind only in wonder and bewildering confusion, unless there is a correct and full acquaintance with
principles or *elements*, or a willingness to apply the mind
to its attainment.   So it is in divine science.   There are, in
regard to the discoveries of the divine word, certain primary
principles, which all who are taught of God know, and which
they hold as principles of explanation for all that that word
reveals.   They who *are* thus "taught of God," perceive with
increasing clearness and fulness, the truth, the rectitude, the
unalloyed excellence of all the dictates of divine wisdom.

All is "plain"—all "right." The darkness that before
brooded over the mind is dissipated. They "see all things
clearly." They "have an unction from the Holy One, and
know all things," 1 John ii. 20.

Wisdom then goes on to recommend her instructions, in
terms very similar to those she had before used:—verses 10,
11.* "Receive my instruction, and not silver; and knowledge
rather than choice gold. For wisdom is better than rubies;
and all the things that may be desired are not to be compared to it."

The first and second parts of the tenth verse are the same
in meaning. The two things are supposed to be brought
into competition. A choice is offered; a decision between
them is to be made. And the instructions of wisdom are
pronounced incomparably superior in real value to the most
choice treasures of earth.

Wisdom next recommends herself and her instructions, by
representing herself as the source of all useful and happy
discoveries:—verse 12. "I wisdom dwell with prudence, and
find out knowledge of witty inventions."

We have already adverted to the following verse, as indicating that Wisdom is to be understood of a *personified attribute*—"I wisdom dwell with prudence, and find out
knowledge of witty inventions."

Wisdom, in the most comprehensive aspect, is to be regarded as giving origin to all arts and sciences, by which
human life is improved and adorned; as by her inventive
skill developing all the varied appliances for the external
comfort and well-being of mankind; as planning the "won-
drous frame" of universal creation, which, with all its varied
beauty, fills us, in the view, with astonishment and delight;
and conceiving, in the depths of eternity, the glorious scheme
—a scheme "dark with brightness all along"—which secures the happiness of man for ever, and in which she
appears in her noblest and most attractive display—the whole,
from first to last, discovering "the manifold wisdom of God."

* Compare chap. iii. 13—15.

Verse 13. "The fear of the Lord is to hate evil: pride, and arrogancy, and the evil way, and the froward mouth, do I hate."—"*Hating evil*," is the practical result of "the fear of the Lord." This is the sentiment; only by identifying the two,*—the *principle* with the *practice*,—the idea is more emphatically conveyed, that the one cannot subsist without the other. If evil is not hated, God is not feared. It is equally true, that if God is not feared evil is not hated: for, indeed, the absence of the fear of God is the greatest of all evil. It is "desperate wickedness;"—"enmity against God," evinced in the neglect of those duties which men owe directly to God,—being necessarily a greater crime than any violation of the claims of fellow-creatures,—greater in the proportion in which the object of the one class of duties is greater than the object of the other.

It is not only divine *Holiness*, observe, that "hates evil;" it is divine *Wisdom*. This conveys to us the important lesson, that the will of God, along with His abhorrence of all that is opposed to it, is founded in the *best of reasons*. All that is evil is contrary to His own necessary perfection, and, consequently, to "the eternal fitness of things."

[Wisdom continues to assert her exalted claims, verse 14 : —"Counsel is mine and sound wisdom; I am understanding; I have strength."—Her "*counsel*" is ever *good*. There is always "*sound wisdom*" in it—the wisdom which guides to right conclusions, both as to the *course* to be taken, and the *means* by which it is to be followed out. To appreciate "sound wisdom," "*understanding*" is essential—a distinct apprehension of the *truth* and *will* of God. In "*understanding and wisdom*" there is "*strength*." (Eccl. vii. 10). "Knowledge is power;" and knowledge in union with wisdom—the ability to use knowledge aright—multiplies the power. In proportion as there is "understanding" and "wisdom," is there "strength"—moral and spiritual strength— strength to act and to suffer—to *do* and to *bear*.

To divine Wisdom, these spiritual treasures peculiarly belong. She alone is their centre and their source. The structure of the sentence is not *uniform;* but the language expresses this idea in the most absolute manner.

"Counsel" and "wisdom;" "understanding" and "strength" are needed by *all;* but to no class are they so indispensable as to those who hold the reins of authority, or occupy the seat of judgment. Hence the following verses—— "By me kings reign and princes decree justice; by me princes rule, and nobles, even all the judges of the earth."—— Are all then who wield the sceptre or exercise judicial functions, guided by the dictates of wisdom? Alas! the history of the Church and of the world alike tell a very different tale. Too often among "kings and princes and judges of the earth," has there been but a slender measure of even ordinary wisdom——worldly discretion——and less by far of "the wisdom that cometh from above." Full many a time have their deeds of oppression and wrong testified of their folly, and discovered their godless spirit——wringing tears of bitterness from many an eye, and groans of anguish from many a heart.

The language may be considered as implying, *First,*——that human government, in all its branches, is the appointment of Divine wisdom;——that, as the Apostle expresses it, "there is no power but of God;" that "the powers that be are ordained of God."——*Secondly,* that all who sustain positions of authority and power, should act habitually under the influence of divine Wisdom——"the fear of God" being the regulating principle of their entire procedure.——*Thirdly,* that no authority can be rightly exercised, and no judicial process successfully carried out,——so carried out as to promote the well-being of man, and the glory of God,——without the direction of Wisdom.——*Fourthly,* that divine Wisdom exercises control over all human agents in the administration of public affairs——from the monarch on the throne to the humblest official——all being alike "ministers of God"——and all their dealings being overruled for the ends which divine Wisdom has to accomplish, so that every act shall tend to further the purposes of Him whose prerogative it is to say, "My counsel shall stand, and I will do all my pleasure."

In the verse which follows, Wisdom gives the gracious assurance of her tender regard for those in whose hearts sincere affection towards herself has a place. She reciprocates their love—"*I love them that love me*," is her solemn declaration: and none ever "seek her face *in vain.*" "*They,*" says she, "*who seek me early shall find me.*" She loves not any for their rank or station:—not the great for their greatness; not the rich for their riches; not the noble for their nobility; not the mighty for their might; not the learned for their learning; not the prince more than the peasant; not the king on the throne more than "the beggar" in his rags: but *all alike*—"high and low, rich and poor together"—who love *her*—"them that love ME:"—them that discern her beauty, that seek her favour, that court her presence, that submit to her will, that learn from her lips, that look to her for guidance, that rejoice in her smile and blessing.

And by ALL her smile and blessing may be "found." From none does she hide herself. She waits to welcome all who come. She bids none from her presence. She proffers to all the hand of kindness. She extends to all the sceptre of her love. She "receives them graciously, and loves them freely:"—"They that seek me *shall* find me:" such is her promise. That promise must stand. It is sure as the word of eternal truth. But she must be "*sought*"—sought "*early*" —*earnestly,* and *now.*

How striking the contrast between the language of Wisdom here, and her utterance in the close of the opening chapter of this Book! Here her voice is that of mild benignity; there it is the voice of stern, unrelenting judgment. Here we have the voice of mercy; there the voice of insulted and offended majesty; here the breathing of tenderness and love, there the dread denunciations of destructive wrath. This is her language *now,* as she stands, in the attitude of condescending kindness, ready to welcome to her embrace the wayward and wandering—the guilty and perishing children of men; that is her language in the view of love rejected, of favour despised, of invitations scorned, of blessing proffered, but trampled in the dust by the spirit of ingratitude

I.   N

and pride. Then will cease for ever "the still small voice,
of Mercy's tender pleadings, and the ear be greeted only with
the startling, thrilling accents of awakened justice.   Then
there are no more invitations, no more gracious promises,
no kind assurances, no words of encouragement, no smile of
benignity, no proffered hand of help.   They "call on her"
but she "hears not."   They "seek her"—seek her with the
agonizing effort of despair—but they do *not* find her."

While we cannot regard Wisdom as the Eternal Word,
yet no language could be more in harmony with His utterances
when, in "the days of his flesh," as incarnate God, He ad·
dressed himself to perishing men—to "the *lost*" whom He
came from heaven to earth to "seek and to save."   In these
words, "I love them that love me, and they that seek me
early shall find me," we seem to hear the voice of Him "who
spake as never man spake,"—of Him "into whose lips grace
was poured,"—of Him who said, with all the deep affection
and tender solicitude of a heart glowing with divine compassion, "Come unto me, all ye that labour and are heavy
laden, and I will give you rest:" "HIM THAT COMETH UNTO
ME I WILL IN NO WISE CAST OUT."—And in the contrasted declaration—"They shall call on me, but I will not hear; they
shall seek me earnestly, but shall not find me," we hear, as
it were, the voice of the same Jesus, when, as the Judge of
all, He shall sit upon "the throne of his glory," and having
"separated the righteous from the wicked," shall say to the
latter, in these words of awful import—filling their trembling
spirits with hopeless agony, "DEPART FROM ME, YE CURSED,
INTO EVERLASTING FIRE.

To induce all to "seek" her, Wisdom anew unfolds the
blessings she has to bestow—blessings of unequalled excellence and unending duration.   Hear her words once more—
"Riches and honour are with me ; yea, durable riches and
righteousness.   My fruit is better than gold, yea, than fine
gold; and my revenue than choice silver.   I lead in the way
of righteousness, in the midst of the paths of judgment : that
I may cause those that love me to inherit substance; and I
will fill their treasures."]

LECTURE XVII.

———◆———

PROV. VIII. 22—36.

" The Lord possessed me in the beginning of his way, before his works of old.
I was set up from everlasting, from the beginning, or ever the earth was. When
there were no depths, I was brought forth; when there were no fountains abounding with water. Before the mountains were settled, before the hills was I brought
forth; while as yet he had not made the earth, nor the fields, nor the highest part
of the dust of the world. When he prepared the heavens, I was there: when he
set a compass upon the face of the depth: when he established the clouds above:
when he strengthened the fountains of the deep: when he gave to the sea his decree, that the waters should not pass his commandment: when he appointed the
foundations of the earth: then I was by him, as one brought up with him: and
I was daily his delight, rejoicing always before him; rejoicing in the habitable
part of his earth; and my delights were with the sons of men. Now therefore
hearken unto me, O ye children: for blessed are they that keep my ways. Hear
instruction, and be wise, and refuse it not. Blessed is the man that heareth
me, watching daily at my gates, waiting at the posts of my doors. For whoso
findeth me findeth life, and shall obtain favour of the Lord. But he that sinneth
against me wrongeth his own soul: all they that hate me love death."

On the principles already explained, I consider the verses
which follow to the thirty-first, as a beautiful and impressive
amplification of the sentiment of the Psalmist, "O Lord,
how manifold are thy works! in wisdom hast thou made
them all," Psalm civ. 24.

Verse 22. "The Lord possessed * me in the beginning of
his way, before his works of old." There is no difficulty
here. The attribute of infinite wisdom was possessed by
Jehovah from everlasting. The "beginning of his way"

———

* Others render *created*. So the Septuagint, εκτισε, the Chaldee and
Syriac. This seems more in harmony with the Hebrew קנה.

evidently means the commencement of creation, when he set out in his course of creative and consequently of providential manifestation of his eternal perfections. *When* this was we cannot tell. We may know the age of our own world, at least according to its present constitution. But *when* the universe was brought into being, and whether by one omnipotent *fiat*, or at successive and widely varying periods, it is beyond our power to ascertain. One thing we know, for a certainly revealed fact, that there were angelic creatures in existence previously to the reduction of our globe to order, and to the creation of man upon it. These holy intelligences contemplated the six days' work of divine wisdom and power in this part of the universe with devout and benevolent transport—"The morning stars sang together, and all the sons of God shouted for joy." How many other creatures, and of what descriptions—how many other worlds, and how peopled, might have existed before man and his earthly residence, we are unable to affirm.—When men, indeed, begin to talk of its being absurd to suppose the universe so recent as to have been only coeval with our own globe or our own system, they forget themselves. They do not speak considerately nor philosophically. There is no lapse of ages, nor any points of measurement, in eternity. The very same absurdity, therefore, remains, how far back soever you carry your conception of the first exercise of creative power. The intelligent beings who lived a few thousand years after the commencement of creation,—supposing that commencement millions of ages remote,—would have stood in the very same predicament as ourselves: seeing there was then a preceding eternity, as there is now, to the beginning of which we never get any nearer, *beginning* being as inconsistent with the very idea of eternity, as termination is. Go as far back, therefore, as imagination, or as numbers heaped on numbers, can carry you, there still remains the previous eternity, during which our speculating and presumptuous minds may wonder that divine power had not been put forth. *Sooner* and *later* are terms of no meaning in eternity. The unsearchable depths of the divine mind it is not ours to fathom. "Such knowledge is too wonderful for us: it is high; we cannot attain unto it." The probability seems to be, that creation, whensoever it began, was progressive; nay even that it still continues so; that the will of omnipotence gives birth to new worlds, and new systems, and new orders and modes of being, from the exhaustless resources of what the apostle denominates "the *manifold* wisdom of God."

The next verse—"I was set up* from everlasting, from the beginning, or ever the earth was," is usually explained of the pre-ordination from eternity of the Second Person in the Trinity to the mediatorial office, to be assumed and sustained by Him, at the needed juncture, in future time. But according to the view we take of wisdom as not a *person* but a *personification*, the meaning seems rather to be, that infinite wisdom directed all the divine counsels,—all the prospective plans of the Godhead being devised by it from everlasting, with unerring, with infinite skill. We are accustomed to speak of a man *consulting* his understanding, his judgment, his good sense and discretion. In the spirit of the figure employed, God, in like manner, is represented as, in the whole of his purposes and plans, "setting up" infinite wisdom to be consulted in every step.

Amplifying still further, and the figure advancing in boldness, Wisdom proceeds—verses 24, 25. "When there were no depths, I was brought forth; when there were no fountains abounding with water. Before the mountains were settled, before the hills was I brought forth."

This is one of the very few passages adduced in support of their doctrine by the advocates of the *eternal generation* of the Son of God; that is, of his having been the Son of the Father from eternity, according to his divine nature alone—mysteriously and eternally begotten in the essence of Deity. But in the first place, there is evidently a *previous question*,—the question, namely, whether *the Son of God*

---

* Or, *I was anointed.*

in person be the speaker. Till this has been clearly and fully established, the words ought not to be quoted in evidence. And in my judgment, the considerations assigned in last lecture render this much more than doubtful. On the authority of the Holy Scriptures, I do firmly believe, that in the divine essence there has subsisted from eternity a threefold personal distinction; but how,—according to what mode, this distinction subsists, I do not think the Bible at all informs us. All that has been said and written, about the Father being the Fountain of deity, about the Son as "begotten but not proceeding," and the Holy Spirit as "proceeding but not begotten," has long appeared to me only as showing the eagerness of men to pry into the mysterious beyond the limits of revelation. Such expressions, there is ground to fear, convey *no ideas.* And yet—as not seldom happens,—the more remote the subject from all human comprehension, the more fiery has been the dogmatism of the different parties, by whom the most hair-splitting niceties of distinction, (distinction often without perceptible difference,) have been maintained and vindicated, as if each of them for himself had succeeded in "finding out God," in "finding out the Almighty unto perfection." Holding firmly the belief I have already stated, I do *not* believe it to be the doctrine of Scripture that any one of the Divine Three possesses divinity *by communication.* I am not for divesting our holy religion of any of the mysteries belonging to it, which have clear Bible authority to support them; but I am very hostile to making mysteries beyond what that authority evidently affirms. And I am strongly inclined to think that the doctrine now referred to is more than a mystery—that it is self-contradictory. I am unable to think of *communication* without the idea of previousness and posteriority, of supremacy and dependence, of inferiority as connected with derivation; nor can I think of such communication, or generation, as *eternal*, without a feeling of contradiction. It was anxiety to maintain the true, underived, independent divinity of the Lord Jesus Christ, that first led me to doubt the prevalent systematic doctrine about "generation and procession from eternity;" and the more I searched, the more I became convinced, that for the latter, the "eternal procession of the Holy Spirit from the Father and the Son," there is not one atom of Scripture evidence—the only text adduced in its support having no relation whatever to any such subject;* and that of the former the proofs are far from satisfactory. The *proper Deity* of the Son of God, eternal, underived, independent, is incomparably better sustained, and the mind freed of all its feelings of impossibility and contradiction, by regarding the title SON OF GOD as belonging to Christ according to *the complex constitution of his mediatorial person*, as "God manifest in the flesh,"—a sense quite peculiar to Himself, and of which the Scriptures abound in proofs.†

When a personification is introduced, and is with any degree of boldness and freedom maintained, we need not be surprised at the appearance, according to the different aspects under which the same thing may be viewed, of *incongruity*. Divine wisdom, belonging essentially to the nature of God, was *from eternity*. But as a person she here speaks of herself as "brought forth" previously to the commencement of creation and providence, with obvious reference to the application of her counsels in the purposes and plans of the Godhead. The language of *figure* is not, of course, to be interpreted literally and strictly.

At the period referred to here, creation was not yet actually framed and executed. It was only planned;—the whole being at once, in all its magnificence and in all its minuteness, before the eye of the omniscient Mind, in its almost *infinite* complexity, extent and variety—yet without the slightest approach to confusion! All there, in one vast and complicated, yet simple idea!

The phrase, "the *highest* part of the dust of the world," is in the margin "the *chief* part;" and by some the phrase has been explained of *man*—whom God made of the "dust"

---

* The passage alluded to is John xv. 26.

† For further discussion of this question the reader may consult Lects. 2, 3, and 4, Vol. ii., of Dr. Wardlaw's "Systematic Theology."

of the earth, and who was the "chief" of his works in our
world.   This seems rather a straining.   It does not hold its
place naturally in the connexion in which it occurs, when so
understood.   The terms probably describe the loftiest parts
of the "dry land," when it had been separated from the
waters, by their retiring, at the Creator's word, to the beds
of their future rest, as the vast and mighty ocean.   And, in
general, the objects selected appear to be those with which,
as emblems, are associated the ideas of the greatest antiquity
and the most stable permanence—"the depths;" "the everlasting mountains;" "the perpetual hills."

And, according to verses 27—30, the same Wisdom that
planned, superintended the *execution* of the whole, "When
he prepared the heavens I was there: when he set a compass
upon the face of the depth: when he established the clouds
above: when he strengthened the fountains of the deep:
when he gave to the sea his decree, that the waters should
not pass his commandment: when he appointed the foundations of the earth: then I was by him, as one brought up with
him: and I was daily his delight, rejoicing always before him."

We stop not to inquire whether by "*the heavens*" we
should understand simply the circumambient atmosphere,
producing the appearance of the blue concave by which the
earth is surrounded—called in the account of the creation,
the *firmament*, and forming the work of "the second day;"
or that blue concave, considered as inclusive of the stars,
with which it appears to be studded—the starry heavens.
From a comparison with other passages, *this* is probably the
meaning;* and the work is often connected with *wisdom*,
as one of its most magnificent displays.†

God's "*setting a compass on the face of the deep*," seems to
refer to His circumscribing the earth when in its fluid state,
assigning to it its spherical form, and fixing the laws by
which that form should be constantly maintained.—I think
it probable that this refers to the earth in the state in which
it is described previously to the beginning of the six days'

---

* Ps. xxxiii. 6.   † Jer. x. 12: Ps. cxxxvi. 5.

work, by which it was reduced to order, and fitted for and stocked with inhabitants.*

How was the fluid element held together in the spherical form? The answer is, God "set a compass upon the face of the deep," saying, "This be thy just circumference, O world!" By the power of gravitation, affecting every particle, drawing it to the common centre, the equilibrium was maintained, the globular form effected and kept; which may here be meant by the poetical conception of sweeping a circle from this centre, and defining the spherical limits of the world of waters. It is the same principle of gravity that pervades the universe, retaining all its movements in unerring harmony, without the deviation of a hair's-breadth, or the error of a second in a millennium!

" *When he established the clouds above:*"—a most important part of the system; by which, through the medium of the solar influence, and the laws of evaporation, condensation, and gravity combined, the ocean is made to supply the land; and without which wonderful and beautiful arrangement, the world would soon become a desolate wilderness. "*Establishing* the clouds," seems an incongruous expression, there being nothing lighter or more unstable than these collections of atmospheric vapour. They are the very emblems of instability and evanescence. But it is the *law* by which the clouds are produced that is established: and that law, like every other, is a proof of "the manifold wisdom of God." †

" *When he strengthened the fountains of the deep.*" This seems to mean, that God so ordered the internal structure of the earth (of which, after the most unremitting efforts of scientific research, reaching necessarily but a short way into the mere crust, we are so extremely ignorant), and the springs and reservoirs on its surface, as to provide a constant supply of waters for the great deep maintaining its regular complement; and, at the same time, preventing its internal reservoirs from bursting their confinement to overflow and deluge the earth.

---

* Gen. i. 1, 2.   † Comp. chap. iii. 20.

Connected with this stands verse 29 :—"When he gave
to the sea his decree, that the waters should not pass his
commandment: when he appointed the foundations of the
earth." The sea is often, with much sublimity, alluded to
in descriptions both of the power and wisdom of God—"Who
shut up the sea with doors, when it brake forth, as if it had
issued out of the womb? When I made the cloud the garment thereof, and thick darkness a swaddling-band for it, and
brake up for it my decreed place, and set bars and doors,
and said, Hitherto shalt thou come, but no further: and
here shall thy proud waves be stayed?" Job xxxviii. 8—11.*
The ocean in a storm, rolling and tossing its proud waves on
high, presents one of the most impressive views of the omnipotence of Him who "measures the waters in the hollow of
his hand." And the wonderful operation of that law, by
which its swelling waters are restrained within their rocky
boundary, (a law which may, perhaps, be most reasonably
explained of the ever and everywhere present operation of
his immediate and almighty energy,) brings before us both
his wisdom and his goodness, preventing them from ever
again overflowing the earth. "The waters could not pass
his commandment," while he laid his restraining charge upon
them; and neither could they resist his commandment, when
he gave them an order of judgment against an ungodly world.
And now that we have God's promise that they "shall no
more become a flood to destroy all flesh," we are as sure
as that God "cannot lie," as sure as that there is no power
that can counteract omnipotence, that they shall never pass
their prescribed limits again.

"*He appointed the foundations of the earth,*" may be
explained in two ways, according to the sense in which the
word *earth* is understood. If it means *the land* as here distinguished from the waters, then it may refer to the appearance presented by the land, when it was separated from the
seas—as if it had its basis in the floods from out of which
it seemed to arise: as the Psalmist says in similar terms,

* See also Ps. xxxiii. 7: civ. 9: Jer. v. 22.

" He hath founded it upon the seas, and established it upon
the floods," Ps. xxiv. 2.   If again *the earth* means *the globe*,
the planet itself made for the residence of man and the inferior creatures, then its foundations may mean its centre,
towards which all parts of its surface and substance directly
gravitate,—all thus resting upon it, and held firmly together
by their attraction towards it, as all the superior parts of a
building, by the very same principle, when adjusted to the
perpendicular by the plumb-line, rest on the foundation on
which it is reared.

All these things were done by the *power* of God; and the
power of God, in all its operations, was directed by God's infinite wisdom; and all the results were a source of satisfaction to the mind of God, as we cannot but conceive the successful putting-forth of His infinite perfections ever to be.
Such seems to be the general sentiment of verse 30—" Then
I was by him as one brought up with him; and I was daily
his delight, rejoicing always before him."   Wisdom was the
constant companion or associate of all God's plans and all
their execution,—inseparable from God in all he purposed
and in all he did; and " was daily his delight."   I cannot
but consider the word *daily* here, in the connexion in which
it occurs, as having immediate reference to the successive
days of the world's creation.   As the products of divine
power and wisdom successively appeared on each of these
days, the almighty and all-wise Creator delighted in the
manifestation of his own perfections.   Even God's intelligent creatures have pleasure in putting forth their faculties,
and in witnessing their successful results.   God's work is
perfect, and His satisfaction correspondingly perfect.   And
what but this divine satisfaction can be meant when it is
said—" God saw every thing that he had made; and behold
it was very good?"—and afterwards that "God rested from
all his work and was refreshed?"

The personification gets still bolder—"*rejoicing always
before him.*"   Wisdom, by her counsels, when carried into
execution, advances the glory of God.   And she is, in the
figure, strikingly represented as rejoicing or exulting in this;

rejoicing in His very presence,—there being nothing in the
results of her counsels of which she has any reason to be
ashamed. This amounts, in effect, to only a stronger expression of the same sentiment as in the preceding clause,—the
satisfaction of Deity in all the products of His united wisdom
and power. It corresponds with the brief but beautiful expression of the psalmist, " The glory of the LORD shall endure for ever: the LORD shall rejoice in his works," Ps. civ.
31. It is added, as the consummation of Wisdom's joy:—
verse 31. " Rejoicing in the habitable part of his earth; and
my delights were with the sons of men." There can be no
doubt that Divine Wisdom delighted, more than in all that
had preceded it, in the last creative effort of the sixth day—

> " In man the last, in him the best,
> His Maker's image stood confest."

In the creation of this wonderful combination of matter
and spirit—of matter in its finest and most exquisite mould,
and its most beautiful, delicate, complicated and perfect ad-
justments; and of spirit, ethereal, intelligent, pure, and active,
to control all the movements of the wonderful mechanism, in
subserviency to the glory of the Maker and the advancement
of the happiness of His creation, was a work fitted to impart
the highest satisfaction of all to the Infinitely Wise. And
when Eden was planted, and fitted up in every way that
could render it a suitable habitation for the holy and happy
creature, and man was placed in this " habitable part of the
earth," the joy of Divine Wisdom might naturally be regarded
as perfect. And so it was. Yet, when I recollect how constantly the Bible, in speaking of the manifestation of the
wisdom of God in reference to man, points to another work,
the work of man's recovery when fallen, I cannot help regarding the language of this verse as *prospective:* as intimating joy in anticipation of a still more glorious display of the
wisdom and other perfections of God, of which this world
was to be the theatre.

Wisdom was displayed in man's creation; but wisdom
was to be magnified still more in man's redemption. The

scheme by which this was to be effected should contain in it
a display of wisdom unparalleled in any of the wonders of
creative power and skill.   It was to be a scheme of mercy
to the last, in which all the perfections of the divine character should be shown—shining forth in blessed harmony, all
equally glorified, all mutually illustrating each other,—providing for the honour, the unsullied honour of justice in the
exercise of mercy; and saving the fallen creature, without the
slightest infringement of the rights of Jehovah's holy government, or the slightest abatement or sacrifice of the claims of
His eternally righteous law:—nay more, not merely without
infringement of the divine glory, but with such an augmentation of it as should fill eternity with the adoring homage of
an intelligent universe.   It was, we apprehend, especially on
this account that Wisdom delighted here: not indeed with
any complacency in the character of fallen man, but with
joy in the anticipation of a temple being reared on the ruins
of his apostate nature, in which higher notes of praise should
sound to God, to the glory of his love and mercy, and justice
and purity, and truth and wisdom and power, than had
ascended to him from Eden itself.   Jehovah as the God of
man's creation was glorious: Jehovah as the God of man's
salvation was to be still more glorious; and the delight of
divine Wisdom was to be proportionally more elevated and
exquisite.

Let the man of mere natural religion think of this.   His
thoughts are not in harmony with those of divine wisdom,
when he is trying to discover the character of God in man
as he now is.   The two states in which man furnishes a true
testimony to the character of God, are—as he was when created, and as he is when redeemed.

The remaining verses of the chapter may be considered as
the practical improvement of the preceding statements:—
verse 32. "Now therefore hearken unto me, O ye children:
for blessed are they that keep my ways."

"*Therefore.*"   The word includes much.   It associates
with it, both what precedes and what follows it.   Consider
the dignity of Wisdom.   Not only does she say, "By me

kings reign, and princes decree justice;" but she appears as
the directress of all the purposes, and plans, and works, and
ways of the infinite God. Consider also the *interest* which
Wisdom expresses in the "sons of men;" her very delight
lying in the union of the glory of God with their present
and eternal happiness. And consider further, the blessedness of those who *do* hearken to her counsels :—verses 34,
35. "Blessed is the man that heareth me, watching daily at
my gates, waiting at the posts of my doors. For whoso
findeth me findeth life, and shall obtain favour of the
Lord."—Shall "find *life*"—life eternal! and "obtain *favour
of the Lord!*" The latter secures the former. "In His favour
is life." O what an acquisition—the smile and love of GOD!
Without these, there is, there *can* be nothing for man that deserves the name of happiness. With these, there can be no
misery in time or in eternity. Well might heavenly Wisdom
say, "Now therefore hearken unto me, O ye children: hear
instruction, and be wise, and refuse it not." Let no tempting Siren voice of the world draw your ear away from the
voice of Wisdom. Mark her solemn and touching conclusion—"He that sinneth against me wrongeth his own soul:
all they that hate me love death."

They that resist her entreaties and warnings, "wrong"—
do violence to, "their own souls." They are guilty—ah! how
often—of *self-destruction!* They "LOVE DEATH!" They
wilfully take the sure way of making it their final portion. They wilfully render themselves obnoxious to it; so
that were it their great aim they could not more effectually
insure it; could not take a more certain road to perdition
were they making it the great object of their search to find
one!

LECTURE XVIII.

---◆---

PROV. IX. 1—18.

" Wisdom hath builded her house, she hath hewn out her seven pillars; she hath killed her beasts; she hath mingled her wine; she hath also furnished her table: she hath sent forth her maidens; she crieth upon the highest places of the city, Whoso is simple, let him turn in hither: as for him that wanteth understanding, she saith to him, Come, eat of my bread, and drink of the wine which I have mingled. Forsake the foolish, and live; and go in the way of understanding. He that reproveth a scorner getteth to himself shame; and he that rebuketh a wicked man getteth himself a blot. Reprove not a scorner, lest he hate thee: rebuke a wise man, and he will love thee. Give instruction to a wise man, and he will be yet wiser; teach a just man, and he will increase in learning. The fear of the Lord is the beginning of wisdom; and the knowledge of the Holy is understanding: for by me thy days shall be multiplied, and the years of thy life shall be increased. If thou be wise, thou shalt be wise for thyself: but if thou scornest, thou alone shalt bear it. A foolish woman is clamorous; she is simple, and knoweth nothing. For she sitteth at the door of her house, on a seat in the high places of the city, to call passengers who go right on their ways: Whoso is simple, let him turn in hither: and as for him that wanteth understanding, she saith to him, Stolen waters are sweet, and bread eaten in secret is pleasant. But he knoweth not that the dead are there; and that her guests are in the depths of hell."

In this chapter Wisdom appears under an aspect entirely new. In the style of Eastern imagery, she is here brought before us, as erecting a house for the reception and entertainment of strangers, and inviting all to become her guests, and freely to partake of her royal provision—" Wisdom hath builded her house, she hath hewn out her seven pillars."

The frequency with which the number *seven* occurs, in special connexions, in Scripture, and the variety of the circumstances of its occurrence—from the seven days of the

week, in the first recorded division of time in the beginning
of Genesis, to the seven living creatures, the seven spirits of
God, the seven candlesticks, the seven churches, the seven
vials, the seven trumpets, the seven last plagues, of the Book
of Revelation, have procured for it the common designation
of *the number of perfection.* Of what, or whether of any
thing, the number may be specially symbolical, it would be
quite out of place at present to inquire. All we need say is,
that it is frequently used as a definite for an indefinite, conveying the notion of *excellence* and *completeness.* Thus it is
evidently used here.

Of the "house" reared by wisdom, the "seven pillars,
hewn out" and decorated, evidently represent *spaciousness,
elegance, grandeur, stability.* I have no doubt, that those
who are fond of the system of *spiritualizing,* would find the
distinct mystic symbol of something spiritual in each one of
the pillars, and bring out of the seven a whole body of divinity. This, however, would not be exposition, but the mere
play of a conjecturing fancy; and how excellent soever the
truths exhibited, they would be educed from that which the
Holy Spirit never meant to contain them. In which case, if
the ingenuity that elicited them made hearers or readers
marvel, the wonder should be, not at the wisdom but the
folly of the discovery:—for ingenuity and wisdom are far
from being always synonymous.

The house is evidently not a *temple,* (a common image
for the Church, taken naturally from the temple at Jerusa-
lem,) but a *place of entertainment* or *festivity.* This is clear.
The second verse shows it—"She hath killed her beasts;
she hath mingled her wine; she hath also furnished her
table."

The blessings of religion—the great and precious blessings
to which divine Wisdom specially invites,—are frequently
set forth under the image of a feast, of which God himself is
the free provider.* These blessings of religion—or, if you will,
(for it is the same thing in effect) the blessings of God's sal-

---

* Isa. xxv. 6: Matt. xvii. 1—3: Luke xiv. 16, 17: Rev. xix. 9.

vation, have been, in all ages, substantially the same,—the same in nature, the same in excellence, the same in enjoyment to the renewed and spiritual mind; they have, therefore, been always, with equal propriety, represented under the same emblems. That by the feast which divine Wisdom provides, these blessings are here intended, will not admit of a doubt in the minds of any accustomed to "compare spiritual things with spiritual." They are blessings comprehending all that sinners of mankind can need to make them truly and for ever happy. What are they?—Pardon of sin; "a new heart;" acceptance with God; peace of conscience; "joy in the Holy Ghost;" "good hope through grace;" all requisite supplies of divine influence; victory over death; resurrection from the grave; acquittal in judgment; and the full fruition of God for ever in knowledge, holiness, love, and joy;—these are the blessings to which men are by divine Wisdom invited.

In the words which follow, Wisdom is represented as joining her own inviting voice with that of her servants; just as God and Christ are represented as doing in other parts of Scripture:—verses 3—5. "She hath sent forth her maidens; she crieth upon the highest places of the city, Whoso is simple, let him turn in hither: as for him that wanteth understanding, she saith to him, Come, eat of my bread, and drink of the wine which I have mingled."

As before, "*the simple*"—the inconsiderate, thoughtless, foolish, infatuated children of men are addressed.

The invitation is *free*. So it is throughout the Bible. The blessings of salvation are the gift of God. They are offered to sinners with the freeness of divine munificence. Not only *may* they be had without a price, but, if they are had at all, it *must* be without a price. This is one of their special peculiarities. In treating with our fellow-men, in the communication of good, we make distinctions. From some, who can afford it, we take an equivalent; from others, who cannot, we take none. We *sell* to the rich, we *give* to the poor. In the present case, there is no distinction. All are poor. All are alike poor; and he who presumes to bring

I.   O

what he imagines a price, of whatever kind, forfeits the
blessings, and is "sent empty away." He who should come
to the House of divine Wisdom, and refuse to enter and to
partake of her feast unless some remuneration should be accepted, must be turned from the gate. The truth is, what
men fancy a price is none. No sinner on earth has, or can
have, any to give. And it is the very freeness with which
divine blessings are offered, that constitutes their suitableness
to our circumstances. If we vainly imagine that we can *buy*,
there is nothing for us, but exclusion, starvation, and death.

The invitation too is *universal;* for all men, in regard to
divine and spiritual things, are naturally inconsiderate and
foolish; negligent and improvident of their best and highest
interests. And it is *earnest, repeated, importunate.* Is not
this wonderful? Ought not the earnestness and the importunity to be all on the other side? Should not we find men
entreating God to bestow the blessings, not God entreating
men to accept them? *Wonderful?* "No," we may answer,
in the terms of the poor negro woman to the missionary,
when he was magnifying the love of God in the gift of his
Son, and naturally put the question, "Is not this wonderful?"—"No, Massa, it be *just like him.*" It is in the true
style of infinite benevolence. But is it not wonderful that
sinners should refuse the invitation? It is not in one view,
and it is in another. It is *not,* when we consider their depravity, and alienation from God. It *is,* when we think of
their natural desire for happiness, and the manifest impossibility of the object of their desire being ever found, otherwise than by their acceptance of them.

Some *do* conceive that there is in the passage an *allusion*
at least to the temple—the place where God, as the God of
grace, dwelt between the cherubim; waited to be gracious;
and dispensed, in virtue of the typical blood and incense,
the blessings of His goodness.

We take the allusion more generally,—to the *Church of
God,* which is often represented under the image of a spiritual building; by the erection of which, of its "living stones,"
and His whole procedure of founding, rearing, stablishing,

and completing it, God's infinite *wisdom* is specially represented as made manifest:—" That now, unto the principalities
and powers in heavenly places, might be known by the church
the manifold wisdom of God."*

The foundation of this glorious structure may be said to
have been laid by the hand of divine Wisdom *in the first
promise*—which is the same thing as its being laid *in Christ*.
Our penitent first parents, we have every reason to believe,
together with their son the "righteous Abel," were the first
"living stones" laid upon the divine foundation. And the
building advanced gradually in succeeding ages, is still advancing, and in due time shall be perfected. It is into this
"spiritual house" that sinners are graciously invited, to partake the blessings of salvation. I shrink not from the use
of this mixed metaphor, which makes sinners at once the
stones that compose the building and the guests that are invited into it; for the Apostle Peter has exemplified a similar
anomaly, in making them at once the *living stones* and the
officiating priests.† It is in the spiritual Church of God that
the blessings of salvation are enjoyed. They who refuse to
enter on divine invitation, can have "neither part nor lot"
in them.

But a participation in the blessings to which Wisdom invites must be accompanied with the practical renunciation of
sin and folly:—verse 6. "Forsake the foolish, and live;
and go in the way of understanding."

"*Forsake the foolish;*" that is, former associates, companions in thoughtlessness and sin. Ah! this is often one of
a young man's chief difficulties. I need not indeed have
restricted the observation to *youth;* for it is a difficulty to the
ungodly at every period of life. And, when men have lived
long, and have long maintained intimacies in irreligion, and
profligacy, and in scorn of what is good, it may be questioned,
in some cases at least, whether the difficulty lessens by age.
How to leave such associates! How to bear their laugh,
their sneer, their ridicule, their sarcastic insinuations, their

* Eph. iii. 10.   † 1 Pet. ii. 4, 5.

alternate coaxing and bantering! How ever to look them
in the face again!—The only difference between youth and
age, in this respect, may be found perhaps in the circumstance, that youth is open, ingenuous, confiding, sanguine;
while the old have had time to discover more of the *heartless-
ness* of those intimacies which have not their basis and their
bond in right principle. Still, in both the one and the other,
it requires a resolution such as divine grace alone can inspire
and maintain. It is one of the cases to which our Lord refers, when, adverting to the difficulties to be overcome in
entering on a religious life and profession, he says—" Strive
to enter in at the strait gate; for many, I say unto you, will
seek to enter in, and shall not be able. When once the Master of the house is risen up, and hath shut too the door, and
ye begin to stand without, and to knock at the door, saying,
Lord, Lord, open unto us; and he shall answer and say unto
you, I know you not whence ye are.*   Mark, however, my
dear young friends, the connexion in the words before us—
" Forsake the foolish, *and live.*"   It *must* be done, if you
would *live;*—not only (although this also is true) if you
would enjoy the present life, but if you would secure the
life that never ends.   The company in the house of Wisdom
is of a different and opposite stamp.   You cannot have a
relish for both.   The society, the pursuits, the practices of
the foolish, will not at all amalgamate with those of the
guests of Wisdom; of those who have been " made wise unto
salvation"—the saints—the " excellent of the earth."   It
is here, in His spiritual Zion, that God delights to dwell; and
he who enters must, in partaking of the provided blessings,
delight to dwell with God.†

When the foolish are forsaken, their *ways* are of course
forsaken.   It follows, " And go in the way of understanding"—the way of faith and love and holy obedience to God;
the way which every man of sound understanding will
choose, because the only way of present happiness, and the
only way to unending bliss.

---

* Luke xiii. 24, 25.   † Psal. cxxxii. 13—16.

There appears a *singular* abruptness in the introduction here of verses 7—9. " He that reproveth a scorner getteth to himself shame; and he that rebuketh a wicked man getteth himself a blot. Reprove not a scorner, lest he hate thee: rebuke a wise man, and he will love thee. Give instruction to a wise man, and he will be yet wiser; teach a just man, and he will increase in learning."

By some, these words are interpreted as cautions to the ministers of God's word and others, who, as the servants of heavenly Wisdom, may be employed in inviting sinners to the feast. They are conceived to signify that, in this important duty, prudence and discrimination require to be used, according to the varieties of character with which they have to deal. To address personal rebukes to the obstinate scoffer, and to repeat and urge them, may, in some cases, serve no other end than that of their being provoked to repay your zeal with abuse and insult, and, it may be, with calumny and slander; or you may even yourself be provoked, in the irritation and haste of an unguarded moment, to utter things of which they may take an ungenerous hold, and turn to their advantage in the most malicious and unmerciful way, to blast your character and mar your usefulness.

Perhaps, with still greater propriety, the verses may be expounded, as containing a similar caution to those who themselves comply with the admonition to "forsake the foolish." One of the most natural and powerful feelings in the bosoms of such persons, is a deep concern for their former associates, and intense heart-burdening solicitude to do them good. When they have themselves experienced the true and exquisite delight—a delight to which before their bosoms had been strangers,—which *religion* has introduced there, they are apt to feel as the youthful Reformer did, when, having found the truth, and the peace and joy imparted by it, he went forth to promulgate it, in the sanguine assurance that what was so self-evidently divine and excellent could not be resisted, but soon discovered to his mortification and sorrow, that " *Old Adam was too strong for young Melancthon.*" Their experience may be like his, as their fond anticipations were. They may therefore, perhaps, be here warned to exercise discretion, lest their love should only be repaid with hatred, and their zeal with such injury as may prove, not distressing merely to their feelings, but prejudicial to their reputation and a hindrance in their efforts to do good.

But the verses may be, after all, but a simple statement of the way in which instruction and admonition *do actually affect* different persons. There are just two ways of it. They may be received wisely, with thankful affection to the reprover, and compliance with his counsel, on the one hand ; or, on the other, foolishly, with scorn, resentment, and stubborn refusal. And in that case, verses eighth and ninth may be, not so much a direction or advice, as a particular mode of stating the fact, that the scorner *does* hate his reprover, while the wise man loves him. In which sense, the words connect beautifully with the closing terms of the address in verse 12—"If thou be wise, thou shalt be wise for thyself : but if thou scornest, thou alone shalt bear it." That is, Since my counsels must be treated in the one or the other of two ways, *mark the results of each:* "If thou be wise"—that is, if thou act the part of wisdom, as here described—"thou shalt be wise *for thyself;*" it shall turn out for thy good; it shall be for thine eternal benefit: "But if thou scornest"—that is, if thou act the part of the *scorner*, as here described, rejecting instruction and admonition, and repaying with despite and hatred the good intentions of your monitor,— "thou alone shalt bear it;" the fearful consequences will be thine own; thine own the loss, thine own the suffering, thine own the ruin. You have been warned; and your blood will be upon your own heads. Thus is it with all in whose ears the warnings and invitations of wisdom have been faithfully sounded. They must "bear their iniquity," in the forfeiture of good and the endurance of merited evil.

In the tenth and eleventh verses, we have the primary lesson of Wisdom repeated ; and what is thus repeated is intended to be *impressed*, as of special importance—"The fear of the Lord is the beginning of wisdom : and the knowledge of the Holy is understanding. For by me thy days shall be multiplied, and the years of thy life shall be increased." *

In the tenth verse, the word in the original rendered "*the Holy*" is in the plural number—"*the Holies.*" Thus, in numerous other passages, plural terms are used in application to the one God. You may take another example, —Eccles. xii. 1, "Remember now thy *Creator;*" literally, "thy *Creators.*" This use of plural terms, and that in union with verbs and adjectives in the singular, has been regarded, and justly, as arising from and indicating the doctrine of the Trinity. And to this correspond the threefold ascriptions of praise to Jehovah, and the threefold repetition of blessing in His name. An instance of the former we have in Isa. vi. 3, "Holy, holy, holy, is JEHOVAH of hosts: the whole earth is full of his glory:"—and of the latter in Numb. vi. 24—26, "JEHOVAH bless thee, and keep thee: JEHOVAH make his face shine upon thee, and be gracious unto thee: JEHOVAH lift up his countenance upon thee, and give thee peace."

Opposed to *Wisdom* (who, as formerly observed, is a female personage,) is "*the foolish woman,*" described in verses 13—15. "A foolish woman is clamorous: she is simple, and knoweth nothing. For she sitteth at the door of her house, on a seat in the high places of the city, to call passengers who go right on their ways."

The "foolish woman" might be understood, in all truth, of the "*strange woman,*" with her enticements; against whom youth are so frequently and so earnestly warned in former passages of this book.

I am strongly inclined to interpret the passage of Folly as an allegorical personage set in contrast with Wisdom:— folly, under all the forms and phases which it assumes in the world; all being included under this personification that entices *from* the gates of that house where Wisdom receives and entertains her guests. The characteristics of this second

---

* Comp. chap. i. 7, &c.

personage are the reverse of those of Wisdom. They are
ignorance, and thoughtless emptiness: what is wanting in
solid and substantial ideas is made up by loud clamour and
noisy importunity. She too hath builded her house. She
too hath provided her entertainment. She too invites her
guests. The houses are over against each other—on opposite sides of the way. Wisdom's is on the right hand;
Folly's on the left.* They are thus in the vicinity of each
other; it being the very purpose of Folly to prevent by her
allurements those who pass by from entering the doors of
Wisdom. Each addresses her invitations; and uses, but
from very different motives, every art of persuasion. Folly
presents all her captivating allurements to the lusts and
passions of corrupt nature; and she shows her skill in seduction by holding out, in promise, the secret enjoyment of
forbidden sweets:—verses 16, 17. "Whoso is simple let him
turn in hither: and as for him that wanteth understanding,
she saith to him, Stolen waters are sweet, and bread eaten
in secret is pleasant." Alas! since the entrance of sin
into the world, there has been amongst mankind a sadly
strong and perverse propensity to aught that is forbidden—
to taste what is laid under an interdict. The very interdic-
tion draws towards it the wistful desires, and looks, and longings of the perverse and rebellious heart.†

There *are* pleasures in sin. It is from these that its temptations arise. And, alas! Folly has the heart of fallen man
wholly on her side. No wonder that her guests are numerous.
"Many there be who go in" by the gates of her voluptuous
abode; stored as it is with all the variety and all the plenitude of vanity and sin. There are all the pleasures of the
sensualist, and all the vanities of the giddy and the gay.—
There are the pollutions of the libertine, and the dainties,
and the wines, and the pastimes of those whose chosen end
in life is to "eat, and drink, and be merry." There are the
glittering honours of the ambitious, and the tempting wealth
of the covetous. There is all that captivates the senses, all

---

* Comp. verses 1, 3, with verse 14.   † Comp. Rom. vii. 5, 8.

that fills the imagination, all that draws the desires, all that stirs the passions of the human heart unrenewed by converting grace.

But O my friends, my *young* friends especially, hear once more the accompanying caution. Hear once more the monitory voice of Wisdom; which is the voice of "the only wise God himself," and of all the wise and good among men. Mark it. He who does comply with the enticements of folly, "knoweth not that the dead are there; and that her guests are in the depths of hell."

"*The dead are there.*" It is a truth that the guests in the house of Folly consist of the "dead in trespasses and sins"—the spiritually dead. But this does not seem to be the meaning of the expression here. The meaning is rather that the guests of Folly *are murdered by her*. She puts them all to death, and to the worst of deaths. She invites them to her house with witching and seductive smiles, and importunate eagerness. She holds out luring promises of unknown and untried but exquisite gratifications—"the stolen waters," and the "bread eaten in secret." But in those stolen waters there is deadly poison,—poison for which, in all her stores, she has no antidote; and her "pleasant bread" has its pleasantness only to the taste; it is bitterness and death within—"the dead are there!" She allures, that she may murder; and that both body and soul—for "*Her guests are in the depths of hell.*" This is the end to which she brings them. Her house is the vestibule of Hell. The pleasures she offers are "but for a season." Behind her mansion of vice and vanity is the prison of everlasting despair. Her guests pass through the one into the other!

Reflect, then, ye reckless votaries of folly and sin; and pause, ye who may be under temptation to join them. Listen not to the voice of the seducer. Stop your ears. Turn away your eyes. Set not a foot upon the steps of her gateway. You would not willingly follow a man whom you knew, or even suspected, to be decoying you to shed your blood. You would not swallow poison for its sweetness, if you knew it *to be* poison, and were warned that, if you took it, you must soon expire in horrible convulsions. Yet in hearkening to the voice of Folly you are doing infinitely worse.

We invite you to the house and to the feast of Divine Wisdom. "The *living* are there." Her guests are instinct with a life that never dies. "They shall not be hurt of the second death:"—and while the votaries of Folly "are in the depths of hell," *their* place is in the "house of many mansions" above, amid "fulness of joy and pleasures for ever-more!"—"Forsake the foolish, then, *and live.*" Linger not a moment. Come to the decision. Halt not between two opinions. Stand not irresolute, midway between the abode of Wisdom and that of Folly. Turn in to the *right*, not to the *left*. And even if you *have* turned to the left; if your foot is on the step; if you have entered the porch; if you have even reached the innermost apartment of the mansion of Folly, and are revelling in the very loosest and wildest of her orgies;—we follow you with the words of Heavenly Wisdom. We shout in your ear—"*The dead are there!*" We call upon you still to escape for your life. Of the other house the door is still open; and "yet there is room!" Flee then from the one, and take refuge in the other. Think not that we speak to you only *officially*. We speak to you as your friends, in the full conviction of the truth of what we say—the truth of all that is alarming, and of all that is encouraging, of all that is damning, and of all that is saving in the word of God:—and we remind you again, in the words before us, "If thou be wise, thou shalt be wise for thyself: but if thou scornest, thou alone shalt bear it."

LECTURE XIX.

———◆———

PROV. X. 1—5.

" The Proverbs of Solomon.   A wise son maketh a glad father: but a foolish son is the heaviness of his mother.   Treasures of wickedness profit nothing: but righteousness delivereth from death.   The Lord will not suffer the soul of the righteous to famish: but he casteth away the substance of the wicked.   He becometh poor that dealeth with a slack hand: but the hand of the diligent maketh rich.   He that gathereth in summer is a wise son: but he that sleepeth in harvest is a son that causeth shame."

IT is here, strictly speaking, that the PROVERBS begin.

The general nature of these proverbs, or sententious maxims, was explained when we entered on the exposition of the Book.   I shall not now resume the subject.

The preceding part of the Book having been, to a great degree, addressed to youth, nothing can be more natural than the position of the *first* of these maxims; and indeed, independently of any such connexion, its place is most appropriate.   The education of the young, the early training of the rising hopes of society and of the church, must begin *at home*, in the bosom of the family, under the parental roof and the parental eye, and the parental care and culture.   In saying so, I cannot withhold my anathema from a system, which, if it has gained any ground at all, has gained all that more than enough;—a system which, under the specious and fascinating name of SOCIALISM, and holding out promises at which men are ever prone to catch, without giving mature thought, if any at all, to the means of their fulfilment, avows principles subversive of the first, most hallowed, most blessed, and most useful, of all social ties;—a system which, inde-

pendently of its atheistical dreariness and impiety, ought to
be scouted and scowled out of existence by every man of virtue and every woman of chastity, by every friend to the
blessings and the benefits of domestic life, and every lover of
social order;—a system which, with an imbecility of argument that is only equalled by its unblushing effrontery,
ventures, in the middle of the nineteenth century, amidst the
advance of all descriptions of knowledge, to propose, as the
sovereign panacea for all the disorder, crime, and misery of
human life, a compound of which the worthily associated
ingredients are—*no God, no marriage*, and *no property—
universal atheism, universal prostitution*, and *the universal
overthrow of the incentives to personal and domestic industry;* with the introduction of all the encouragements to idleness and plunder, by a state of things which, were it possible
to bring it into being even for an hour, could not beyond
that hour be continued!   My present plea is for DOMESTIC
LIFE;—for all the sweets of connubial intercourse, and all
the " charities of father, son, and brother," which such a system would, at one fell sweep of its loathsome principles,
annihilate.   We must take things on a large scale.   It will
not do to argue from exceptions.   If it must be called benevolence that does so, it is the benevolence of a distempered
brain.   Every rightly thinking man will admit, as the result
of all reason and of all experience, that if the sacred distinctions of *domestic* society were once destroyed, the order and
the benefits of *all* society would quickly perish with them.—
But I must return from this digression.

Solomon speaks, in the first verse, his own *observation* and
his own *experience*.   He had witnessed the gladness, and he
had witnessed the grief of his father David; and for his own
offspring he had felt all the racking solicitudes of a pious
heart, and wept many a bitter tear for their follies.   Yes,
brethren; and if his own example, in what he terms "the
days of his vanity," had served, as it would not fail to do, to
encourage in evil those who were "bone of his bone and flesh
of his flesh," and whom it was his duty to train in the fear
of Jehovah, the bitterest of all his tears would be those with

which he lamented, on *their* account, his own criminal folly.
And both in the introductory warnings of *this* Book, and in
the solemn and affecting text, with its illustrative and impressive lessons, of the Book of Ecclesiastes, I discern the
bitterness of spirit, that would fondly remedy the mischief
which his example of misconduct so grievous had occasioned.

He begins at the beginning;—with maxims for youth
relative to their *entrance into life:*—verse 1. " A wise son
maketh a glad father: but a foolish son is the heaviness of
his mother." What does Solomon mean by *" a wise son ?"*
Is it a child of precocious intellect?—taking up, quickly and
largely, the various branches of his education?—a superior
scholar? Or is it one who learns aptly how to manage for
this world?—shrewd, sagacious, prudent, smart, in all temporal concerns?—holding out every fair promise of a good
man of business—the buds and blossoms of future earthly
well-doing and prosperity? Do not suppose that by asking
such questions, it is my purpose to make light of indications
like these. They are in themselves good, and where they
are discovered cannot fail to be gratifying to parents. But
every one who attends to the previous lessons of this
Book, and to the general tenor of the Bible, will be satisfied
that such qualifications are far from being those chiefly
meant. Thus in the immediately preceding verses, we have
the maxim which repeats and embodies the lessons of all the
nine chapters, "The fear of the Lord is the beginning of
wisdom; and the knowledge of the Holy is understanding."
—" A wise son," then, is one who early discovers this " fear
of the Lord" as having taken possession, and assumed the
dominion, of his heart; who loves, reads, and understands
God's word; and who walks in God's ways.

Such a son " maketh a *glad father.*" When this is said,
there is evidently something more implied in the father's
character, than at first sight appears.—*Worldly* parents rejoice, when their children excel in the wisdom that, in a
temporal view, promises well for their future life. But for
all that bears the aspect of *really serious religion,* such parents are terrified. Instead of being *glad* when they discern

the symptoms of it, they are beyond measure distressed and alarmed; they are vexed, fretted, mortified, as if something had occurred quite dishonourable to their family, and which, of all things, they must studiously conceal, if they cannot avert it; which, however, they do all in their power, with a cruel and criminal assiduity of varied means, to accomplish. They mourn over their poor child, as having got its head turned; and they curse in their hearts the methodists and fanatics by whom such notions have been instilled into his mind. And all this, just at the time when, in the estimate of the God of heaven, their child is beginning to be wise! This is an awful case. How *un*natural in one sense! In another how sadly *natural!* It is quite what might be expected. They who are unimpressed by the words of the Redeemer, in reference to themselves, "What is a man profited, if he shall gain the whole world, and lose his own soul? or what shall a man give in exchange for his soul?"—cannot reasonably be expected to feel their application to others. They who love and seek for themselves, as their own portion, the wealth, and honours, and pleasures of the world—how can it be supposed that they should adopt another standard of desire and enjoyment for their children! The father whom "a wise son makes glad," must be a *pious* father— a fearer of God. Parents who are themselves religious, can alone rejoice in the true spiritual religion of their children.

The same observations require to be carried forward to the second clause of the verse, which is the opposite side of the alternative:—"*But a foolish son* is the heaviness of his mother." The "foolish son," is the son who *fears not God*, —who is without the principles of piety. In this sense, it is no uncommon thing to find a youth whom Solomon would have pronounced a fool, abundantly wise in regard to all that pertains to this world, both its learning and its business. Now, a godly parent, how grateful soever he may be for this wisdom, yet will not be satisfied with it. He cannot. So long as he sees the heart not given to God—no indications of that spiritual change without which there is no admission to the kingdom above, he will still heave the sigh of disappointment and grief, and long and pray for the happy day when his eyes may behold it.

I need hardly say, that in the style of parallelism in this verse, *both parents* are to be considered as meant in both clauses. They are supposed to be one in character, and consequently in feeling and desire, respecting their common offspring. The father who is glad for his son's wisdom, will be grieved by his folly; and the mother to whose heart his folly is heaviness, will fully sympathise in the gladness imparted by his wisdom.—The two clauses might be transposed, and retain all their truth: "A wise son maketh a glad *mother;* but a foolish son is the heaviness of his *father.*"

There is here, then, a lesson for *children,* and a lesson for *parents:*—1. I am far from meaning that the young should be religious, *merely to please their parents.* They might be hypocrites for this purpose; but for this purpose *alone* they could not be religious. The first considerations by which youth should be induced to prefer a life of true religion, should be their relation to the blessed God, and the inestimable worth of their own immortal interests. The first and most sacred and imperative of their obligations are those under which they lie to Him; and for the happiness of their undying spirits, which is indissolubly connected with true religion, He, desirous ever of their good, has graciously provided, and has commanded them to seek, and to seek supremely. But we are more than warranted to urge on the young, as a collateral motive, the concern which their parents feel for their happiness, and the propriety of laying to heart, that by an ungodly course, along with the ruin they bring upon their own souls, they bring heart-break to those whom it is their first earthly duty to love; that thus, in a most affecting sense, they incur the guilt at once of *suicide* and of *parricide.* Why should not this consideration be urged, to deter from irreligion and vice? I *do* urge it, my young friends. I urge it earnestly. Ah! it will be a bitter bitter drop in the cup of future woe to many an ungodly youth, to recollect how ill requited were all the tender anxieties, the godly counsels, the fervent prayers, the faithful admonitions, the melting tears of pious fathers and mothers, who would fain have won them to God and to happiness, but whose affectionate solicitations and remonstrances they resisted, going on frowardly in the way of their own hearts.

2. We have a lesson for *parents*. Let them see to it, that they put spiritual interests *first* in their desires, and efforts, and prayers in behalf of their children. Let them beware of all the biassing and misguiding influences of parental partiality, that would lead them to overlook, or to palliate the evils discernible in the characters of their children; and of that easy, listless hoping for good in future, that would make them deal with present faults, even of a serious description, with a seemingly kind but really cruel indulgence. Let the cords with which you draw them from evil to good be the cords of love; but never let go your hold of them. Let the rod with which you seek to drive folly from their hearts be the rod of love; and, while on no account you use it when it is *not* necessary—that is, when you can accomplish the desired effect without it,—do not withhold it when it *is;* for the highest authority assures you, "He that spareth the rod hateth his child."

In this Book of Proverbs, we are not, in general, to look for any very strict connexion between the maxims that are successively introduced. Sometimes, however, an associating link, sufficiently natural, may be discerned. It is so here. The following verses might readily be suggested by the first.

Verse 2. "Treasures of wickedness profit nothing: but righteousness delivereth from death." Worldly parents covet for their children, as they do for themselves, the wealth of this world. They wish them to be rich. In all their plans for their settlement in life, this is the main concern, the *summum bonum*—the "one thing needful." And not a few even of Christian parents seem to act as if, on this subject, they had adopted the world's maxims. All else is made to yield to this. If, in a situation that promises to be lucrative, there are temptations of a moral and spiritual kind specially hazardous, how ingeniously they impose on their consciences! "What situation," say they, "is there in this world *without* its temptations? If this has one kind, others have other kinds:—and then, *grace is free.* Situation, however free of temptations, cannot impart it, and situation, however full of temptations, cannot keep it back." These are but flattering unctions. You would not, for any earthly consideration, set down your child amidst barrels of gunpowder, while sparks were flying in all directions around them. You hurry him away from a situation, when any violent and deadly epidemic makes its appearance, and his life is imminently at stake. Had you a right feeling in regard to his *eternal* interests, your first inquiries would ever relate to the security of *them;* and your weightiest solicitude would be to avoid exposing them to risk. Let both parents and children ponder the truth in this verse. Forget not that, how honestly and fairly soever acquired, riches bring with them many temptations and perils. The terms used in God's word on this subject are very strong; and the strongest of all are from the lips of Him who "spake as never man spake:"—"How hardly shall they that have riches enter into the kingdom of God! It is easier for a camel to go through a needle's eye, than for a rich man to enter the kingdom of God."*—Above all, let parents be on their guard against instilling into their children's minds such a love of riches as might tempt them, in "*hasting* to be rich," to use unjustifiable means for their acquisition.

"*Treasures of* wickedness" may mean, either treasures wickedly *got*, or treasures wickedly *spent*, or *both*. Such treasures "profit nothing," that is, evidently for the bestowment of true happiness. It is a saying of divine truth, confirmed by universal experience, "that a man's life consisteth not in the abundance of the things which he possesseth:" and it is specially true, when the abundance is of the kind here described. There cannot fail, in that case, unless conscience has become "seared as with a hot iron," to be many misgivings, much inward remorse, self-dissatisfaction and self-reproach—a sting in the treasure.

* Luke xviii. 24, 25.

The connexion of the two parts of the verse intimates, that "riches profit not" in "delivering from death." They cannot save even from temporal death, and far less from death eternal. Probably *both*—though the latter rather as an inference from the former—are included in the Psalmist's words, "They that trust in their wealth, and boast themselves in the multitude of their riches; none of them can by any means redeem his brother, nor give to God a ransom for him: (for the redemption of their soul is precious, and it ceaseth for ever:) that he should still live for ever, and not see corruption."* So far from profiting *then*, they only serve, by making a man more reluctant to quit *this* world, and less prepared for another, to sharpen the sting of death, and to surround the grave with thicker horrors. They chain the spirit to earth, and torture it with the anticipation of the chains of hell.†

On the contrary—"righteousness delivereth from death." —"*Righteousness*," in this connexion, evidently means, not mere *justice in dealings* with fellow-men; but, as in many other places, all that is included in a course of right principle; a course of faith and love and practical obedience. This "delivers from death"—not merely saving from the gallows, preserving from the punishments which human laws inflict upon the wicked; but taking the sting from death, and victory from the grave; at once preserving "from the second death," and leading to "life everlasting."

Another collateral and closely associated consideration is presented in verse 3. "The Lord will not suffer the soul of the righteous to famish: but he casteth away the substance of the wicked."

Among the children of men, in their natural unregeneracy, "there is none righteous, no, not one." *They* are "the righteous," who are justified from condemnation, and sanctified from pollution, by the pardoning mercy and the renewing grace of God, "through the redemption that is in Christ

---

* Psal. xlix. 6—9.
† Compare 1 Tim. vi. 9, 10: Jam. v. 1—5.

Jesus." For *them* God provides present peace and joy; and all the means of maintaining and perfecting spiritual life, with the influences of the Spirit to render means effectual, for nourishing them up unto "life eternal,"—the higher life He has reserved for them, with himself in heaven. Surely, then, God will not leave them destitute of what is needful for them in "the life that now is." He who gives them the greater blessings, will not withhold the less. He who gives life to the soul, will not neglect the body. He who bestows heaven's bliss, will not deny that measure of earth's good which he sees will prove for the greatest benefit.* It is of temporal supplies the wise man is here speaking. The "famishing of the soul," indeed, might be understood, with great truth, of the proper and peculiar life of the soul. But the connexion rather demands a different interpretation: and in similar connexions, the word *soul* is often used (very frequently especially in the Old Testament Scriptures) to signify the *person*, and the *animal life*. The famishing of the soul, at the same time, may have reference to that weakness and fainting of spirit, which is the result of the corporeal exhaustion produced by the extremity of want.† It is of God's people it is said in divine promise—"Bread shall be given him; his waters shall be sure." "The young lions do lack, and suffer hunger: but they that seek the Lord shall not want any good thing."‡

On the contrary, " He casteth away the substance of the wicked."—The righteous have blessings as *their* " substance," that are *permanent*. They belong to their immortal nature, and shall continue theirs for ever. So that to the poorest of them the Lord says, "I know thy poverty—but thou art rich." Though "having nothing," they "possess all things." " All things" are theirs.§ But "the substance of the wicked" is "of the earth earthy." It pertains not to the soul, and partakes not of its imperishable vitality. O the miserable, but sadly common mistake of the rich man in the parable,

---

* Psal. xxxvii. 3, 16: Matt. vi. 33.   † Psal. cvii. 5.
‡ Psal. xxxiv. 10: Isa. xxxiii. 16.   § Comp. 1 Cor. iii. 21—23.

when he addressed his *soul* in terms of congratulation, as if,
in the abundance of worldly good, it had got what would give
it real and permanent satisfaction—"Soul, thou hast much
goods laid up for many years, take thine ease, eat, drink, and
be merry!"*

"*Casting it away*" is an act indicative of regarding it as
worthless. The substance of this world is that on which the
hearts of the sons of men are set. But God will "cast it
away." He will not only bereave them of it—and that, it
may be, suddenly:—but what is there, in all this substance,
that can avail as purchase-money for the soul and for heaven?
Had a man "the world" to offer, God would "cast it away."
He would say, "Thy money perish with thee!" "Riches
profit not in the day of wrath." The famished soul must
then die, and die for ever!

But we are ever in danger of extremes. Riches must not
be our *portion;* but neither are they to be despised. They are,
in themselves, a good. Many a time are they included among
the blessings which God promises to bestow; and when so
promised, they cannot be considered as an evil. This remark is necessary, to render the verses now expounded consistent with those which follow; in which the attainment of
this good is made the motive to diligence, and such diligence
one of the ingredients and characteristics of wisdom.

While habits of early industry are a means of *preventing
vice*—for "to be idle is to be vicious,"—they are also the
preventive of poverty, and the way to the enjoyment of temporal comfort and abundance:—verse 4. "He becometh poor
that dealeth with a slack hand: but the hand of the diligent
maketh rich."

While it is dangerous to have the spirit of "them that *will*
be rich"—who set their hearts on wealth, and make it the
determining point of all their plans and pursuits, yet if, by
the blessing of God upon honest and well-principled industry, riches *do* come, they are to be received gratefully, as a
boon from the hand of God, to be employed for His glory,

---

* Comp. Luke xii. 16—21.

and for the good of others—relatives, friends, fellow-Christians, and fellow-men.   This is the true benefit of riches. They put it into a man's power to effect more extensive good. They give their possessor the privilege of resembling God the more as THE UNIVERSAL DISPENSER—"the Father of lights, from whom cometh down every good and perfect gift"—the bountiful giver of all that is enjoyed throughout creation. He who is animated by the godlike virtue of benevolence, must rejoice when he has it in his power to indulge it in more extensive exercise.

That the connexion is such as I have intimated with the principles of early training, is apparent from verse 5. " He that gathereth in summer is a wise son: but he that sleepeth in harvest is a son that causeth shame."

Prudence and sober industry will enable a youth, as the apostle expresses it, to " requite his parents," and thus, by the reciprocations of practical affection, to gladden and comfort their hearts ;—and nothing ought to be a source of purer or more exquisite gratification to a son than this, specially when, in divine providence, his parents come to be placed in circumstances that require it.   Such a son too, by the universal respect which his character draws upon him, will be a credit and an honour to them.   On the contrary, the indolent and slothful in his disposition—the "sleeper in harvest," becomes an idle unprofitable vagabond, or possibly what is worse, a cunning artful knave, or a vacant, mindless, and heartless sot—a reproach of all himself, and (although it may be sometimes undeservedly) a discredit and shame to those who brought him up.

The remark suggests itself afresh, that the virtues of industry, and sober application to business, are closely connected, as practical results, with the " fear of God."   There may be diligence and sobriety where there is no religion ; but there is, assuredly, no religion, where there are not diligence and sobriety.   When the fear of God reigns in the heart, the prosecution of a man's worldly calling, being conducted under the influence of the religious principle, becomes a *religious act*, and industrious activity a part of godliness.

LECTURE XX.

———◆———

Prov. x. 6—12.

" Blessings are upon the head of the just: but violence covereth the mouth of the wicked. The memory of the just is blessed: but the name of the wicked shall rot. The wise in heart will receive commandments: but a prating fool shall fall. He that walketh uprightly walketh surely: but he that perverteth his ways shall be known. He that winketh with the eye causeth sorrow: but a prating fool shall fall. The mouth of a righteous man is a well of life: but violence covereth the mouth of the wicked. Hatred stirreth up strifes: but love covereth all sins."

THE preceding verses have reference to industry and idleness; and of these we have a comparison, as to their present and future effects, in the opening verses of the passage before us, —" Blessings are upon the head of the just: but violence covereth the mouth of the wicked. The memory of the just is blessed: but the name of the wicked shall rot."

" *The just*," as we formerly observed, is not the mere rigidly equitable man; but the man who, under the influence of the principles of true religion, unites benevolence with righteousness, and seeks, in acts of kindness as well as of equity, to fulfil "the royal law." He is the " *good* man," as distinguished from the merely " *righteous* man," for whom, the apostle says, "some would even dare to die." Such a character was the patriarch Job;* in whom righteousness and goodness appear blending in lovely practical union. " *Blessings are on the head*" of such a man. His value is appreciated; his real usefulness felt. If he prospers, he enjoys

* Job xxix. 11—17.

his prosperity with a blessing from God, and with the gratulations and plaudits of men. He sees and enjoys the general favour in which he is held. It gives him confidence, so that he can open his mouth without being ashamed.

"*But violence covereth the mouth of the wicked.*" Of this clause a different rendering has by some been proposed. That of our received version, however, seems preferable, and we retain it. It yields a natural contrast with the *first.* Some conceive that there is an allusion to the practice of *covering the face* of the condemned.* According to this view, the import will be, that the violence of the wicked will bring him to condemnation. More probably, however, "covering the mouth" means *making ashamed—putting to silence.* His detected and exposed iniquity, and rapacity, and selfishness, shall be like a muzzle upon his mouth, shutting it in silent confusion.

And the blessing that is on "the just" is not confined to the period of his earthly life. It follows him to the grave. It hallows his ashes. It rests upon his name, when he himself has bidden a final adieu to the world. "*The memory* of the just is blessed." His memory is blessed of God, who smiled complacently on his life of faith and love and practical godliness, and took him to himself at its happy close. It is blessed of his family, his kindred, his friends, his companions. It is blessed of the Church of God. It is blessed by mankind at large. For even the world, although incapable of appreciating the excellence of those principles by which the conduct of the truly good, the just, the children of God, is influenced and regulated, yet cannot but approve and admire the characteristic consistency which these principles produce, as their legitimate result, and with which the profession of them, unless the profession of hypocrisy or of self-delusion, will invariably be associated.

I may here observe, that perhaps the blessings which rest on the "memory of the just," are purer than even those

---

* See Esth. vii. 8: Job ix. 24. The latter passage seems to mean, that the wicked man, into whose hands the earth is given, condemns, silences, puts down, those by whom righteous judgment was executed.

which came upon him while he lived. While a man lives, there are, in this our fallen world, envy and malice, misapprehension and calumny enough to taint, at times, even the fairest reputation; but death, in general, disarms these enemies to living fame, and justice is done to the dead which was withheld, or but stintedly and partially bestowed, during life. Death is a smoother-down of asperities and alienations. Few are so thoroughly embittered as to carry their malice, in all its rancour, to the grave. And, in regard to those who knew and admired, esteemed, and loved the departed, there is, as all feel, a keenly sensitive jealousy of his memory,—a tenderness that shrinks from doing it wrong, and that is wakefully on the alert to vindicate it from the very slightest aspersion. It is embalmed in the sweetest of the heart's affections; and the intrusion of aught that would taint the sweetness is resented with a sensibility specially acute.

On the contrary, "*The name of the wicked shall rot.*" The expression is strong, but far from unduly so. It becomes loathsome,—offensive as the putrid carcase of a dog. It is cast out and forgotten. Men have no pleasure in taking the name into their lips, or recalling the memory of the character with which it was associated. Whatever, during life, had been his greatness, (falsely so called, for there is no true greatness independent of goodness,) his name, even if recorded in his country's annals, excites disgust instead of satisfaction, and his course is like a vile, stagnant, putrid kennel in the field of history—nauseous to every well-ordered and rightly-thinking mind.*

Let all remember, not the posthumous blessing of fellow-men only, but, in a special manner, the infinitely more desirable blessing of the living and life-giving God. "The Lord taketh pleasure in his people." Their names are in his "Book of life." There they stand enrolled, in connexion with the name of "the Lamb that was slain." It is in this connexion that their names are well-pleasing to God, and that

* For a commentary on these two verses read the 112th psalm.

his blessing rests upon them. There is in the very best of men enough, and infinitely more than enough, to *rot* their names, and render them offensive to the God of taintless purity. But He delighteth in his beloved Son. And those who give their names to Christ in the profession of the gospel, are blessed for his sake, and held in everlasting remembrance. His name is "as ointment poured forth;" and theirs, in Him, partake of the fragrance. And moreover, God delights in his own image, in the measure in which, in each of his people, it is produced. He cannot but delight in "the beauty of holiness." "The righteous Lord loveth righteousness; his countenance doth behold the upright."

In this Book the *wise* and the *foolish* are brought before us under very many points of comparison and contrast. We have several in the verses that follow:—verse 8. "The wise in heart will receive commandments: but a prating fool shall fall."

It is one of the marks of true wisdom, and none of the least, that it is not *self-sufficient* and *self-willed*. This is the evident import of the former part of the verse. We might consider the disposition in reference both to *God* and to *men*, —to the Supreme Ruler and Lord of the conscience,—and to existing human authorities. The "wise in heart will receive" *God's* commandments. *This*, true wisdom will do *implicitly*. It will never presume on dictating to God, or on altering and amending His prescriptions: but, proceeding on the self-evident principle that the dictates of divine wisdom must, in all cases, be perfect, will bow in instant acquiescence. With regard also to *earthly superiors*, a humble submission to legitimate authority, both in the family and in the state, is the province of wisdom. There is a self-conceit that spurns at all such authority. It talks as if it would legislate for all nations. It would *give* commandments rather than receive them. It likes not being dictated to. It plumes itself on its skill in finding fault. There is no rule prescribed at which it does not carp; no proposal in which it does not see something not to its mind; no order in which it does not find something to which it cannot submit. This is folly; for, were this temper of mind prevalent, there would be an end to all subordination and control.

To the "*wise in heart*" stands opposed "*the prating fool;*" —"but a prating fool shall fall." The phrase in the original is a *fool of lips*, a *lip-fool*. It may be understood in two ways. First, the self-conceited are generally superficial. There is much talk, and little substance; words, without sense; plenty of tongue, but a lack of wit. Light matter floats on the surface, and appears to all; what is solid and precious lies at the bottom. The foam is on the face of the waters; the pearl is below. Or secondly, the reference may be to the *bluster* of insubordination; the loud protestations and boastings of his independence on the part of the man who resists authority, and determines to be "a law to himself."

In either sense it is true, that "the prating fool shall fall." His words are a stumbling-block to his own feet. He exposes himself by his recklessness and rashness. He is in constant danger of falling into self-made mischief, or of exposing himself to the effects of individual resentment, or to the punitive visitation of the laws. The distinction at which he aimed, as a self-sufficient authoritative oracle, not being sustained by any such weight of intellect as is necessary for such pretensions, he *falls* from his fancied elevation into derision and neglect.

I have said that the "wise in heart" will receive the commandments of God *implicitly*. This may be considered as corresponding to the character in verse 9. "He that walketh uprightly walketh surely: but he that perverteth his ways shall be known." "*Walking uprightly*" stands opposed to all duplicity, all tortuous policy, all the crooked arts of *manœuvring*, for the purpose of promoting reputation, interest, comfort, or any other end whatsoever.*

He who walketh thus—"*walketh surely.*" He walks with a comfortable *feeling of security*—a calm unagitated serenity of mind. This springs from confidence in that God whose will

---

* Comp. chap. ii. 7.

he makes his only rule. In the path of implicit obedience, he feels that he can *trust*.* And further, the way in which he walks is the *surest* for the attainment of his ends.—-Proverbs are generally founded in observation and experience, and express their ascertained results. Hence, even though not inspired, they have generally truth in them. It has become proverbial, that "honesty is the best policy." The meaning is, that the acts of deceit very frequently frustrate the object of him by whom they are employed, and land him in evils greater than the one he meant, by the use of them, to shun. Let it be deeply impressed on all minds, and an ever-present thought, that the way of safety, of reputation, of happiness, of honour, and, generally speaking, of success, is the way of evidently commanded *duty*. In the opposite course,—the course regulated by the ever-shifting maxims of a worldly expediency, and the tactics of an accommodating policy, there can be nothing of that sweet confidence in God, which is the peculiar enjoyment of the "upright;" but the consciousness of evil interdicting all such confidence, separating between the soul and God, and distracting it with unceasing solicitudes.

And *detection comes at last!*—"He that perverteth his ways *shall be known*." Artifice and guile seldom succeed long in screening themselves from discovery. The feet of the artful man are caught in the meshes of his own net; and his very efforts to disentangle himself discover his wiles. And then come, as the necessary consequences of the discovery, loss of character, loss of confidence, loss of interest, loss of comfort, loss of society, loss of friendship, and loss of the very end which all his arts had been plied to obtain,—the very object for the sake of which he *perverted his ways*.—And all this is no more than righteous retribution. The results, and the sufferings to which they give rise, are *self-produced*. The man has not even the comfort of not having himself to blame.

We have had the "prating fool" in contrast with the "wise in heart." In the next verse, we have a contrast of a

* Comp. Psal. xxxvii. 1—7.

different kind:—"He that winketh with the eye causeth
sorrow: but a prating fool shall fall." We might, indeed,
avoid the appearance of contrast altogether, by simply rendering the "*but*"—"*and*." I am disposed, however, to
think the *but* may be retained. The characters brought into
comparison are *the sly artful man*—the man of looks, and
nods, and hints, and inuendoes,—and the *open, loquacious,
chattering fool.* The former is incomparably the more dangerous and mischievous to others;—the harm from the folly
of the latter falls principally upon himself. We had the
former already before us.* There is no character more odious, and none more pernicious in any society, domestic,
ecclesiastical, or civil. The "winking eye" sows jealousies,
foments dissensions, introduces distrust, separates friends,
divides families, troubles churches, agitates kingdoms. It
"*causeth sorrow*"—often the keenest inward anguish, and, it
may be, the most serious outward broils and calamities.
Surely *that* eye—as well as "the eye that mocketh at his
father, and despiseth to obey his mother, the ravens of the
valley shall pick it out, the young eagles shall eat it." The
folly of the most reckless is not so perilous as the studied
art of the "double-minded." Still forget not that the "prating fool shall fall." Let both evils be avoided. Be *straight-
forward*, yet be *circumspect.*

The image in the 11th verse is a very beautiful one,
"The mouth of the righteous is *a well of life*"—or a living
fountain. In Hebrew idiom, "*living* water" means, as various
passages show, *springing* water.† As a well or fountain,
then, of springing water, clear, cool, and refreshing to the
exhausted traveller, so to the weary soul is "the mouth of
the righteous." Thus precious, thus salutary, thus cheering,
thus invigorating and bracing, are the instructions, consolations, and counsels, of the wise and good. The mouth
"speaking from the abundance of the heart," brings forth
the stores of a well-informed mind, and of a pious, kind,
affectionate spirit. It is a striking figure which is used by

---

* Chap. vi. 12—14.   † See in the margin, Gen. xxvi. 19.

Job, to express his disappointment on the failure of those friends to administer consolation and strength, from whose lips he had eagerly and fondly anticipated it.* The caravan in the wilderness, with their tongues cleaving to the roof of their mouth for thirst, see water at a distance. Their spirits rise at the sight. They hasten forward. But, ere they reach the spot, it has passed away. "The mouth of the righteous" will not thus disappoint the expectations of those who look for its refreshing words. The mouth of God's servants and of God's people ought, in this respect, to be like His own. His mouth is indeed "a well of life." His instructions are all truth, and they are all life-giving. It was of them, as accompanied by the teaching and influence of the Spirit, that Jesus said—speaking of the water of the well of Sychar— " He that drinketh of this water shall thirst again : but whosoever drinketh of the water that I shall give him shall never thirst; but the water that I shall give him shall be in him a well of water springing up into everlasting life.†"

In the original, the latter part of this verse is the same as the latter part of the sixth. The words may be rendered either, " *violence covereth* the mouth of the wicked," or, " the mouth of the wicked *covereth violence.*" As they occur here, the latter seems the more natural meaning, as standing in more distinct and suitable contrast with the other clause of the verse :—" The mouth of a righteous man is a well of life," but "the mouth of the wicked covereth violence." From the one there proceed the words of comfort, truth, and joy; under the tongue of the other there lie concealed cursing and bitterness, wrath, and clamour, and evil-speaking. There is something more fearful in the idea of the mouth *covering* violence than in that of its *uttering* it. If the mouth is kept close, it is only covering, till a convenient season, the violence that is within;—intimating, that the wicked is well aware *when* it is most for his nefarious purposes to keep silence, as well as when to speak out. Even when he compresses his lips and says nothing, there is no good there. It is but a cover to violence.

* Job vi. 15—20.   † John iv. 13, 14.

The connexion is natural between this and the following verse—" Hatred stirreth up strifes: but love covereth all sins." Hatred and love are opposites, in their nature and in their effects. Here we have *one* of the many points of contrast.

" *Hatred stirreth up strifes.*" It will not allow its object to rest. It is ever jealous and touchy; catches impatiently at every trifle; lets nothing pass that can possibly be construed amiss; magnifies and misrepresents; is easily provoked; thinks evil; rejoices not in the truth but in iniquity; cherishes resentment; looks out for modes of retaliation; seizes every opportunity to pick quarrels; easily irritated, it is *not* easily appeased,—taking fire in a moment, but difficult to quench, and slow to cool. It blows up the kindling fuel, and stirs the dying embers of strife.

" *Love,*" on the contrary, " *covereth all sins.*" It is ever disposed to overlook, to pardon, to forget. This must, of course, be understood in harmony with such other parts of Scripture as Lev. xix. 17.—" Thou shalt not hate thy brother in thine heart: thou shalt in any wise rebuke thy neighbour, and not suffer sin upon him." *Suffering sin upon a brother*, is an act, not of love but of hatred—and one of its very worst. By " love covering all sins," is meant the *general disposition to pass over personal wrongs;* not to be quick in taking offence, and, when offended, to be quick to reconciliation, " easy to be entreated"— every wish and desire set upon restored agreement.[*]

This passage in Proverbs affords the explanation of a much-abused passage in the New Testament; the latter being a quotation of the former—" Above all things have fervent charity among yourselves: for charity shall cover the multitude of sins."[†] Men have interpreted this of almsgiving; and have represented gifts to the poor as covering the sins of the charitable from the eye and vengeance of Divine justice. There is in this a twofold error. *Charity* is not alms-

---

[*] 1 Cor. xiii. 4—7: Eph. iv. 31, 32: Jam. iii. 13—18.
[†] 1 Pet. iv.

giving; it is *love*:—and it is not from the justice of God that it covers the sins of him by whom it is exercised, but from public exposure to others that it covers the sins of its object. The words in Proverbs show this: the "hiding of the multitude of sins" standing in contrast to the "stirring up of strifes."—The sense affixed, in thoughtlessness, to the words of Peter is most pernicious. But the true sense, as here made apparent, presents one of the most important of love's exercises, and one most salutary amongst the Lord's people in the fellowship of his churches—essential, indeed, to the preservation of peace, and union, and social prosperity.

Let this spirit, then—the spirit of *love*, be increasingly cultivated. "Love as brethren." "Let brotherly love continue." Let the world see in you "how Christians love one another." This is the evidence of your own discipleship,* while it is one of the means of the world's conviction, and conversion to Christ.†

Mark here the identity of the great principles of Old and New Testament morality. Many speak of them as if there were essential differences between them. It is not so. They are *the same*. When Peter says, "Charity covereth the multitude of sins," he quotes Solomon. When Paul says, "If thine enemy hunger, feed him; if he thirst, give him drink: for in so doing thou shalt heap coals of fire on his head,"‡ he quotes Solomon. When our Lord himself says —"Ye have heard that it hath been said, Thou shalt love thy neighbour, and hate thine enemy;"§—he does not quote the saying with approbation, as if it were a true interpretation of the law, and then lay down a law of his own in distinction from it. "Thou shalt love thy neighbour, and hate thine enemy," was *not* the law of Moses;—no, never, and in no wise. Love to personal enemies was inculcated by the law of Moses as well as by the law of Christ.‖ Our blessed Master is to be understood as only reprobating the false gloss, and restoring and confirming the true sense of the

---

* John xiii. 35.
‡ Rom. xii. 20.
‖ Exod. xxiii. 4, 5.

† John xvii. 20, 21.
§ Matt. v. 43, 44.

law.   The whole law is summed up by Him in the two great
precepts of *love to God* and *love to men;* or in the *one* great
principle of *love.**   And in the parable of the good Samaritan, He shows that this love included enemies and aliens,
as well as friends, and countrymen, and kindred.†   And
this is the Book whose morality is to be set aside by the
atheistical and heartless novelties of the "New moral world!"
O the deceitfulness and presumption of the human heart!

But of God's Law, "holy, just, and good," we are violators.
We have incurred its sentence of condemnation.   Vain is
every attempt to justify ourselves before God, by any appeal
to our own characters when tried by it—either by the one
or the other of its great precepts.   We cannot stand.   There
must be something else for us than the Law, or our case is
desperate.   It is not enough that the excellence of the Law
shows the book which contains it to be of God: its very
excellence is what condemns us.   It is a comfort, however,
that it does prove the book which contains it to be divine;
for the same book which contains the LAW contains the GOS-
PEL.   The same book that shows us the ground on which we
are condemned, tells us the ground on which we may be justified.   The same book which reveals God as a Judge, reveals
him as a Saviour.   The same book that tells us of judicial
wrath, tells us also of pardoning grace.   The same book that
appointed "the ministry of condemnation," appoints also the
"ministration of righteousness."   The same book that reveals
SINAI, with its "blackness and darkness and tempest," reveals CALVARY, with its propitiatory LAMB OF GOD, and its
"still small voice" of love and mercy!

---

* Matt. xxii. 35—40.
† For the full discussion of this subject, see Wardlaw's Syst. Theol.
Lects. x, xi. vol. 3.

LECTURE XXI.

Prov. x. 13—18.

" In the lips of him that hath understanding wisdom is found: but a rod is for the back of him that is void of understanding. Wise men lay up knowledge: but the mouth of the foolish is near destruction. The rich man's wealth is his strong city: the destruction of the poor is their poverty. The labour of the righteous tendeth to life: the fruit of the wicked to sin. He is in the way of life that keepeth instruction: but he that refuseth reproof erreth. He that hideth hatred with lying lips, and he that uttereth a slander, is a fool."

THE sentiment expressed in the beautiful figure of the eleventh verse—" The mouth of the righteous is a well of life," is here, in the thirteenth verse, conveyed with more literal simplicity—" In the lips of him that hath understanding wisdom is found."

Where there is "understanding" in the *mind*, there will be "wisdom" in the "*lips*." The lips will utter what the mind contains. The possession of a sound understanding, that has been employed in laying up useful knowledge, not only provides a man with a source of constant enjoyment to himself, but enables him also to benefit others. It is not right that the lips of the man who "has understanding" should be always closed. He will know, indeed, when to speak and when to be silent; but to keep his knowledge entirely to himself, would be "lighting a candle and putting it under a bushel." It is no uncommon thing to find a proneness to talk, not in proportion to the fulness but to the emptiness of the mind. But no duty can be clearer than that the man who *has* understanding should make his understanding *useful*. And

I.   Q

he who, truly wise, puts GOD first among the objects of his
knowledge; and his own eternal interests first among the
objects of his desire and pursuit, is the man who will, by his
lips, be most truly serviceable to others.   Speaking the dictates of an understanding enlightened by the Spirit of God,
he may be the instrument of making others "wise unto
salvation."

"*But a rod is for the back of him that is void of understanding.*"   The sentiment is similar to that in the latter
clause of verses eighth and tenth,—"A prating fool shall fall."
"*Void of understanding*," does not mean destitute of natural
intellect.   The rod is not for the back of him who is thus naturally incapable of comprehending the lessons of divine wisdom.

The character brought before us is that of the man who is
full of himself, and who, in the vanity of his ignorant and
self-sufficient mind, will not listen to the lessons of true wisdom.   In childhood, this temper requires "the rod" of parental
discipline, and will ever be exposing the subject of it to the
necessity of such infliction.   And in the community, when
the self-will that has refused to receive instruction, or to be
subject to salutary restraint, gives way to the indulgence of
its evil propensities, it must be dealt with by the punitive
coercion of the magistrate, for the general security and the
public good.   And in a sense still more serious, the man
"void of understanding," who casts off the fear of God, who
walks "in the sight of his eyes, and the imagination of his
heart," exposes himself to penal visitations in a quarter infinitely higher.   He is amenable to God for the use of his faculties; and by the abuse of them,—by their desecration to
ignoble and worthless, or to wicked and ungodly ends,—he
"treasures up unto himself wrath against the day of wrath;"
and, in agreement with the allusion of the wise man in the
words before us, he shall be "beaten with many stripes."

The sentiment is still similar in verse 14. "Wise men lay up
knowledge: but the mouth of the foolish is near destruction."

To "*lay up* knowledge," very obviously implies that value
is set upon it.   Men never think of seeking and accumulating
what they regard as worthless:—and in proportion as an ob-

ject is prized, will be the degree of eagerness with which it
is pursued, and of jealous vigilance with which it is "laid up"
and guarded.   Thus the *Miser*.   With what an eye of restless and eager covetousness does he look after the acquisition
of the idol of his heart's desires!—with what delight does
he hug himself on his success!—with what avidity does he
add the increase to his treasures—carefully secreting them
from all access but his own!   With a care incomparably
more dignified and useful, how does the man of science
mark and record every fact and observation, whether of his
own discovery and suggestion or of those of others!   How
he exults in every new acquisition to *his* stores!   He lays all
up in his mind; or, fearful of a treacherous memory, in
surer modes of record and preservation.   Hints that lead to
nothing at the time may lead to much afterwards.   Some one,
in another generation, may carry out into practical application, or into the formation of valuable theories, the facts and
conjectures that are now, in apparent isolation, "laid up"
for such possible future use.   The true philosopher, to use a
colloquial phrase, "has all his eyes about him."   He allows
nothing to escape notice, and nothing, if he can help it, to
pass into oblivion.   "He *lays up knowledge*."

But alas! in this respect as in others, "the children of this
world are, in their generation, wiser than the children of
light."   Surely, if such be the practice of the wise men of
the world, much more ought it to be of the *truly wise*, in regard to divine knowledge, the best and highest of all!*

It is the Christian's duty to seek knowledge in all directions, and by whatever helps he can be enabled to find it.   It
is his duty to lay it up for use—first for the purposes of self-
improvement and self-direction, and then for the further
purpose of enabling him to contribute to the instruction and
guidance of others.   And every Christian should make it a
point of conscience, to find out the particular sphere in which
the knowledge he *has* laid up may be best turned to account
for others' benefit—whether in the occupations of a Christian-

---

* Chap. ii. 1—4.

instruction agency, or in those of a Sabbath-school teacher, or in any other more private or more public department.

"*But the mouth of the foolish is near destruction.*" The expression is forcible, and its meaning sufficiently plain. The fool babbles without discretion—with reckless inconsideration and rashness. He expends his shallow stock thoughtlessly and at random. You can place no confidence in him. He speaks when he should be silent, and is silent when he should speak. He blabs out secrets, forgetting till it is too late that they were confidentially entrusted to him. He suits not his talk to time, place, or company, but comes out with communications to parties the very opposite to those for whom they were intended, or to whom they are appropriate; and is in constant danger of saying just the things he ought not to say. Thus you are ever trembling for him—never sure but the very next opening of his lips may run him into a snare, and expose him to mischief.

Standing opposed as this does here to "laying up knowledge," it clearly relates to the propensity to talk without knowledge and without thought. And while the words of folly may prove the ruin of the fool as to this world, by the injudiciousness of their utterance, and by the breach and destruction of confidence;—"the fool's mouth is near destruction" in a sense much more alarming. "For every idle word," says Jesus, "that men shall speak they shall give account in the day of judgment;" "for by thy words thou shalt be justified, and by thy words thou shalt be condemned." There may be a vast amount of guilt in words: and thus "the mouth of the fool is near destruction," inasmuch as its very next utterance of profane and ungodly thought or feeling may place him on the very verge of hell; so that, were he cut off with the words on his lips and in the state of heart they indicate, he must sink into everlasting woe.

There is a pursuit that is incomparably more prevalent in the world than that of the "laying up of knowledge." To this Solomon refers in the next verse. It is that of *wealth:* —verse 15. "The rich man's wealth is his strong city: the destruction of the poor is their poverty."

"Wealth" is pursued, as if there were the general and rooted conviction that it drew every thing in its train that heart could desire; as if it were the security for all that is necessary to the attainment and enjoyment of happiness, and the preservative from all that nature deprecates and dreads—a source of perfect security—a "strong city." It is evident that the wise man does not here express the sentiment that there *is* real security in the rich man's wealth. It is the *state of mind* that is intended—the confidence which the rich man places in his riches. This is clear from the connexion in which the same words stand elsewhere—"The rich man's wealth is his strong city, and as an high wall *in his own conceit.*"*

No doubt the possession of riches preserves from the evils which are specially incident to poverty. The rich are free from the distresses of the poor. Even from these, however, the protection is, in the last degree, precarious; for the riches themselves which constitute it, are every instant insecure. The "*strong city*" is exposed perpetually to be assailed and taken; the high wall to be overthrown; the citadel invaded and rifled; and he who trusted to its munitions left exposed, defenceless, disappointed, and, in proportion to the amount of his previous confidence, forlorn, and wretched;—driven, at times, even to insanity, or tempted to self-murder; and, to avoid the privations of time, plunging into the infinitely more fearful privations and woes of eternity!

Besides, insecure as the bulwarks are, there are multitudes of evils, common to rich and poor, from which, even while they stand, they are no protection. They cannot keep out disease, either of body or of mind, or ward off relative any more than personal afflictions. They can neither keep away nor cure, neither alleviate nor remove, the agony of the gout or the stone. They cannot quench the burning fever. They cannot arrest the progress of insidiously mining consumption. They can neither hinder nor heal the still more affecting maladies of the mind, and replace Reason on its vacant throne. They cannot purchase exemption from

* Chap. xviii. 11.

the grave, for the wife of the bosom, for the child, the parent, or the friend.   And, if they are incompetent to ends
like these, far less can they SAVE THE SOUL.   *Death*—the
"king of terrors"—"the last enemy," shall scale the walls
of the "strong city," and surprise its confiding occupant in the
very citadel of his strength.   Where can he find a barrier
that can prevent *his* entrance; where among all his treasures a bribe that will stay *his* dart! And when "after death
comes the judgment," what shall he have, when he stands,
stript of all his worldly possessions, and, what is infinitely
worse, stript of every plea of defence—which, but for the
temptations of the world, he might in time have provided,
—a poor, naked, helpless, trembling culprit, before the tri-
bunal of a neglected God—what shall he have to stay judgment—to avert damnation?   "Riches profit not in the day
of wrath!"

   "*The destruction of the poor is their poverty.*" The word
rendered *destruction* being the same as in the preceding
verse, it would be arbitrary to change the sense.   Retaining it, the words are capable of *two meanings*.   First,
there are temptations peculiar to poverty as well as to riches.
Agur was aware of these when he prayed, "Give me not
poverty—lest I steal and take the name of my God in
vain."*   He who gives way to such influences of poverty,
insures "destruction" as much as he who is "full and denies
God, and says, Who is the Lord?"   Secondly, as we found
the preceding clause of the verse to refer to the *state of
mind*—the *confidence of safety* inspired by his wealth in the
bosom of the rich, it seems fair and natural to understand
the latter clause on a similar principle.   "The destruction of
the poor" will then mean, that which, *in their own eyes*, is
their destruction; that which engenders their fears and apprehensions—their constant dread of destruction.   They are
ever apt to contrast their circumstances with those of their
wealthy neighbours, and to deplore their poverty, and
fret at it as that which keeps them down, depriving them

---

* See chap. xxx. 7—9.

of all good, and exposing them to all evil. And, without doubt, it is the source of many and heavy sufferings, both in the way of privation and of endurance. But the poor may indulge their fears, and make themselves unhappy without cause. Their forebodings may be more than groundless. If by their poverty they are exposed to some evils, they are exempted by it from others. If they but trust in God, they have a far surer ground of confidence than wealth can ever afford to the richest on earth. They are under the eye and the care of that Providence, without which even "a sparrow falleth not to the ground." "The name of the Lord is a strong tower"—how much stronger and more inpregnable than any which *wealth* can construct! Thither running, they are safe. "Their place of defence is the munition of rocks."

And as riches cannot save, poverty, blessed be God! cannot hinder salvation. No, nor can it shut out the soul from the present joys of salvation, or the consolations that spring from the "exceeding great and precious promises" of God's covenant. On the contrary—"Hearken, my beloved brethren, Hath not God chosen the poor of this world rich in faith, and heirs of the kingdom which he hath promised to them that love him?" James ii. 5.

The poor have, at times, been *so* pressed by their fears, as to allow themselves to be tempted to sin, in order to shun the "destruction" they dread. But Oh! let sin be ever more dreaded than all the ills, in all their accumulation, of poverty. Remember,—sin *will* do, what poverty *cannot* do: it will ruin the soul. Let the poor seek the peace, and comfort, and safety which are imparted by the gospel; and thus, possessing the "true riches," they will not need to "fear what man can do unto them." The worst of all destructions will be far from them. They shall know, in their experience, that "godliness with contentment is great gain;" and when "heart and flesh fail; God will be the strength of their heart, and their portion for ever."

Verse 16. "The labour of the righteous tendeth to life: the fruit of the wicked to sin."

"The *labour* of the righteous" may be understood in either a more restricted or a more general sense; either of his daily labour in his worldly business, or of all his active engagements. The words are alike true as to both. With regard to the former—it "*tendeth to life*," inasmuch as it is conducted on right principles, and with a view to right ends; not to those of mere selfishness, but to those of piety and benevolence. It "tendeth to life," by contributing to the truest happiness of his own life, in correspondence with the words of Him who said, "It is more blessed to give than to receive;" and it "tendeth to life" also, by imparting, as far as his means and opportunities extend, happiness to the lives of others.

There is a higher sense too in which it "tendeth to life." And in saying this, I refer, not solely to ordinary labour, but to the whole of the active engagements of the child and servant of God. They all bear a certain relation to his final acceptance, and attainment of life everlasting. I need hardly say—on no ground of *personal merit*. The only ground of acceptance and life to any son or daughter of fallen man is found in the merit of the divine Mediator—in the righteousness, the sacrifice, and the intercession of Immanuel. But genuine faith in that Mediator—whether existing *before* or *after* his manifestation in the flesh, according to the amount of existing revelation—must be shown by the "work of faith and the labour of love." And the "labour of the righteous" —of which the true principle is known to the Judge, "the searcher of hearts," who distinguishes between the false and the true, according to the motive in operation,—will be graciously accepted, as the labour of one "accepted in the Beloved," and whose works are recognized as having their source, not in the spirit of self-righteousness, but in the power of faith. God the Father will then testify his regard to righteousness in *two ways:*—first, in justifying sinners on the ground of a righteousness fully commensurate with all the demands of his law, in their full amount of spirituality and purity—the perfect righteousness of his own Son:—and secondly, by making personal righteousness of character, or the holy influence of the truth, the necessary evidence of interest in the righteousness thus provided in Christ for the justification of the ungodly;—acknowledging the good works of his people, as works conformable to the precepts of his law, but evangelical in their dictating motive; and bestowing the reward of free grace, according to the measure both of rectitude in the *act* and rectitude in the *principle.**

On the other hand, *the fruit of the wicked* (tendeth) *to sin.*" The contrast is striking. It is not directly said, as the previous clause might lead us to expect, "tendeth to *death,*" but "to *sin.*" This, by the wise man, is considered as the same thing. It "tendeth to sin," *and consequently to death.* Thus it is said, "When lust hath conceived, it bringeth forth sin: and sin, when it is finished, bringeth forth death."† Between the two there is an intimate and inseparable connexion.

The "*fruit* of the wicked" means here, apparently, the immediate proceeds of his labour—his *income*—his *revenue.* And the idea intended, seems to be, that when the wicked man prospers, and so acquires possessions, they only *enlarge his means of sinning;* only increase the amount of his selfish, worldly, vicious indulgence. The fruit of his labour, neither first nor last, is given to God, for the glory of His name, or for purposes in harmony with His will. The modes of using it, therefore, only serve to augment guilt, and aggravate the sentence of *death.* To such, by their abuse of it, prosperity proves a curse instead of a blessing. Whatever *tends to death* must be so regarded. Oh! it is an affecting sight, to behold men, as they call it, *enjoying life,* when their real occupation is—fitting themselves for destruction, "treasuring up wrath," forging for themselves "chains of darkness," ensuring death—the death that never dies, and adding virulence to the venom of its eternal sting.

The sentiment of the next verse is very similar to some that have already come under review—"He is in the way

---

* Comp. Luke xii. 33; xix. 12—19: Rom. ii. 3—11: 1 Tim. vi. 17—19: Heb. vi. 10—12. † Jam. i. 15.

of life that keepeth instruction: but he that refuseth reproof erreth."

The *instruction* meant, I need not say, is the instruction
of wisdom—salutary, saving instruction—the "counsel of
God." He who humbly hears and "*keeps*" it, "is *in the
way of life*"—in the way of present happiness, and in the
way to life eternal. "But he that *refuseth reproof*"—the
reproof that would admonish and bring him to God, "*erreth.*"
Under the influence of a miserable delusion, he wanders
farther and farther *from* "the way of life." He is not, like
him who "keepeth instruction," *in* that way: he is already
out of it; and he diverges from it more and more widely.
He is like a traveller who has missed his road, and yet
will persist in taking his own course, pertinaciously refusing
all direction from those who are able to give it him. That
traveller may fall into the pit or over the precipice; or, over-
taken by the darkness and the storm, become desperate, and
lay him down and die. We pity him; but his blood is on
his own head. Thus it is with the sinner who "refuses reproof," who shuts his ear to remonstrance, however affectionate and earnest, and to every voice of faithful kindness that
calls him to the way of life.*

Verse 18. "He that hideth hatred with lying lips, and
he that uttereth a slander is a fool."

In the character depicted in this verse there is a threefold evil. There is, first, the indulgence of a sinful passion—
the passion of *hatred*. God's word gives it no countenance.
Its injunction is—"Love your enemies." There is only one
description of *hatred* that is there tolerated. God himself
is said to "*hate* all the workers of iniquity." But He hates
them only *as such*. It is the *character*, not the *person* that
is hated. If God hated the wicked personally, He would
have pleasure in his death, a sentiment He solemnly ab-
jures, as foreign to his nature. It is in a corresponding
sense then, that we must understand the Psalmist when he

---

* The verse here commented on, may be rendered, "He that keepeth instruction is a way of life," i. e. is a guide to the way of life; "but
he that refuseth reproof *causeth to err*."—Comp. marg. of E. V.

says, " Do not I hate them, O Lord, that hate thee? . . . I hate them with perfect hatred."* It was simply *as the ene-mies of God* that he hated them. Could he have converted them into friends of God, and thus brought them to the en-joyment of His favour, and to the life which it imparts, he would willingly have done it: and that would have been the act, not·of hatred, but of the truest love. We are not al-lowed to *hate any human being.*

Superadded to this, there is the guilt of hypocrisy and falsehood: he " *hideth* hatred *with lying lips.*" The lips that cover hatred by lies—that is, by words that are in op-position to the true state of the mind and heart,—must of course be the lips of *flattery*—pretending love and friendly feeling, while mischievous devices, the dictate of cherished malice, are revolved in the mind. There can be few things more despicable or more detestable than this malignity of falsehood—oil on the lips and venom in the heart—all that is good in words, all that is evil in inward wish. There are not terms in language strong enough to express the abomi-nation and the guilt of such conduct.

There is too the further guilt of *treachery.* I am disposed to take the words, " *and he that uttereth a slander,*" in this connexion, not as a new and distinct character, but an addi-tional feature only of the former. The man is supposed to " hide hatred by lying lips" from him who is the object of it, while, at the same time, he is *slandering him to others.* This is an addition to the diabolical wickedness. And at the same time, he who acts the part described is emphati-cally " *a fool.*" Even in a worldly sense—even on the prin-ciples of common discretion, he is foolish; for the slander is almost sure to reach the ear of the person whom he flatters; and then he stands in the unenviable position of one self-betrayed, and procures himself contempt, indignation, deser-tion, and mischief, for his pains. He becomes an outlaw from all reputable society; is put under the ban and the dis-grace even of the world.—But in a higher sense " he is a

* Psal. cxxxix. 21, 22.

fool." The odious want of principle displayed by him brings him under a ban more fearful than that of the world,—fixing upon him the curse of that God who "abhors the deceitful man;" and who hath doomed all liars to have their part in the "lake that burneth with fire and brimstone."*

Where is the man who will not join in the strongest terms of reprobation in regard to this hypocritical and treacherous villany? The world, as well as Christians, are open-mouthed against hypocrisy. There is often, however, a great deal of it practised under less obnoxious designations, —a great amount of dissimulation and flattery that passes under the names of needful prudence, and the etiquette of compliment and courtesy; in which, fair and fulsome words to the face, are followed by the curse of dislike, or the jeer of scorn, or the tale of slander, or the self-gratulation of good riddance, as soon as the back is turned.

But the hypocrisy which has the largest measure of the world's sarcastic virulence is—*religious hypocrisy.* And assuredly, no one can go beyond due bounds in the condemnation of it, wherever it really discovers itself. It is to be feared, however, that the detestation of hypocrisy is, in the case of many, only a convenient cover for the *dislike of religion.* They hate hypocrisy. And yet, how comes it that they have such a chuckling delight in the detection of instances of it? Were it the object of their serious hatred on right principles, such detection should fill them with sincere, heart-felt grief. But the manner in which they are affected by such discoveries, real or supposed, shows that they are not shocked by the dishonour done to God by such false pretensions, nor by the guilt brought by them on the consciences of those by whom they are made, and the fearful consequences to which they are thereby exposed. They avail themselves of such detections to throw out their general sarcasms and their sweeping inuendoes against the professors of religion at large. They shrewdly suspect that "it is not all gold that glitters;" that where there is most

* Psal. v. 6: Rev. xxi. 8.

show there is often least substance.   And, where there is more than ordinary appearance even of humble and unostentatious devotion, they are ready with another proverb, alleging, with a meaning wink of the eye, that "deep waters flow smoothly;" but that these *saints* (possibly the designation preceded with an epithet of vulgar malediction) are all, if one but *knew* them, much alike.

Now, my friends, we go fully along with you in your strongest reprobation of hypocrisy, of false and treacherous pretensions, whether to men or to God,—and especially, if you will, *the latter.*   But forget not that *the very idea of hypocrisy implies a reality of which it is the simulation.* We have no objection that you be as cautious as you please in crediting the professions of religion; but it were a very unwarrantable abandonment of all charity to deny that there is *any* sincerity to be found.   When you know that a forgery exists on the notes of any Bank, or on any department of the national Coinage, it is natural, and it is right, that you should be the more jealous in examining and distinguishing the counterfeit from the true.   But why are you thus careful?   It is because you *set a value on the true.* You never think of concluding that all are forged together. It would be well, if your abhorrence of hypocritical profession arose from your really setting a value on true religion itself—loving it, and deploring its desecration.   But, if *this* were your state of mind and heart, it would carry you farther than even to the unfeigned admiration of it in others.   You would *be* religious yourselves.   You would feel at once its true dignity and its true happiness; and, not with "lying lips," but with lips of truth, giving utterance to the feelings of devotion, cherished in "simplicity and godly sincerity," you would unite with all "that in every place call upon the name of the Lord."   You would give yourselves, heart and hand, to His service, under the influence of the "faith that worketh by love."

LECTURE XXII.

Prov. x. 19—32.

" In the multitude of words there wanteth not sin: but he that refraineth his lips is wise. The tongue of the just is as choice silver: the heart of the wicked is little worth. The lips of the righteous feed many: but fools die for want of wisdom. The blessing of the Lord, it maketh rich, and he addeth no sorrow with it. It is as sport to a fool to do mischief: but a man of understanding hath wisdom. The fear of the wicked, it shall come upon him: but the desire of the righteous shall be granted. As the whirlwind passeth, so is the wicked no more: but the righteous is an everlasting foundation. As vinegar to the teeth, and as smoke to the eyes, so is the sluggard to them that send him. The fear of the Lord prolongeth days: but the years of the wicked shall be shortened. The hope of the righteous shall be gladness: but the expectation of the wicked shall perish. The way of the Lord is strength to the upright: but destruction shall be to the workers of iniquity. The righteous shall never be removed: but the wicked shall not inhabit the earth. The mouth of the just bringeth forth wisdom: but the froward tongue shall be cut out. The lips of the righteous know what is acceptable: but the mouth of the wicked speaketh frowardness."

THREE of these verses relate to the same subject. It is one which has come before us more than once already—*the use of the tongue*—its mischievous and its beneficial effects.

The maxim contained in the first is, like many similar ones, of a *general* character. It is no easy matter for a man to be a great talker, without saying both foolish things and faulty. The more especially, that men who are full of talk are in most cases (for there are exceptions) superficial men, without much solidity of judgment to direct and regulate their speech. Their extreme propensity to talk makes them forgetful of the common but just and needful maxim, " Think before you speak." They speak without thinking. To hear them, one would fancy they had some pleasant sensation in the very movements of the organs of utterance; or that they were using them for the sole purpose of giving them volubility by practice; or that the sound of their voices was peculiarly grateful to their own ear, or, in their vain fancy, to the ear of others. Talk they *must*. And what is nearest the surface comes forth, be it right or wrong.

"*But he that refraineth his lips is wise.*" To "refrain the lips," is to be "sparing of words." He is truly wise who speaks with due consideration of *when, where,* and *what*.

There is one case in which "the multitude of words" is singularly inappropriate. I mean, *in worship:*—when a man pours out a volume of talk to God; as if *this* were what God desired and would be pleased with; as if the worshipper (if such he should be called) were vain of his fine and fluent speech, even before the throne of the Infinite Majesty, and imagined he should be "heard for his much speaking"—either for the quantity or the quality of his words!* How beautifully is the truth of this remark exemplified in the pattern of prayer given us by Jesus himself—the great, the Divine Teacher!†

Verse 20. "The tongue of the just is as choice silver: the heart of the wicked is little worth."

The *sentiment* in the former clause is very similar to that in verses 11 and 13. The *figure* is different. The lessons of instruction, the counsels, consolations, directions, and reproofs "of the just" are precious as silver—as "choice silver,"—"silver tried in a furnace of earth purified seven times." They effect ends which silver, ever so refined, cannot attain.—The contrast, in the second clause, is striking:—"But the *heart* of the wicked is little worth." Why is the contrast not between the *tongue* of the wicked and the *tongue* of the just? Simply because the state of the heart gives its character to the tongue. If the one be "little worth," so will be the other. There is a beautiful correspondence between the language of our Lord and that of Solomon. Jesus speaks of the "*good treasure*" that is in the heart of the good man;‡

* See Eccl. v. 1—3.   † Matt. vi. 9—13.   ‡ Luke vi. 45.

and Solomon speaks of his tongue being as "*choice silver.*"
What he utters, is just a part of the "good treasure" brought
out from within for use.

Men admire *talent,* and are loath to think ill of him who
possesses it, and to whom they feel themselves indebted,
perhaps, for both pleasure and information.   They weave
the golden threads of genius into a vail, which they throw
over the moral corruptions and defects of the heart and
character.   They allow talent to stand as a compensation for
vice, and palliate irreligion for the sake of mental eminence.
But it is to the *heart* that GOD especially, and in the first
instance, looks.   It is a heart renewed by grace ; a heart in
which the truth dwells by faith, and works with holy power ;
a heart under the dominant influence of heavenly wisdom ;—it
is *such* a heart that, in God's sight, renders the tongue "as
choice silver."   It is not the facts or demonstrations of
science, nor the selectest beauties of elegant literature, that
are here meant ; but the lessons of *divine truth.*   The most
brilliant display of parts in conversation would not, in the
Bible, receive the designation here used, were not the eloquence of the lips seasoned with the salt of genuine piety ;
and so calculated, not to minister amusement and intellectual gratification merely, but what the Bible calls "*grace* to
the hearers."   And when, in any case, the tendency is of
an opposite nature,—were all the brilliancy of genius ever
possessed by the human mind concentrated in the one individual speaker, and flowing with all captivating sweetness
from his lips,—this would be no protection to him, from the
severest reprehension, and the heaviest denunciation of
Heaven.   Nay, the reprehension would be all the severer,
the denunciation all the heavier, in proportion to the
amount of intellect thus unsanctified, and withheld from
God,—unbaptized by the Spirit, unconsecrated to God's glory.
Genius thus unhallowed, becomes only the more perilous, the
more pernicious, the more guilty.

In the same strain it is added, verse 21. "The lips of the
righteous feed many : but fools die for want of wisdom."

This is the same sentiment, under still another, and a

very natural figure. Instruction, counsel, and comfort are represented as the *food and nourishment* of the soul. The righteous man may be a *poor* man:—yet he possesses what may render him, on many occasions, far more valuable, because far more useful, than the possessor of the largest amount of " choice silver." The silver may provide " the meat that perisheth;" but the lips of the righteous furnish that which " endureth unto life eternal." The words of his mouth give life to the dead, and they strengthen the life of the spiritually living. He directs the perplexed by wholesome counsel, and he soothes the afflicted with seasonable and tender sympathy,—thus feeding and cherishing the drooping and fainting spirit. The righteous man, by the wisdom of his lips, " both saves himself and them that hear him." On the contrary, " Fools *die* for want of wisdom." That is, of the *true* wisdom—" the fear of God." In spite of all their acquisitions in science, and all their reputation and honour, applause and flattery, for their worldly sagacity, they " *die.*" No power in the range of science or art can ward off either the first or the " second death"—no devices of the wiliest sagacity, can elude the detection, or perplex the councils, and nullify the judgment of the Omniscient and Almighty!

With the character of the righteous comes, in sufficiently natural connexion, " *the blessing of the Lord:*" for it is on them His blessing rests:—verse 22. " The blessing of the Lord, it maketh rich, and he addeth no sorrow with it."

The expression—" the blessing of the Lord *maketh rich,*" is evidently susceptible of two meanings;—either that God's blessing *constitutes* true riches; so that he who possesses it has in that blessing itself the best and most desirable wealth; or, that by the blessing of God *riches are acquired.* Men fancy that the requisites to such acquisition are *in themselves.* The Bible ever inculcates an opposite lesson—reminding them of their dependence, and of the necessity of the divine favour to success.*

The meaning of the latter clause will, of course, be modi-

---

* Deut. viii. 14, 17, 18: 1 Chron. xxix. 12—16: Dan. v. 22, 23.

fied according as we affix the one or the other of these senses
to the former.   If the *first* be the true meaning, then the
words, " *He addeth no sorrow with it*," must signify, that this
blessing is in itself the source of the purest and richest joy.
The child of God, indeed, feels, like others, the sorrows of
life.   His religion is not the parent of apathy, but rather of
more acute and tender sensibility ; but the blessing of his
heavenly Father sweetens every bitter cup that is mingled for
him ; sustains him under the pressure of the heaviest calamity ;
nay, even converts the sorrows of life themselves into grounds
of praise, by rendering them the means of spiritual benefit.
The Lord " adds no sorrow."   It gives no real *cause* for sorrow ; inasmuch as, " all working together for good," all shall be
joy in the end.   And then the blessing shall be realized in
its fulness—sorrow and sighing having for ever fled away.

If the *second* be the meaning, then this latter clause will
signify, that the riches obtained by the good man, who
sought them in dependence on the divine blessing, being
acquired with a good conscience, and used to God's glory,
are enjoyed by him without the agitations of perplexing
anxiety and care, the secret gnawings of self-accusation and
remorse, or the harassing distraction of spirit arising from
the haunting apprehension of their loss.   Both senses are
good, and both equally true and natural.

Cultivate, brethren, a spirit of *dependence*, and a spirit of
gratitude.   Amid the bustle and excitement of worldly
business, Christians themselves are in danger of forgetting
their entire dependence ; in danger of losing sight of God ;
of taking undue credit to their own sagacity in scheming
and following out their schemes ; of " offering sacrifice to
their own net, and burning incense to their own drag ;" but

> " Fond mortals but themselves beguile,
>   When on themselves they rest ;
> Blind is their wisdom, weak their toil,
>   By thee, O Lord, unblest ! "

And mark—no wealth can be comfortably enjoyed, that has
not been acquired, in dependence on the divine blessing, by

means which have the sanction of God's law; and that is not used in a manner and for ends in accordance with God's will.

We should reckon a man deranged in mind who should, in the way of pastime, break those laws of human society which are guarded by the sanction of death. Yet how much more are they chargeable with derangement, by whom the laws of God are violated with reckless mirth, although the sanction which guards them is one so incomparably more fearful! To do this in sport!—how inconceivably infatuated! Such folly, however, is to be found:—verse 23. " It is as sport to a fool to do mischief: but a man of understanding hath wisdom."

The " *mischief*" here spoken of is not, I apprehend, to be understood, exclusively at least, of that in which the giddy, volatile, thoughtless minds of youth are prone to indulge; which, however annoying, ends in no very serious consequences to those who are the subjects of it. Even this youthful propensity, however, is one constantly in danger of running to an extreme, and requires to be curbed and restrained. If parents and guardians treat any of its mischievous tricks as mere sources of amusement, there is a temptation to set the wits to work to devise a still better one next time; so that what began in jest may come to end in something more serious; and the young may be tempted to adopt and act on the unprincipled and vexatious maxim— " *No sport without mischief!*" But "the fool," considered as the man who "has not the fear of God before his eyes," goes much further than this. He makes "sport" of injuring the character and reputation, the property and interest, the personal and domestic comfort and happiness, of others. And, in still more general terms, he commits sin with a sportive and inconsiderate lightness, and heedlessness of consequences. Such men injure and disquiet their neighbours. They tempt others to crime, and laugh at the success of their temptation—enjoying the sport so much the more if they see any thing like remorse in those whom they have seduced. They treat with merriment even acts of nefarious turpitude, if they can be perpetrated with present impunity.

They hear with derision the admonitions and expostulations of the godly—jeering at them as all cant and hypocrisy; and, to show their superiority to restraint, and their proud defiance of threatened danger, they will sometimes repeat the evil reproved in the very face of the reprover, and that too with aggravations; or commit some other act still worse, and delight in laughing at the gravity of countenance and the heaviness of heart with which their conduct is contemplated. Alas for human nature!—there *is* such folly.   But on the contrary, " The man of understanding"—the man enlightened by the truth and Spirit of God, " *hath wisdom;*" wisdom which prevents his acting so infatuated and ruinous a part.   He considers all that belongs to his neighbour as by the law of God—the law of love—rendered sacred; and " *mischief*" which he would not like as practised upon himself, he shrinks from practising upon others.   All sin, too, he regards with any feeling but that of sportiveness—any eye but that of mirth and encouragement.   He dreads it, as of all evils the worst; hateful to God; ensuring His displeasure and curse; polluting and ruining the soul.

Sport and *happiness* are not one.   When there is laughter in the mouth, there may be no joy in the heart. There is such a thing as laughing away terror; hiding real alarm by assumed gaiety; concealing anguish of conscience by the mirth of social revelry.   The reflection is suggested by next verse—" The fear of the wicked, it shall come upon him: but the desire of the righteous shall be granted."

The wicked, then, *has* his fears—secret suppressed forebodings—the " fearful looking-for of judgment."   " Even in his laughter, the heart is sad; and the end of that mirth is heaviness."   Till he has arrived at that most appalling of all states—" having the conscience seared with a hot iron," he *will* have his misgivings, his disquieting apprehensions, scaring, like a sudden phantom, his maddest mirth.   And his fears are far from groundless: — they " *shall come upon him.*"   And not merely his fears *in life;* but the worst and most overwhelming of his fears—the fear that assails his spirit, when he comes to the verge of an eternal world, (the great testing-time of human principles, human joys, and human hopes,) all, and more than all, "shall come upon him." During his career of iniquity, he might affect to call such alarms, whether he saw them in others or at times felt them rising within himself, superstitious and womanish fears; but there is a *reality* in them. Conscience is in them; God is in them. They "*shall* come upon him."

While the "God with whom we have to do" is true to his *threatenings,* he is no less true to his *promises.* The righteous are as sure of the fulfilment of their hopes, as the wicked are of the realization of their fears:—"*But the desire of the righteous shall be granted.*" This might be taken comprehensively. "This is the confidence that we have in Him, that, if we ask any thing according to his will, he heareth us: and if we know that he hear us, whatsoever we ask, we know that we have the petitions that we desired of him."* The good man's "desire," in regard to all spiritual supplies and blessings here, and for the enjoyment, not of temporal mercies merely but of God's love in them, "shall be granted," in answer to believing prayer. But the connexion leads us to consider the words as having special reference to the fulness of his desire, in the completion of all his hopes of future blessedness. And that blessedness shall be something far surpassing the thoughts of the most capacious mind, and the flights of the loftiest imagination.

And let me here apply a test of present character. The sources of the happiness of heaven will be the same things with those which are the desire of the righteous *now.* Is "the desire of their souls," for instance, to their Lord and to "the remembrance of him?" *There* the desire shall be satisfied:—they shall "see him as he is," and be "for ever with him."—Is their desire after communion with God? *There,* "He that sitteth on the throne shall dwell among them!"—Is their desire after freedom from sin, and perfection in holiness? *There* they shall be "like Him" who is "holy, harmless, undefiled, and separate from sinners."—Is

* 1 John v. 14, 15.

their desire after the joy of pure and holy fellowship with the family of the redeemed? *There*, all shall be clothed with the white robe, not only of imputed righteousness but of personal sanctity—all pure, even as God is pure!—Is their desire after perfect and permanent deliverance from all the sorrows and sufferings of time? *There*, "they shall hunger no more, neither thirst any more ; neither shall the sun light on them, nor any heat. For the Lamb which is in the midst of the throne shall feed them, and shall lead them unto living fountains of waters: and God shall wipe away all tears from their eyes," Rev. vii. 16, 17.

This last may be considered as the desire of *nature:* the others are the desires of *grace*. And what we earnestly wish all to bear in mind is—that unless these spiritual and heavenly desires are in the heart *now*, there can be no well-grounded anticipation of the possession of the blessings hereafter.

Many and striking are the figures employed in Scripture, to impress on the mind the transient nature of the prosperity of sinners, as contrasted with the stability and security of God's people. Here is one :—verse 25. "As the whirlwind passeth, so is the wicked no more: but the righteous is an everlasting foundation."

The whirlwind is rapid and impetuous, mighty and destructive, while it lasts. But it lasts not long: it "passes away." Such is the course of the wicked. Their triumphs, their boastings, their sportive mischiefs, are only as the short-lived fury of the hurrying tempest.*

In the latter clause—"But the righteous is an everlasting foundation," the verb is supplementary: "But the righteous—an everlasting foundation." Some supply *has;* making the words mean that he builds on a firm and permenant basis; he trusts in the "rock of ages"—in the "precious corner-stone, the sure foundation." But the antithesis in the verse leads us rather to the idea of *his own* stability and endurance, as represented in other passages ;† and in verse

* Comp. Job xxvii. 16—21: Psal. xxxvii. 35, 36; lviii. 9.
† Psal. xv. 5; cxii. 6—8: Matt. vii. 24, 25.

30th of this chapter, "The righteous shall never be removed." Perhaps there may be a reference to the violence of the wicked being directed against him, and his remaining, under the protection of the divine power, unmoved, unharmed. The whirlwind assails the mountain; sweeps and eddies along with impetuous and tearing fury; leaves here and there slight traces of its raging course:—but the mountain stands unshaken on its deep-laid and immoveable basis. Such shall be the amount of the wicked's power; such the harmlessness of its results, against those who are under the protection of Jehovah. It shall spend itself, and pass away ; and the righteous shall not be moved. "If GOD be for him, who can be against him?"

And reversing the question—as with awful truth it may be reversed—in regard to the wicked themselves :—if GOD be against them, who can be for them? Could they succeed in rousing the universe to take their part, what would all its combined powers and resources avail against the MAKER of the universe? — against Him who says, with divine majesty, of all the opposition that can be brought to bear against Him—"Who will set the briars and the thorns against *me* in the day of battle? I will go through them,—I will burn them up together!"

It is worthy of being noticed, how often the two ideas of *wickedness* and *sloth* present themselves together to the mind of Solomon; the one apparently suggesting the other. Having spoken of the *wicked,* he brings before us the *sluggard*— "As vinegar to the teeth, and as smoke to the eyes, so is the sluggard to them that send him."

There is no difficulty as to the meaning of the comparisons here used. *Vinegar,* or the *sour grape,* sets the teeth most unpleasantly on edge ;—*smoke,* and especially smoke from particular descriptions of fuel, smarts, pains, and injures the eyes. All have felt this: and all who have employed a sluggish messenger for the execution of their business, instantly feel the appropriateness of the comparisons. He is sent for something you long to have, and are in special haste to obtain. You wait, and wait; you look out, and look out again, and again; but he is never like to return. You get impatient, irritated, fretful, angry. He is commissioned on some business that requires despatch,—in which, indeed, expedition is every thing: he lingers and loiters, and saunters away his time in listless lounging or trifling, till the opportunity is lost, and we are mortified and harassed by disappointment. And apart from the consideration of actually evil effects, the very sight of the yawning, lazy loiterer, whether engaged on our own business or that of others, is teasing and provoking. One is ever disposed to push him out of the way. He is a perfect annoyance—"as vinegar to the teeth, and as smoke to the eyes."

The sentiment in next verse—"The fear of the Lord prolongeth days: but the years of the wicked shall be shortened," has been already fully illustrated.* We pass on.

Verse 28. "The hope of the righteous shall be gladness: but the expectation of the wicked shall perish."—"The hope of the righteous" is *present* "gladness." O what gladness! above all that earth can grant, and springing from a source with which earth cannot interfere! And it shall *end* in "gladness:" not in disappointment and shame, but in all the joy of a glorious fulfilment. What gladness has the "hope of the righteous" imparted to many a soul, in passing through the valley of the shadow of death; enabling the happy combatant with the king of terrors to sing in the very midst of his conflict, as in triumph over an already conquered and fallen enemy—"O death, where is thy sting? O grave, where thy victory? The sting of death is sin; and the strength of sin is the law. But thanks be to God, which giveth us the victory through our Lord Jesus Christ!" 1 Cor. xv. 55—57. And what a day of exulting gladness will that be, when, "the hope of the righteous" having been completed by the resurrection from the dead—the "multitude which no man can number shall stand before the throne and before the Lamb, clothed in white robes, and palms in their hands; and cry with a loud voice, saying, Salvation to our God which sit-

---

* Comp. chap. iii. 2, 16; ix. 11.

teth upon the throne, and unto the Lamb!" Rev. vii. 9, 10.
"*But*," on the contrary, and in contrast with the fulfilled
anticipations and perfected joys of the righteous, "*the expectation of the wicked shall perish.*" What a striking and
affecting counterpart to the statement in verse 24th—
"The fear of the wicked shall come upon him!" He has
his *fears;* they are realized:—he has his hopes; they are
frustrated and lost. The fears are well-founded; the hopes
delusive and vain. They are based and built on false and
deceitful views of himself and of God. They have no
foundation in truth. They are like the house built on the
sand, which may stand in the summer's sunshine and calm,
but gives way, with tremendous and utter downfall, before
the storm and the flood of winter. His "expectation
shall perish." He flattered himself with its stability;
but it was while it was untried:—in the end he is buried
in its ruins. "His hope is as the giving up of the ghost."
The vision that has deceived him,—the unreal phantom
that has cheated his eyes and allured his wandering steps
onward and onward to the gates of hell, shall vanish then
in "the blackness of darkness for ever!"—all his fears fulfilled; all his hopes for ever blasted!

The next verse may be taken in connexion with this, as
assigning a sufficient *cause* for the "hope of the righteous,"
being "gladness" in their end—"The way of the Lord
is strength to the upright: but destruction shall be to
the workers of iniquity." The connexion may not very
readily appear as the words stand in our translation. They
may be rendered—"*Strength to the upright, is the way of
the Lord;*" "*but destruction to the workers of iniquity.*"
Either rendering holds out the communication of divine
strength as the ground of the final perseverance of the righteous, and their happiness at last. It is the "*way* of the
Lord"—his usual mode of dealing with his people, to give
strength to them when they seek him, and thus "keep them
through faith unto salvation."* And the other part of "the

---

* Comp. Isa. xl. 28—31: Deut. xxxiii. 25.

way of the Lord" is, " destruction to the workers of iniquity."
" Evil shall not dwell with Him." As "the just God,"—
" a God of truth and without iniquity," this *must be* his way.
Under his holy and equitable administration, the righteous
and the wicked can never possibly *fare alike.*

The sentiment is still similar in verse 30. " The righteous
shall never be removed : but the wicked shall not inhabit the
earth."—The word "*removed,*" might be interpreted of his
confidence and security under the protection of Omnipotence.
But the contrast, or antithesis in the verse leads to a somewhat different interpretation. " The *earth* " should be
rendered " the *land.*" The reference in the words appears
to be to the promises made by Jehovah to his people, of continued and permanent possession, on condition of their
continued obedience; and his threatenings against them
on the ground of unbelief and rebellion. These promises
were made *to the righteous.* Canaan was the land of *promise.* It was obtained *by faith;* and "*by the obedience of
faith*" it continued to be held; and by *unbelief and disobedience* it was to be forfeited and lost.* Accordingly, the
various *removals* of Israel were for their failure in faith and
obedience,—for their unrighteousness and wickedness, as the
indication of a heart departing from the Lord. The language,
addressed to the people at large, always, of course, implies
God's regard to *the righteous* considered *individually,* and
the assurance of his blessing to *them.*

Even the present world the people of God enjoy better
than the wicked; inasmuch as they enjoy it with his blessing
and the assurance of his love, imparting to all its lawful possessions and enjoyments a zest and relish of which the men
of the world, even " when their corn and their wine are increased," know nothing. And then, " the land " shall be
inherited by them *for ever*—the " better country, even the
heavenly "—the " inheritance incorruptible, undefiled, and
that fadeth not away." And when they once set foot on the
inheritance above; when they once settle *there;* thence they

---

* Comp. Deut. ix. 4—6, with chap. xi. 8, 9, 26—28, and chap. xxix.
24—28.

shall never be removed.   They shall have it in everlasting
possession, by the charter, sealed with blood, and sure as the
word and oath of Him "with whom it is impossible to lie."
And *that* land "the wicked shall not inhabit."   No foot of
the "uncircumcised and the unclean" shall ever tread its
holy soil.   There shall be a full and final separation of the
vile from the precious.   Into the "holy city,"—the "city
which hath foundations, whose builder and maker is God,"
there "shall in nowise enter anything that defileth."   All
there shall be "holy and without blemish."   *That* land shall
never need to rest by the banishment of its inhabitants, that
it may enjoy its Sabbaths, which had been desecrated by
the ungodly and profane.   Its one universal and perpetual
Sabbath of holy rest shall never be disturbed; and it shall
be enjoyed alike by all the blessed inhabitants,—being, in
its character and in all its holy exercises, in full harmony with
the pure and delighted feelings of every individual of the
countless multitude of the redeemed.

We dwell not on the closing verses, as the sentiment they
contain is very similar to what has been repeatedly before us.
Let a single remark suffice.—While the tendency of all
that "the righteous" utter, from the "good treasure of the
heart," is to profit souls, and to "save them from death"—
the tendency, on the contrary, of the "corrupt communication"
that proceeds out of the mouth of the wicked,—of the words of
the "froward tongue" and the "perverse lips,"—is to spread
spiritual death;—every word bearing upon it a taint of evil
that carries pestilential infection to the heart.   O! that men
would but consider, not only the direct sin committed against
God by the utterance of evil, but the amount of moral mischief of which such utterance may prove the present and
ultimate occasion!   As by the slightest puncture, the *virus* of
putrefaction may find its way into the entire animal frame,
inflaming, swelling, fevering, mortifying, killing; so may the
virus of moral contamination and corruption be conveyed to
the soul by a single word, and effect its present disorder and
its final destruction; while, from that infected soul the contagion may spread to the injury and ruin of thousands.

LECTURE XXIII.

PROV. XI. 1—9.

" A false balance is abomination to the Lord: but a just weight is his delight. When pride cometh, then cometh shame: but with the lowly is wisdom. The integrity of the upright shall guide them: but the perverseness of transgressors shall destroy them. Riches profit not in the day of wrath: but righteousness delivereth from death. The righteousness of the perfect shall direct his way: but the wicked shall fall by his own wickedness. The righteousness of the upright shall deliver them: but transgressors shall be taken in their own naughtiness. When a wicked man dieth, his expectation shall perish: and the hope of unjust men perisheth. The righteous is delivered out of trouble, and the wicked cometh in his stead. An hypocrite with his mouth destroyeth his neighbour: but through knowledge shall the just be delivered."

IT is common for a *general sentiment* to be conveyed under a *limited form of expression;* for an individual case to be selected, to illustrate and enforce a universal principle. Thus it is in the first of these verses. The general affirmation is manifestly couched under a particular one, that *all unjust dealing* is " an abomination to the Lord;" while *all righteous dealing* is "his delight." The God of the Bible is—" the righteous Lord who loveth righteousness, and whose countenance doth behold the upright." And the pervading injunctions of his word are in harmony with this representation of his character. Under similar terms to those before us, the divine injunctions and prohibitions are frequent and strong,* and the violation of this maxim is one of the sins which we find complained of by the prophets, as amongst the causes of the divine judgments upon Israel.†

---

* See Lev. xix. 35, 36: Deut. xxv. 13—16: Prov. xvi. 11, &c.
† Hosea xii. 7: Amos viii. 4—6: Mic. vi. 10, 11, &c.

I speak to many who are *men of business.* Do not, pray, take the language literally, as if it had application only to such as, in their business, actually require the use of scales and weights? It involves the *principle* of *all* your mutual dealings. In all these, the eye of GOD is upon you.

Many are pleased at the *dexterity* with which they practise their deceptions. The fraud is undiscovered; and, being undiscovered, is *unfelt* by those on whom it is practised:—and what is never known and never felt, can be *no harm.* So *they* think. But God sees it; and He estimates the action on no such principle:—no; nor is it the principle on which you would estimate it, were you the party defrauded. You have no idea, in your own case, of admitting that what is not missed is not lost; or that the cleverness of the fraud is any palliation of it. You do not think the better of the merchant with his " balances of deceit," that the unfairness of the balance is ingeniously concealed. You do not regard it as a compensation for the property abstracted from your plundered house or warehouse, that the impression of your keys has been adroitly obtained, or the mode of entrance skilfully devised and expertly executed. You do not approve of the laws of ancient Sparta, which, to encourage cleverness and sleight of hand, rewarded instead of punishing the youthful thief who could steal without detection. Depend upon it, if you plume yourself on the dexterity with which you have contrived and executed a plan for cozening your neighbour, it will be no palliation with God, nor will any amount of such dexterity produce any abatement of His sentence of condemnation. It is the *moral principle,* or *want* of principle, in which the evil lies; and the very measure of thought and contrivance expended for the purpose of ensuring success in the contravention of God's law, instead of diminishing, will serve to aggravate your guilt in His sight. The " abomination " will be only the more loathsome.

Many are the subterfuges, many the quirks and evasions, to which men betake themselves, with a view to shelter their consciences and keep them easy in the practice of iniquity. And amongst others may be particularized the *commonness* of certain modes of deception and fraudulent dealing. Oh! say they, there is *no man in the line* by whom it is not more or less done; and if we do not conform to the custom, we shall be undersold by our neighbours, and may shut shop at once. Then, I reply, if you are Christians, *do so*. Run all risks, incur all losses, rather than offend God. What you do is not the less "abomination" to Him, that it is done by many as well as by you. That is only so much the more lamentable; and the stronger is the reason why Christians should, by their stern adherence to integrity, rebuke the prevalent practice, by acting as exceptions to it.—There are few departments, for instance, in which fraud is so little thought of, as when it is practised upon the *revenue of the country*. And yet there is nothing as to which the requisitions of the Bible are more peremptory, and which is more distinctly and strongly put under the regulation of a sensitive conscience. The difference between the man who cheats a single customer and the man who cheats the revenue is, that the former defrauds *one*, while the latter defrauds *millions*. Let not your question be, fellow-christians, What is *interest?* but, What is *duty?* not, What will *men* think? but, What will *God* think? Shun every approach to what you know, from His word, to be " an abomination " to Him; and practise unvaryingly, in defiance of human opinions and of all apprehended consequences, that in which He delights;—for of all evils the worst is God's displeasure, and of all blessings the richest is God's favour. The latter is cheaply purchased by the loss of every earthly good; nor is there any amount of such good that can be a compensation for the former. Let it be the sentiment of every mind, and the feeling of every heart, that one frown of God is enough to annihilate every kind and degree of benefit than can arise from transgression.

If there is anything in which the phrase an *honourable pride* might be used with propriety, it is the case now mentioned of unbending, uncompromising integrity of principle. But the very next verse teaches us that pride, in every form, must be denied—" When pride cometh, then cometh shame: but with the lowly is wisdom." The entire Bible,

from the beginning to the close, points against pride.   All that
is said in it of what man *is;* and all that is revealed of the
way of salvation, both as it regards the ground of the sinner's
hope, and as it regards the means of the believer's preservation to the end, has the same tendency—" to hide pride from
man,"—to " lay him low, and keep him there."   It is the
avowed design of the gospel, that " the lofty looks of man
should be humbled, and the haughtiness of man bowed
down, and that the Lord alone should be exalted."   Against
pride shafts are aimed at every turn.   God frowns upon
it; and shows it to be His purpose throughout to mortify
and humble it.   It is the pervading maxim of the Divine
word—" Every one that exalteth himself shall be abased."
In the end, pride *must* bring " shame."

Perhaps, however, the reference in the words before us,
may especially be to the influence of pride in our intercourse
with men.   And in this view of them, they are verified in
different ways.   For example—The manifestation of pride,—
of supercilious loftiness and self-sufficiency, strongly tempts
others to spy out defects, and to bring down the haughty
man from his imaginary elevation.   Every one takes a
pleasure in plucking at him, and leaving the laurel-wreath
which he has twined for his own brow, as bare of leaves as
possible; and thus to cover him with " shame."

Another way in which it tends to "shame" is, that it
leads him who is the subject of it to undertake, in the plenitude of his confident self-sufficiency, to fill stations for which
he is incompetent; by which means, he ere long exposes
himself to the derision or the pity of his fellows.   He
shortly finds himself in the position of those described in our
Lord's parable who " choose for themselves the highest seats,"
but in the end, abashed and crest-fallen, " begin with shame
to take the lowest rooms." *—That parable is a graphic commentary on the words before us.

On the contrary, "*with the lowly is wisdom.*"   In the
highest departments this is true.   The lowly, distrustful of

* Luke xiv. 7—11.

themselves, ask wisdom of God, who "giveth to all liberally
and upbraideth not." And wisely distrustful of their own
strength as well as knowledge, they receive strength from
above, and are "strong in the Lord." And moreover, the
lowly act otherwise than has been described, in *their* intercourse with *men*. They remember the words of the apostle,
"I say, through the grace given unto me, to every man
that is among you, not to think of himself more highly than
he ought to think; but to think soberly."* The man of
this character all are disposed to take by the hand—to respect,
to encourage, and to put forward.

I have recommended a principle of unbending rectitude,
as the principle which the God of truth and righteousness
approves. I may further recommend it, as *the best of all
casuists*,—our surest and most ready director in the right way.
Such is the spirit of the third verse—"The integrity of the
upright shall guide them: but the perverseness of transgressors shall destroy them."

Or even, in regard to "transgressors," suppose the contrary—so far as this life is concerned. Suppose them by their
well-contrived and well-covered arts to succeed and to accu-
mulate wealth—still, "Riches profit not in the day of wrath:
but righteousness delivereth from death."†

"The day of wrath" evidently means the day of judgment!‡ O my friends, what an affecting commentary will
the transactions of that day read to an assembled world
on the solemn question of our Lord,—"What is a man
profited, if he shall gain the whole world, and lose his own
soul?" Matt. xvi. 26.

The same general sentiment—of the superior advantages
of the righteous, both now and in the end, is expanded in the
next two verses—"The righteousness of the perfect shall direct
his way: but the wicked shall fall by his own wickedness.
The righteousness of the upright shall deliver them: but
transgressors shall be taken in their own naughtiness."

---

* Romans xii. 3.
† For further illustration of verses 3, 4, see chap. x. verses 2, 9, 15.
‡ See Rom. ii. 5.

"*The perfect*" are those whose hearts are *sincere*, and *undivided;* given up in their dominant principles and affections, decidedly and unreservedly, to God. They are the same with the *upright;* whose uprightness, as before shown, "directs their way"—*in* safety, and *to* safety; while the wicked, by their worldly and crafty devices, often involve *themselves* as well as others in mischief. And while, in their progress through this world, they are many a time ensnared in the meshes of their own arts of deceit, their feet are entangled in a snare from which, in the end, there is no deliverance—the "snare of the devil." By him they are "taken captive at his will;" and, having abandoned God, have their part with him and his angels. They "fall by their own wickedness"—fall beyond recovery. They are "*taken*"—taken finally and irretrievably, "in their own naughtiness." The frequent repetition of this truth should impress it on the memory and heart. Let it be indelibly impressed on *yours*. Nothing can be more certain than that lies, deceptions, breaches of promise, plans of double-dealing and artifice, however they may seem to prosper for a time, are the *sure road to ruin*. The man who has recourse to them is weaving the shroud for his reputation, and digging the grave for his interest here,—while he is fitting himself for destruction hereafter, "treasuring up wrath against the day of wrath."

The same strain of thought is still followed in verse seventh—"When a wicked man dieth, his expectation shall perish; and the hope of unjust men perisheth."*

There have been some who have questioned whether the doctrine of a future state was understood under the former dispensation. They have regarded that economy as to such an extent carnal, worldly, and temporary, as to have excluded from it all reference to that subject. I might show you, from many passages, the falsity of such a sentiment. In this verse we have *one* of them. Nothing can be clearer than that, were there not such a future state, the expecta-

---

* Comp. chap. x. 28.

tion and hope of righteous and wicked alike must perish to
gether, and that the very distinction so evidently made here
between the one and the other, proceeds upon the assumption of a state beyond the present. The maxim of wisdom
would otherwise be—"Let us eat and drink, for to-morrow
we die." Such expressions, having evident reference to expectations and hopes entertained *at the time of death*, clearly
evince that a future state was matter of full conviction with
Solomon himself, and that its sanctions were by no means
held back, but were pressed upon the people.

The next verse may be taken *by itself*, as expressing a
frequently occurring case—"The righteous is delivered out
of trouble, and the wicked cometh in his stead."

This was a thing which Solomon had often observed;
and which harmonized to such an extent with general observation as to have become *marked* and *striking*. The *general* state of things was *then* what it is now;* yet had it
been frequently noticed, how singularly good men had been,
by divine interposition, preserved from trouble, and delivered
out of it,—and especially when the trouble had arisen from
the conscientious exercise of principle; while the wicked,
especially if in any way they had been the authors of the
trouble, impending or suffered, have "come in their stead,"
and found their feet taken in their own snares. Thus was
it in the case of Mordecai and Haman; and thus in the
case of Daniel and his unprincipled accusers.

But the verse naturally connects with the preceding verses
to complete the *antithesis* between the righteous and the
wicked occurring so regularly throughout the passage. When
thus taken together, they may be considered as having reference to the same period—the period of *death*. "When a
wicked man *dieth*, his expectation shall perish; and the
hope of unjust men perisheth: the righteous," *when he
dieth*, "is delivered out of trouble, and the wicked cometh
in his stead." This will express the same sentiment as that
of the prophet, "The righteous perisheth, and no man layeth

* Eccl. ix. 1—3.

it to heart: and merciful men are taken away, none considering that the righteous is taken away from the evil to come. He shall enter into peace: they shall rest in their beds, each one walking in his uprightness," Isa. lvii. 1, 2. And while *he* is thus "taken away," the wicked, his enemy, succeeds to the trouble of which that enemy had been the cause; or, if not to it, to some other. Thus has it many a time been with blood-thirsty persecutors, when they have succeeded in their vindictive plots of death against God's servants. They have dismissed the saint from his sins and sorrows; but have themselves become the victims of divine visitation. Thus it was with Herod. Thus it was with the persecuting Jews, who "both killed the Lord Jesus and their own prophets," and pursued with the same unrelenting malignity the apostles of the Lamb.

But of true religion there is the semblance as well as the reality: and the semblance is worse than worthless. It avails not the professor himself, and is injurious to others:—verse 9. "An hypocrite with his mouth destroyeth his neighbour: but through knowledge shall the just be delivered."

This verse, indeed, may be understood with a reference to all insincere professions of friendship and good intentions—to all insinuating and flattering pretensions, adopted for the purpose of effecting a particular end. How many are there, who for objects of their own deceive others; no matter what the result may be to the deceived, provided the deceiver but accomplishes his selfish aim:—though even that is frequently lost to the hypocrite, injuring and destroying both his neighbour and himself,—the flattered and the flatterer alike suffering. In religion, the hypocrite has a purpose. His religion is not real. He assumes the cloak to cover some secret design. The verse itself suggests the design—*the undermining of the principles of others.* He makes great pretensions. He insinuates himself into confidence. He gets a character. The confidence increasing, he becomes by degrees more and more bold, till, by slow steps, he unsettles the principles, shakes the faith, dissipates the seriousness, and ruins the souls of others. Moreover, hypocrites are awful stumbling-blocks. Full many has the detection of their true character hardened in sin and worldliness, and established in infidelity. Full many have they thus "destroyed."*

"*But by knowledge shall the just be delivered.*"—By general knowledge, the result of experience, and observation of character, and natural and acquired sagacity,—the just man is placed on his guard against false and flattering professions, and is enabled to detect and expose them, and to shun the consequences. And still further, by the knowledge of God's word, he is enabled to discern the symptoms of false professions of religion, and so to avoid the insinuations of the religious deceiver. He repels by his knowledge the assaults of "the wicked one," and of his crafty and malignant emissaries; as the Lord Jesus foiled Satan by the sword of the Spirit.

Observe in conclusion—

1. None can condemn hypocrisy more severely than the Bible itself does. What character is there that is branded in this Book with a broader and deeper brand of divine reprobation? But the same Bible which condemns and reprobates hypocrisy, recommends godliness, and affirms and urges its necessity. My friends, all would be well, if, agreeing with the Bible in the one sentiment, you agreed with it also in the other. The Bible is consistent. It proportions the vehemence of its reprobation of hypocrisy to its right estimate of the thing that is desecrated and dishonoured by the false assumption of it. Oh! that you would but show the genuineness of your hatred of hypocrisy by your admiration and love, your adoption and practice of the reality of which it is the semblance—TRUE RELIGION!

2. Fellow-Christians, see to it, that you let the world have no such cause of offence as the world are so disposed to find. Be honest. Be upright. Be consistent. "Give no occasion to the adversary to speak reproachfully." "Be sincere and without offence until the day of Christ!"

* The *character* of the hypocrite is given, Matt. vii. 15: 2 Cor. xi. 13—15. The tendency of it may be illustrated from such cases as that of the *lying prophet* in 1 Kings xiii. 18, &c.; xxii. 6, &c.

LECTURE XXIV.

———◆———

Prov. xi. 10—17.

"When it goeth well with the righteous, the city rejoiceth: and when the wicked perish, there is shouting. By the blessing of the upright the city is exalted: but it is overthrown by the mouth of the wicked. He that is void of wisdom despiseth his neighbour: but a man of understanding holdeth his peace. A talebearer revealeth secrets: but he that is of a faithful spirit concealeth the matter. Where no counsel is, the people fall: but in the multitude of counsellors there is safety. He that is surety for a stranger shall smart for it: and he that hateth suretiship is sure. A gracious woman retaineth honour: and strong men retain riches. The merciful man doeth good to his own soul: but he that is cruel troubleth his own flesh."

THE first of these verses states *a fact*. The fact is, that the life, the safety, the well-being of righteous rulers,—of men in high station and of extensive influence, actuated by the principles of justice and goodness,—are much set by on the part of the members of a community; that the general wish is for their preservation in life and office; and that their deliverance from any danger occasions congratulation and joy; while, on the contrary, "*when the wicked perish,*"—when unprincipled men, selfish, unjust, and cruel oppressors, are cast down from their "high estate,"—even though it should be by sudden and violent death,—instead of grief, there is gladness; instead of wailing, "there is shouting." He "departs without being desired;" and the people, when the fear that before restrained them is removed, speak out their feelings. Delivered from the malaria of despotic oppression, they breathe freely, and quickly discover in each other's minds at once the unanimity of hatred, and the unanimity of satisfaction.

For this fact the reason is assigned in next verse—" By the blessing of the upright the city is exalted: but it is overthrown by the mouth of the wicked."

Upright men—men of sound principle, alive to the rights and solicitous for the happiness of all over whom their power or influence extends, and above all, men animated by the highest of all principles, the fear of God,—are an eminent blessing to a community. By their means " *the city is exalted;*"—the commonwealth advanced and elevated in character, in honour, and in general prosperity; and especially in the " righteousness that exalteth a nation." The rule of such men is in itself an inestimable benefit. Their prayers, their example, their pious efforts, their self-denying devotedness to the public good, all bring down the blessing of Heaven. They are men for whom, on principles of personal attachment and of public-spirited patriotism, not a few might even " dare to die."

On the contrary, " *by their mouth*"—that is, by their unsound counsels, their pernicious maxims, their false sentiments, and, it may be, their lewd, irreligious, blasphemous talk,—" the wicked" corrupt the public mind and morals, and subvert the true glory and the true prosperity of a country. This accords with the anticipations of reason, and with the general recorded experience of mankind. The decline and fall of states have to be traced, in most instances, to the misgovernment of unprincipled men.

Let it be our constant and earnest prayer for our country, that right principle may direct her councils, supreme and subordinate, as the surest means, under the blessing of God, of elevating her character, prolonging her existence, and augmenting her prosperity!

Verse 12. " He that is void of wisdom despiseth his neighbour: but a man of understanding holdeth his peace." From the antithesis in the verse it is evident, that the word " *despiseth* " is not to be understood of *secret* and *silent* contempt, but of contempt *expressed*, whether in words, in actions, or in looks. The man who is destitute of wisdom, or sound discretion, ridicules and exposes his neighbour, for every little failing he happens to discover in him.   In this he not only violates "the royal law," but acts unwisely on his own account.   The man of prudence—the wise man, "holdeth his peace."   He considers, in the first place, that *every one* has his failings, of which, from the power of custom, he may not be sensible; and that *he*, therefore, may have *his*,—notorious enough to others, though unperceived by himself: and under this impression, he is tender toward others from a sense of his own defects and his liability to more.   He is further aware, that by the expression or manifestation of scorn, he may bring upon himself odium and resentment, and even serious mischief; or at any rate, were he indulging in this satirical and contemptuous disposition, render himself universally disagreeable, and reap, as his merited reward, a studied exclusion from the social circle. No man can be a more unpleasant member of society, in the private walks of life especially, (of which free and confidential familiarity is the very zest) than he who makes it his business to spy out failings, to detect and fasten upon every thing that is ridiculous or ludicrous in the appearance, the motions, the character, or the manners of all with whom he comes into contact, and to expose it.   "The man of understanding"—the man who has a proper regard for his own comfort and enjoyment, who duly appreciates the principle of "the golden rule," and considers how large an amount of the social happiness of mankind arises from things that are in themselves of minor importance,—even when the failings of others do not escape his notice, but may be such as strongly to tempt the propensity to exposure—will lay a restraint upon himself, and "*hold his peace.*"

This is *one* case, then, in which *silence* is *wisdom*.   It does not stand alone.   There follows another:—verse 13. "A talebearer revealeth secrets: but he that is of a faithful spirit concealeth the matter."

But, while in this case there is wisdom, there is *more*. There is the principle of *fidelity*.   The "*talebearer*" is at once one of the most odious and most mischievous of characters; —the man with whom no secret is safe; who cannot be at ease, till he has it out; who goes from one to another, and from party to party, big with it, and watching his opportunity to introduce it appropriately; and when no such opportunity offers, unable to contain himself any longer, and forcing it in, "in season or out of season."

The propensity to reveal secrets—to a certain degree common to all, though in some discovering its unsubdued power by an unrestrained indulgence—is imputable to different causes. In the first place, we are ever apt to be vain of knowing what others are ignorant of;—but this of course cannot be known to others, and can procure no gratification to this vanity, without disclosure. Then, further, we are equally apt to be vain of the confidence reposed in us—of our having been made the confidants of others,—and especially when these are persons of any name and notoriety. This is a very self-contradictory vanity; for it is impossible to give indulgence to the propensity inspired by it, without, in the very act of doing so, showing that the confidence placed in us, and on which we are pluming ourselves, has been *misplaced*. The very revealing of the secret is an avowal that we should not have been trusted, and a warning against trusting us again.

There are various ways of acting the "talebearer." There is that of *open blabbing.* And this, as it is the simplest, is, in truth, the least dangerous. The character becomes immediately known; and all who have secrets which they *really wish kept* will take care to withhold them from him.

There is next that of *confidential communication.* The secret-holder affects to look this way and that, to ascertain that no one is within hearing; and then, with many whispered *doubts* whether he is doing right, and whispered *no-doubts* that he is perfectly safe with the dear friend to whom he speaks, imparts it in a breath that enters only his solitary ear, as a thing received in the profoundest secrecy, and not, on any account whatever, to go further, to be kept still as the grave;—thus setting the example of broken confidence as the encouragement and inducement to keep it! Then he goes, and finds out some other dear friend, with whom the same scene is repeated.

There is that also of *sly insinuation.* The person who has the secret neither openly blabs it, nor confidently whispers it, but throws out hints of his having it—allusions more or less remote to its nature,—by which curiosity is awakened, inquiry stimulated, and the thing ultimately brought to light; while he who threw out the leading notices plumes himself on his having escaped the imputation of being a talebearer. The story was not of his telling! Now these, and whatever others there may be, *are all bad;* and the greater the amount of pretension and hypocrisy, so much the worse.

A *"faithful spirit"* is what all should cultivate, and maintain at whatever risk or cost. But all should be cautious. It is very wrong, generally speaking, to come under an obligation to secrecy, without knowing what it is that is about to be imparted.* We may thus bring ourselves into a snare, entrammelling our consciences; for the secret may be something which *ought not* to be concealed. It may involve the interests of others; it may involve the cause of religion and the honour of God. Beware, then, of rashly *receiving* secrets. It cannot be the duty of any man to *keep* a secret which he has thus ignorantly and indiscreetly pledged himself to keep, on his discovering what it is, and what are its bearings and results. Yet it may cost him a severe struggle to bring himself to break his word. To keep a secret of the description in question, however, would evidently be to add a greater sin to a less;—to add to the sin of rashly committing ourselves, the further and heavier sin of allowing others to suffer undeservedly by our silence, or the interests and honour of religion to be compromised and injured. And again, if a man is sensible of the strength either of his propensity to reveal what he knows, or of the temptations to discovery to which he has the prospect of being exposed, let him at once decline being the confidential depositary of *any* secrets. As for the known "talebearer," the hunter after secrets, of

* Hence one strong objection on the part of Christians to the system of *Free-masonry,* which withholds its secrets till those who seek initiation take solemn oath *never* to reveal them.

which he immediately, and of previous purpose, manifests his unworthiness of having intrusted to him—his desert is to be shunned and detested, to be hissed and hooted out of society.

Many things in this Book—as from Solomon's own official station might have been anticipated—have an immediate relation to RULERS. Generally, however, the principles of what is said relative to *them*, are capable of easy transference, and sufficiently pointed application to ordinary life. Thus—

Verse 14. " Where no counsel is, the people fall: but in the multitude of counsellors there is safety." It is obvious enough that there is something here to be understood. The *counsel* that keeps the people from ruin must be *wise and good;* and when given, it must be taken and followed. There may be no lack of counsel; but it may be counsel that " causeth to err from the way of understanding;" and both ruler and people would have been better without it. But the case supposed, appears to be that of a self-willed, self-sufficient, head-strong ruler, who glories in his power; who determines to wield the rod of that power in his own way, and who plays the hasty, jealous, resolute, sensitive, and vindictive tyrant; who disdains to call in counsel, or who does it only for the pleasure of showing his superiority to it by setting it at nought. I conceive the phrase " *where no counsel is* " to be intended to convey not a little of the character of him by whom it is declined or disregarded. He is a character under whose rule " the people fall." We have an example of such a character—foolish, high-minded, insolent—in Solomon's own successor *Rehoboam.*

And yet, at the same time, in his case we are taught the necessity of understanding all such maxims as maxims that admit of exceptions. Rehoboam *did* take counsel;—and his counsellors were not few. Had they been *fewer*, there would, in that instance, have been *more safety.* Had he stopped with the " *old men* who had stood before David his father," all would have been well.—But in the verse before us—" *the multitude of counsellors* " stands contrasted with " *no counsel;* " and the sentiment is in accordance with reason and with experience. The character intended is that of one who, instead of, in his own self-sufficiency, refusing counsel, betakes himself, especially in cases of difficulty, to different judgments; compares their respective decisions, and adopts, after due deliberation, what appears to recommend itself as the best, or frames a measure from the hints and dictates of the whole.   Still it is implied that the counsellors be selected, as men of understanding, prudence, and principle.   " In the multitude of counsellors," unless they are suitable characters,—not a multitude taken capriciously and at random, or under the influence of any improper disposition,—there might be distraction and hazard rather than guidance and security.—How much better would it have been for Ahab, had he taken for his sole counsellor Micaiah the son of Imlah,

> ————— "faithful found
> Among the faithless—faithful only he,"

—than it was when he preferred the four hundred prophets of Baal! " The multitude of counsellors " was, in that case, his destruction.

The maxim, therefore, is *general*.   It affirms the danger of solitary self-sufficiency, and the safety of deliberate and, in proportion to the complexity and difficulty of each case, and the nature and amount of its consequences, of extensive and diversified consultation.   And the principle applies to *all* as well as to rulers.   Consultation is right in regard to what may materially affect *our own* interests.   It is specially incumbent when the interests of others, whether as to character, or property, or personal and domestic comfort, are implicated.   These are never to be sported with—never to be treated with hasty indifference; and a truly right-hearted man will be anxious to avoid having on his conscience the painful reflection, that others should have suffered through any over-confidence on his part in his own judgment.

The *fifteenth* verse we had occasion to take in formerly, in connexion with a previous passage, on which the general principles regarding suretiship were discussed;—the desirableness and even duty of shunning it; the impropriety and cruelty of urging it; and the special instances in which it might, and even ought, to be complied with.*

In verse sixteenth, agreeably to a Hebrew idiom far from uncommon, a *comparison* is manifestly designed :—"*As strong men retain riches, so doth a gracious woman retain honour.*" The immediate allusion probably is to *spoil taken in battle.* The valiant and powerful, by whose prowess and might it has been gained, defend their booty—their wealth —against all aggressors and plunderers. They will not suffer it to be touched. They watch it with an eye of fire and an arm of strength. And thus is it as to the honour of a virtuous and pious woman. She holds it dearer than the riches of the wealthy; dearer than the prey of the warrior, which not its own value merely but the point of honour renders precious in his eyes, and the object of vigilant sensitiveness; dearer than life itself. She holds it as a jewel of inestimable value, maintaining it in unsullied purity; repels, with dignified and indignant determination—with the appalling firmness of sensitive and offended principle, indicated by an eye that flashes with the quickness of lightning, and a cheek that flushes with the vehemence of unutterable scorn—every act, or word, or look, that presumes on a freedom, or dares a reflection on her untainted fame.

True religion has ever been associated with assigning to the female portion of the community their due estimation, and rank, and influence in society. It was so under Judaism; it is so still more under Christianity. If Christian women would but contrast their situation, as daughters, wives, and mothers, with that of females under any of the forms of idolatry and false religion, they could not but be thankful for the amount of "*honour*" they have of which to be jealous; and thankful for the religion to which they are indebted for the treasure. And as the character of human society depends to so very great a degree on the illumination, the dignity, the purity, and the influence of the female mind,—I cannot avoid again, in "words that burn," or at least that utter the

---

* See Lect. on chap. vi. 1—5.

indignation of a burning heart, denounce that brutal and brutifying system, which has presumed of late, with an unblushing effrontery, to offer itself to the acceptance of an enlightened and civilized and Christian community, and which, by degrading the dignity, tainting the purity, and quenching the vestal flame of womanhood, would more than annihilate its salutary influence; and, inflicting on human society a corresponding degradation, assimilate it, in the extinction of all its holiest and happiest ties, to the promiscuous herding of the beasts that perish. The subject is one on which, I freely own, I cannot speak with patience. When I think of the feature of the system of *Socialism* to which I have just adverted, independently of its atheism, its fatalism, and its anarchy, I again denounce it as meriting alike the contempt of every person of understanding, and the abhorrence of every person of principle.

Verse 17. "The merciful man doeth good to his own soul: but he that is cruel troubleth his own flesh." There are two descriptions of mercy. There is mercy to *sufferers*, and mercy to *offenders*. Mercy to sufferers is the disposition to *relieve;* mercy to offenders is the disposition to *forgive.* The two are infinitely united in God. Under his government all sufferers are offenders. It is only *as* offenders that they are sufferers; and when he pardons the offence, he cancels the sentence to suffering. And in every good man the two are united. They should, indeed, be regarded as one principle, operating in different departments.

Now, "the merciful man," whether considered in the one light or in the other,—in exercising forgiveness or in relieving distress—"*doeth good to his own soul:*" he effectually consults his own interests. He does so, even for present enjoyment; for in the exercise of the generous and kindly affections there is a genuine and exquisite happiness. The divine sentiment of the Saviour,—"It is more blessed to give than to receive," has its full application here. Jesus himself, above all that ever lived on earth, experienced its truth. He "delighted in mercy." He came from above on an errand of mercy. The divine authority of that errand of mercy he proved by innumerable works of mercy, diffusing around him an incalculable amount of blessing. His heart melted over human suffering; and he "went about doing good." "The merciful man" participates in this blessedness of the Son of God!

"The merciful man," moreover, procures favour with his fellow-men;—he "makes himself friends of the mammon of unrighteousness;" he causes society to feel an interest in him,—to regard and treat him as its friend and benefactor. This is eminently gratifying and pleasing;—to know that in the hearts of fellow-men our names are associated with affection and blessing, and that when we "fail," there will be some ready to welcome us into "everlasting habitations," who had been made friends by our kindness during their sojourn in the wilderness.

But above all, the mercy of the merciful is associated with the enjoyment of the favour and blessing of God.—"Blessed are the merciful, for they shall obtain mercy." Thus in the most emphatic sense, "the merciful man doeth good to his own soul." With regard to the *un*merciful it is in every way the reverse: "The cruel *troubleth his own flesh*." He ensures his own wretchedness. He stirs up resentment, instead of conciliating favour; so that on every hand, in every face, he sees an enemy, from whom, on his own account or on account of others, he dreads the fulfilment of the Saviour's maxim—"With what measure ye mete it shall be measured to you again." How can he be happy? There is *un*happiness in his very passions. The opposite of the character of God, they cannot but be associated with misery. They are the counterpart of his who was "a murderer from the beginning." And as likeness to God in mercy is joined with likeness to God in blessedness; so likeness to the devil in malignity is joined with likeness to the devil in misery and ruin. "He shall have judgment without mercy who hath showed no mercy."*

* See Matth. xviii. 21—33.

LECTURE XXV.

Prov. xi. 18—23.

"The wicked worketh a deceitful work: but to him that soweth righteousness shall be a sure reward. As righteousness tendeth to life: so he that pursueth evil pursueth it to his own death. They that are of a froward heart are abomination to the Lord: but such as are upright in their way are his delight. Though hand join in hand, the wicked shall not be unpunished: but the seed of the righteous shall be delivered. As a jewel of gold in a swine's snout, so is a fair woman which is without discretion. The desire of the righteous is only good: but the expectation of the wicked is wrath."

The expression in the first of these verses, "a *deceitful work*," does not mean a work of deceit practised by the wicked upon *others*, but a work *deceitful to himself*. By some the phrase is rendered "an *unprofitable* work," which, in point of effect, is much the same; *unprofitable* meaning, obviously, the reverse of that which he himself anticipates: hence "*deceitful*." As to present happiness, his course proves so; for even amid wealth, should he acquire it, and the temporal honours and earthly benefits which wealth brings with it, he still feels the truth of *His* words who never uttered aught but what was in accordance with fact—" A man's life consisteth not in the abundance of the things which he possesseth," Luke xii. 15. And if he looks for anything else in the end than the final ruin of all to which he had trusted, he will find himself still more *deceived*,—his fondest hopes blasted for eternity! Although it was not all truth that was spoken by Job's three friends, and though even of what *was* true the principle and motive were wrong; yet much of what was true they *did* speak; and their descriptions are at

times very forcible and striking. Such is that of Bildad
the Shuhite, "Can the rush grow up without mire? can
the flag grow without water? Whilst it is yet in his
greenness, and not cut down, it withereth before any other
herb. So are the paths of all that forget God; and the
hypocrite's hope shall perish: whose hope shall be cut off,
and whose trust shall be a spider's web," Job viii. 11—14.
And the apostle Paul represents the connexion between wickedness and final destruction as of the same certainty with that
between the seed and the harvest—"Whatsoever a man
soweth, that shall he also reap. For he that soweth to his
flesh shall of the flesh reap corruption; but he that soweth
to the Spirit shall of the Spirit reap life everlasting," Gal.
vi. 7, 8. The connexion is equally sure on *both* sides of the
alternative. The reaping must be according to the sowing.
He who, with the hand of faith, "*sows righteousness*"—
sows the seeds of spiritual obedience—shall, as his "*sure
reward,*" reap *life;* while he who scatters in this world
the seeds of earthly-mindedness and sin shall reap, as *his*
"sure reward," in the world to come, a harvest of *death.*
This is a law of the moral world as infallible in its operation as any law of the physical world.

The same general thought is continued in verse 19. "As
righteousness tendeth to life: so he that pursueth evil pursueth it to his own death."

The "sure reward" in the preceding verse is "*life*" in
this: and as that reward is *sure* in the one case, the "*deceitfulness* of the wicked's work" lies in its effecting "death" as
its result, instead of "life." He who "*pursueth evil*" may
overtake it, and may boast himself in the success of his
pursuit. But the very evil that he overtakes shall slay him.
It is as if a man were to pursue a serpent, captivated by
the beauty of its appearance in its shifting and glistering
hues, but ignorant of the venom of its sting or its fang, and,
in the act of laying hold of it, were to receive the deadly
wound. Death treads on the very heels of the man who
"pursueth evil;" and when *he* overtakes the evil, Death
overtakes *him.* And in the next verse we have the reason

why "*life*" is attached to "*righteousness*," and "*death*" to "*evil.*" It is, that God, from the holiness of his nature, infinitely loves the one, and infinitely hates the other. "They that are of a froward heart are abomination to the Lord: but such as are upright in their way are his delight." Many a time, and in various and striking ways, has God given testimony to the truth of this declaration, but no-where and at no time was it so impressively displayed, as in the deeply awful scenes of Gethsemane and Calvary. On the cross it was written in blood—the blood of His own Son!

And while God's hatred of sin is infinite, his determina-tion to punish it is immutable, and his power on the part of sinners irresistible, verse 21. "Though hand join in hand, the wicked shall not be unpunished: but the seed of the righteous shall be delivered."

The terms "*though*" and "*join*" are supplementary. The words stand literally—"Hand in hand the wicked shall not be unpunished." It is said that no fewer than *sixteen* in-terpretations have been given of the words; and, as not seldom happens, the most *common* seems to be by far the most *natural*. "*Hand in hand*" is the emblem of union; of united power; of pledged combination:—and the senti-ment seems to be, as expressed in our authorised version, that sinners, combining their counsel and their power,— encouraging one another in evil,—braving the "terrors of the Lord,"—jointly laughing away their fears, and perpe-trating evil with a high and determined hand, shall not be the more secure from the penal consequences of their sins. "There is no wisdom, nor understanding, nor counsel," no, nor might, whether personal or combined, "against the Lord." They may combine successfully against human au-thority and vigilance, and may successfully resist the power of an earthly government; but if God be against them, escape they cannot.

To the counterpart of the sentiment in the previous verses an addition is made in the second clause of this. It is not said merely "*the righteous*," but "*the seed of the righteous*

I.   T

shall be delivered." This implies the divine favour and
blessing to the righteous themselves in the first instance :—
and then there is a regard to "the seed" for their sakes. Their
offspring have many a time been regarded and kept from
evil *on their account.* We see in the divine conduct, at
times, the principle operating which David expressed when
he said, "Is there yet any that is left of the house of Saul,
that I may show him kindness for Jonathan's sake?"
2 Sam. ix. 1. Thus it was in the case of Noah. Thus it
was in the case of Lot. Thus it was of old, and thus it
is still, in the case of Abraham, Isaac, and Jacob, whose
posterity, even in the midst of their continued unbelief and
rebellion, are "beloved for the fathers' sakes." The promise of the covenant to Abraham was—"I will be a God
to thee, and to thy seed after thee in their generations;" in
which promise, although it related to the spiritual seed,
there was evidently a *primary* reference to the natural offspring, among whom, both in the outset and at the end, the
spiritual children and their appropriate blessing were to be
found. "Salvation was of the Jews;" and it was "*to* the
Jews first." And among the proofs that God "had *not*
cast away his people," Paul says, "For I also am an Israelite, of the seed of Abraham, of the tribe of Benjamin."

The promise of the covenant remains.* But "let not the
seed of the righteous"—the children of the godly—deceive
themselves. God may act kindly and mercifully towards them
for their parents' sakes :—they may, on their account, enjoy
many blessings, and be dealt with in much patience and long-
suffering. But let them not fancy they can be *saved* in
virtue of any connexion whatever, even with the very best
of men,—the holiest saints that ever lived. No, my young
friends. If you do not make a right use yourselves of the
privileges with which God is pleased to favour you—no
such relation can give you safety in the end. Your advantages will only aggravate your guilt and your condemnation.
Your godly parents shall have their place on the right hand

---

* Psalm ciii. 13—18, and Psalm cxii. 1, 2.

of the Judge, while—-O heart-rending thought!—heart rending to both parent and child!—severed from them, you shall find your station on the left, and be banished, not from them only, but from the God of light and love, the source of all the happiness in the universe, for ever.   O join heart and hand with your parents in the love and service of God; and a double blessing will rest upon you for their sakes.

In the idiom of the Hebrew and of other Eastern languages, a comparison was sometimes expressed by the simple juxtaposition of the things intended to be compared.   Thus it is in the next verse—"As a jewel of gold in a swine's snout, so is a fair woman which is without discretion."

The "*as*" and the "*so is*" are supplementary.   The original stands thus:—"A jewel of gold in a swine's snout—a fair woman who is without discretion."—I doubt not, you may find expositors by whom this simile will be traced out in not a few ingenious and some far-fetched points of resemblance.   This, however, is more a display of ingenuity than of wisdom.   Obviously the great general idea intended to be conveyed by it, is that of *offensive and disgusting incongruity*.   Nose-jewels, sometimes very elegant and costly, were, as they are still, worn by females as a part of Eastern finery.   They are mentioned among the ornaments of the vain and wanton daughters of Zion, for whose light and ungodly walk the judgments of God were denounced, in Jehovah's name, by the prophet.   Nothing can well be more expressive than the simile, when understood as the image of *incongruity*.   "*Discretion*" must here be understood in its largest and best sense; not of mere *worldly prudence*,—though even in that or any other restricted sense, there would be truth in the comparison,—but of true feminine propriety, both of sentiment and feeling, and deportment, springing from and guided by a pious and well-ordered mind.

A nose-jewel in a swine's snout is *ridiculously out of place*, the subject of merriment and laughter.   And is it not thus with *beauty without discretion?*   The features may be admired; but the words and acts of imbecility, absurdity, and folly expose their possessor to the titter and the mirth mingled in some bosoms with pity, but in more with scorn, of the company,—and are many a time enjoyed afterwards as the topics of jest, and sarcasm, and scandal. But this is not all. The nose-jewel in the swine's snout,—as it alters not the nature of the animal nor abates its propensities to filthiness, must be for ever raking amidst mud and gar- bage and all manner of pollution. And thus beauty without discretion—unguided by the firmness of principle or any correct and consistent sense of propriety—is ever liable to be degraded by the artful designs of flattery, to serve, by its own degradation, the basest and most unworthy purposes.

We cannot, if we are ourselves right-minded,—if we have even good sense, apart from piety,—admire such beauty. It hardly deserves the name. True loveliness consists not in the mere exquisite symmetry of features. It cannot exist without *expression*. To constitute true beauty, the counte-- nance must be the index of the mind and the heart—of what is intellectual and what is amiable. The very finest and best-turned assortment of features can inspire no com- placency, no admiration, if there looks out from them, or even looks in them, the expression of unlovely passions,—of pride, of impiety, of vanity, of cruelty, of revenge. The in- congruous unseemliness of such expression in such features, makes us turn away with loathing, instead of hanging on the countenance with admiration and love.

And the woman here described—the mindless, heartless, senseless beauty (if we *may* use terms so self-contradictory) becomes one of the most pitiable objects in nature, when the flower fades; when the bloom departs and the wrinkles ap- pear; when the food of her vanity, and the source of her attraction, such as it was, is gone; when admiring fools cease to flatter, and to her own quenched eye and fretted spirit the mirror too faithfully reveals the cause. Whether the want of discretion be considered as meaning silliness, empti- ness, an unfurnished mind,—in which case there are no in- ward resources of enjoyment when what was merely outward is gone; or whether it be understood of the absence and violation of propriety and feminine seemliness,—in which case there is the forfeiture of all esteem, and the substitution of unmingled contempt—unmingled unless with pity,—and the consequent absence of all that can impart solid satisfaction in the intercourse of others. In either case, there is not a more wretched being than a *faded beauty;* whose place, when thus unceremoniously thrown aside, others come forward to fill, awakening the spirit of heart-consuming envy—the "rottenness of the bones." O my female auditors, seek the beauties of the mind, and heart, and character; and especially those of true piety. These will never fade; but will increase in attraction to the end. These will ensure esteem, respectability, and comfort, when encroaching age has defaced the outward charms of youth. Such a character possesses within itself resources of enjoyment, and will command the interest of affectionate regard, whether in single or in wedded life. Above all remember— "favour is deceitful and beauty vain; but the woman that feareth the Lord, she shall be praised."

The 23d verse is capable of *two* meanings:—1. It may refer to the *matter* of the desires cherished, respectively, by the righteous and the wicked. "The desire of the righteous," *for others*, "is only good." They cherish the principle of benevolence. They delight in seeing all around them happy. This is part of the character of the good man, that he wishes well to all—evil to none, not even to his enemies. Nor is he satisfied with desiring good. He shows the sincerity of the desire in "*doing* good to all as he has opportunity." On the contrary, "the expectation of the wicked is *wrath*"—or, as those who take this view of the passage understand the word,—*misfortune, disappointment.* These are what he seeks, waits, longs for in regard to others, and enjoys when they come upon them.

2. It may refer to the *issue* of their respective desires and expectations. The desires of the one—of "the righteous," terminating in the possession of *good*, only good; and good infinitely surpassing all that those desires could take in or anticipate; while the expectation of the other, his vain and groundless expectation, issues in *wrath*—in the fearful

effects of the anger of God, incomparably exceeding all that his apprehensions could forebode, and in spite of all his self-flattering hopes and fond delusions.

We close with two reflections :—

1. True honour lies, not in *condition*, but in *character*. This is the maxim of wisdom. " Better is the poor that walketh in his integrity, than he that is perverse in his ways, though he be rich." One of our poets has expressed the same sentiment thus—

" Honour and shame from no condition rise ;
    Act well your part—there all the honour lies."

But O do not forget, that *character* must be estimated on Bible principles. All that, in the sight of God, is truly good, must have its basis in TRUE RELIGION.

2. Let sinners beware of the danger and the inevitable result of fighting against God ! " He is wise in heart, and mighty in strength; who hath hardened himself against Him, and hath prospered ?" What fearful odds—the creature against the Creator !—the sinner against his rightful Judge !—the arm of flesh against the arm of omnipotence ! "Hand in hand, the wicked shall not be unpunished." Though they could league all creation with them in the conspiracy and rebellion, how powerless the combination ! " He that sitteth in the heavens should laugh ; the Lord should have them in derision. He should speak unto them in his wrath, and vex them in his hot displeasure." Companions in sin shall be companions in banishment and in suffering. " Forsake the foolish, then, and live." Choose another fellowship. Give your hand to God's people, giving your heart to God himself. " Hand in hand" with them in God's service here, you shall be one with them in the enjoyment of His love and blessing hereafter. This is the only fellowship that can end well. All the people of God, with one heart and one soul, concur in saying to you—" Come with us, and we will do you good; for the Lord hath spoken good concerning Israel."

LECTURE XXVI.

———◆———

Prov. xi. 24—31.

" There is that scattereth, and yet increaseth; and there is that withholdeth more than is meet, but it tendeth to poverty. The liberal soul shall be made fat; and he that watereth shall be watered also himself. He that withholdeth corn, the people shall curse him: but blessing shall be upon the head of him that selleth it. He that diligently seeketh good procureth favour: but he that seeketh mischief, it shall come unto him. He that trusteth in his riches shall fall: but the righteous shall flourish as a branch. He that troubleth his own house shall inherit the wind: and the fool shall be servant to the wise of heart. The fruit of the righteous is a tree of life; and he that winneth souls is wise. Behold, the righteous shall be recompensed in the earth: much more the wicked and the sinner."

THE farmer who is desirous to have an abundant harvest, must not sow his seed with a sparing and niggardly hand. A thin sowing must of necessity produce a scanty crop. Now, according to the representations of the word of God, that which is the case in nature, in the physical world, is the case also in regard to the use which a man makes of the means of doing good which providence commits to his care, in regard to the virtue of *liberality*, or *practical charity.*

Such is the general sentiment in the first two verses of this passage; and the sentiment is in harmony with the statements of the New Testament on the same subject.*

The fact which Solomon states is, that there is such a thing—nay, that it is frequent and reasonably to be expected, —as *gaining* by *giving;* as *augmenting* substance by its *free distribution.*

* 2 Cor. ix. 6.

The fact has its origin in the promised smile and blessing
of the Lord on the labours and the pursuits of the man of
diffusive benevolence.   That man, in the use he makes of
his means, resembles the Divine Being himself, the universal
Giver; and he acts in conformity to His will and purpose in
the bestowment of His benefits.   When He fills the clouds
with rain, it is that they may " empty themselves upon the
earth," " that it may give seed to the sower and bread to the
eater."   So, when He blesses a man, it is that he may be a
blessing.   Mere selfish enjoyment is in no case God's purpose.   He constitutes every man a debtor to his fellow-men,
in every case in which He puts it into his power to do them
service.   " God is love."   " His tender mercies are over all
his works."   And God's word is like himself.   It is full of
love; full of the principles, the precepts, and the examples
of benevolence.   Mark the fact, then, here stated.   *Scattering*, does not seem a likely way of *increasing*—*giving away*,
a likely means of *acquisition*.   Yet here stands the declaration, " There is that scattereth, and yet increaseth."   On the
other hand, it seems a natural and reasonable sequence, that
the more a man *keeps* the more he should *have*, that the less
is given away, the more should remain; yet, " there is that
withholdeth more than is meet, and it tendeth to poverty."

It is a question, then, for the serious consideration of
God's people—whether, in this matter, they have sufficient
confidence in Him; whether they trust Him as they ought to
do.   I fear not.   They have more reliance on their own
plans of saving than on God's blessing on giving; more dependence on the *bank* than on the *promise*.   But is not the
injunction of Jesus fully applicable here—" HAVE FAITH IN
GOD?"   Is not this just one of the appropriate ways of putting faith to the test on God's part, and showing its reality
on ours?   Is it not precisely the defectiveness of this faith
that makes us timid, cautious, parsimonious in giving? ever
fearing that we may stint ourselves, and feel the want of
what we expend on suffering humanity and on the cause of
God?   Is it not thus by unbelief that we are tempted to
sow sparingly?   And ought it to be, that the husbandman

trusts more to the laws of nature than the Christian does to
the covenant of his God? Might He not say to each of us, in
terms of gentle but merited reproof, "O thou of little faith,
wherefore didst thou doubt?" Even when we do give, give
we nót with a *misgiving*, as if we were not quite sure whether
we were right,—rather hoping that God's promises *may* be
fulfilled than believing that they *will?* Alas! if the principle of proportion contained in the words, "According to
thy faith be it unto thee," were applied in the present case,
could we expect a large return? And may not this be the
very secret of seeming failures, when they do occur?—He, be
assured, who gives to others in proportion as God gives to
him, takes the surest method of opening still more widely
the fountain of the divine benevolence to himself.

The next verse continues and further developes the same
thought—"The liberal soul shall be made fat; and he that
watereth shall be watered also himself."

"The liberal *soul*" may signify, according to a common
acceptation of the term, the liberal *person;* and "*fat*" being
considered as a metaphor for *rich*—full of substance, the
sentiment would simply be, the *liberal* man shall be the
prosperous man. Or we may render the words thus, "The
soul of the liberal shall enjoy abundance;" that is, he shall
both best attain it, and best relish it.

"*And he that watereth shall be watered also himself.*"
The man of unaffected, unostentatious benevolence, who lays
himself out, in the use of his substance, for the good of
others, attracts to himself general favour, both for his own
sake, and for the sake of the community of which he is so
useful a member.

And further, he shall be compensated by blessing from
God. God will smile upon him; and will so order His
providence as to maintain and promote his prosperity. Or,
if, to God's infinite wisdom, that should not seem best for his
higher interests, He will give him, in lieu of worldly prosperity, when that is abridged or suspended, such an amount
of spiritual benefit as shall infinitely more than countervail
the loss. Thus "he that waters shall," in one or other of

two ways, " be watered himself;" either in *kind* or in *kind-ness;* either in increase of earthly acquisition, or in the flourishing condition of his soul by the very privation of his worldly joys. The streams of his bounty flow all around, to refresh and gladden the parched wastes of poverty and affliction;—and streams of supply keep flowing in, more than adequate to supply the waste. His wealth is like a reservoir, which, while it is ever sending out, is ever receiving; —and, to supply it, the God of love will even " open fountains in the wilderness, and springs in the desert,"—bringing its tributary rills from the most unexpected sources. O! it is a vile maxim, and at utter variance with the entire tenor, and most explicit and energetic statements of the word of God,—that stinting, and saving, and griping, and holding is the way to wealth. The plan may indeed at times succeed. Immense sums may be amassed. But what enjoyment is there in them? There is no blessing with the riches, either from God or man:—no disposition to promote the miser's interest; no regret when his losses and disappointments come; no tear of pity; no hand to help in time of need. O how much happier the man who can say—" The blessing of him that was ready to perish came upon me, and I caused the widow's heart to sing for joy;" and of whom it is said—" Blessed is he that considereth the poor; the Lord will deliver him in time of trouble," Psal xli. 1.

The beneficence to which the divine favour is pledged is, of course, beneficence practised on *right principles.* The same thing done from self-righteousness or ostentation, is *not* the same thing in God's sight with what is done in the spirit of the gospel—the spirit of self-renouncing humility, of lowly and lively gratitude for God's redeeming grace. When, therefore, there appear, in the providence of God, cases that seem like failures in the promised prosperity of the liberal, there are two considerations which we do well to bear in mind. The *first* is, that the Lord, who corrects his children not for " his pleasure but for their profit,"—their *spiritual* profit, that is—may at times, in his unerring wisdom, see trials in their *substance* to be the trials most appro-

priate for the effectual attainment of this end; in which case
it would be unkind in the highest sense, and a breach of
promise instead of a fulfilment of it, were he to allow
them to gain *this* world at the risk of the next,—to grant
them temporal prosperity at the expense of their soul's well-
being in time, and safety for eternity. This is what they, if
rightly minded, could not desire; and what He, in the exercise either of faithfulness or love, could not possibly do.
The *second* is,—that we, who cannot search the heart, can
never tell how far, even in the characters of God's people,
there may be the intrusion and intermixture of those less
pure and hallowed impulses, of which they are ever so
much in danger, and which *He* may see operating in no
small degree, even when they are escaping *our* detection.

The *specific case* mentioned in the following verse, contains still an illustration of the same principle as in the two
preceding, "He that withholdeth corn, the people shall curse
him: but blessing shall be upon the head of him that selleth
it." The prevailing maxim of the world ever since the first
murderer gave utterance to the tendencies of human nature
after its fall, in the question, "Am I my brother's keeper?"
—has been, *"Every man for himself."* And sometimes they
who are loudest in denouncing this maxim when nothing
immediately affects themselves, afford the most melancholy
examples of its operation when they are put to the test.
The identity of human nature in all ages is stamped on
almost every sentence of this book of Proverbs. What presented itself to view in Solomon's days is no rarity still.
There are such selfish wretches now, as there were then;
who, when multitudes are famishing around them, will retain
such supplies of the "staff of life" as are in their possession;
aye, and, if they have any spare capital, will buy up as much
as they can obtain from others, for the purpose of wringing
a still higher price from a starving and dying community.
There can hardly be a more affecting exemplification than
this, of the power of an avaricious disposition in hardening
the heart—in draining it of its last warm drops of sympathy.

The man may gain his end. He may get a high price for

his corn. But he pays a still higher for his money:—he pays for it in the forfeiture of character and sympathy and good-will. He is banished from the affections of his towns-men and his countrymen,—driven with curses out of their hearts. He may affect to despise this. He may hug him-self in self-gratulation, that he has secured the pelf, and that their curses can't take his money from him. But this only renders him the more odious and despicable;—and, although for the time pluming himself on his independence, the time may come when he will be made to feel the truth of the saying, " A good name is rather to be chosen than great riches, and loving favour rather than silver and gold." What a contrast to his is the situation of the man, who, content with a moderate profit, disdaining, or rather conscientiously dreading, to take advantage of the pinching necessities of others, and to starve them into compliance with his unconscionable demands, feels for prevailing dis-tress, opens his granaries, and supplies the market for the poor and the famishing; who will rather do this at a loss than see others perish for want that *he* may have abundance. How enviable *his* emotions! How precious the blessing of the poor,—how sweet to the ear and to the heart!

The word rendered " *selleth* " is by some interpreters un-derstood of distributing or *breaking* bread to the hungry. This of course obtains a still more spontaneous and abun-dant blessing, than parting with it at a small profit, or even at cost. It was such disinterested kindness that brought a blessing upon Job from those who experienced it.* And it is this with which is associated the promised blessing of God.†

What in the verse before us is said of individuals is true also of GOVERNMENTS. As there are few things in a com-munity so fearful as famine, the government that, in a season of dearth, makes it its first concern to provide supplies of corn and provision for the poor, will bring on itself the bless-ing of the poor, and establish itself in the affection and con-fidence of the people. On the other hand, laws of which

* Job xxix. 11—13.   † Isa. lviii. 6—11.

the tendency and the effect are to keep up the price of bread, and which thus press hard on the labouring classes,—whose families, on low wages, are scantily fed, and deprived of education to their minds by the difficulty of providing sustenance for their bodies,—it would require very clear and strong grounds indeed to justify. And, when their operation is felt, and the dissatisfaction is indicated by universal and indignant remonstrance,—as there is nothing so unhappy and so perilous as a discontented and murmuring population, cursing their rulers instead of blessing them,—there would require to be very cogent reasons for refusing the trial at least of a change.—This is not the place for discussions on political economy. One thing, however, is clear, that laws which "withhold corn" can never be popular, and that it is the very first principle and duty of every paternal government,—of every government that would settle itself in the confidence and affection of its subjects,—to " DO NOTHING BY PARTIALITY."

The sentiment is similar, though more general, in verse 27. " He that diligently seeketh good procureth favour : but he that seeketh mischief it shall come unto him."

" *He that seeketh good*" stands here in contradistinction to " *him that seeketh mischief.*" There can be no doubt, therefore, that the meaning is, " He that seeketh good *to others;* that is, makes the good of others his aim. The word rendered " diligently" signifies *in the morning,* or *early.* This is a Hebraism, and a natural one. When we make anything our business—when we set our hearts upon it—we set about it immediately; we give it our *morning* energies,—beginning the day with it, and occupying it as it was begun. The character designed, then, is that of one who desires, and industriously and perseveringly seeks, the well-being of all around him. That man "*procureth favour*" —favour both from men and from God ; not only the kindly and grateful affections of men, but, in time of need, the practical manifestation of those affections. And as to God —it stands on record in his own word, that " with the merciful man he will show himself merciful."

The connexion thus explains the meaning of what follows.
No man ever "seeketh mischief" *to himself.* And he that
seeketh it *to others* does in effect seek it to himself. "*It
shall come unto him:*" that is, his attempts to do harm will
recoil upon himself. Enmity will be the result, instead of
favour. All about him will be made his foes. And, what
is worse, he will be exposed to the divine displeasure; for it
also stands recorded in the same word, "He shall have judgment without mercy who hath showed no mercy."

The *trust in riches* mentioned in the 28th verse, we have
already had before us.* How prone is the possessor to "say
to the gold, Thou art my hope, and to the fine gold, Thou art
my confidence!" The possession ought, according to its proper and legitimate tendency, to lead the heart *to* God, from
whom cometh down every good gift; but alas! it too often
draws it away from Him, and produces confidence in itself
instead of the giver. The giver banished by his gift!

From the connexion in which the words stand, there may
perhaps be a special reference to riches gained by means such
as those that had just been specified. And in that case, the
language of Jeremiah becomes peculiarly appropriate, "As
the partridge sitteth on eggs, and hatcheth them not; so he
that getteth riches, and not by right, shall leave them in the
midst of his days, and at his end shall be a fool," chap. xvii.
11. If a man so trusts in his wealth, as to be emboldened
by his confidence to acts of high-minded oppression and injustice—that man "*shall fall.*" He shall fall into decay.
His riches shall "make themselves wings." God shall blight
and blast his hopes and wishes. Or, if he continues to
maintain his eminence, he shall *finally* fall with the more
tremendous and frightful ruin.

"*But the righteous shall flourish as a branch*"—a vigorous,
fresh, extending, blossoming, fruitful branch. The image is a
beautiful one. It is applied, in the dying blessings of Jacob,
to his favourite son, "Joseph is a fruitful bough, even a
fruitful bough by a well; whose branches run over the

---

* Chap. x. 15.

wall," Gen. xlix. 22. Whether understood temporally or spiritually, it is equally true and equally beautiful. God shall bless that man. He shall "spread out his roots by the waters, and the dew shall lie all night upon his branch." "His beauty shall be as the olive-tree, and his smell as Lebanon." He shall be "filled with the fruits of right-eousness," and at the same time with those of peace and joy in his own bosom.

Verse 29. "He that troubleth his own house shall inherit the wind: and the fool shall be servant to the wise of heart." There are many ways in which a man may " *trouble his own house.*" He may by the violence and irritability, the pee-vishness, fretfulness, and selfishness of his temper; he may by his avarice on the one hand, or by his reckless prodi-gality on the other—involving his family in starvation and suffering by opposite means; he may by intemperance, with all its horrid attendants; he may by sloth, and idleness, and indisposition to work. "*He shall inherit the wind.*" The expression is a very strong one. Could any words more im-pressively convey the idea of loss, disappointment, and ulti-mate destitution and misery?—*heir to the wind!* Beggary shall be his portion. He shall be "clothed with rags."—The result he himself deserves. A man's family is his first charge from heaven, and ought to be his chief and constant solicitude. The only evil to be lamented is, that he brings the destitution upon *them* as well as upon himself. It often happens, however, in the providence of God, and by the natural operation of human sympathy, that the family is looked after and provided for, while the "troubler of his house" is left to the consequences of his guilt and folly.

"*And the fool shall be servant to the wise of heart.*" The meaning evidently is—and it accords with what has more than once been under notice,—that the prudent and discreet, the just and good, shall have the superiority. The posts of station and influence,—the *mastery* shall be theirs. They get on in society; while the foolish, the indiscreet, and un-principled, are left behind in the race of competition.

Verse 30. "The fruit of the righteous is a tree of life;

and he that winneth souls is wise." An eminent com-
mentator thus expounds the verse—connecting its two
clauses ingeniously and happily together;—" The good example, pious discourse, wise instructions, fervent prayers, and
zealous good works, of the righteous, become exceedingly
beneficial to those around them: they are as fruit from the
tree of life; they promote the salvation of sinful men. And,
as immortal souls are valuable beyond all estimation, he
who thus wins souls, and allures them into the way of eternal
life, is emphatically the *wise man;* he proposes to himself
the noblest end; he uses the only proper means; he perseveres, and is prospered by God himself."

I am aware that of the last clause the expositions have
been various; but there is no occasion. "*The wise winneth*"
or gaineth "*souls,*" is literal; and it accords sufficiently well
with the former part of the verse. It expresses the very
best and highest effect of wise benevolence—the benevolence
of "the righteous." The soul outweighs the world in value.
So was its preciousness estimated by the most competent
of all judges. It is not enough, however, to admit this
in words. The admission must be *followed out* in action.
I know not which is the more foolish—to deny the position, or to admit it in words and contradict the admission
in conduct. There is a difference in the *kind* of folly. The
former, could we conceive it possible, would indicate a disordered *intellect;* the latter is more the product and indication of a disordered *heart.* There is in it more of criminality.—The wise men of the world may set at nought the
efforts of him who makes it the aim of his life to "win souls;"
they may hold in scorn the kind of knowledge by which
souls are won; they may scoff at futurity and at the Gospel
provision for securing its happiness; but their scorn is only
a fulfilment of the intimations of the very Book they despise;
which has prepared us to expect that "not many wise men
after the flesh" should be found in the number of its believers, and the subjects of its saving influence,—and which
pronounces "the wisdom of this world foolishness with God."
Surely he who views man as immortal, and moreover as

sinful and guilty, acts *wisely*, when he sets his heart on *winning* him from sin to holiness, from guilt to forgiveness, from the "fearful looking for of judgment" to the possession of inward peace, from the desire and pursuit of things temporal to the desire and pursuit of things "unseen and eternal;" from death to life, from hell to heaven. He who thus "winneth souls" is wise in regard even to his own interests—for they that turn many to righteousness shall shine as the stars for ever and ever," (Dan. xii. 3.)

This Book is ever impressing our minds with the character of God as "the righteous Lord, who loveth righteousness." In every form does this sentiment come before us. We have it in the last verse. "Behold, the righteous shall be recompensed in the earth: much more the wicked and the sinner." The meaning here is not, that in the present world there is a regular and constant distribution of reward and punishment. This is not *the fact;* nor is it any part of the doctrine or Scripture. The reference evidently is to the convictions of chastisements of God's people; which are the results of sin remaining in them; the testimonies of their heavenly Father's displeasure against *it*, but love to *them*. He hates their sins, but loves their souls; and seeks the final salvation of the latter by the means adopted by him to deliver them from the former. The expression, "How much more the wicked and the sinner," *may* be interpreted of *temporal judgments* —present tokens of the divine displeasure. But for the full sense we must look further. The text is quoted by the apostle Peter, according to the version of the Septuagint,— "If the righteous scarcely be saved, where shall the ungodly and the sinner appear?" 1 Pet. iv. 18. Here, the connexion leaves us at no loss as to the ultimate and most important reference of the words. The sin even of God's people is visited with the indications of God's displeasure; so that the righteous are saved with difficulty—by a series of inflictions involving in them at times a large amount of heavy suffering; which the Lord is not willing to employ, were it not that He sees them to be necessary for the attainment of the great end of his love in their final well-being. If so—if sin be thus, in

I.   U

God's sight so "exceeding sinful,"—"where shall the ungodly and the sinner appear?"   How can they "escape the
damnation of hell?"

Let the people of God, then, hold in abhorrence that which
exposes them to the displeasure and frown of their heavenly
Father—a frown the more distressing that it is the frown of
love; and implore the accompanying influence of the Holy
Spirit with every stroke of paternal discipline, that it may
work in them the peaceable fruits of righteousness, and make
them "partakers of the divine holiness.   And let "the ungodly and the sinner" be assured that their sin will *find
them out.*   No covering can vail it from the eye of " Him
that sitteth on the throne;" nor is there any power in the
universe that can protect from his righteous vengeance.

If he that "winneth souls is wise"—the souls of *others;*
surely, the first province and the first mark of wisdom must
be, for a man to seek the salvation of his own soul.   This is
indeed " THE ONE THING NEEDFUL."

Ye who have felt the preciousness of your own souls, and,
in solicitude for their security, have committed them where
alone they can be safe,—even into the hands of that Saviour
who " *is* able," and who *alone* is able, " to keep that which
is so committed to him against that day,"—seek the wisdom
necessary to "win the souls" of others; and be in earnest in
the use of it.   Selfishness is the reigning sin of fallen nature;
but it is dislodged from its throne by the power of the cross.
Then " *no one liveth to himself.*"   Every believer's life is
felt by him to be no longer his own.   He lives for God, for
Christ, for souls,—for the temporal and eternal well-being of
his race.   O live thus.   Identify the happiness of all around
you with your own.   Seek the latter in the former.   In
seeking and finding the good of others, you will most effectually seek and find your own.   Your own substance will
grow, while you " deal your bread to the hungry;" and you
will experience that the spiritual life in your own souls is
never more prosperous than when you are engrossed in the
benevolent work of doing good to the souls of others,—of
" seeking the profit of many, that they may be saved."

LECTURE XXVII.

———◆———

PROV. XII. 1—19.

" Whoso loveth instruction loveth knowledge: but he that hateth reproof is brutish. A good man obtaineth favour of the Lord; but a man of wicked devices will he condemn. A man shall not be established by wickedness: but the root of the righteous shall not be moved. A virtuous woman is a crown to her husband: but she that maketh ashamed is as rottenness in his bones. The thoughts of the righteous are right: but the counsels of the wicked are deceit. The words of the wicked are to lie in wait for blood: but the mouth of the upright shall deliver them. The wicked are overthrown, and are not: but the house of the righteous shall stand. A man shall be commended according to his wisdom: but he that is of a perverse heart shall be despised. He that is despised, and hath a servant, is better than he that honoureth himself, and lacketh bread. A righteous man regardeth the life of his beast: but the tender mercies of the wicked are cruel. He that tilleth his land shall be satisfied with bread: but he that followeth vain persons is void of understanding. The wicked desireth the net of evil men: but the root of the righteous yieldeth fruit. The wicked is snared by the transgression of his lips: but the just shall come out of trouble. A man shall be satisfied with good by the fruit of his mouth: and the recompence of a man's hands shall be rendered unto him. The way of a fool is right in his own eyes: but he that hearkeneth unto counsel is wise. A fool's wrath is presently known: but a prudent man covereth shame. He that speaketh truth sheweth forth righteousness: but a false witness deceit. There is that speaketh like the piercings of a sword: but the tongue of the wise is health. The lip of truth shall be established for ever: but a lying tongue is but for a moment."

IT is by "*instruction*" that "knowledge" comes. He who fancies he has all in himself will never learn. He who fancies he has already got from others all he *can* get, will cease to learn.—Again, in proportion to the *love* of instruction will be the acquisition of knowledge. Thus must it be in every department: thus it is in regard to the knowledge of divine things—the truth and will of God.*—Further, the love of instruction implies *humility*. It argues a sense of ignorance and need of information. It is a common thing for men to allow pride to cheat them of much valuable knowledge. They like not to be thought ignorant; unless it be in regard to the knowledge of divine truth. Some absolutely plume themselves upon their ignorance on *such* subjects. They would be ashamed were they supposed acquainted with the Bible, and will at times put questions for the very purpose of showing how ignorant they are of its contents! Surely a more melancholy or affecting view of the perverseness of our fallen nature there cannot be, than appears in the fact, that the highest, the greatest, the best of all the possible subjects of thought or investigation, GOD HIMSELF, is that which last and least engages human attention and interest! Were man what he ought to be, this of all subjects would be the one on which he would most "love instruction," and delight to find "knowledge."

That the knowledge of *duty* as well as of *truth* is here to be included, may be inferred from the latter part of the verse—"but he that *refuseth reproof* is brutish." Such conduct is "brutish," as irrational, senseless, unworthy of a creature endowed with intellect; distinguished by reason from the beasts of the field, and distinguished from them too by his immortality. It was when Asaph recovered from that strange temptation, under the power of which he seemed to forget the eternity of man's being, and to confine his estimate to the present life, that he exclaimed, " So foolish was I and ignorant; I was *as a beast* before thee!" Psal. lxxiii. 22. And the same comparison is repeatedly used respecting the ungodly. They sink themselves even below the level of the brutes. I say *even below*, for the brutes fulfil the ends of *their* being, under the impulse of their respective instincts and appetites; but the man who forgets his immortality and forgets his God, does *not* fulfil the end of *his*. He acts a part infinitely beneath it, and is emphatically " *brutish*." †

---

* Comp. chap. ii. 1—6.　　　　† Comp. Psal. xlix. 10—12; xcii. 5, 6.

There may also be comprehended in the expression, the absence of what every rational creature ought to have—*spiritual discernment and taste;* the destitution of all right sentiment and feeling in reference to God and divine things. This is the character of him whom Paul denominates "the natural" or *animal* " man," who "receiveth not the things of the Spirit of God: for they are foolishness unto him."

Verse 2. "A good man obtaineth favour of the Lord: but a man of wicked devices will he condemn."

God *must* delight in goodness. Goodness is His own nature. He cannot but take pleasure in resemblance to Himself. On "*the good man*" His blessing descends,—on his person, on his labours, on his substance, on his family, on his temporal enjoyments, and on his temporal trials and corrections.

The character with which "the good man" stands here contrasted seems to show that *good* has at least a special, if not exclusive reference to *benevolence;* "But the man of wicked devices will he condemn." Such a man was *Judas,* to whom, knowing the treachery of his heart, Jesus so early said, "Have not I chosen you twelve, and one of you is a devil?" The false-hearted attended Jesus to the last, and then, with the kiss of false friendship, having first sold, betrayed him. They too were "*men of wicked devices,*" who " consulted how they might take Jesus by subtlety and kill him"—kill the very pattern of all goodness! God "condemned" *him* who betrayed, and *them* who paid the bribe. Both became the victims of righteous vengeance.

The *principle* of the next verse is the same—" A man shall not be established by wickedness: but the root of the righteous shall not be moved."

The prosperity that is obtained by wickedness shall not be permanent. There is rottenness in the "*root*" of it. The hidden curse of God is in it: and that curse has in it a secret power of blight and wasting, which no wit of man can anticipate, and no power contravene. Where that curse is nothing goes well: everything fails; and no one can divine the cause. The very means devised for safety turn out means of insecurity and loss. A kind of *fatality* appears to wait upon every step of the man's course. A fire, blown he knows not how, consumes his substance. His ' *wicked devices*" for his own aggrandizement turn out like plans contrived for his own destruction.—The words indeed may have a different meaning. " *Established*" may have reference not to the stability of his fortunes, but to that of his *mind*—to tranquil self-possession and firmness. The steadfastness of the righteous, in this view, is finely expressed in the latter clause of the verse—" *But the root of the righteous shall not be moved.*" Even if, in the providence of God, his substance should fail, he himself remains unshaken and entire, in all his best blessings and in all his hopes. He loses nothing. He gains. What injures him in one way, benefits him in another and a better. And his spirit remains unbroken; his confidence loses not its hold. He resembles the mighty oak of the forest, that has stricken its roots wide and deep into the soil: the raving tempest may assail it, may shed its leaves, may snap a few twigs and slender branches; but it stands itself firm in all its unblemished majesty.*

Verse 4. " A virtuous woman is a crown to her husband: but she that maketh ashamed is as rottenness in his bones."

" A woman of *virtue*." The word is to be understood as including, along with strict conjugal fidelity in affection and conduct, *good principles* in general, in their practical operation;—piety and consistency; industry, economy, prudence, and good management; steadiness, propriety, and becoming dignity; all the affections, all the duties, and all the delicate seemliness, belonging to her station, as a wife, as a mother, and as a mistress.

Such a woman is " *a crown to her husband.*"—There is supposed by some to be an allusion in the expression to the practice of crowning bridegrooms on the occasion of their nuptials, as an emblem of the new authority and honour with which they were conceived to be invested. Be this as it may, the meaning is plain. A crown is a mark of dignity: and a " virtuous woman" being " a crown to her husband,"

* Comp. Jer. xvii. 5—8.

represents the respectability, credit, reputation, which accrue
to a man from such a connexion;—not only from his having
made so suitable a choice, but from the inevitable association of the one with the other, and from the discreet and
generous conduct of the wife, in at once hiding her husband's failings, and in giving prominence to his excellencies
and virtues.   In this respect wives have much in their
power, in either maintaining or letting down the respectability and honour of their husbands.   It is a miserable case,
when there is *contested superiority* between man and wife.
The woman that does contest it can never answer to the
description here of a "*crown*" to her husband."   No woman
can that aims at assuming the crown to herself; and especially when, instead of keeping her usurpation a secret, she
evidently aims at letting everybody know of her success.
Such a woman does what she can to stamp her husband
with degradation and littleness.   Husband and wife are *one;*
and they are so associated in the minds of others as to be,
in a certain measure, *identified;* the respect, or the disrespect,
felt for the one, almost unavoidably and insensibly, extending itself to the other.   It is the duty of the husband to
"give honour unto the wife, as unto the weaker vessel;"
and the husband who is not sensitively jealous of all that
touches the respect due to his wife, and is not solicitous to
make the best of her character in the eyes of others—in-
dignantly protecting her from every act or word or look of
insult, signally fails in a most essential element of conjugal
love and duty.   But it is best when husband and wife so
feel themselves one,—their interests, their honour, their happiness one,—that *superiority* and *inferiority* are words unknown in their conjugal vocabulary; when authority never
needs to be asserted, and subjection is never felt, the one
being exercised, the other rendered *in love;* and when husband and wife are thus reciprocally "a crown" to each other,
each adding to the other's reputation and honour.

But there may be more in the "*crown*" than the idea of
honour.   Garlands were also worn on occasions of festivity
and joy; and on this very account they graced the nuptial

ceremony, which, in all ages, has been one of gladness and social mirth. In the metaphor, therefore, *joy* and *honour* may be considered as combined;—the former as well as the latter arising to a husband from the character of the wife of his bosom, the joint head of his family, the worthy partner of his earthly lot. He feels and values the honour; and the joy is one of the richest sweeteners of his earthly pilgrimage.

The contrary part of the alternative is expressed in strong, yet not *too* strong, terms:—"*But she that maketh ashamed is as rottenness in his bones.*" The first thing that here presents itself to the mind is *unfaithfulness to the marriage vow.* And, assuredly, to the man who truly loves his wife, this must be one of the most agonizing wounds it is within the range of possibility to inflict upon him. And I would have husbands to remember—for there is at times to be found abundant sensitiveness on the one side, when there is comparatively little, if any at all, on the other,—that *the obligation to fidelity is the same on both parties;* and that the contrary is "rottenness" in a *wife's* bones, as well as in a husband's. I enter into no questions of comparison and casuistry, but affirm the general law, and assert the equal deference due to feeling on the part of both.

But there are other ways in which a wife may "make ashamed," and, although not to the same degree, may be "rottenness in the bones." She may be otherwise depraved and unprincipled. She may be a slattern; she may be a drinker; she may be a waster; she may be improvident; she may be vain, and light, and frivolous; she may be contentious, imperious, peevish, passionate; she may be a gossip and a scandal-monger. Her husband sees this, and sees the effects of it on the minds of others: and the sight brings vexation and anguish of heart; especially when he connects the character with the education of a rising family, on the members of which the example of a mother exerts so early and so powerful an influence. "It is rottenness in his bones."

The figure is strong. We may consider it as conveying *two* ideas: 1. The "bones" are the *strength* of the frame. Upon them the whole is built. There is, therefore, in the

idea of *caries,* or rottenness in them, that of the *wasting* of the
vigour of body and mind, and the bringing of the man pre-
maturely to his grave; and that too by means which cost
him, ere this result is effected, exquisite suffering.   Then—

2. "The bones" are *unseen.* The poor man is pierced with
inward and secret agony, which he cannot disclose; pines
in unseen distress,—distress, of which the cause is hidden,
while the *effects* are sadly and rapidly visible.   Too often
has it happened, that wives, who by their conduct have deprived *home* of its attractions, and made it the scene of annoyance and wretchedness, rather than of comfort, peace, and
social joy,—have been the temptations of their husbands;
have driven them to the ale-house and the evening club, to
bad company and excess, to the ruin of business, of family,
of character, of health, of life.   Ye wives, beware: ye have
much in your power.   Let the beautiful description of conjugal duty, and consequent conjugal union and happiness,
drawn by the pen of the inspired Apostle, in writing to the
Ephesian church, be realized under the domestic roof of all
husbands and wives calling themselves Christians.

Verse 5. " The thoughts of the righteous are right: but
the counsels of the wicked are deceit."

The verse has been rendered—" *The policy of the just is
honesty; the wisdom of the wicked is cunning.*"   And this
rendering marks more strikingly the intended distinction.
The " righteous man," in all his " thoughts," keeps by what is
" *right.*"   He deals in rectitude, as opposed to " *deceit;*" and
from his actions you may know his thoughts.   It is not so
with " the wicked."   He thinks one way and acts another.
His words and deeds are not the fair index of his thoughts.

In the next verse, the same evil is depicted, only rising a
step higher,—I should say, perhaps, sinking a step lower—in
turpitude—" The words of the wicked are to lie in wait for
blood: but the mouth of the upright shall deliver them."

The *principles* of murder are in the heart of the wicked
man, and the words of murder are in his lips.   The idea in
the latter part of the preceding verse is evidently retained
here.   In the words that suggest and advise " laying wait for

blood," there is "deceit;" and deceit for the most atrocious of all ends, the death of the hated object. Before the purposes of a wicked selfishness even *life* will not be permitted to stand.* " *But the mouth of the upright shall deliver them.*" It is clear that " *the mouth of the upright*" implies the simplicity and commanding power of truth. It is not *entreaty* by which he is supposed to prevail, but the pleadings of *truth.* In such pleadings there is a power that is ever fitted to produce the effect; especially in cases where the death of the good man is sought under the forms of law; when they plead their own cause, with wisdom, with the internal evidence of simple truth, and with the mien and the majesty of real and conscious innocence. Even in such cases, however, it is far from having always been so. From the first martyr to the Christian faith, onward through the entire history of persecution, numberless instances of the contrary present themselves: but there are not a few also of the overawing and disarming power of the "mouth of the upright." When Jesus fulfilled his promise—"I will give you a mouth and wisdom which all your adversaries shall not be able to gainsay nor resist," there was a power which, though it might not convert opponents, or even conciliate such favour as should ensure protection for the future, yet laid a restraint upon the indulgence of vindictive fury :—and many a time truth has *silenced,* when it has not *saved;* has promoted the cause even when it has not preserved its present advocate.

At all events, the words suggest the idea that " the *mouth* of the upright" is the only weapon the upright is warranted to employ. It is his to plead, and to plead in simplicity and sincerity, leaving his cause thus pleaded, with GOD.

Verse 7. "The wicked are overthrown and are not: but the house of the righteous shall stand."

Solomon had a signal exemplification of this in the case of *Saul,* and his father *David.* Possibly this instance might be in his eye at the time. Saul seemed to have the mastery; and David to be forsaken, and in constant and imminent

* See chap. i. 10—19.

peril.   Yet the house of Saul was overthrown so as *not to be;* while David and his house were established; established in the divine favour and in the promised throne of Israel. Thus has it *often* been.

Verse 8. " A man shall be commended according to his wisdom : but he that is of a perverse heart shall be despised." This is capable of two interpretations.   It may refer to commendation by *men,* or to commendation by *God.*   When understood in the one or in the other, *wisdom* requires to be somewhat differently interpreted.   If a man possesses a sound judgment and proves a prudent, discriminating, faithful, and salutary adviser, in times of difficulty, perplexity, and trial,—that man will be *" commended according to his wisdom"* by his fellowmen.   But if commendation from *God* be intended, wisdom must be taken in its higher sense,—as signifying not mere *secular discretion,* but *religious principle;* according to the invariable testimony, not of Solomon only but of all the inspired penmen, that *" the fear of the Lord, that is wisdom."*   This is not the wisdom that secures the eulogy of men ; but it will ever secure the commendation of God—the Infinitely Wise, the Infinitely Good.

And indeed, the two things may be united.   A man who has " the fear of God before his eyes " will always be a *faithful* counsellor ; and if, at the same time, he have sound wisdom and discretion in regard to the affairs of life, fitting him for counsel and arbitration—this will form the perfection of character.   There will be commendation both from *men* and from *God.*   Forget not the counterpart of this statement, *" But he that is of a perverse heart shall be despised.."*

In the pride of your hearts, you may affect to hold very cheap the contempt of men ; though even that is often more pretension than reality—disappointment rankling at the heart, while scorn is curling the lip.   But what must it be to be " lightly esteemed " at last—to be *" despised"* by that God who has in His hands the destinies of the universe.

There are expressions that have got into currency as the words of Scripture, that are not to be found in Scripture. Of this we have an instance in the way in which the former part of the tenth verse is usually quoted, — "*The merciful man is merciful to his beast.*" No such words exist in the Bible. The nearest to them are the words which occur here. You will say, it is but a difference of words; and I am ready to admit that the sentiment as it has obtained currency, is in the fullest harmony with Bible principles. But there is more in the sentence as it stands in the Bible than in its ordinary form. That a merciful man is "merciful to his beast" expresses no more than that a kind and benevolent disposition will extend its exercise to the inferior creation as well as to fellow-men. Now, this is *almost* a truism. We may occasionally, in consequence of certain perverse habits of thought and feeling, acquired by incidental circumstances, or by injudicious training, or unfortunate example in early life, find the anomaly of a person kind to men and harsh to brutes. But it *is* an anomaly; and, as an anomaly, a comparative rarity. The man who really deserves the character of a *merciful man,* we expect to derive the very character from his kindness to the inferior tribes of creation as well as to men,—to the whole range, as far as within his influence, of sensitive existence. But the maxim contained in the words "A righteous man regardeth the life of his beast" is, *that practical kindness, extending to the brute creation, is an essential part of the character of a scripturally good man.*—He deserves not the designation of a "*righteous man,*" who is destitute of *mercy.* He is without one of the most important features of resemblance to God. When the Scriptures describe His character, He appears before us as extending a benevolent care over all creatures. His word is full of this. Read the 104th Psalm. You will find throughout a beautiful and sublime illustration of the general sentiment, "The LORD is good to all; his tender mercies are over all his works." And the lips into which grace was poured, have said in terms of lovely simplicity, and pregnant with meaning, "Are not five sparrows sold for two farthings? and not one of them is forgotten before God"—"one of them shall not fall to the ground without your heavenly Father." Each one of His children should delight to witness the joys of all creation, and strive by every means to promote them. The poet deprecates the friendship of the man "who needlessly sets foot upon a worm."

There are few things more shocking than the wanton barbarity practised upon animals that are employed in the service of man. How useful!—how ill treated! There are two systems of treatment pursued, both of which, after all, are but different descriptions of mere self-interest. There is the system that works them hard and gets most labour out of them in the shorter time they last:—and the other is the system that by working them less severely, exacting from them a smaller average of toil, makes them last the longer time. But with "the righteous" there ever will be, more than a mere calculation of self-interest. It will not be merely "the life of *his* beast," because it is his, and because he considers gentle treatment as the most economical, that "the righteous man will regard." That would not be mercy, but mere prudential management for his own advantage. Higher motives will influence him. It will not even be *mere sensibility*. It will be sensibility associated with principle, and a regard to the authority and the example of God.

The latter part of the verse is a singularly strong expression for *hard-heartedness*—"The tender mercies of the wicked are cruel." Mercy, if ever exercised at all, is exercised with a surly and grudging reluctance; and the extent of its doings and its gifts is so restricted and parsimonious, that they will appear to the man of generous spirit, who "delights in mercy," no better than "*cruelty*."

The expression may perhaps also mean, that of wicked men even *the kindness* is frequently injurious. As they have no thought beyond the body, the world, and time, they often express their kindness in a way that may prove prejudicial in the extreme to those who are disposed to accept of it. As it is said that "he that flattereth his neighbour spreadeth a net for his feet;" so may it be said of the kindness of the ungodly. It makes no account of the highest of all interests; and will propose and urge plans of worldly benefit fitted to ensnare, and damage, and finally ruin the soul. Of such kindness let all beware. It is "*cruelty*" in disguise.

The former, however, is probably the true meaning; and the language has special reference to the treatment of inferiors, and of dependent brute creatures. What affecting exemplifications might be found for illustration in the treatment of *slaves*. How often have the very descriptions of *kind* treatment — treatment on which the owner highly plumed himself, been such as only to fill with indignation and shame the bosoms of all possessing a truly compassionate and generous spirit! And how often has the iron-hearted tyrant vaunted of his "mercy" in the course pursued towards his captive victims, or those who have offended him; when he was only presenting a practical commentary on the words, "The tender mercies of the wicked are *cruel*."—And have you never met with a monster in human form, who, when reproved for merciless severity to his "beast," has laughed at you, and told you, with manifest self-complacency, how much harder he could make his blows if he chose; as if he had whereof to glory in the mere fact of his not putting to his entire strength in venting his passion, or enforcing his merciless determination with the still worse coolness of a fiend?

Verse 11. "He that tilleth his land shall be satisfied with bread: but he that followeth vain persons is void of understanding." *Industry* again!—A general principle is illustrated by a particular case. The principle is, NOTHING WITHOUT LABOUR—a principle applicable alike to business, knowledge, and religion. Bread-corn will not spring up, ripen, and yield its produce spontaneously. There must be ploughing, sowing, harrowing, cleaning, reaping, thrashing, grinding, before a morsel of bread is obtained. And so business will not prosper, knowledge will not increase, religion will not thrive, but by the sedulous, persevering use of all instituted means.

The antithesis between the two parts of the verse is plain, " But he that followeth vain persons is void of understanding." By "*vain persons*" we understand *idle*, dissipated, frivolous, time-killing persons. I warn young men espe-

cially to beware of such. They may present themselves
under different aspects:—as low profligates; as aspiring,
would-be, gentlemen; as men of station who can afford to
be idle, who glory in it, and who flatter others by assuming
them as their associates, and so giving them a distinction of
which they are in danger of being vain.—Take care. "He
that followeth them" is "*void of understanding.*" He acts
in opposition to all the plainest dictates of prudence and
common sense, which testify the evil tendency of idleness,
both as to present comfort, as to future success in life, as to
true respectability, and as to moral and spiritual character.
He flies in the face of all the lessons of experience; lessons
the most striking and multiplied; lessons written many times
in bitter tears, and not seldom even in blood.

The next verse naturally enough connects with this:—
"The wicked desireth the net of evil men: but the root of
the righteous yieldeth fruit."

The word "*net*" may be understood of *any means* by which
the wealth and honours of the world may be acquired. Thus
it is used in Habakkuk i. 13—17. The net described in
this passage is emphatically "*the net of evil men.*" It is that
of the oppressor, who regards his fellow-men as of any value,
only as he can render them conducive to his own benefit and
aggrandizement, and who uses them accordingly; and, when
his oppressive measures prove successful, vaunts himself in
the power and the skill by which the success has been
secured, taking the entire credit, unenviable as it is, to himself.—There seems to be a special reference, in the verse before us, to *illegitimate* or *fraudulent* means. In "the net of evil
men," this is evidently implied. When "the wicked" see the
devices of "evil men" succeed, they desire to try the same arts.
Instead of any moral detestation of the *means*, they look only
at the *end*. They see that attained. They are envious. They
are tempted to imitate; and, there being little or no principle
to offer resistance, the desire is at once put into practice.
The violation of right sits but lightly on their consciences.
The barrier of what men call duty and conscience, is easily
thrown down. The sole question is, whether the plan be

feasible,—whether it holds out a fair prospect of success. If objections are urged on the score of principle, they give a careless shrug and say, "Leave that to me; you have no business with my conscience; *my* question is—*Will it answer?*" If, in any case, conscience *should* remonstrate and restrain, and will not allow them to go quite so far, they yet envy, and regret their restraints. They still "*desire* the net" even when they can't bring themselves to use it. They wish they could get over their scruples; and, in this state of mind, the probability is that by and by they will.

"*But t/e root of the righteous yieldeth fruit.*"—The "*root* of the righteous" might be understood as meaning the fixed, settled, stable *principle* of the righteous; and the sentiment may be, and it is an important one, and in harmony with much to the same purpose in this book—that *acting on rooted principle*, the righteous man will ultimately prosper; or, even if, in regard to this world, he should fail of success, his principle will yield the fruit of true happiness to him in the blessing of the Lord and the "peace which passeth all understanding." I incline, however, to think, that, as "*the net*" signifies the varied artifice, cunning, and fraud employed to gain riches quickly and easily—"the *root* of the righteous," as contrasted with the "*net* of evil men," may represent rather the *source of his revenue or income:* and—in opposition to the art of making rich quickly, to excite the surprise and the envy of others—a steady, firmly established, regularly and prudently and justly conducted business, bringing in its profits fairly and moderately; as a tree deeply rooted in the soil, draws thence its natural nourishment, and "receiving blessing from God," brings forth its fruit in due season. The two views are closely, if not inseparably, connected.

Verse 13. "The wicked is snared by the transgression of his lips: but the just shall come out of trouble." There may possibly, in these words, be an allusion to "the net of evil men" in the verse preceding. One of the means used by such men in attaining their ends—one of the meshes of the net which they weave for the purpose—is equivocation, falsehood, sometimes even perjury; and the defamation of persons; and the cheapening and abusing of goods; with a variety of other modes of untruth and dishonest chicanery. But often such men outwit themselves. They are "*snared by the transgression of their lips.*" Their own words take them in. They are detected; and by detection their ends are frustrated, and reversed.

"*But the just shall come out of trouble.*" The contrast is striking. "*The just*" is the man of principle. How often has the man of known integrity been released on the credit of his own word in times of suspicion and "trouble," when the man of known duplicity and deceit has been committed and retained; and, even when innocent, has got off with difficulty and is followed by doubt!

The following verse presents another advantage of right words—the words of "the just." Their salutary counsel; their wholesome advice; their expressions of encouragement, consolation, and kindness, bring a rich reward into their own bosoms. They enjoy the satisfaction of seeing the happy effects of their words—a sweet gratification to a benevolent spirit!—and reap a precious return of esteem and affection, of gratitude and cheerful benefaction—for "*a man shall be satisfied with good by the fruit of his mouth.*" And what is true of *words* is true of *deeds;* what is true of the *tongue* is true of the *hands*—"*The recompense of a man's hands shall be given unto him*"—a principle equally applicable to the *wicked*, who shall have both of man and God "according to their doings."

In the next verse we have brought before us afresh one of the distinguishing characteristics of *folly*, on the one hand, and *wisdom* on the other. That of the former is a proud, high-minded self-sufficiency, which disdains all admonition, deems its own ways and plans ever and certainly the best, and can brook no control. That of the latter is the self-diffident humility that seeks guidance, courts instruction, and is ready to yield to good counsel at the hand of man, and renders entire and implicit submission to the mind and will of God—without which there is nothing that deserves the name of wisdom—"The way of a fool is right

I.   X

in his own eyes; but he that hearkeneth unto counsel is wise." *

Another mark of folly is brought before us in the 16th verse:—" A fool's wrath is presently known: but a prudent man covereth shame." The fool has no proper command of his passions. His self-sufficiency renders him impatient of contradiction—irascible, and headstrong; and he is incapable, from want of the vigour of self-control, of suppressing his auger. He allows it to burst forth in whatever place, time, or circumstances; and no matter in whose presence.—In contradistinction from the touchy and overbearing fool is "the prudent man who *covereth shame.*"—Shame here means *any affront.* He does not, by his quick and blustering resentment, make it immediately known to all the world that he has been insulted, and that he has *felt* it. He stifles his passion; restrains the bursting out of wrath; lest he should utter hastily what may put him more to shame than any word or deed of insult from another ever could.— The virtue here commanded is that of *self-command.*

The following verse—" He that speaketh truth showeth forth righteousness: but a false witness deceit," needs little comment, as we have had the same subject already under consideration.† We are reminded of the special necessity of *truth in witness-bearing* in order to the right decision of any cause. He who "tells the truth, the whole truth, and no-thing but the truth," subserves the interests of equity; "*shows forth righteousness*"—contributing as far as lies in *him* to a just result: while a "*false* witness" misleads and deceives—drawing judge, and jury, and audience into a wrong train, and producing a false and unrighteous verdict, which acquits the guilty or condemns the innocent.

The two following verses are closely connected with the preceding, and with each other:—" There is that speaketh like the piercings of a sword: but the tongue of the wise is health. The lip of truth shall be established for ever: but a lying tongue is but for a moment."

The language of keen irritation, reproach, invective, and scorn, often inflicts wounds on the heart that are deep and hard of cure—wounds *"like the piercings of a sword."* This is especially the case, when the words are from the lips of a friend, or of one we love, when heated by sudden passion. The utterance of a moment may embitter the future of a life-time—the remembrance "piercing" the heart of him whose lips the words have escaped, even more severely than that of the object of them.

Wit, too, when not chastened and controlled by an amiable disposition, often wounds deeply, and is as "the piercings of a sword." Jibes, jests, irony, raillery, and sarcasm, fly about. No matter what the wounds, or where they be inflicted, if the wit be but shown. A *happy hit,* a clever, biting repartee, will not be suppressed for the sake of the feelings, or even the character of a neighbour, or, as it may happen, a friend. The man of wit *must* have his joke, cost what it may. The point may be piercing in the extreme; but if it *glitters,* it is enough; to the heart it will go.—The man of such a character, whose wit is for self-display, to the sacrifice of every feeling but his own, never can be loved. He is feared, hated, avoided. *" But the tongue of the wise is health."* It has no keen "piercings." It composes differences, allays resentments, vindicates character, soothes the sorrowful, comforts the afflicted, cheers the drooping and desponding spirit, promotes peace and concord, justice and piety, personal and social happiness.

In the last verse the value of *truth* is re-asserted. They whose lips are *" the lips of truth "* hold a position of pre-eminent security and peace. With those of a "lying tongue" it is all the reverse—momentary success—final ruin! The verse has been differently rendered:—"The tongue of truth is ever steady: but the tongue of falsehood is so but for a moment," (Hodgson). There is unvarying consistency in the one case; for truth is always in harmony with itself; while there is shifting evasion, vacillation, self-contradiction, in the other. Truth is ever at once the *easiest* course and the *safest.* Cleave then to TRUTH.

LECTURE XXVIII

---◆---

Prov. xii. 20—28.

" Deceit is in the heart of them that imagine evil: but to the counsellors of peace is joy. There shall no evil happen to the just: but the wicked shall be filled with mischief. Lying lips are abomination to the Lord: but they that deal truly are his delight. A prudent man concealeth knowledge: but the heart of fools proclaimeth foolishness. The hand of the diligent shall bear rule: but the slothful shall be under tribute. Heaviness in the heart of man maketh it stoop: but a good word maketh it glad. The righteous is more excellent than his neighbour: but the way of the wicked seduceth them. The slothful man roasteth not that which he took in hunting: but the substance of a diligent man is precious. In the way of righteousness is life; and in the pathway thereof there is no death."

WHAT is the precise point of the designed antithesis in the first of these verses? I am disposed to think, that the word rendered " *deceit*," may be understood as including deceit practised on a man's self as well as on others; and that here it may have the sense of *self-deceit*. Eminent translators, accordingly, in exact conformity with this idea, have rendered the word, in its present connexion, *disappointment; frustrated hope.* Should this rendering be questioned, —the word being generally used for *fraud*, or *mischievous dissimulation* and *double dealing*,—the principle of interpretation is still sufficiently obvious. Those who "*imagine evil*," dare not avow their designs. Dissimulation and craft are productive of incessant apprehension and anxiety. They necessarily engender self-dissatisfaction and tremor; and that from the very dread of detection, frustration, and consequent evil to themselves, instead of to those against whom they were plotting.—While such is the unhappy condition of the man who "imagines"—that is, who *devises* evil; who seeks to foment discord; to sow the seeds of dissension, and to encourage their germination and growth till they bear all their bitter fruits—on the other hand, "*To the counsellors of peace is joy.*"

God is "the God of peace." Christ is "the prince of peace." "The fruit of the Spirit is peace." In harmony with His own character and with the character and ends of the dispensation He was introducing, Jesus pronounces a blessing upon the "maker of peace."* When the angelic host ushered the new-born Saviour into the world, they proclaimed " Glory to God in the highest, and on earth peace!" All the exhortations of the divine word accord with this. Peace is the spirit of the Bible. Peace is the very element of the gospel. Peace is the bliss of heaven—" They shall enter into peace." The *joy* which the " counsellor of peace" possesses, springs from the inward satisfaction of having felt and acted in harmony with the will and the word of God, and with the best interests of men ; and from complacency in the blessed results of his counsel and mediation. What a spirit that must be that has pleasure in the opposite! The very pleasure is misery. The very sweet is gall and wormwood.

Verse 21. " There shall no evil happen to the just: but the wicked shall be filled with mischief."

This verse has been variously rendered. The rendering of the English version seems to have as fair a title to preference as any. The difference arises from the word for *evil*, —like that word itself—signifying either *evil done*, or *evil suffered.* Our translators have understood it in the latter sense; and we keep by it.

It will be evident that, in this understanding of the word, the sentiment in the first clause of the verse must be taken, like others, in a *general* sense. It is a fact in providence that many distresses come upon the righteous, and that, in the ordinary acceptation of terms, and according to the or-

* Matt. v. 9.

dinary feelings of mankind, these are *evils*. They are, in themselves, "not joyous, but grievous." But viewed in their bearing on the higher department of human interests, the declaration may be considered as of exceptionless universality: the import being, in the terms of Matthew Henry —"The worst troubles shall be overruled for their good." In this sense it can be truly said of "the just"—"*All things are theirs.*" "The world" is theirs. "Life and death" are theirs. "Things present and things to come," whether in themselves good or evil, are theirs, for " ALL THINGS work together for their good."

On the contrary—"The wicked shall be filled with mischief"—mischief *to himself.* The expression is strong. But when considered as inclusive not merely of present evils but of final results, what expression can be *too* strong? What expression can go at all beyond the truth; nay, can ever reach it?*

Mark still again, in the next verse, the vileness of *falsehood,* the excellence of *truth;* and truth in *act* as well as in word. The two parts of the verse taken together suggest the remark:—"Lying lips are abomination to the Lord: but they that deal truly are his delight." *Honesty* is just *truth in conduct;* and *truth* is *honesty in words.*

Verse 23. "A prudent man concealeth knowledge: but the heart of fools proclaimeth foolishness."

" *The prudent man,*" the man of modest and diffident discretion—"*concealeth knowledge.*" He is not forward and ostentatious in the display of it. When he does bring it to view, it is on suitable occasions, when it is really required; and in a suitable manner,—not with vain-glorious parade, but with blended self distrust, and a measure of confidence proportioned to the amount of certainty.

There are persons with whom the growth of knowledge is only the increase of food for vanity. Every new acquisition pampers their self-conceit; and, indeed, is sought after, in a great degree, with that view—to gratify self-esteem, and

---

* Comp. chap. i. 31.

to fit for display. True are the words of Paul, "Knowledge puffeth up:" and the augmentation of it may only puff
up the more. This produces a very anomalous and incongruous combination—a mind filled with solid information,
and a heart distended with the emptiness of vanity. And
this generates the *pedant*,—one of the most contemptible and
disgusting of all characters—the man who is ever showing-
off; ever aiming at effect; ever speaking as nobody else would
speak; ever dwelling on his own themes in his own terms;
and in every word, and look, and movement, courting notice
to *self*, as the only object of his own admiration, or worthy of
the admiration of others. What a fool even the man of
"*knowledge*" does at times make of himself!—exemplifying
the truth of the old quaint adage, "*An ounce of mother-wit
is worth a pound of clergy.*"

Still it is true, that the more extensive the knowledge
which a man acquires, he is, generally speaking, the more
conscious of remaining ignorance, and consequently the less
vain; that it is in the early stages of acquirement that self-
sufficiency and conceit are most apparent. It is the *empty*
that are usually the most prone to vain-glory: "*The heart of
fools proclaimeth foolishness.*" The *heart* desires and dictates
the proclamation. The heart is the fountain from which the
shallow, noisy, babbling stream of folly is ever welling out.
It is the ready indulgence of the heart's intense propensity
to talk that betrays the folly. The fool becomes thus the
herald of his own emptiness. "Even a fool, if he hold his
peace," Solomon says elsewhere, "may be counted wise."
But then, alas! to hold his peace is just the difficulty! He
will speak; and he cannot speak without making his folly
apparent. What is *in* will be *out;* and what is in is *foolishness.* "A fool's voice is known by the multitude of
words"—the words being out of all proportion to the sense.
"Yea also, when he who is a fool walketh by the way, his
wisdom faileth him, and he saith to every one that he is a
fool."

There is a connexion, brethren, in which the former part
of the verse ought to be very cautiously interpreted. I mean,

in its relation to divine knowledge—or rather the knowledge of divine truth. Even in regard to the use of that knowledge, there *is* such a thing as "*prudence.*" There *is* such a thing as introducing religion inappropriately, in places and at seasons, when its introduction is likely to do harm rather than good—such a thing as "casting our pearls before swine." And in many instances has the want of discretion,—the want of a due discrimination of the "time to keep silence" and "the time to speak,"—only produced derision on the part of the enemies of religion, and the blush of shame on the cheek of its friends. And yet the ill-timed mistake of the well-meaning but weak and indiscreet, ought not to be used as a cover and apology, as we fear it too frequently is, for "*concealing knowledge*"—for refraining from speaking, and for keeping our mind to ourselves, when a legitimate "prudence" does not at all impose silence; and when the real cause of the reserve, although it shelters itself under the protection of such texts as this, is no other than *shame*—a dastardly shame. O let us beware of *this* extreme. "A word spoken in season, how good is it!" Forget not that our Master has said—"Whosoever shall be ashamed of me and of my words, of him also shall the Son of man be ashamed when he cometh in the glory of the Father, with the holy angels," Mark viii. 38.

In the following verse we have, in a fresh form, an oft-repeated maxim—"The hand of the diligent shall bear rule: but the slothful shall be under tribute."

Industry is the way to preferment; sloth to degradation. Sloth makes a man the subject, not the ruler; the tail, not the head; the vassal, not the master; the subjugated, not the conqueror; the bearer of the yoke, not the bearer of the sceptre. *Would you rise?—be diligent; would you sink?— be idle.* The maxim holds alike in the church and in the world.

Verse 25. "Heaviness in the heart of man maketh it stoop: but a good word maketh it glad."

The figure here is a natural one, and is common in all languages. The "*heaviness*" may arise from different causes;

from the pressure of severe afflictions, whether personal or relative; from apprehensive fears of threatening calamities; or from distress of conscience under the conviction of sin. Such causes " *make the heart stoop.*" They weigh it to the dust.   On the contrary, in these circumstances, — "*a good word maketh it glad.*"   A "*good* word" is a word of sympathy and kindness, of encouragement and consolation, spoken in the ear, in the spirit of friendship.   Above all, "a *good* word" is a word from God.   O! there is no word so good, so pregnant with consolation and strength, and peace and joy, as "the word that cometh forth from the Lord." Have not you felt this, my fellow-christians?   When the heaviness of sorrow has been weighing your spirits down, and you have been ready to sink into despondency, if a friend has whispered into your ear one of the sweet and faithful promises of your covenant God, has it not lightened the burden?   Has it not lifted the crushing weight from your heavy-laden heart?—brought the smile of peace over your countenance, and the tear of joy to your eye?—What an important and interesting duty then does it become, to impart such "good words and comfortable words" to the downcast and heavy-hearted!   It is a delightful designation of our God—" God who comforteth them that are cast down!" And this is one of the characters in which we should seek to resemble Him;—to "visit the fatherless and widows in their affliction;" and "to comfort them who are in any trouble with the comfort wherewith we ourselves are comforted of God."

For sinners convinced of sin, and oppressed with conscious guilt and fear—O how *good* the word of the truth of the gospel! It is the only word that can relieve and lighten it.   Many an oppressed and agitated spirit has it set at rest.   There are in this book of God, indeed, words that may well make the hearts of sinners "*heavy*"—words of solemn import—of fearful denunciation.   O that we but saw them "stooping" under this "heaviness;" sensible of sin, feeling the hand of a righteous and holy God upon them; conscious of the justice of his condemning sentence and trembling in the ap-

prehension of its execution! Then should we be sure of a
ready entrance to the "good word" that tells of mercy for
the chief of sinners through a divine Saviour;—the word
that stilled the trembling spirits of the convicted murderers
of "the Prince of life;" that sent the eunuch of Ethiopia on
his way rejoicing; that filled with gladness the alarmed
jailer at Philippi—giving a satisfactory answer to his question
of agitation and dread—"What must I do to be saved?"—
"the word of reconciliation"—"the faithful saying, and worthy
of all acceptation, that Christ Jesus came into the world to
save sinners." O listen, listen to the "good word" that
came from the lips of Him who spake as never man spake
—"Come unto me, all ye that labour and are heavy laden,
and I will give you rest. Take my yoke upon you, and
learn of me; for I am meek and lowly in heart: and ye
shall find rest unto your souls. For my yoke is easy, and
my burden is light."* Surely, when he uttered these words,
the prediction of the prophet was fulfilled, in which Messiah
is introduced as saying—"The Lord God hath given me the
tongue of the learned, that I should know how to speak a
word in season to him that is weary!" Isa. l. 4.

Verse 26. "The righteous is more excellent than his neighbour: but the way of the wicked seduceth them."

The word rendered "*excellent*" is on the margin translated
"*abundant*." And although it is a truth that in regard to
character, in all its principles and their practical results, "the
righteous is more *excellent* than his neighbour;" yet such
a statement is almost a *truism.* Taking the word as referring to *possessions* and *prospects,* as meaning that the righteous excels his neighbour, or men in general around him, in
his *lot* as to happiness and hope—blessings in enjoyment
and blessings in anticipation—it then becomes a statement of
very great importance. It presents an inducement to the
godly to "hold fast their profession," and an inducement
to others to join their society, and cast in their lot with
them. "The righteous" may belong to the lowest grade in the

* Matt. xi. 28—30.

community of this world; for "to the poor the gospel is preached." But even the poorest of the people of God has a lot that may well be envied by the wealthiest and the noblest of the sons of earth. When we view them as the possessors, in the promises of God, and in the experience of their own hearts, of "all spiritual blessings,"—rich *in* faith and rich *by* faith, and the heirs of an everlasting and celestial inheritance, of a crown and a kingdom above,—we feel the truth of the position.

The wicked themselves are convinced of it. But, as Solomon here adds—"*the way of the wicked seduceth them.*" Their way is the way of sin—"the course of this world." By this their way they are beguiled. There is something tempting in it always before them, by which they are lured forward. The pleasures of sin—the fascinations of the world—its riches, its honours, its company, its amusements, its present gratifications, its promises for to-morrow—all work upon, and "*seduce*" them.*

Another graphic description follows of the effects of *sloth:* —verse 27. "The slothful man roasteth not that which he took in hunting: but the substance of a diligent man is precious."

Even the sluggard, roused by particular circumstances, will at times make an effort; but having made it, he relapses into his habit of indolence, and the effort is rendered nugatory. He goes out a hunting; he catches prey; he brings it home. But he lets it lie, from sheer laziness, till it becomes useless. His labour is lost. "*But the substance of a diligent man is precious.*" He turns his "substance" to good account. What he gains becomes, in his hands, by the use he makes of it, "precious," as the means of further increase. And his substance becomes "precious" to others as well as to himself. It is industriously, profitably, benevolently used. In *this* lies the true value, the real "preciousness," of a man's substance;—not in the *acquisition*, but in the *use*.

* Comp. chap. i. 31, 32.

We have had the sentiment of the 28th verse repeatedly before us:—"In the way of righteousness is life; and in the pathway thereof there is no death."—The words have no meaning, unless they be understood as implying, and having reference to, a *future state*.   In one sense, you are all aware, there *is* death to the righteous as well as to the wicked.   "Wise men die" as well as "the fool and the brutish person."   But "the righteous" are in possession of spiritual life—a life which never dies—a life which the death that dissolves for a time the union of soul and body cannot injure, but only advances to perfection, setting the living and happy spirit at liberty in "the beauty of holiness," and meetness for the life of heaven.

And thus, in regard to *them,* even now all that is tormenting in the fear of death—of the first or of the second death—the second imparting its terrors to the first,—is taken away; so that "*in the pathway* of righteousness there is *no* death."

That "pathway," remember, begins at CALVARY; and your entrance on it must begin with faith in HIM who died there. You must start in it from the Cross.   THERE ARE A THOUSAND PATHS TO HELL; ONE ONLY TO HEAVEN.   "Enter ye in at the strait gate—strait is the gate and narrow the way that leadeth unto life, and few there be that find it."

In giving you such counsel we are, in the highest sense, "counsellors of peace."   We are seeking your peace, present and future—your peace for time, and your peace for eternity; your peace with God, your peace with yourselves; peace of conscience, peace of heart, peace on earth, and peace in heaven!   Let us have joy of you in the Lord!   If any poor wanderer shall be prevailed upon by what has been said to flee from the paths of sin and ungodliness and the world, and to choose henceforth "the way of life"—"my heart shall rejoice, even mine."   That joy shall be shared by all who have experienced the happiness and the hope of true religion,—and by the spirits of the just and the angels of light above:—for "there is joy in heaven over one sinner that repenteth."

LECTURE XXIX.

———◆———

PROV. XIII. 1—15.

" A wise son heareth his father's instruction: but a scorner heareth not rebuke. A man shall eat good by the fruit of his mouth: but the soul of the
transgressors shall eat violence. He that keepeth his mouth keepeth his life:
but he that openeth wide his lips shall have destruction. The soul of the sluggard desireth, and hath nothing: but the soul of the diligent shall be made fat.
A righteous man hateth lying: but a wicked man is loathsome, and cometh to
shame. Righteousness keepeth him that is upright in the way: but wickedness
overthroweth the sinner. There is that maketh himself rich, yet hath nothing:
there is that maketh himself poor, yet hath great riches. The ransom of a man's
life are his riches: but the poor heareth not rebuke. The light of the righteous
rejoiceth: but the lamp of the wicked shall be put out. Only by pride cometh
contention: but with the well-advised is wisdom. Wealth gotten by vanity
shall be diminished: but he that gathereth by labour shall increase. Hope
deferred maketh the heart sick: but when the desire cometh, it is a tree of life.
Whoso despiseth the word shall be destroyed: but he that feareth the commandment shall be rewarded. The law of the wise is a fountain of life, to depart
from the snares of death. Good understanding giveth favour: but the way
of transgressors is hard."

THE language of the first verse is capable of two meanings:
either, that hearing instruction and not hearing reproof are
the effect and manifestation, respectively, of a wise or a
scornful mind;—the wise son showing himself to be so by
"*hearing his father's instructions*," and the scorner showing
himself to be so by " *not hearing rebuke;*"—which interpretation, on reading the words, strikes the mind as most
natural. Or, (reversing cause and effect) that wisdom and
scorning are the results, respectively, of hearing or not hearing instruction and rebuke. In other words—"*The son that*

is instructed by his father turns out wise; he who receives no correction turns out a fool."

In the first of the two senses the admonition is chiefly to *children,*—in the second to *parents.* Let both, respectively, receive, and ponder, and act on, the admonition as from GOD.

The sentiment of verse *second* is similar to that expressed in the *fourteenth* verse of the preceding chapter—" A man shall eat good by the fruit of his mouth; but the soul of the transgressors shall eat violence."—A single remark must suffice in further illustration of it. Although the spirit and practice of *retaliation* are nowhere vindicated in Scripture, but everywhere explicitly and strongly condemned; yet a treatment corresponding to their own conduct towards others, is what every one may expect, even independently of what deserves the name of *retaliation.* In the nature of things it cannot be otherwise. It is not in *human* nature, nor in *any* nature, not even in the *divine* itself, to love (with the love of complacence, I mean) that which is *unamiable.* An amiable disposition alone can secure love: and amiability of disposition is greatly indicated by the *tongue.* The man who is charitable in his judgments, and disposed to speak well of others, will be himself the subject of charitable judgment and of cordial commendation. All will love, and honour, and bless the man "in whose tongue is the law of kindness." Thus he "shall *eat good by the fruit of his mouth.*" On the contrary, against the man who is a "*transgressor*" with his lips, making them the instruments of malice in the utterance of slander and the fomenting of alienation and strife—against that man are unavoidably kindled all the feelings of indignation, all the angry passions; of which the result is "*violence*"—the violence of vindictive pride and sense of wrong.

This interpretation of the latter part of the verse harmonizes best with the language of that which follows— "He that keepeth his mouth keepeth his life: but he that openeth wide his mouth shall have destruction."

Verse 4. "The soul of the sluggard desireth, and hath

nothing; but the soul of the diligent shall be made fat."
Here the important maxim—*Nothing without labour,* is
again repeated. It is the original law of man's nature.
The *fatigue* and *distress* of labour are, no doubt, the result
of sin. Not so *labour itself.* Even in the garden of prime-
val innocence "the man was placed, to dress it and to keep
it:" not to bask idly in the sun, and see everything spring
and prosper around him—the ground dressing itself, and the
plants trained and pruned by the hand of nature, and nothing
left for him to do but enjoy the beauty, and the fragrance,
and the fruit. No; his enjoyment was to be enhanced by
his having a hand in all, and obtaining all as the reward of
his own care and tending—his own "delightful task." It
was by his "dressing and keeping" that everything was to
thrive.

On the two following verses it is equally unnecessary to
enlarge. They bring up afresh very frequently recurring
thoughts*—"A righteous man hateth lying; but a wicked
man is loathsome and cometh to shame. Righteousness
keepeth him that is upright in his way; but wickedness
overthroweth the sinner."

The "hatred" of the "righteous" to "*lying*" arises from
his sympathy in all things with God. He is "of one
mind" with God; and to Him "lying lips are an abomination." He covets God's approving smile more than all that
earth can yield, and would not lose it one moment for all
the most successful duplicity could ever gain. And that
smile a course of uprightness and integrity secures; but
"*the wicked,*" meaning here especially *the liar,* by his very
lies, his deceit and falsehood, to say nothing of the varied
crimes, for the concealment of which these are employed, is
emphatically "*loathsome.*" He is loathsome to God, loathsome to all the truly good, and even according to the con-
ventional morality of the world, from which "lying" is
excluded on the principle of *expediency,* "loathsome" to
men in general:—and "*cometh to shame;*" loses confidence;

---

* Comp. chaps. xi. 3—6; xii. 22, and other passages.

is distrusted, shunned, nicknamed, scorned, and ruined. Destitute of the "righteousness" which "*keepeth the upright in the way*," he is, like all other "sinners," overthrown, discomfited, and destroyed by his "wickedness."

Verse 7. "There is that maketh himself rich, yet hath nothing: there is that maketh himself poor, yet hath great riches." This verse bears a close resemblance to the 24th verse of the eleventh chapter, but the sentiment it expresses is not the same. That verse assures us of the favour of the Lord to the generous and liberal—who, under His blessing, prosper by *giving*, make rich by "*scattering;*" and of His displeasure at the niggard, whose blessings He curses, and whose accumulated stores He dissipates, making the very care he takes of them the means of their diminution and failure. But here the wise man brings before us quite different developments of character, — *the ostentation of riches where there are none; and the affectation of poverty in the midst of riches.*

Some make a great show of wealth, with little if any capital—living on false credit. Enamoured of the "lust of the eyes and the pride of life," they contrive to keep up an external appearance far beyond any means they actually possess. They affect *high life* on *low finances*. Even, at times, for the sake of commanding credit, they put on such an appearance to give the world the impression that they are prospering. They live at great expense; launch into extensive speculations; make a show of large dealings, great warehouses, great stock, and distant connexions. But all is hollow; there is no substance, no reality. It is only a gay bubble, sparkling in the sunshine, but lighter than vanity; which bursts anon, and its emptiness is discovered. What seems bullion is but a covering of gold leaf. What dazzles is but a passing meteor.

Such a course is nothing better than a species of *swindling* on a large scale; and surely the largeness of the scale should not diminish the guilt in our eyes. It is frequently adopted by men of little principle, when they find themselves sinking. Instead of *giving in* in time—they *make a dash;* they

assume a higher and more splendid style of living than
before, that they may thus avoid suspicion, and maintain
their credit; while they know that they are only augmenting
risks, hastening their own downfall, and more largely and
seriously involving others. *This is wickedness.*

On the other hand we have the *miser.* He scrapes, he
holds, he hoards, he "*has great riches.*" But he "*makes
himself poor;*" not only feigning poverty, and assuming its
garb and appearances before others, that he may not raise
expectations by his wealth being known, but actually *living
in poverty;*—denying himself the comforts and even the
necessaries of life,—pinching and starving to add to the
store which lies unused, of no service either to himself or
others. *This too is wickedness,* but of another type. It
must be ranked among the varieties of mental derangement,
and yet it is derangement which, like some other descriptions of it, is of a *moral* kind, originating in the perversion
of moral principles.—And akin to it, on this ground, is the
love of money, and the eagerness to hoard, induced by the
preposterous vanity of *dying rich.* I have called the vanity
preposterous because of the strange incongruity of a man
breathing his last in the conceit of being the richest he
knows, and aware, at the same time, that the instant
his last breath is drawn, the extent of his earthly possessions will be the length and breadth of his grave! And
further, because the man who is vain of dying rich, is
vain of that which is his *shame.* His dying rich is the
very *proof* of his sin and shame. Had he done with his
riches what God always intends when he bestows them,
he would not have died *so* rich. Had he hearkened
to the claims of benevolence and piety; had he dispersed
and given to the poor, to relieve both their temporal and
their spiritual need, he might have had less in his coffers,
but an incomparably more enviable reputation on earth, and
a better and more enduring substance in heaven.

Verse 8. "The ransom of a man's life are his riches: but
the poor heareth not rebuke."

The verse has been understood in different ways. The

I.   Y

import of it has been given thus:—"*A rich man when he fears any evil from his enemies, can divert it by a sum of money; but the poor man, when he is threatened, dares not stay, but runs away.*" He does not stay to defend or buy himself off; but the moment he hears "rebuke" or threatening, aware that he has no resources, he stops not to hear it out, but immediately makes good his escape—*takes himself off.*

I prefer another interpretation—according to which the verse sets forth the comparative benefits of poverty and riches.—The rich are objects of envy; exposed to false accusation, to robbery, to theft, and to the risk of life. It is true that in their circumstances, they may, in seasons of public calamity, redeem their lives by "a ransom" from their abundant store. But the poor are still better off. They are *not* exposed to danger. They are not envied; they are not "looked at askance with jealous leer malign,"— with the "evil eye" of covetousness; nor are they molested with the harassing disquietudes arising from such causes. Who thinks of envying, or prosecuting, or defrauding, or taking the life of the man who has nothing? Who ever thinks of robbing or murdering a beggar? *He* is every-where safe and free from molestation, from whom there is nothing to be had. Poverty, then, is not without its advantages. They are, to be sure, of a *negative* kind; and not likely to make men give the preference to poverty; nor do I mention them because it should, or that it may. All that is meant is, that such considerations should contribute to reconcile the poor to their providential lot.—Another consideration is this—that *there is a death from which no riches can ransom, and a life which no riches can purchase.* Here "the rich and the poor meet together." They stand on the same footing. They must both obtain life and salvation on the same ground. The rich cannot purchase it; the poor need not riches to procure it. It is "the gift of God," "without money and without price." By *the same ransom* all, "high and low, rich and poor," must be redeemed —"not with corruptible things, as silver and gold; but with the precious blood of Christ, as of a lamb without blemish

and without spot." O let rich and poor come to the same
cross, and the same throne; to the same Saviour, and the
same Father in heaven; and, trusting in the same foundation of hope, anticipate together the same eternal home.
Believe in Christ and the riches of eternity are yours. HE
has paid the ransom.

Verse 9. "The light of the righteous rejoiceth: but the
lamp of the wicked shall be put out." Here *light* is joy.
The meaning is, that of "the righteous" the joy is steadfast,
permanent, increasing; while that of the wicked is destined
to final and perpetual extinction—leaving him in the blackness of darkness.—Of the former " the light *rejoiceth*,"—or
" burns brightly;" shines with growing lustre—"more and
more unto the perfect day." Of the latter the joy shall close
in misery and despair—his lamp extinguished in a darkness,
of which the intensity will be deepened by contrast with the
previous light.*

Even amid the gathering and brooding gloom of adversity,
" the righteous is more excellent than his neighbour." He
possesses, in his hours of sorrow, a light of spiritual gladness which many a time shines most brightly and cheeringly
when the lights of this world's prosperity are dim or extinguished. Have you not found it so in your happy experience,
ye friends of Jesus and children of God? Yes; and by
and by, the gloom shall have passed away, and the light
of your blessedness shall shine forth in all its splendour
for ever and ever! Death, instead of quenching it, only
removes whatever obscured the brilliance of its lustre ; that
in the purer atmosphere of heaven it may send forth all its
radiance. There your " joy shall be full."—On the contrary,
the light of " *the wicked*" is worldly prosperity alone. It is
a " lamp " which every passing breath may extinguish, and
which, even if no such accident befall it, is rapidly consuming
—burning to a close. And when this only light fails, all is
darkness—darkness without a single ray to relieve it—the
darkness of unending night.

* Comp. Job xviii. 5, 6: and chap. xxi. 17.

Verse 10. " Only by pride cometh contention: but with the well-advised is wisdom." This verse has been rendered —" A fool, through pride, stirreth contention: but with the considerate is wisdom."—An immense proportion of the quarrels and disputes found in families, in circles of relationship and friendship, in churches, and in communities, have their origin and their continuance in " *pride*." And where it does not operate in producing them *alone*, it mixes itself up with other principles and motives—tainting and vitiating even such as are in the main good. There is a quick and touchy jealousy which cannot brook a word, or act, or look, that bears the slightest semblance of disrespect or deficiency of deference. *This* is " pride." And resentment, revenge, envy, ambition, are all to a great extent, resolvable into " *pride*." From the contending interests of the world, bringing into operation these and other principles, arise so many unhappy strifes and alienations. And then, when there might be reconciliation and peace, " pride " interferes and prevents it. The question, Who is to yield?—or, Who is to yield *most ?*—comes to be asked; and pride makes it difficult of reply. The adjustment might be easy, but for pride. Some point of honour—or what to pride seems such—must be maintained. The required apology must be complete in matter and in manner; not a word omitted or qualified; and the bow of humiliating submission must not want a hair's-breadth of its due profoundness. The offender must be thoroughly prostrated, that the triumph of pride may be complete!

And, as might be expected of our fallen nature and deceitful hearts, we are full of excuses for this pride. We are fond to exempt it from condemnation under some of its varieties; and we contrive to screen it under palliative epithets. We call it a *becoming* pride; a necessary self-respect and regard to our own dignity; a manly assertion of our own rights; a spirit that will not submit, and *ought* not to submit, to be trampled upon; and thus, under pretexts which involve a certain amount of truth, we cover from censure a larger amount of what is wrong. And the very manner in which even a Christian man may be seen, at times, to draw himself up, and toss his head, and look consciously great, when he is putting in this plea, should be enough to show him that there is a spirit working within not quite in harmony with the "meekness and gentleness of Christ."—Our pride and vanity naturally prompt to an over-estimate of wrongs of which *we* happen to be the objects; so that what, did it happen to another, we should never so much as notice, assumes much of consequence when it affects *us;* and we cherish the vindictive remembrance of little matters, which the wing of the passing moment has swept from every memory but our own. Nor do we only magnify the real,—we imagine injuries that were never meant, and have no existence; and impute to the worst motives what had either little or no motive at all, or a motive which, though mistaken, was good.

" *But with the well-advised,*" or the considerate, " *is wisdom.*" They show the wisdom of thinking more rightly of themselves; of putting a curb upon their pride and passion; of shunning disputes and quarrels, and, when they have unhappily occurred, of bringing them, by every possible means, to a speedy termination.

Verse 11. "Wealth gotten by vanity shall be diminished: but he that gathereth by labour shall increase."

In this verse "*vanity*" evidently means *all iniquitous methods of acquisition;* and perhaps these are all called "vanity," because the expectations of him who uses them of real enjoyment in what he acquires, when successful, are so utterly vain.

And what is true of private is no less true of public possessions. When such possessions are obtained, on the part of any country, by self-aggrandizing and unprovoked aggression, extermination, and conquest,—what are such means but injustice, oppression, and murder on an extended scale?—and surely, we say again, the largeness of the scale should not abate our abhorrence of the evils! Gaining possessions by a violation of the rights of others,—of the principles of equity, and honour, and good faith—or, in one word, of the "royal law," is turning a country's glory into shame; and, under the righteous and retributive administration of Heaven, the extension of dominion is but the extension of danger.[*]

"*But he that gathereth by labour shall increase.*" The phrase for "by labour" is in the original "*with the hand.*" But it signifies of course labour of all descriptions, all that comes under the designation of *honest industry.*

Verse 12. "Hope deferred maketh the heart sick: but when the desire cometh, it is a tree of life."

HOPE is the great cheerer of "the heart." And who has not experienced the sinking and "*sickening*" of the spirit from long-delayed expectations; and the joy that springs up in the soul, on the arrival of the long-looked-for good? A beloved friend, who has been for many a year in a distant land is returning home. How tardy then the flight of time!—days are weeks, and weeks months! "The heart" gets "sick" with "deferred hope." Then, when the hour of arrival and meeting does at length come, how vivid the ecstasy of delight!

We have, in Scripture, recorded illustrations of the sentiment. We have the case of Abraham in regard to God's promise. O! the time was long! The delay looked strange. And, although his faith did not fail, yet at times his spirit seems to have felt the encroaching weariness of protracted waiting without any appearance of fulfilment.[†] Then, we have Hannah, pining at heart, amidst the insults and provocations of her "adversary," with the "deferred hope" of a son—when she "wept and did not eat" and her spirit was "grieved."[‡] We have David too in the wilderness, heart-sick in longing for Jerusalem and the courts and ordinances of God's house.[§] And then we have Simeon, "waiting for the consolation of Israel"—fervently desiring his departure to heaven.[||]

Whither, in all cases, under the pressure of "hope deferred," shall we look? Whither but to our gracious God? He is the source, and He alone, of resignation and comfort, of patience and strength.

---

[*] Hab. ii. 6—12.   [†] Comp. Gen. xii. 1—3. with xv. 2, 3.
[‡] 1 Sam. i. 4—12.   [§] Psal. xlii. 1, 2.   [||] Luke ii. 29, 30.

And suppose, my Christian friends, the trouble, be it what it may, under which we suffer, and the " deferred hope" of whose removal makes us feel the "sickness of heart," the languor of spirit, here described—suppose it should continue with us even to the last; suppose the hope still and still "deferred," even on to the hour when "heart and flesh shall fail;" then the "*desire cometh*," in the highest sense the expression can bear. What was Paul's desire should be ours. The object on which *he* set his heart supremely, should be that on which *ours* are set—"*to be with Christ.*" And when *that* "desire cometh," it will be "a tree of life" indeed. For what says the Saviour himself, in engaging for the future peace and blessedness of his people?—"To him that overcometh will I give to eat of the tree of life, which is in the midst of the paradise of God."

Verse 13. "Whoso despiseth the word shall be destroyed : but he that feareth the commandment shall be rewarded."

The "*word*" is the word of God—whatever comes with His authority. Of the sinner who despises that word the "destruction" is sure. "*The commandment*" has the same meaning in the latter clause with the *word* in the former; and the expression "*shall be rewarded*" is on the margin, as in the original, "*shall have peace.*" This agrees with the language of the Psalmist—"Great peace have they which love thy law; and nothing shall offend them."

Whatever comes with divine authority is a divine *command*. The *truth* that comes with the authority of God, it is the *duty* of man to receive. Let it not, then, be forgotten that the Bible is the revelation of God's mind to man *as a sinner;* and that the very first thing to which man as a sinner is bound, is to accept the terms of forgiveness and life there prescribed. The gospel is, on this as well as other accounts, called "the law of faith ;" being the *divine prescription* for the pardon and salvation of sinners. It has in it all the authority of *a law.** The faith of the gospel is now the principle which produces obedience to the law. It

* 1 John iii. 22—24.

"worketh by *love*," which is "the fulfilling of the law." And as it is in being "justified by faith" that we find "peace with God;" so it is in obeying God under the influence of this faith that we retain "the peace of God."* Thus, we have "in the keeping of His commandments a great reward."

Verse 14. "The law of the wise is a fountain of life, to depart from the snares of death."

"*The law of the wise*"—the law which they choose, and follow, and recommend as the rule of eaith and duty, can be nothing else than this Holy Book—the Book of God. It was the law of the wise *then;* and now that it has been completed, it is more emphatically than ever "the law of the wise" *still.* They are truly wise who understand and believe its doctrines, and conscientiously obey its injunctions: for it is "a fountain of life, to depart from the snares of death." It is a fountain whose streams are salubrious. and life-giving;—not like the waters of Jericho *before,* but *after* they were "healed" by the prophet's "cruse of salt." Nothing but life flows from the fountain of divine truth. To all who refuse to drink of that pure and vital fountain there is *death.* To all who partake of it there is *life.* Death is to those only who disbelieve and disobey. All who receive and love the truth have life. The word of God is essentially life-giving. Its design is not to confirm and publish the sentence of death, but to show how death may be escaped. The declaration of the sentence of death is only intended to show the necessity, and to impress the importance and value of the tidings of *life.* LIFE is the end—the all-gracious end—of divine revelation.

"*The snares of death,*" is a phrase in which allusion is made to nets set for animals meant to be taken and killed. Such are all the temptations of "the Wicked One"—all the allurements of sin; they are "snares of death." He who is taken in them perishes. Now "the law of the wise"—this holy and blessed Book of God—conducts far from these snares all who take it for their guide. It is "a foun-

---

* Phil. iv. 6—9.

tain of life, *to depart*," or to lead "from the snares of death."
He who partakes of the healing waters of this fountain,
and follows along the course of the stream that flows from
it, will escape these "snares." On the margin of that
stream they are not to be found. Its course is away from
them. It is only when induced by strong temptation to forsake it that we are in peril. If, through the devices of
Satan and the allurements of the world, we wander from
this "pure river of water of life," our feet are sure to be en-
entangled in the intricate meshes of those toils that are laid
for us; and so we may never more find our way back again
to its safe and peaceful banks. *There* all is life. *There*
there is *no death*.

Verse 15. "Good understanding giveth favour: but the
way of transgressors is hard." The meaning is not obvious;
and different senses accordingly have been affixed to the words.

1. "Good understanding giveth" or *showeth* "favour"—
say some,—that is *to others;* it is mild, gracious, kind, and
conciliatory, while "the way of transgressors is"—still *to
others*, "*hard*,"—harsh, severe, repulsive, unyielding, stern.

2. The verse has also been rendered—"Ingenuous manners procure favour, but rugged is the path of the artful"—
that is, *it is unpleasant both to himself and to them with
whom he associates;* exposing to incessant troubles, anxieties,
and perplexing difficulties; while open, fair, ingenuous dealing makes a man's way plain before him, and finds him favour and help from all.

3. More probably the meaning in both parts of the verse
terminates on the person's self. "Good understanding"—an
intelligent and sound judgment, enlightened by principle and
instructed by observation and experience,—by fitting a man
to be a wise and able and useful counsellor—procures
"favour." Such a man comes to be valued, esteemed, and
loved. While, on the contrary, "the way of transgressors is
hard"—hard to themselves. Like "by-path meadow" in the
Pilgrim's Progress, it presents at its entrance all that is
tempting to allure into it; but it is "hard." It supplies no
true enjoyment to the traveller in it at last.

If we take "good understanding" as the same with *wisdom*—the wisdom that teaches to "fear God and depart from evil;" we may consider "favour" as meaning *divine* favour. It is on them only who fear him that God "lifts up the light of his countenance." It is to them he gives peace. It is in their hearts that he sheds abroad his love; it is to them he imparts the hope that maketh not ashamed. Them he "guides with his counsel;" them he "brings to glory." "Blessed the people that are in such a case!"—But *the way of transgressors is hard;* and for this very reason—enough, were there no other—that the *favour of God* is not to be found in it. He smiles not on that path, nor on a single soul that chooses it. There is no light of his countenance there. And the way terminates—at that world of woe, in which all the ingredients of the curse are concentrated for ever. The wrath of God which is but *revealed* on earth, is *felt* in hell. It is revealed here, that you may escape it there. This is the design of the Gospel. It unfolds the "way of salvation." They are fools who disregard it. They are of "good understanding" who consider and choose it. It is the way of favour and life here. It leads to favour and life for ever. Examine it. Choose it. Press into it. Flee for it "the way of transgressors." Keep in it. Let nothing drive, let nothing draw you out of it. All will then be well. The way conducts to Heaven—terminates at the gates of the Celestial City.

LECTURE XXX.

PROV. XIII. 16—21.

"Every prudent man dealeth with knowledge: but a fool layeth open his folly. A wicked messenger falleth into mischief: but a faithful ambassador is health. Poverty and shame shall be to him that refuseth instruction: but he that regardeth reproof shall be honoured. The desire accomplished is sweet to the soul: but it is abomination to fools to depart from evil. He that walketh with wise men shall be wise: but a companion of fools shall be destroyed. Evil pursueth sinners: but to the righteous good shall be repaid."

THE first of these verses contains a sentiment in reference to *conduct*, similar to that expressed in chap. xii. 23. with regard to *speech*. "*Prudent men*"—men of discretion, who look before and after—do not either act, or commit themselves to action, rashly. They deliberate. They apply all their sagacity, and all their information, to determine previously how they should resolve, and how they should proceed. And in proportion to the importance of the case—the magnitude of the interests involved, and the consequences likely to ensue, they are the more solicitous that their deliberations should be enlightened and mature; especially when these interests and these consequences affect not themselves alone or chiefly, but others.

On the contrary—"*A fool layeth open his folly*." His whole conduct exposes him, or shows what he is. He leaves nobody at a loss about his character. Even when he tries to be wise,—assuming the air, as fools sometimes do, of an oracle,—he fails. His very airs of wisdom betray "his folly;" and what is good that he has got from others, he mixes up with something incongruous and out of keeping of his own, by which he betrays himself. He disarranges his borrowed feathers in the very attempt to display them, and lets every one see what is below. *Prudence*, of course, has no reference to *principles*, but only to times, and means, and modes of acting. When any principle is in question, and the course prescribed by that principle is clear, prudence is out of place, when allowed to put in a single word to delay, or dissuade from, action. Principle admits of no compromise. Our prudence must never presume to interfere with the dictates, the wisdom, or authority of God. It then becomes an insult to Heaven. The cardinal *virtue* is converted into a cardinal *vice*. The province of prudence is only to consider well, and ascertain surely, that the act we are about to do, or the course proposed to be followed, *is* in harmony with divinely sanctioned principle,—*is* required by divinely enjoined precept.

Folly and wickedness are often, in this book, found in close alliance, and mutually suggesting each other to the mind. It follows:—verse 17. "A wicked messenger falleth into mischief: but a faithful ambassador is health."

"*Wicked*" and "*faithful*" stand here in contrast.—When a man is entrusted with any commission, and undertakes for its execution, *un*faithfulness, falsehood, treachery, is wickedness; is *the* wickedness peculiarly belonging to the position he occupies. "A wicked messenger" is one who betrays his trust,—who, either with intention from the first, or influenced by temptations afterwards, acts a part different from his instructions, and contrary to their design.

Such a messenger, it is said here, "*falleth into* mischief;" as if the evil results came upon *himself*. And true it is, and what might be expected, that in very many cases he does. His treachery, though meant for present benefit, and even, it may be, bringing it, is ultimately ruinous to his own interests. He is detected, cashiered, disgraced, and punished. But this does not yield so direct a contrast or antithesis with the latter clause of the verse—"a faithful ambassador *is health;*" which evidently relates, not to benefit accruing *to himself,* but to those by whom he is employed. On this principle—to bring the two clauses into more direct and natural connexion—the former has been rendered, " A wicked messenger *precipitates into* mischief"—*causes* to fall into it. Thus, the result to the prince, or whoever else may have employed him, is expressed. The embassy may be one, in its principle and in its details, eminently fitted for effecting ends the most desirable,—a wise and salutary measure: but the treacherous conduct of the diplomatist to whom it is entrusted,—whether dictated by a regard to his own interest, or by an overweening conceit of his own sagacity,—spoils the plan, and frustrates the object; and, instead of securing the intended benefit, exposes to injury, dishonour, and loss. He acts a double part. He carries a contrary or a different message. He manages in a way of his own, and not according to his instructions. Thus did *Ziba* to *Mephibosheth*—misrepresenting, falsifying, slandering; and, instead of procuring favour to his master, seeking favour and profit to himself, at the expense of interest, and character, and honour to him that sent him; and moreover, throwing the king into error, and inducing him to act unkindly and unrighteously to one, who, had the truth been told at the time, would have fared very differently at his hands.

I cannot pass this verse without applying it—as it is capable, in all its force, of being applied,—to the ambassadors of Christ of old, and the ministers of his cross still. Unswerving was the fidelity with which the former executed their trust.* And their example, laying apart the *inspiration* and *authority* implied in the idea of an "ambassador," ministers of Christ ought still to follow. "Faithful messengers are," in the highest of all senses in this department, "*health.*" In other and ordinary departments, they are so. They at once *please* and *profit* those by whom they are sent; and they promote the benefit of the community. Their diplomatic fidelity contributes to the healthy soundness and prosperous condition of the body politic. In the kingdom

---

* See chap. iii. 17; iv. 1—5: 2 Cor. v. 18—21.

of Christ, they advance his glory, promote the progress of his cause, and accomplish the salvation of men; by which, indeed, it is, that both his cause is promoted and his glory advanced. Unfaithful ministers, on the contrary, by whom his doctrine is not fully and fairly stated, and by whom ends are pursued different from that for which he himself came into the world, and suffered and died,—bring dishonour on his name, hinder the progress and influence of his truth, injure the spiritual interests of his kingdom, produce unhappiness to the church, and destroy human souls.

Verse 18. " Poverty and shame shall be to him that refuseth instruction: but he that regardeth reproof shall be honoured."

Had you the opportunity of tracing back to its origin the poverty and wretchedness of multitudes, you would find that origin in the neglect or the spurning of faithful and salutary instruction, admonition, and advice, in the morning of life. How very many of those who come to the gallows, or to the hulks, or to transportation, begin their confessions and regrets, by lamenting over their early disobedience to parental counsel, their disregard of a father's and a mother's entreaties and tears!—and in all cases in which such unhappy persons, when not utterly hardened, have enjoyed the benefit of early instruction, their first and most earnest entreaty to others is, to beware of the disposition to make light of, to slight and disown such early privileges; their own sad experience giving point and poignancy to their warnings.*

Verse 19. " The desire accomplished is sweet to the soul: but it is abomination to fools to depart from evil."

Of this verse various interpretations have been given. Two or three I shall mention; and leave you to choose between them.

1. Solomon has been thought to express this sentiment— that the final attainment and enjoyment of a desired good abundantly compensates for all the self-denial, the difficulty, and the privation, endured in waiting for, and in pursuing

* See on chap. v. 7—13.

it. This is a truth of practical importance; holding out, as it does, encouragement to perseverance, through trying and disheartening hindrances, in the anticipation of the recompense. And it is a truth which holds with unfailing certainty, in regard to *spiritual* blessings, the happiness of true religion, and the everlasting felicity in which these are consummated in a future world. But, notwithstanding all this, infatuated, self-willed fools persist 'in evil; pursue present pleasure; discover a rooted aversion to all spiritual duties and spiritual enjoyments; and cannot be induced to deny themselves the gratifications and indulgences of the passing moment, even for the sake of the best and highest of blessings and hopes, how affectingly soever exhibited. They "will not hearken to the voice of the charmer, charm he ever so wisely."

2. Some render:—"It is sweet to the soul to enjoy what we love; therefore an abomination it is to fools to depart from evil."* In this rendering, *the reason* or *principle* is assigned, from which it arises that fools will not depart from evil. Their enjoyment is in it. They feel there are pleasures in sin. These pleasures they love. And, as these pleasures arise from sin, sin is what they like;—sin is sweet; and they *will* indulge their sinful propensities, for the sake of the present pleasure they yield. The present has the entire ascendency. The future is driven from their thoughts, and left to provide for itself, as it best may. They are resolved to take their pleasure now, and take their chance for the future when it comes. They wince, and fret, and are provoked by every admonition to reflection and anticipation. They dislike and spurn their faithful monitors. Their maxim is—"Let us eat and drink, for to-morrow we die."

3. "Desire" *subdued*, restrained, or overcome, "is sweet to the soul: but it is abomination to fools to depart from evil."† According to this translation the former clause expresses the inward satisfaction arising from the successful curbing and subjugation of any sinful desire—any evil pro-

---

* Hodgson.   † Schult. and Schulzius.

pensity. This forms a fine and striking antithesis to the
second clause. While the good man can hardly enjoy a
greater satisfaction than is imparted by the exercise of self-
control, and the overcoming of any powerful and imperative
desire that has tempted and endangered his virtue, — on
the contrary, to the ungodly the exercise of self-restraint is
irksome, the denial of whatever worldly and sinful propensity demands gratification, is misery : it cannot be endured.
They "draw iniquity with cords of vanity, and sin as it
were with a cart rope." They give the reins to all their
lusts, and, hating all restraint, "say to the Almighty, Depart
from us, for we desire not the knowledge of thy ways." The
character is portrayed with great spirit, in the tenth psalm.*

The lesson of the following verse is one of the comparative effects of *good* and *bad* company ; a subject on which
we have found Solomon touching more than once already.
He knew and felt its importance :—" He that walketh with
wise men shall be wise : but a companion of fools shall be
destroyed."

It is a fair and encouraging symptom of begun wisdom
and piety, when a disposition is discovered to "*walk with the
wise;*" to associate with them ; to court and frequent their
company ; to prefer them as companions and intimates. As
"two cannot walk together unless they be agreed," such association augurs well. It is one of the ways, and one of
the first ways, in which when there is, in any heart, "some
good thing toward the Lord God of Israel," it begins to
show itself.

By such association also, good principles will be confirmed
and strengthened ; virtuous and holy habits formed and established ; and all the affections which constitute the spirit
and essence of true religion settled and matured. The spirit
of the wise, or pious, is imbibed ; the encouragement of their
countenance felt; and the benefit of their conversation and
example, in every way experienced. The interchange of
thought augments its useful stores ; and the interchange of

* Comp. verses 1—6, and 11—13.

true sympathy, and prayer, invigorates every right feeling, every pious and virtuous resolve.

On the other hand—"*the companion of fools shall be destroyed.*" Let the young mark it. "Evil communications corrupt good manners." "The companion of fools" learns their ways; drinks in their spirit; becomes familiarized with their principles and specious reasonings; loses the shrinking timidity of previous educational virtue; follows their courses; shares their doom. His heart is corrupted, and his soul is lost. Many scriptural illustrations press for notice. We have the *family of Lot,* suffering the fearful contamination of Sodom, from his "love of this present world" guiding his choice of a residence, instead of higher principles.* We have *Rehoboam,* following the counsel of his young companions, in preference to that of the aged and experienced counsellors of his father, and losing, in consequence, five-sixths of his kingdom.† We have *Jehoshaphat,* associating with Ahab, "helping the ungodly, and loving them that hated the Lord;" "wrath, therefore, coming upon him from Jehovah."‡

The lesson is equally applicable to the prudential knowledge and regulation of secular affairs. The associate of the wise and intelligent in the business-pursuits of the present world will learn, by conversation and example, many profitable facts, and truths, and principles, which may be turned by him to good account; while "the companion of fools"—of the idle, the profligate, the dissipated, will lose all these, and is in the direct road to temporal disgrace and ruin. But the higher application of the words in their bearing on man's spiritual and eternal destiny, is incomparably the more important.

Let youth take warning. When anything in their situation exposes them to the company of the ungodly, they are in danger. Let them not *choose* the exposure; and, should it unavoidably come in their way, let them fortify themselves by resolution and prayer. And as parents would not for any earthly consideration, wilfully and knowingly, place

---

* See Gen. xiii. 10—13.   † 2 Chron. x. 6—19.
‡ 2 Chron. xviii. and xix. 1, 2.

their children amidst the infection of the plague, far less should they, for any such consideration, set them down amidst the contaminations and enticements of vice and impiety. Too often, alas! this is little thought of, even by Christian parents, in choosing situations for their children. For the sake of a *lucrative place*, they will subject them to the most imminent risks of moral and spiritual pollution and death! O beware. You have no right to expect divine interposition to preserve your children from an evil to which you willingly, and wantonly, and from worldly motives, expose them. How *can* you expect to be heard for them? The Lord will shut out your prayer.

Many, as we have seen, are blinded to the dangers of evil company—blinded to the final consequences of associating with men of evil principles and evil deeds, by witnessing the present prosperity, and seeming enjoyment of such men in the course of this world, and the pleasures of sense and sin. The language of the next verse may well counteract any such illusion and forgetfulness:—"Evil pursueth sinners: but to the righteous good shall be repaid."

The representation here is very striking. "Evil *pursueth* sinners." It follows their every step; and will infallibly overtake them in the end. It keeps pace with the progress of time. Each moment it comes nearer. Silent and unperceived, it tracks them through their whole course,—through all the windings and doublings of their wicked career. Insensibly it gains upon them. And at last—it may be suddenly and when least expected, it seizes and destroys them. The stroke of vengeance may be suspended; but it will only fall the heavier when it comes. "Because sentence against an evil work is not executed speedily, therefore the heart of the sons of men is fully set in them to do evil. Though a sinner do evil an hundred times, and his days be prolonged, yet surely I know that it shall be well with them that fear God, which fear before him: but it shall not be well with the wicked, neither shall he prolong his days, which are as a shadow; because he feareth not before God," Eccl. viii. 11—13.

LECTURE XXXI.

———◆———

Prov. xiii. 22—25.

" A good man leaveth an inheritance to his children's children ; and the wealth of the sinner is laid up for the just. Much food is in the tillage of the poor: but there is that is destroyed for want of judgment. He that spareth his rod hateth his son: but he that loveth him chasteneth him betimes. The righteous eateth to the satisfying of his soul: but the belly of the wicked shall want."

OF the former clause of the first of these verses, the sense may be either *metaphorical* or *literal:*—that is, it may refer to a *better* inheritance than wealth, or it may refer to wealth itself. By the careful and pious education of his children,— bringing them up in the fear of God and the habits of virtue —the "good man leaves them an inheritance" of *right principles.* And these are, in reality, a far more valuable inheritance than the largest amount of riches ever accumulated by human industry or speculation, or the largest number of acres that earthly estate ever contained. By bringing up his children thus, he bequeaths to them the very best of all legacies ;—valuable, even as it respects this world; for better surely are the principles of which the right application may, by the blessing of God, *acquire* wealth, than the largest amount of wealth *left* to a child, with principles that unfit him for the right use of it, and fit him only for squandering it away: and, when regarded in relation to the world to come, *in*valuable, insuring the blessings which " cannot be gotten for gold, neither shall silver be weighed for the price thereof." Ye who have been "trained up in the nurture and admonition of the Lord," value—O value

this inheritance. Retain it with a miser's care, that none of
it be lost. If you throw it not away, it will last you for
ever. And more than this—it is an inheritance that may
be transmitted, with due reliance on the promises of God, to
generations to come. You have had it from *your* parents;
you may transmit it to "children's children."*

There is another sense too, in which "a good man leaves
an inheritance to his children"—in the savour and influence
of *his name*. The same affectionate veneration that has
attended him in life, attaching to his memory when he is
gone, will recommend his family to the sympathy and generous good-will of the community. They will be "beloved
for the fathers' sakes." To the sympathy thus divinely
secured, the psalmist seems to refer, when he says—"I have
been young, and now am old; yet have I not seen the
righteous forsaken, nor his seed begging bread. He is ever
merciful, and lendeth; and his seed is blessed," Psa. xxxvii.
25, 26.

Important as this is, and general in its application to *good
men*, who may all leave their children *this* inheritance, if
no other, the antithesis in the latter clause of the verse leads
more naturally to the *literal* interpretation.

In this view, there are *two* things implied. First, that
the blessing of God on his labours, enables him to *obtain*
the inheritance which he has to leave. The proverb clearly
implies this, the inheritance requiring to be *made*, ere it can
be *left*. The second thing implied is, that *with* the inheritance the blessing of the Lord descends to *his children*. What
would the inheritance be without this? an evil, rather than a
good—a curse, rather than a blessing. If parents be faithful,
affectionate, prayerful, spiritually-minded, and persevering in
the religious education of their children, the character and
the blessing will generally be found descending with the
instruction. Many parents, I fear, are fond of "laying the
flattering unction to their souls," when their children fail
to evince the influence of the principles of godliness, and to

* Compare Psa. lxxviii. 1—7.

keep their consciences easy by this means—that "*grace does not run in the blood*." Very true; but it accords with the entire tenor of God's covenant, that *grace accompanies means;* and that, where the means are rightly used, we may look for the grace.

It is quite clear, that in this and other passages, an inheritance is regarded *as a good*, and that no blame is attached to "the good man" who leaves it to his children and "children's children." We are to understand it as a good *in itself*. And so it is. But this is no reason for overlooking the danger associated with it. Christians should not forget it in their own case; parents should not forget it in their children's. What I wish earnestly to impress upon all parents, is this—that, while it may be a good thing to "leave an inheritance" to their children, they will do their children infinitely more service, by leaving them an inheritance of *principles without wealth*, than an inheritance of *wealth without principles;* and further, that they must not lay up an inheritance for their children by depriving God, and the cause of God, of their due,—by parsimonious stinting in the promotion of the claims of piety and benevolence; for by doing this, they will forfeit the blessing of the Lord upon their substance for themselves, and prevent the blessing from descending with it to their offspring.

While the "good man" thus "leaveth an inheritance to his children's children"—"the wealth of the sinner is laid up for the just." This proceeds on the same great principle with that laid down by the apostle—"*All things are yours:*" and, amongst other things, "*the world.*" They are so, in the sense that they are all wisely ordered for the ultimate attainment of their highest good. That may most truly be called mine, from which I derive the greatest possible benefit it can be made to yield. It would be strange indeed, were I to wish anything else, or anything more. The assertion here made must be interpreted in a similar manner. "The earth is the Lord's, and the fullness thereof." His, among other things, is "the wealth of the wicked." The wicked man calls it *his own*. But it is God's. God retains the entire right to it, and the sole disposal of it. He can

do with it what pleaseth him. God is the friend of his own
children; and holds *that* property, like every thing else, *for
their good;* so that it is *theirs* by being *his.* By the secret
arrangements of his providence, he *can,* whensoever he *will,*
transfer property from one owner to another; and in all cases
in which it will be for his people's benefit, He will make
the transference. Whensoever anything is wanted for his
own cause, he can bring it into the hands of those—" the
just "—to whom he has given grace to use it for its advancement.*

Verse 23. " Much food is in the tillage of the poor: but
there is that is destroyed for want of judgment." There
seems an interesting connexion, and perhaps a twofold connexion of suggestion or association, between the former verse
and this. Talk of *inheritances!* says the poor man, with
his scanty means and hard daily toil,—*we* have *no* inheritance, neither *from* our fathers, nor *for* our children: all is
homely with us, and likely to remain so. Well, says Solomon, the poor man is not without his consolations, even of
a temporal nature—" *much food is in the tillage of the
poor.*" The maxim, though under a particular form, like
many others, is general; not to be confined to the one
kind of labour specified, but extending equally to all the
different modes in which the poor make their daily bread.
The poor peasant, who cultivates his plot of ground industriously and by the " sweat of his brow," will, through the
divine blessing, procure thereby an ample supply of " food "
for himself and his family ; and, if a child of God, he will
have this with the sweet relish of his heavenly Father's
smile. Industry and tidy economy will make the cottage
fireside and table snug and comfortable; and its lowly ten-
ants will enjoy plenty, though in a plain and homely form,
without luxurious delicacies.—On the other hand, how often,
in the case of those who obtain *inheritances,* may the poor
see the saying verified, " *There is that is destroyed for want
of judgment.*" By prodigality and excess, by careless neglect,

* Comp. Eccl. ii. 26.

by bad management, by injudicious and ill-conducted plans and projects, they waste and ruin their fortunes. Their lands are extensive, but they are unproductive; or if productive, the product is mis-spent and squandered: it goes, no one can tell how. To such persons, the homely comfort of "the tillage of the poor" is a just object of envy; far more so than, in many cases, the wealth of the rich is to the poor.

Verse 24. "He that spareth his rod hateth his son: but he that loveth him chasteneth him betimes." There is no subject of deeper interest and importance than the EDUCATION OF THE YOUNG. It is so for their own sake; for the sake of their family and kindred; for the sake of society; for the sake of the Church; for the sake of the glory of God. In their systems of education, some are for excluding the "*rod*" altogether. But such would be wiser than God; for He has sanctioned its use. They, indeed, who consider Solomon as merely giving *his own mind*, are at liberty, how high soever his wisdom may be ranked, to dissent from his judgment, and to decline following the course he prescribes. This might be somewhat presumptuous; but there would be no impiety in it,—no resisting the dictates of the *divine* mind. But if Solomon wrote by inspiration, and the truths and precepts delivered by him are the truths and precepts of the Spirit of God, we must beware of gainsaying any of his prescriptions, in any of the various departments of duty.

For the Scripture authority, not warranting only, but enjoining the use of the "rod," I might quote many passages besides that before us.* I might also refer to such passages as, in speaking of the dealings of God with his people, contain allusions to this part of parental duty.† It should be noticed that the "rod" is to be taken for *correction* or *punishment in general;* not specifically for *corporal* punishment. The blessed God employs a great variety of kinds of chastisement in dealing with *His* children, suiting the correction in nature as well as in degree, to the peculiarities of each character, and the circumstances of each case;—so may Christian

---

* Prov. xix. 18; xxii. 15; xxiii. 13, 14; xxix. 15, 17.
† Prov. iii. 11, 12; Heb. xii. 7, 8.

parents consider themselves warranted to employ whatever description of punishment experience may teach them to be best fitted to answer the end. Of the observations now to be made, some refer to the "*rod*" more specifically, and some to all kinds of correction.

1. *The rod should be the last resource.*—In this remark I refer of course to the "*rod*" properly so called. Perhaps the most suitable season for the use of it may be in the early stages of education, when the mind is but beginning to open, (as soon as the meaning and design of it can be distinctly understood) with the view of forming a habit of subjection, such as may enable you afterwards to rule easily and effectually without it. Still, whenever it *is* used, it should be as *the last* resort. If conviction and sorrow, sufficiently pungent and deep, can be produced otherwise; if you can reach the heart, and draw the tears of a tender and contrite spirit to the eyes—it would, generally speaking, in such circumstances, be cruelty to super-add the pain of correction, the end having been gained, in all respects more pleasantly and more effectually, without it. Cases are supposable, in which it may be necessary to pro-ceed to the correction even amidst the tears and the sobs of submissive distress. I know nothing more acutely agonizing to a parent's feelings than when such necessity exists; and the cases in which it does exist are very rare. To inflict correction in spite of the confessions of weeping penitence, —which may, in most instances, be readily enough distin-guished from the affected acknowledgments of a selfish and heartless hypocrisy,—is obviously in the face of the apostle's admonition—" provoke not your children to anger, *lest they be discouraged:*" for nothing can well be more discouraging, —more calculated to engender a secret sentiment of inward dissatisfaction, as if greater severity had been used than was needed by the offender,—a rising emotion, which checks the full and free flow of affectionate and penitential tenderness, the tenderness which melts into the open bosom of offended but conciliated love.

2. When the "rod" is used, or any punishment inflicted, *be sure that a fault has been committed.*—Strange direc-

tion!—you may say: who requires to be told this? Do
you suppose any of us so unnatural, so fond of putting
our children to pain, that we would punish them for nothing? My answer is, that there is no parent who does
not require the counsel. My full conviction is, that children are often chastened, and chastened at times severely,
when they have committed *no fault.*—A fault I would have
you remember, that justifies punishment, should involve the
manifestation of *some evil disposition.* In every other case,
correction is wrong; and the parent who inflicts it would
himself be a fitter subject for it.—To illustrate my meaning
by two or three exemplifications. There is in children, when
in good health, *a principle of activity,*—a restless buoyancy
that invites and impels them to lively exercise. It is an important instinctive propensity, intimately connected with
bodily health,—with the strength of the bones, the firmness
and pliancy of the joints, the tension of the nerves, the
energy of muscular action, and the general growth and vigour
of the entire frame. The indulgence of this propensity may
make them at times a little noisy and turbulent. It may be
indispensably necessary, on occasions, to lay it under temporary restraint. But authority should be reluctantly interposed; and, unless when authority is violated, or incumbent
duty neglected, it should never be visited with punishment.
You would be punishing your child for exhibiting nature's
indications of health; which it should rather please you
to see, as young people are seldom *well,* when dull and
disinclined to romping and active exercise.—Again, evil
is sometimes done *in ignorance.* The child has no idea
that it has been doing any harm. You happen, I shall suppose, to leave a bank-note in your child's way. He finds the
bit of paper. He finds it where it should not have been.
He has no notion whatever of its value. He takes it up
and throws it into the fire; and he laughs and claps his
hands, in innocent glee, at the pretty blaze. The *loss,* in
such a case, is yours; but don't forget that so is the *fault.*
You should not have left anything of the kind thus exposed.
You may warn your child strongly, never again to burn any

bits of paper he may find, till he has asked you whether they
are of use; and you may impress the lesson by teaching him
the extent of the damage he has done. But take care. Let
not rising passion at your loss lead you to inflict hasty and
summary punishment on the child. He does not deserve it.
And let not the punishment and the passion be proportioned
to the amount of the loss. One pound or fifty was the same
to the child. The more valuable the note, the more inexcusable was your own carelessness. A severe infliction, in such a
case, would be the extreme of unrighteousness; and it would
be the greater culprit punishing the less.——Things, again, may
be done by children from want of *mature discretion*. A child,
when you are not at hand, may have his sympathies touched
by the tale, and the apparent distresses, of some impostor;
and knowing where money is to be found, and thinking,
from what he may have seen you do, that if you only knew,
you would afford relief, may give a great deal more than discretion, even in a really deserving case, would warrant. Would
you be severe on him for this? It would be barbarous. It is
one of the loveliest of principles, operating, as might be expected in a child, without due acquaintance with the acts of
imposture or the value of money, to guide the exercise of his
charity. I remember hearing of a fine little child who gave
a beggar in this way *half-a-crown;* and, in telling what he
had done, called it a *white penny*. In such a case, it would
be right to inculcate the lesson that children should be on
their guard in making use, even for charity, of what is not
their own; and to teach the offender (if such he should be
called) the difference between white and brown. But to
correct him with the rod, would be worse than cruelty; it
would be selling for half-a-crown a principle which it should
be one of the main ends of education to cherish.——Still further, things may be done, that are much to be regretted,
by accident. Here too correction is wrong, or should be very
discriminatively inflicted. If the accident has happened in
doing that which had been previously warned against or forbidden, there may be room for it. But to punish for what
has been purely accidental, where there has been no evil

principle or intention, is most unjust. Let children be
trained, by all means, to caution and care. But O beware of
assuming, in such cases, as the measure of punishment, the
actual extent of the mischief done. A greater punishment
may be deserved, where the damage has been ever so small
than when it has been ever so great; because in the one case
there may have been evil intention or great and culpable
carelessness, and in the other neither. Nay the intention
may even have been good; good may have been intended, and
harm done. In this latter case, there should rather be reward for the intention, than punishment for the accidental
mischief. Whatever may be your loss, do not add to it an
evil much greater,—the evil of spoiling your child by correcting for no fault. For example. Your child, watching your
employment, sees by your looks and motions, that you are in
want of something. He knows, or he guesses what it is;
and with the lively glee of childhood, and affectionate eagerness to serve you, he sets off full speed to fetch it. By and
by he comes back—slowly, and in altered mood. He hangs
down his head beside you in hesitating silence, and fears to
tell what has happened. He has alas! stumbled in his haste,
and has let fall and broken the article he ran to bring. You
feel your spirit rise at the loss and the disappointment. An
article, it may be, of some value, is destroyed, and your process is interrupted and spoiled. But again take care. Lift
not your hand. Call not for the "rod." His very eagerness
to serve you has occasioned the misfortune. Would you
punish him for *that?* Poor dear child! he is more to be
pitied than you. The mortification and shame,—the sudden
sinking of his little heart from lively gaiety to sadness and
vexation, indicated by the slow creeping step, the downcast
look, the tearful eye, and the faltering tongue,—are punishment enough for his undue haste, when that very haste was
prompted by a praiseworthy principle. Caress him for his
kind intention, whilst you join in lamenting the accident;
restore, if you can, the smile to his countenance; and caution
him not to be quite so quick in his motions, even to serve
you, next time he happens to have brittle ware to carry.

3. Let there always *be a due proportion between the fault and the correction.* It should be laid down as a general principle, that all punishment *beyond desert* is punishment of innocence. The *just* degree of punishment is, in all cases, the smallest degree by which the desired effect may be produced—a proper impression, that is, of the evil done, humble submission, and promise of amendment. The kind and the degree may thus be different with different children. The *repetition* of an offence may, of course, warrant greater severity than the first commission of it. But in the conduct of some parents, there is an indiscriminate severity, a general system of rigour and harshness, which knows no rules of proportion; which acts as if the greatest punishment in its power to inflict were little enough for the smallest offence; and whose only reason for not inflicting a greater, in cases of more heinous fault, is its not having a greater to inflict. Nothing can be in more direct contrariety to the important warning already quoted—" Provoke not your children to anger, lest they be discouraged." What could more effectually either spoil their temper, or break their spirit?

4. *Never chastise in a passion.*—There are few cautions of more difficult observance; but few of more essential consequence. If you are unable to govern yourselves, are you fit for governing your children? *Rage* may frighten. It may even, by the mere power of terror, keep from outward trespass; but it never will reclaim to right feeling or right principle. Do not, then, deal in furious rebukes and angry blows. If you correct while the fit of passion is on—what is the effect? You are sure to appear to your child to be merely indulging and gratifying your own anger, instead of having in view the only legitimate object of all correction. And moreover, you are quite sure to *exceed bounds,* and thus at once to " provoke your child," and " to discourage him," while you lay up cause for vexation, and shame, and self-reproach, when you have leisure to cool. If you feel passion rising, lay a firm command upon it; restrain yourself; let the correction stand till you are calm, and fit to do it with judgment. Never forget that correction is *for an end;* that that end is the

conviction, repentance, and recovery of the offender. This
end is not to be effected by passion. All must be done, after
the example of God, *in love;* with displeasure indeed, proportioned to the evil of the transgression, but with calm
and unruffled dignity. The fuming heat of passion, beating a
child, and renewing the beating, for relief to itself, only
lets down the parent in the child's eyes, lessening his filial
respect for him; and is thus most injurious. True affection
will mingle grief with displeasure, tenderness with discipli-
nary coercion. This is strikingly expressed in the words—
" My son, despise not the chastening of the Lord; neither
be weary of his correction: for whom the Lord loveth he
correcteth, even as a father the son in whom he delighteth."
This should teach you the lesson of impressing your child's
mind with the conviction that it is your very *delight* in
him that obliges you to do violence to your own feelings in
correcting him. This leads me to notice—

5. The propriety of always *preceding* or *accompanying*
chastisement with *convincing the offender of his fault.* Show
him, seriously and affectionately, *why* you chastise him. If
you feel yourself at all at a loss to do this, you may be very
sure you are doing wrong. Correction must never either *be*
or *appear to be,* a mere arbitrary display of authority. In
all the precepts respecting " the rod," *the child's good* is the
object; and all should be regulated by a regard to this end.
The spirit of it, on the part of parents, should be that which
dictates the corrections of God, who chastens, not for " His
own pleasure," but for his children's *profit.*" And in seek-
. ing this end, mark the terms of the verse before us—" he that
loveth him chasteneth him *betimes.*" Oppose the *beginnings*
of evil. Check propensities to it early; before they have
time to acquire strength, and to form and settle into habits.

6. That correction may have the surer and happier influence, let it be accompanied with a system of *encouragements.*
It is not fair to correct, and to correct severely for faults,
and to express and manifest no satisfaction and pleasure in
the right discharge of required duties. Children should be
judiciously commended, as well as judiciously reproved;

judiciously rewarded, as well as judiciously punished. There is, with different parents, a danger of the opposite extremes —of commendation and reward without reproof and punishment, and of reproof and punishment without commendation and reward. It requires much discretion duly to blend the two. The good sense of parents must distinguish between just commendation and what would only minister to vanity. But it is evident, that few things can possibly be more dispiriting to a child, than for a parent to be ever prompt to punish evil, but never to reward good; severe and forward to chide, but reluctant and backward to commend. Children should be stimulated by praise, as well as restrained by censure. You may be assured that this will eminently contribute to the right reception of your chastisements, and their salutary influence upon the character. I only add—

7. That *correction* is one of the *most delicate and difficult of parental duties.* It is easy to do it; but far, very far from easy, to do it *well.* Therefore, let parents *keep it in their own hands.* It must ever, in order to answer its appropriate ends, be associated with the blended faithfulness and tenderness of love. When transferred to improper hands, it is almost sure to produce the very opposite effects to those designed by it.

Let Christians, as the children of their heavenly Father, rejoice that their parental discipline is in the hands of One who cannot err, either in the time, the manner, or the measure of His corrections; who will make every stroke of " His rod" tell upon the best interests of his people; promoting their spiritual, and securing their eternal interests. And let their submission, in all their sorrows, correspond with this assurance.*

The last verse must not detain us long—" The righteous eateth to the satisfying of his soul: but the belly of the wicked shall want."

The two states contrasted in these evidently proverbial expressions, are a state of *satisfaction and contentment,* and

* See Heb. xii. 5—11.

a state of *dissatisfaction and discontent:*—the former that of the good man—"*the righteous*"—who enjoys his repast with a true relish arising from the love and blessing of his heavenly Father; the latter that of the "*wicked*" who in that love and blessing has no share! The particular expression here used respecting "the wicked," implies his never being satisfied; ever desiring, ever wanting, how much soever he obtains. What a fine contrast Paul presents to us in describing his own feelings, "I have learned, in whatsoever state I am, therewith to be content. I know both how to be abased, and I know how to abound: every where and in all things I am instructed both to be full and to be hungry, both to abound and to suffer need!" Phil. iv. 11, 12.

To the possession of this perfect satisfaction there is but one way. It is the enjoyment of GOD'S FAVOUR. Nothing can satisfy the soul of man but this; and when this is obtained, it will infuse the spirit of satisfaction into every thing. It will enrich every joy; it will alleviate, and sweeten, and sanctify every sorrow. Here lies the secret of true contentment and happiness. GOD IN ALL THINGS, AND ALL THINGS IN GOD, is the sum of the divine lesson. And the lesson, like all the other lessons of Christian virtue, must be studied at the foot of the CROSS. There must the grand principles of them all be imbibed and settled in the soul.

LECTURE XXXII.

Prov. xiv. 1—6.

" Every wise woman buildeth her house: but the foolish plucketh it down with
her hands.   He that walketh in his uprightness feareth the Lord: but he that
is perverse in his ways despiseth him.   In the mouth of the foolish is a rod of
pride: but the lips of the wise shall preserve them.   Where no oxen are, the
crib is clean: but much increase is by the strength of the ox.   A faithful witness will not lie: but a false witness will utter lies.   A scorner seeketh wisdom,
and findeth it not: but knowledge is easy unto him that understandeth."

THERE is a *fulness* in the word of God, of which the conviction grows on every fresh perusal, and becomes still the
stronger, the closer and more minute our investigation of its
various parts.   It addresses itself (though, for the best possible reasons, under no systematic and formal arrangement,)
to persons in all the various relations and conditions of life.
Sometimes we find important preceptive directions conveyed
in simple descriptive touches of character, in which approbation on the one hand, or disapprobation on the other, is
manifestly designed to be implied.   Thus it is in the first
verse of this chapter:—"Every wise woman buildeth her
house: but the foolish plucketh it down with her hands."

Here we have *female wisdom* and *female folly* contrasted,
with special reference to their appropriate department—the
management of *domestic concerns.*   It is a common saying
amongst ourselves, and it is a pithy and a true one, that
"a fortune *in* a wife is better than a fortune *with* one."
From the situation which women occupy in the household,
it might previously be supposed (and the supposition is
daily verified in fact) that a vast deal depends on them, for

the comfort, the independence, the respectability, the honour, and the advancement of families. We understand "*house*" here, as in many other places, to mean *family;* the "*building*" of the house, the raising of the family; and the "*plucking down*" of the house, the depression of the family, in the various ways just enumerated.

Suppose, what many a time happens, to use the word, of the saying just quoted, "a fortune *with* a wife," but the wife herself, the owner and bringer of the fortune, destitute of discretion, incapable of managing her domestic affairs, or of keeping account of her expenditure; without *home* habits; vain, extravagant, fond of finery and show, and rivalry of her superiors; ever gadding about, and ever squandering money with thoughtless indifference, — the *fortune* will give anything but domestic happiness while it lasts, and that will not be *long*. It will be the same, indeed, if such a woman have her will and her way, whether the fortune be her own or her husband's. Many a time have females been the means of bringing families down that before were thriving, and rising in comfort and respectability. This has arisen from their total want of the domestic virtues of activity, economy, and discretion,—of all that passes under the general name of *management*. "Many a family," says Matthew Henry, "is brought to ruin by ill housewifery, as well as by ill husbandry." On the contrary, a prudent, industrious, frugal, domestic, *managing* wife, animated in all her duties by affection, conjugal and maternal, dignified by the graces of true religion, and guided in all her daily course by a wise discretion, has often essentially aided in bringing forward a family, even from a condition of inferiority, to respectability, independence, and honour, and of retrieving its affairs, when by previous *mis*management brought low.

It is at once the duty and the interest of husband and wife, to co-operate in promoting the common benefit of the family. They must be *one in principle and in aim*. If not, while the one is "building," the other will be "pulling down;" the one will overturn what the other has reared : while the one gathers, the other will scatter. Too often may husband and wife thus be seen counterworking each other; the one doing, the other undoing; the one bringing in, the other throwing out. The verse before us relates only to the *wife's* side of the house. Let wives remember, that all the industry and toil of their husbands will be vain, unless, on their part, it is seconded by management and economy. It is wonderful, in the families of the workman and the peasant, to see the difference of appearance and of real substantial comfort, on the same means, between one where the wife is cleanly, active, orderly, thrifty, and cheerful, and another where she happens, unfortunately for her husband and her children, to be an idle, dirty, disorderly, peevish slattern. The latter character should never be seen, nor any approach to it, in " women professing godliness."—Christian wives, emulate one another; and emulate those "godly women" who are commended in Scripture, in sedulous attention to the tempers and duties that become you in your domestic relations. Let the family, next to the soul, be the first care. And beware of allowing even a professed concern for the interests of the soul unduly to interfere with, and jostle out of place, any of your incumbent domestic duties. Everything is beautiful in its place and time. I have no idea of that religion which allows a woman, under pretext of enjoying spiritual privileges, and making the most of time and means for the soul, to gad about, visiting, and calling, and talking, and hearing sermons, and attending committees, when her presence and active superintendence are wanted at home, and imperative domestic claims and duties are neglected. Wives must make their families their first care; and if, by regularity and diligence in the discharge of their respective trusts at home, they can redeem time for the more private or more public calls of general benevolence, or for hearing a sermon, or attending a meeting, or enjoying the benefit of a little Christian society, it is well. When the two are thus made compatible, " her own works will praise her in the gates." But if, by attending to other calls, her husband is left comfortless, and the food and clothing and education of her children are neglected,—she may be "building" elsewhere, but not where she should be; she is "the foolish" woman whose hands "pull down" her own house,—and who is, in the world, a discredit to the religion she professes, and in the church, a stumbling-block to fellow-professors.

Verse 2. " He that walketh in his uprightness feareth the Lord; but he that is perverse in his ways despiseth him."

The pronoun "*him*," in the second clause is capable of two references. It may refer either to the "upright who feareth the Lord;" or, as is more probable, to *the Lord;* in which case there will be a marked antithesis between the character of the man who *feareth* the Lord, and that of the man who *despiseth* Him. In the first part of the verse, then, we have again the only true, satisfactory evidence of "the fear of the Lord"—of genuine religious principle. It lies not in words or professions, but in *conduct.* That man alone fears the Lord, who "*walketh in his uprightness.*" "This," says the apostle John, " is the *love* of God, that we *keep his commandments.*" This is equally the *fear* of God. Hear you a man making great professions; wondrously devout; his prayers many and long; his psalm-singing loud; his attitudes and looks and gestures the perfection of acted sanctity? *Test* him. Mark his conduct. See what he is in the family and in the market,—*is all right there?* If not, note that man; he is a man of words; his religion is the religion of words; his fear toward God is taught only by the principles of interest and expediency, or by that of compromise; of words for God and actions for himself;—which is the same thing as a compromise, to honour God *verbally* for liberty to *dis*honour him *practically.* Let it be laid down as a settled principle, that whatever be a man's professions of reverence and devotion—" he who is perverse in his ways despiseth God." *Disobedience* is the sure proof of contempt. You judge of the professions of children to parents not by what they *say*, but what they *do.* Thus judge of men's religion. Ask not how frequent, how long, how loud, or how austere and rigid his devotions are;—ask what his *practice* is. There have been men who in the sanctuary have seemed the very patterns of all that is devout, (only that in general it is

overdone) whom, when you follow them into the world, you
find in the meanest of its mean and the dirtiest of its dirty
doings.   This is not to "fear" but emphatically to "despise
the Lord."   It is the greatest of all the affronts that can be
put upon Him—the grossest of insults, the most injurious of
wrongs.   The child dishonours his father more who speaks
fair to his face and rebels behind his back, mocking at the
very success of his fair speeches, than if he were openly and
consistently hostile and regardless.   And so does he dishonour
God more who says to Him, "Lord, Lord, but does not the
things which He says," than if he made no profession at all.
He adds *hypocrisy* to *rebellion*.   Actual "perverseness," or
disobedience, is contempt of God's *authority;* contempt of
God's *glory;* contempt of God's *threatenings;* and contempt
of God's *promises*.   It shows a scornful disregard of *all*.
They who despise God's WILL despise GOD HIMSELF.

Verse 3. "In the mouth of the foolish is a rod of pride :
but the lips of the wise shall preserve them."

"*Pride*" may be regarded as one of the attributes of folly.
It was the original folly of man; the principle which Satan
succeeded in introducing, and by which he seduced man from
God.   And it has been, in reference to God, his folly ever
since.   And from the pride which, in their folly, men too
frequently indulge towards one another, comes haughty, contemptuous, violent, abusive language;   the language of
haughty command, haughty censure, haughty scorn.   This
is "the *rod of pride*" which is in "the mouth of the foolish."
The foolish smite with it; and by doing so, they expose
themselves to many dangers, from envy, resentment, and the
spirit of strife.   By some the word rendered "*rod*" is understood of a *shoot* or *branch*, from the only other place in
which it occurs—"And there shall come forth a rod out
of the stem of Jesse, and a Branch shall grow out of his
roots," Isa. xi. 1.   But even in that passage, there is probably in the shoot springing from the stem of Jesse, an in-
direct reference to the *sceptral rod*—the emblem of the roy-
alty of which the prophet proceeds to speak ;—and the figure
of smiting with the tongue as with the "*rod* of pride" is far

more natural (when the mouth is spoken of) than that of a branch springing from pride as a " root of bitterness."

The general import of the antithesis in the second clause is sufficiently plain:—" but the lips of the wise shall preserve them." " *The lips of the wise*" are the lips, not of pride, but of humility—not of the contempt and wrath which arise from pride, but of meekness, gentleness, kindness, and peace. And there are two senses in which the *preservation* spoken of may be understood. First, by prudent and humble-minded dealing—by language well-weighed and well-adapted to the characters of the individuals with whom they have to do, and to the circumstances in which they happen to be placed,—they preserve themselves from this very " rod of pride," and from its sometimes mischievous consequences. Or, *more generally;* while by their proud and overbearing insolence the foolish bring severe retaliation and correction upon themselves, by the provoking use of their " rod of pride,"—the discretion of the wise, laying restraints upon their tongue, " setting a watch at the door of their lips," preserves them from many contentions, perplexities, troubles, and wrongs; it gives them favour and good understanding, and thus brings upon them benefit and blessing, instead of ill-will, and angry frowns, and muttered curses—the natural returns of pride.

Verse 4. " Where no oxen are, the crib is clean: but much increase is by the strength of the ox."

The most natural interpretation of these words seems to be that which proceeds on the principle that two things are put in contrast, between which men are left to choose.

If oxen are not employed, " *the crib is clean;*"—there is no trouble in feeding, and tending, and cleaning, and keeping all in order from day to day. Here, then, is gratification for indolence and the love of ease. " *But much increase is by the strength of the ox.*" Here is the expense at which the indolent love of ease is to be indulged. It must be purchased at the expense of all that the labour of the oxen would produce. He who would have *the increase*, therefore, must submit to the labour of this feeding, and tending, and cleaning. We have thus again, in a fresh form, the great general lesson of everyday use—*Nothing without labour.*

Wealth will not come of itself. The good things of life do not drop into the mouth of the yawning sluggard. Reputation and honour must be won by deeds that deserve them. Discoveries in science and art must be effected by experiment, observation, reflection, and research. Progress in general knowledge must be attained by reading, conversation and inquiry. And if we would, as believers, grow in the divine life, and in holy meetness for heaven, we must obey the command to "work out our own salvation with fear and trembling," in the use of all appointed means, "giving all diligence to make our calling and election sure."

Verse 5. "A faithful witness will not lie: but a false witness will utter lies."

We have had this subject repeatedly before us:—chap. vi. 16—19; xii. 17—19; xiii. 5. The statement in the verse before us may be regarded as somewhat stronger in regard to the characters contrasted. The meaning is that a "*faithful* witness"—that is a man of sterling integrity and truthfulness, will adhere to truth in all his statements, at whatever risk, and at whatever cost. Nothing will tempt him to depart from it—neither the fear of threatened suffering nor the hope of promised reward. On the contrary, "a *false* witness"—a man addicted to falsehood, regarding merely what is expedient—and what at the time promises most benefit, whether negative or positive,—such a man *will* utter lies, let the temptation be ever so small;—sometimes from the very pleasure he has in deceiving others, and seeing them perplexed and confounded, and led astray in their judgment and counsels. A habit of *lightness* in regard to truth is one which, once admitted even in the smallest matters, grows insensibly,—becoming less and less thought of in matters of greater importance. He who lies in little things is only *learning to lie* in great things.

Verse 6. "A scorner seeketh wisdom, and findeth it not: but knowledge is easy unto him that understandeth."

The "*scorner*" is the same description of person as in chap.

i. 22.   There are indeed two descriptions of the character.
There are "scorners" of *truth*, from *pride of intellect;* and
there are "scorners" of *authority*, from the *pride of self-will.*
They are nearly allied; and they are frequently united. It
is the former that is chiefly meant here; seeing the subject
is *knowledge* rather than *duty.*

There is a certain spirit and frame of mind necessary
to the understanding and successful investigation of divine
truth.   It is the spirit that counts our own wisdom folly—
laying it down at the feet of our divine Instructor, and taking our place as listeners and learners.   It is the spirit of
Samuel, when he said—" Speak, Lord, for thy servant heareth."   It is the spirit of the apostles when they said, "Lord,
to whom shall we go but unto thee—thou hast the words of
eternal life."   It is the spirit of Mary, when she sat at the
Lord's feet, and " heard his words."   It is the spirit of Cor-
nelius, when he said, " Now, therefore, are we all here present before God, to hear all things that are commanded thee
of God."

To him who submits his understanding to divine teaching,—who, sensible of the many biassing and blinding influences to which he is subject, and by which his mind is in
danger of being perverted, looks humbly for promised illumination, and whose mind is disciplined to an implicit ac
quiescence in all that divine wisdom reveals:—to *him* " the
entrance of God's word will give light;"—and "knowledge
will be easy."   One truth will lead to another; and " the
word of Christ will dwell in him richly *in all wisdom.*"

But is not " *a scorner seeking wisdom*" a species of contradiction? We answer—in *one* sense it is. But words must be
understood as their connexion will bear. A " scorner seeking
wisdom," is a man inquiring after divine knowledge under
the influence of a spirit opposite to that we have been describing—a self-sufficient, critical, censorious, sneering spirit.   We may exemplify the difference by instancing the
case of those who came to Christ, in the days of his flesh,
with humble-minded desire of instruction, and that of those,
on the contrary, who came to him with questions, not for

the sake of information, but for the purpose of "entangling him in his talk," and of "catching something out of his mouth that they might accuse him." These were not inquiring learners, but prying and evil-minded "scorners."

The "scorner" is the man who has a high notion of his own understanding; an overweening conceit of himself; trusting "in himself that he is *right* and despising others;" determined to follow the dictates of his own vaunted reason; having formed his opinions, and holding in disdain whatever contradicts them, and whatever presumes to be above his comprehension;—measuring truth, even should it relate to the infinite God himself, by the line of his own capacity. Such a character, actuated by such a state of mind, may reject divine revelation altogether, and seek wisdom elsewhere without finding it:—or supposing him to have the conviction, from external evidence or from education, that in the Bible we have a revelation from God, he may, in such a frame of spirit, seek wisdom even *there* without finding it. The man is not in a state of mind to be satisfied with taking the truths made known in their simple and obvious meaning. He scorns that. He must have something of his own; something out of the common course; something that is the product of his own ingenuity and originality. And he who is determined to make something else of the discourses of the Bible than the language of it plainly expresses,—*will* succeed in misinterpreting and explaining them away.

Beware of this spirit. "Be ye not mockers, lest your bands be made strong"—the bands of ignorance and darkness, and a self-deluded heart. It was when the heathen "did not like to retain God in their knowledge," and preferred counsels of their own, "that God gave them over to a reprobate mind." It was when the followers of the man of sin "received not," when they had the opportunity, "the love of the truth that they might be saved," that God "gave them up to strong delusion, that they should believe a lie." It was when "Ephraim was joined to his idols," that God said, "Let him alone." It was when the Jews "heard and understood not, saw and perceived not," wilfully closing their ears and eyes to the truth of the messages of Jehovah, that Jehovah pronounced their sentence of judicial abandonment and blindness.

The poet's language is fearful but true :—

> " Hear the just doom, the judgment of the skies ;
> He that hates truth shall be the dupe of lies :—
> And he who *will* be cheated to the last,
> Delusions, strong as hell, shall bind him fast."

There is one who is called, by way of eminence, in the Bible, " THE FAITHFUL WITNESS." It is He by whom, in these last days, " God has spoken unto us ;" He " whose name is called the Word of God." All that he declares is *truth*— truth without mixture. He bears testimony for God ; and " we know that his testimony is true." He is true in his declarations, and true in his promises. His word is " not yea and nay." "All the promises of God in HIM are yea, and in HIM Amen !"

LECTURE XXXIII.

PROV. XIV. 7—12.

" Go from the presence of a foolish man, when thou perceivest not in him the lips of knowledge. The wisdom of the prudent is to understand his way: but the folly of fools is deceit. Fools make a mock at sin: but among the righteous there is favour. The heart knoweth his own bitterness; and a stranger doth not intermeddle with his joy. The house of the wicked shall be overthrown: but the tabernacle of the upright shall flourish. There is a way which seemeth right unto a man; but the end thereof are the ways of death."

THE counsel in the first of these verses might be enforced on both negative and positive grounds. First of all, the company and conversation of " *a foolish man* " can do you no good; you can derive *no profit* from it. At the best, therefore, the time spent in his society can be only time wasted and lost. But this is not the full amount of the reason. While he *can* do you *no good;* he *may* do you essential harm: for " the foolish " are the *unprincipled;* and the " *knowledge* " not found in their lips is especially the knowledge of the mind and will of God.—Be ye the " companions," as the Psalmist was, of " them who fear HIM." From such choose your associates. Let their society be the society you love. They say, " Come with us, and we will do you good." O comply with the invitation, if you would imbibe their spirit, learn their wisdom, and participate in their happiness.

True wisdom is *practical.* Thus here :—" The wisdom of the prudent is *to understand his way.*" He first of all estimates, according to their real worth, those abstruse or airy speculations, which terminate in nothing but diverting the attention of him who is fascinated by them from the consideration of the "*way*" which he ought to be pursuing. Every man has a way to go; has a department in life to fill up. It is "*wisdom*" to know how to do this with sense, with propriety, with safety, with honour, with advantage to self, with benefit to others. He who does not thus " understand his way," may have *knowledge,* but he has not *wisdom.*

And, to apply the words (as I cannot doubt they were meant to be applied) in the highest of all departments— every man has a *final destination* before him. The way of all is the way to the grave, and to eternity. But in that eternity in which the present short course must terminate, there are *two* widely differing states;—the one of perfect purity and perfect bliss, the other of growing sinfulness, and unmingled and unmitigated woe. To these opposite states there are *two* ways—" the narrow," and " the broad." O the infinite value of true wisdom here!—the wisdom that " understands" both ways, and rightly chooses between them!

" *But the folly of fools is deceit.*" These words may mean that the folly of fools *proves to them deceit.* They fancy and call it wisdom. But they impose upon themselves. Their confidence in it, and their expectations from it are sheer delusion, and this they will find by bitter experience in the end. Or the sense may be, " *Deceit* is the folly of fools." The truly wise and prudent man is an enemy to policy and craft. He is upright and straight-forward; ever acting up to our own established adage—that " *honesty is the best policy.*" Craft and policy mislead, entangle, and ruin men. They are " taken in their own craftiness." " New stratagems," says Lord Bacon, " must be devised, the old failing and growing useless; and as soon as ever a man hath got the name of a cunning crafty companion, he hath deprived himself utterly of the principal instrument for the management of his affairs,—which is *trust.*" *Policy,* therefore, on this as on other accounts, is " *the folly of fools.*"

Verse 9. " Fools make a mock at sin: but among the righteous there is favour." This verse has been differently rendered, and of course differently understood. The word for *sin* signifies either *the trespass* or the *guilt* involved in the trespass, and which exposes to penal consequences. Both at the sin, the guilt, and the consequence, "*fools make a mock.*"—The chief difficulty in the verse is the point of the antithesis in the two clauses of it. The general import, however, seems to be, that the friendship of wicked men, of scorners, and scoffers, is destitute of principle. You can have no dependence on the man who "makes a mock at sin;" and between men of this description there can be no lasting, sacred, confidential attachment. They feel that they can have no sure hold of each other, neither word nor deed being trustworthy. Between them mutual *esteem* cannot exist, there being nothing on either side on which such a sentiment can find a basis. On the contrary— "*Among,*" or *between* "*the righteous there is favour,*"—genuine, disinterested, benevolent regard,—attachment founded on principle, and respect for each other's character. In the former case, each knows the other's worthlessness; distrusts, and is distrusted; despises, and is despised. In the latter, there is mutual esteem. Each cleaves to the other in admiring and confiding affection.

The conduct of the man who "makes a mock at sin," involves *impiety, cruelty, and infatuation.*

1. That it involves *impiety* is sufficiently obvious. "Sin is the transgression of the law." It is contrariety to the divine holiness, opposition to the divine authority, ingratitude for the divine goodness, the object of the divine abhorrence, the declared and denounced subject of the divine curse and vengeance. To "mock at sin," therefore, is to despise God's holiness, to set at nought God's authority, to abuse God's goodness, to disregard and slight God's glory, to make light of God's curse and threatened vengeance; which implies a denial of God's truth and a scornful defiance of God's power. There cannot be a more profane insult on the infinite Majesty, than is involved in *every sin,* and especially in *mockery* at this worst of evils.

2. It involves *cruelty*—cruelty the most atrocious. The scoffer may be a *great* pretender to humanity and kind-

heartedness. But there breathes not on earth a more in-
human, a more iron-hearted monster, than the man who
"makes a mock at sin." He may profess to feel for the
miseries of mankind; for the ravages of disease and death
over their bodies; of fire and flood and storm over their
means of life and comfort; of melancholy, and idiocy, and

> "Moody madness, laughing wild
> Amid severest woe,"

over their minds; and the vast endless catalogue of ills by
which the lot of man in this world is afflicted. But he
"makes a mock" of that which is the *cause*, the prolific and
accursed cause of all. There is not an ill that man is called
to suffer, that does not owe its origin to SIN. Like the
"star called wormwood," in the Apocalyptic vision, it has
fallen on every "fountain and river" of human joy, turning
all their waters to bitterness. It is the sting of conscience.
It is the venom and barb of the darts of the king of terrors.
It is the very life of the "worm that dieth not." It is the
kindling and fuel of the flames of hell. Oh! the miserably
mistaken flattery, that can speak of the kind-heartedness
and humanity of the man who laughs at that which is the
embryo germ of all the sufferings of time, and all the woes
of eternity! Abuse not language thus. Assail not the unhappy wretch with irony so bitter. Call himself what he
will, he is "cruel as the grave," who "makes a mock at sin."

3. Such mockery is most *infatuated*. Sin is the evil that
is ruining the poor sinner himself—hurrying him to perdition.
It is the disease that, whether he is sensible of it or not, is
preying upon his own vitals, and must terminate in "the
second death." It is the secret consuming fire, that is wasting his eternal all. Sin has separated him from God. Sin
has doomed him to toil, to trouble, to sorrow, to death, and
to the grave. And sin will "destroy both soul and body in
hell." Yet the deluded victim of its power laughs at it—
"makes a mock" and a jest of it! O the infatuation, the
self-murderous madness of mocking at sin! Beware of it, my
hearers. It is mockery of God, mockery of all the sufferings

in the universe, mockery of your own damnation!—And let the mutual "favour" that subsists between the people of God, manifest itself in their keeping each other from sin; in their cherishing in each other's bosoms right impressions of its exceeding sinfulness, and such a holy dread and detestation of it, as shall lead them to seek, with all earnestness and assiduity, its crucifixion and destruction in themselves, in one another, and in all around them!*

Verse 10. "The heart knoweth his own bitterness; and a stranger doth not intermeddle with his joy." We may connect this verse with the preceding; and in this connexion, it naturally suggests the thought of the "bitterness" of a spirit wounded by the accusations of conscience—the stings keen and rankling, of remorse; of the inward, secret, dark anticipations of death and judgment, hell and eternity, unacknowledged, but acutely felt by the fools who "make a mock at sin." His mockings are many a time but the flimsy cover of a spirit ill at ease, and the poor expedient for alleviating for the moment the "bitterness" which his own heart alone knows, and which he is proudly anxious to conceal. And this may be contrasted with the heartfelt "*joy*" of the righteous—"the joy of the Lord"—the joy of God's salvation—the "peace that passeth all understanding,"—the delightful sense of God's pardoning mercy and paternal love—the cheering "hope of glory, honour, and immortality."

Or the words may be taken more generally, as expressing a distinct and independent sentiment.—We are not competent judges either of the happiness or the *un*happiness of others. The sentiment is emphatically true of the latter. All is not happiness that bears the semblance of it. How often are there secret griefs concealed in the inner chambers of the heart, and engendering there a "bitterness" unknown

---

* The verse has been rendered, "Sin-offering mocks fools; but among the upright there is ready acceptance," the meaning being, that "when sin-offering is presented formally by fools, it mocks their hopes because it is not accepted;" whereas the offerings of the upright "find *good will*, that is, ready acceptance." Some consider that the structure of the Hebrew sentence makes this rendering imperative. Be this as it may, it in no way affects the solemn truth so forcibly illustrated.

but by him who feels it! How often are fondly cherished desires and hopes frustrated!—and, as no one knew the sweetness of the sanguine anticipation, no one can duly estimate the "bitterness" of the disappointment. How many circumstances are there which give special poignancy to sorrow which another cannot appreciate! The remark might be illustrated from the feelings that arise out of the peculiar *relations* of life. Who but a parent can fully know the " bitterness " of his grief who " mourneth for an only son " —of him who is "in bitterness for his first-born!" O, who but a parent can sympathise with the " bitterness " of the royal mourner's anguish, when over a son that had died in rebellion against his father, and his God, he exclaimed, " O my son Absalom, my son, my son Absalom! would God I had died for thee, O Absalom, my son, my son!" Who but a widow can realize the exquisite " bitterness " of a widow's agony, when bereft of the loved partner of her joys and sorrows, her cares and her comforts ; and when gazing with tearful eye and bleeding heart on her fatherless babes! Who but a pastor can know, in all its intensity, the " bitterness " of soul experienced in seeing those on whom he counted as genuine fruits of his ministry, and on whom he looked with delighted interest, as his anticipated " joy and crown " in " the day of the Lord," falling away—" going back and walking no more with Jesus!"—the " blossom of his hopes going up as dust," or ripening into the " fruits of Sodom and the clusters of Gomorrah!"

But still, amid all descriptions of secret woe—of heart-felt and heart-hidden " bitterness," the child and servant of God possesses " a joy " with which " a stranger doth not intermeddle." It is a joy imparted to the heart by the Spirit of God. It is many a time most sweetly and exquisitely felt, when other joys are withdrawn,—when the springs of earthly pleasure are stinted or dried. The world cannot give it ; nor can the world, blessed be God! take it away. Who?—what " stranger?"—what creature, in heaven, earth, or hell—can " intermeddle with the joy " of the believer, when, in the darkest and most desolate of the hours that pass over him—his

dearest joys all swept away and his fairest hopes blasted,—he
can still sit down and sing, "Though the fig-tree shall not
blossom, neither shall fruit be in the vines; the labour of
the olive shall fail, and the fields shall yield no meat; the
flock shall be cut off from the fold, and there shall be
no herd in the stalls: yet I will rejoice in the Lord, I will
joy in the God of my salvation?" Hab. iii. 17.

The language may also be applied to the gracious and
divinely awakened convictions of sin, and the secret anguish
thence arising, when the conscience is aroused, the "heart
pricked," and the cry of distress wrung from the inmost soul,
" What shall we do?"—and to the peace and joy, contrasted
with this, which arise from the spiritual discernment of the
gospel, in the freeness and richness of its grace, and the
adaptation of its provisions to all the sinner's exigencies—

> " When in that trembling sinner's view
>   The wonders of the cross arise,
>   His agonizing fears subdue,
>   And change to joy his hopeless sighs."

In the verse following, the " *house* of the wicked " stands
in contrast with the " *tabernacle* of the upright." The one
may be a palace, the other a hut; but, as we had occasion
before to remark, the lowly mud-walled cottage of the pious
poor is, with the blessing of heaven abiding under its roof
and resting on its inmates, incomparably better than the
splendid and spacious mansion of the man of the world,
who is living without God, and enjoys not His favour and
love :—" The house of the wicked shall be overthrown ; but
the tabernacle of the upright shall flourish." *

Verse 12. " There is a way which seemeth right unto a
man; but the end thereof are the ways of death." There are
some ways which can hardly " *seem right* " to any man,—
the ways, namely, of open and flagrant wickedness :—although
even in these the presumptuous sinner may delude himself,
with false, self-flattering views of the divine mercy,—fondly
assuring himself that God will not be hard upon him, and

---

* Compare chap. xiii. 33; xii. 9.

that all, no doubt, will be well at last !   But many are the ways which, under the biassing influence of pride and corruption, "*seem* right," and yet their "*end*" is "*death.*"

There is the way of the *sober, well-behaved worldling.* He thinks of the law as if it had but one table, the first being entirely overlooked.   He passes among his circle for a man of good character.   He flatters himself in proportion as he is flattered by others, that all is right, and that there is no fear of him.   And yet he lives "without God"—a stranger to the spiritual feelings and exercises of a renewed heart; without regard to the divine authority as his rule, the divine glory as his end, the divine love as his motive, the divine blessing as his portion.   And, with all his earth-born virtues, goes down to the grave " with a lie in his right hand."   His way " seems right;" but it is not the way of life, for GOD is not in it.

There is the way of the *formalist.*   He follows, strictly and punctually, the routine of external religious observance. He reads his Bible.   He goes pretty regularly to church and sacrament.   He maintains, perhaps, " by tradition from his fathers," a form of family worship, and even, possibly says a prayer when he rises, and when he goes to bed.   But his heart has not been given to God.   The world still has it. He compromises the retention of its affections for the things of the world and of sense, by giving to God the pitiful and worthless offering of outward homage.   It will not do.   The services cannot *terminate in life,* which *have no life in them.* The way of mere form is the " way of death."

There is the way of the *religious speculatist*—or *the speculative religionist.*   From education, or as a matter of curiosity, he has made himself an adept in theological controversy —especially, it may be, in the particular questions of the day.   He holds by the creed of orthodoxy, and is ready-armed at all points in its defence : and he imagines that this kind of knowledge is religion.   " His way seems right to him."   And yet there may not be in all his knowledge and in all his talk one atom of religion—one " vital spark " of its "heavenly flame."   The heart may not be touched—

I.   2 B

neither warmed nor purified in any one of its affections; nor the conscience rendered sensitive and tender in its submission to the dictates of the divine will. Speculative opinion is not saving knowledge;—is not the faith which "worketh by love" and "overcomes the world." It is not the way of spiritual life; and the "end thereof are the ways of death."

There is the way of the *self-righteous*. It is, we shall suppose, a combination of all the other three—of sobriety, formality, and knowledge,—and of self-confidence thence arising. Such was the way of the Pharisees in Christ's time; on whom, notwithstanding their high pretensions, he de- nounces the heaviest and most terrific woes. And such was the way of the unbelieving Jews of that age more generally; of whom Paul in his Epistle to the Romans presents such a graphic and powerful description.*

In the "way which seemeth right unto a man" may be comprehended, in short, all that bears the semblance of re- ligion and may be mistaken for it, but *is not the reality*. The "*end*" of everything of *this* kind is and must be "the way of death."

GOD's way must be the *only right way*. It is, we re- mind you anew, the way of faith and obedience; of faith pro- ducing obedience—of obedience springing from faith. The way to heaven—the way of life, is measured from CALVARY. From the foot of the cross alone can any sinner set out in it. The course of holy obedience commences with the acceptance of mercy *there*. It is there, through faith in atoning blood and mediatorial righteousness, that the sinner is freed from the burden of conscious guilt and heart-sinking fear; and thence, under the spring and elasticity of a light and joyful heart, he starts in "the narrow way"—the one and only divinely provided way to heaven. "I AM THE WAY," says Jesus; "NO MAN COMETH UNTO THE FATHER BUT BY ME."

---

* Romans ii. 17—24.

LECTURE XXXIV

———◆———

Prov. xiv. 13—24.

" Even in laughter the heart is sorrowful; and the end of that mirth is heaviness. The backslider in heart shall be filled with his own ways: and a good man shall be satisfied from himself. The simple believeth every word: but the prudent man looketh well to his going. A wise man feareth, and departeth from evil: but the fool rageth, and is confident. He that is soon angry dealeth foolishly; and a man of wicked devices is hated. The simple inherit folly: but the prudent are crowned with knowledge. The evil bow before the good; and the wicked at the gates of the righteous. The poor is hated even of his own neighbour: but the rich hath many friends. He that despiseth his neighbour sinneth: but he that hath mercy on the poor, happy is he. Do they not err that devise evil? but mercy and truth shall be to them that devise good. In all labour there is profit: but the talk of the lips tendeth only to penury. The crown of the wise is their riches: but the foolishness of fools is folly."

It is, at times, unavoidable, and all but a duty, to assume external appearances not quite in harmony with inward feelings. For the sake of his company, a man is often obliged to keep his secret sorrows in abeyance, and to *seem* cheerful when in reality his heart is depressed and sad; and often, from the painful effort it costs to maintain the semblance of a joyous spirit, deeper is the dejection into which he sinks. Even thus, "*in laughter the heart is sorrowful; and the end of that mirth is heaviness.*"

But such is not the case here intended. The " laughter " is that of *violent and boisterous merriment*—what Solomon elsewhere calls " the laughter of the fool.* And well might he

———

* Eccl. vii. 6.

say of such laughter—the laughter of intemperate mirth—
"it is mad." In such a world as this,—in such a condition
as that of fallen man, and with such prospects before him,
it becomes a species of *insanity*. It is often, Solomon
alleges, but the veil of a heart ill at ease—a heart fretted
by the stings of an accusing conscience, and oppressed with
the forebodings of futurity which conscious guilt engenders.
The jovial merriment of the social board is courted for the
very purpose of repressing these—of drowning care, and
silencing the inward monitor, whose voice, in solitude and
quietness, is too well heard for the sinner's peace. When
the glass, and the jest, and the laugh go round, there is a
partial, and to others it may seem an entire suspension of
these inward gnawings and secret fears. But even then the
success is seldom complete. Could you look within; could
you see the inner depths of the sinner's heart—you might
find there something widely different from what outward
appearances indicate. You might find the begun tortures
of the undying worm, and real sadness in the very midst of
the most boisterous revelry.—And when left to himself;
when the song and the glass, the joke and the laugh have
ceased with the breaking up of the company, and solitude
and reflection follow, how emphatically true—"*the end of
that mirth is heaviness!*"

And may we not apply the words to the case of the deluded sinner, who attempts to be jocular and merry even on
the bed of death? Ah! surely, in such a case, the lips and
the heart belie each other. Jesting and levity, in these circumstances can be only the symptoms, while they are the
attempted concealments, of internal disquietude. This is
what we might naturally and fairly suspect; and many a
confession, from those who have been brought back from the
gates of death, and have subsequently come to a better mind,
has confirmed the suspicion into certainty. There can be
nothing more out of all reason,—nothing more affecting and
shocking to every pious, and even to every soberly-thinking
mind. Emphatically might it be said of *such* mirth—"it is
mad." Even were the system of infidelity and annihilation

true, the very thought, were there no more, of the final and irrecoverable extinction of conscious being, might be enough to render any man at least thoughtful and serious.

O how different from the "laughter" and "mirth" of the men of this world *the joy of the Christian!* that cheerful serenity of soul—that inward sunshine, which diffuses on every hand its benign and smiling influence!

What was before affirmed respecting the wicked and impenitent generally, is in the next verse affirmed specially of "*the backslider*"—of him who has "left his first love," and declined from the ways of God—"The backslider in heart shall be filled with his own ways: and a good man shall be satisfied from himself."

Temporary backsliding may take place in the true children of God; but the "backslider" *here* is evidently he who, in the language of the Apostle, "goes back unto perdition." Solomon alludes to such "*perpetual* backsliding" on the part of those who thus prove themselves to have been no more than professors—"having the form of godliness, but denying the power thereof." Such characters, whatever appearances they present to the eyes of men,—even of the people of God, with whom they associate, never were vitally and savingly one with Christ, and one with true believers in Him. This is as plainly affirmed as it is in the power of language to affirm it: "They went out from us, but they were not of us; for if they had been of us, they would no doubt have continued with us: but they went out, that they might be made manifest that they were not all of us," 1 John ii. 19. It is of *such* characters, therefore, that we must interpret other passages that describe final and fatal backsliding.*—O let professors be upon their guard; jealous of themselves; "keeping their hearts with all diligence;" "working out their own salvation with fear and trembling;" "building themselves up on their most holy faith." Let them ever remember, there may be a great deal of what Solomon here calls "backsliding *in heart*," that does

* As Heb. x. 26—30: 2 Pet. ii. 20—22.

not discover itself to the view of others in the outward conduct:—a declension in the inward vitality of true godliness,—a deadening of the tender sensibilities of the new nature,—the sensitiveness of conscience, the warmth and interest of heart in spiritual things. And backsliding, though temporary and partial, will be the occasion of severe though salutary correction, and bitter distress of soul. Thus it was in David's case; and thus it was in Peter's. And the general threatening from the Lord is, "Thine own wickedness shall correct thee, and thy backslidings shall reprove thee: know therefore and see that it is an evil thing and bitter, that thou hast forsaken the Lord thy God, and that my fear is not in thee, saith the Lord God of hosts," Jer. ii. 19. Even when restored, "the backslider" is "*filled with his own ways.*" He returns through the valley of humiliation, with a burdened, aching, broken spirit, and may, as the merited result of his sin, be allowed to go mourning many a weary day in the bitterness of his soul. Of the *final* apostate the doom is the most fearful of all that the word of God describes.

Mark the antithesis:—"The backslider in heart *shall be filled* with his own ways; and a good man from himself." For the supplement "*shall be satisfied*" there is no need. "*From himself,*" some would render "from *above* himself," and refer it to his receiving *from God,* from the divine fulness of blessing and grace. This, however, though the original may bear it, seems rather a straining, to insure orthodoxy. It is unnecessary. For as "the backslider" is he who *departs from God,* the "good man" is he who *cleaves to God;* and as the one is "filled with his own ways," in their sad results, so are there in "the good man"—in his heart, and in his ways, which are the ways of God,—springs of true satisfaction and delight. He enjoys present happiness,—flowing from a sanctified state of mind; from the holy exercise of its renewed affections; from what the Apostle declares to have been *his* rejoicing, "the testimony of conscience" to the "simplicity and godly sincerity" of his conduct; from growing evidence of interest in the salvation of God, and in the well-founded hope of eternal life; and from the pleasure, pure and blessed, of pious and benevolent deeds. And, when he acts under the influence of Gospel principles, —having learned what it is to renounce self and to serve God from grateful love and glad devotedness,—he knows that "God is not unrighteous to forget his work and labour of love;" that He will own all at last, and say to every one who, instead of backsliding and apostatizing, perseveres in the right course, "Well done, good and faithful servant: thou hast been faithful over a few things, I will make thee ruler over many things: enter thou into the joy of thy Lord!"

Verse 15. "The simple believeth every word: but the prudent man looketh well to his going."

The words may first be applied to the *concerns of the present world*. "*The simple*"—the thoughtless and inconsiderate, are easily imposed upon by the specious and the artful—by their plausible representations, their confident protestations and assurances, their flattering and fawning speeches, insinuating address, and fair and ample promises. Possessing no depth of discernment for the discrimination of character, and no steadiness of observation and comparison to enable them to profit by experience, they are credulous of all. This is a very different thing from the "*charity* which *believeth all things*." Charity, assuredly, should be more prone to believe good than evil, and ever disposed, where two views present themselves of any case, to credit that most favourable to the character of another;—but *not against evidence;* not so as to flatter any one into a false conception of his spiritual state, or even of his temporal affairs. What we have here described is the *credulity* of the *simple*, not the *candour* of the *charitable*.

Now "the simple," on finding himself often deceived and imposed upon, and thus injured by those in whom he unwittingly confided—"believing every word"—not unfrequently degenerates into the contrary extreme. He has his temper fretted and soured. He becomes universally and without distinction distrustful. From having, in his simplicity, taken the word of all men for honesty and truth, he comes to reckon all men cheats, liars, rogues; and appears in the wretched character of an imbittered, jealous, all-suspecting misanthrope.

"*But the prudent man looketh well to his going.*" We may liken "the prudent man," when at all in perplexity, to an intelligent traveller who has lost his way, or is not at least *sure* of it. He reflects. He brings before his mind the relative positions of places,—the time of the day with the direction of the sun in the heaven; and, laying all things together, considers which of two or three roads is the most likely to conduct him to his destination. Or, if he is in possession of a map, he examines it for his guidance. He does not, like "the simple," strike at once into the first way that offers itself, or choose without thought, or rashly take the advice of any one who may chance to give it him. In every matter of importance, he "looks well to his going;" first to *find* the right way, and next to *keep* it.*

We may apply the verse, in all its emphasis of meaning, to *eternal concerns.*—"The simple" hear different persons on the subject of religion, and take it for granted that all they hear is right. They are easily bewildered by sophistical arguments; led away by appeals to feeling; swayed and mastered by false eloquence; seduced by flattering assurances, palatable to the selfishness of the heart. They get thus entangled in error and delusion, or in a strange confused jumble of error and truth, between which they have no clear discernment. They are the sport of all that is novel—"tossed to and fro, and carried about with every wind of doctrine." On the contrary, when interests so vast are at stake, as those of the whole man, body and soul, for an interminable existence, the "*prudent* man" will inquire earnestly and cautiously; will feel his way; will ponder every step; will deliberately examine every statement, and every argument, taking nothing upon trust. He first bends his earnest thought to the question of the divine authority of the Bible—a question next in importance to that of the being of God; and having ascertained its authority,

---

* Comp. chap. iv. 26.

he will go to it, with humble-minded candour and anxiety,
to learn its lessons. Having the map, he will examine for
himself the way to heaven as there delineated. Having a
divine directory, he will trust no human guide.

Verse 16. "A wise man feareth, and departeth from evil:
but the fool rageth, and is confident." In this verse, the
evil from which the "wise man departeth," may mean either
suffering or *sin*. Both may with propriety be included, the
one being the cause of the other—all suffering having its
origin in sin.

We might take the maxim as only a further illustration
of *prudence* and *folly*. Thus, in regard to temporal evils,
the wise man estimates aright the magnitude of the mischief
and the degree of the danger; and, by discreet precaution,
shuns impending harm. The fool, on the contrary, sees no
danger; dreads no harm; pushes recklessly forward, and falls
into mischief. The wise man, again, will take, and will profit
by a hint of caution and friendly direction or dissuasion;
but the fool, in his self-sufficiency, is impatient of every
thing of the kind. He resents it, as implying a reflection
on his own penetration. He takes it short and high. He
breaks out into passion—as if, forsooth, *he* could not see
that! He calls the adviser, how modestly soever he may
have ventured the hint, officious, vain, forward, pragmatical.
He frets and blusters. And though sensible of the goodness of the advice, he will go directly against it rather than
appear to act by the counsel of another. He prefers being
wrong in his own way to being right in another man's. *He*
"*rageth, and is confident.*"

Then, with regard to *evil* in the sense of *sin*. Set before
the considerate—"prudent" man the nature and extent of
its consequences,—its fearful results—here and hereafter—
present and eternal—he thinks, he pauses, he trembles, he
"departs from it." If sin is brought home to his conscience,
he confesses and forsakes it. The fool, on the other hand,
spurns all restraint. He is provoked and offended by every
thing in the form of prohibition or threatening. The very
commands of God irritate him. He foams, and winces, and

champs the bit that checks him in his wild career. The
secret stings of conscience goad him to madness. He is
galled and chafed by the suggestions of this inward monitor,
but not held back. He is only driven to pursue sin with
the more headstrong and frantic avidity. Reproof is like a
spark struck amongst combustibles. The man's irritable
passions are inflamed; and, in return for the reproof how
gently and kindly soever administered, he only repeats the
sin in word or act, whatever it may happen to be, with
strong manifestations of displeasure at the presumption that
has ventured to find fault,—repeats it in an aggravated
form, from pure spite and passion. He "*rageth, and is
confident.*" Thus too it often is when any one hints at the
danger of the way in which he is expecting salvation, and
presumes to recommend another—even when the hint is
given from an avowed and heart-felt solicitude for the welfare of his soul and his eternal happiness. "What business,"
he mutters, "have people with me and my soul? Let them
mind their own, and leave me to mind mine; impertinent
intermeddlers with matters they have nothing to do with!—
every man's religion is his own concern!" And thus, the very
presumption, as he regards it, that would set him right, con-
firms him in wrong. He "rageth, and is confident." Suppose
he *is* on the way to hell—that is his own concern; and if he
chooses to keep that way, who has a right to hinder him?—
No one certainly, poor sinner. But neither have you a right
to hinder us from wishing you well;—*that is all.* It is duty
to give you the counsel, whether you hear or forbear. And
when you angrily adopt the poet's words, and say—

> " 'Twere well, would you permit the world to live
>   As the world chooses;—what's the world to you?"

we might adopt the poet's answer—claiming kindred and
brotherhood with you, and insisting on the privilege of
kindred love. You surely cannot but approve the conduct
of the servants of *Naaman*, when their master on receiving
the prophet's order—" Go, wash in Jordan seven times, and
thy flesh shall come again to thee, and thou shalt be clean,"

—"raged and was confident," saying, "Behold, I thought, He will surely come out to me, and stand, and call on the name of the Lord his God, and strike his hand over the place, and recover the leper." "My father," said these decreet counsellors, "if the prophet had bidden thee do some great thing, wouldst thou not have done it? how much rather then, when he saith to thee, Wash, and be clean." Now this is all we would say to you. We point you to the divinely appointed remedy for the deadly malady of sin, common to you with us all, and entreat you to avail yourselves of it. If you *will* "rage and be confident;" if you *will* rather retain the distemper and die eternally than be cured by any other means than your own; if you *will* prefer going to hell in your own way than to heaven in God's way—we cannot help it; we have delivered our own souls, and are clear of your blood: but you cannot prevent our still pitying and praying for you!

Verse 17. "He that is soon angry dealeth foolishly: and a man of wicked devices is hated."

In the Septuagint Greek the verse is otherwise rendered, but without sufficient reason. The antithesis, as it stands in our own translation, which appears faithful to the Hebrew text, is abundantly manifest.

"*Foolish*" indeed is the conduct of the man of a quick, touchy, irritable temper. O! what would the irascible man many a time give to have his hasty words recalled!—His anger, however, vents itself in the vehement bluster of the moment. He utters rash and mischievous things, it may be; but people come to know him, and to appreciate these. His burst of passion is quickly over. The storm soon spends itself. The calm returns; and perhaps an apology for his haste and violence. How troublesome and unpleasant soever such a temper may be, it is not to be compared with that of the "*man of wicked devices*,"—the man, that is, who studiously conceals and covers up his passion; broods over it; nourishes and cherishes it in the secret recesses of his bosom; waits his most favourable time for vengeance; watches, and contrives plans of retaliation; and all the while, perhaps, shows no external symptoms of the internal ferment, but

possibly assumes the very opposite—is all smiles and
courtesy. Than such a character none is more odious; and
it is dangerous as it is odious. Such a character cannot
but be "*hated.*"

In the following verse, *simplicity* and *prudence* are again
presented in a somewhat fresh point of contrast. "The simple
inherit jolly." This means not, as some would have it,
that folly is theirs *by hereditary possession,* as part of the
heritage of their fallen nature; but that through their inconsiderate and vacant listlessness, folly becomes their patri-
mony—with its full train of serious consequences—scorn,
perpetual imposition, deranged affairs, distress and calamity,
bankruptcy and ruin. The very designation of *fool* is the
inheritance of the thoughtless simpleton, with all the
derision that accompanies it. He stands as a neglected
cipher in the intercourse of life, or becomes the dupe of every
unprincipled deceiver.—On the contrary, "*the prudent are
crowned with knowledge.*" They acquire knowledge; and
this knowledge becomes their *crown.* It brings them respect
and honour; advances and elevates them in society.

The language, as in other cases, is equally true of the interests of the world to come. "The *simple*"—*careless sinners,* who pursue heedlessly "the course of this present world;"
who disregard the gospel message, "the word of truth and
love;" who, if hearing it at all, hear it with an ear between
which and the mind the avenue is closed—in the end "*inherit folly.*" All they find awaiting them as their portion, is
the exposure of their folly, by the verdict of Heaven, before
the assembled world,—with the "shame and everlasting contempt" which is the necessary consequence. While the "*prudent*"—the truly thoughtful and wise in heart—are raised
to the most exalted honour—honour far transcending what
belongs to earth; have placed on their brows a diadem of
glory—the "crown of life that fadeth not away:"—all the
result of that divine "knowledge" to which they lent a willing ear, and welcomed to their hearts. "For this is life eternal
to know thee, the only true God, and Jesus Christ, whom
thou hast sent."

Verse 19. "The evil bow before the good : and the wicked at the gates of the righteous."

All that Solomon intends by this language, so far as what is merely *temporal* is concerned, is, that not seldom the real, sterling superiority of righteousness and goodness over vice and impiety is made apparent. It does frequently happen, that "*the wicked*," by whom "*the righteous*" were scorned, have come, by a reverse of circumstances, to feel their need of their counsel and aid; to feel the excellence of that which they had contemned—the true nobility of goodness. They have been fain to have recourse to them; to fawn where they had despised; to cringe at the gate of those from whom they would have withheld even a passing look; to petition where dependence would have been disdained, and the very proposal of application for help resented as an insult.

Such instances may be only occasional, but the superiority of the righteous to the wicked is *universal*. And its universality will appear in the " judgment of the great day,"—the day when the light of eternity shall be thrown upon the honours and the possessions of time. O the agonizing regret with which the miserable mistakes of the past will *then* be recollected!—and how utterly will every thought be absorbed in the awful present and the still more awful future —the *eternal* future!

Verses 20, 21. "The poor is hated even of his own neighbour : but the rich hath many friends. He that despiseth his neighbour sinneth : but he that hath mercy on the poor, happy is he."—Taking these two verses together, the connexion shows that the former of the two is not to be understood as if by *all* his neighbours in every case, the poor were hated. Those there are who " have mercy on the poor," and who are sensible that to "despise " them is to be guilty of sin. But, alas! for the selfishness of human nature!—the case supposed, and the principle involved in it, are far from rare. From the poor there is *nothing to be got*. There is not only no share of property to be had from them, by any process of attention and flattery, but no respectability; no distinction arising out of any connexion with them. Nay, even to be seen in their company is to insure being shunned by all who love the honours of the world, and are set upon what the world calls good society.—"*The rich hath many friends.*" There is keen satire in these words; but there is no slander. They are words of truth.   The rich have friends, on both the accounts mentioned—interest and honour.   If they are bountiful, the friends they have are not those who are attracted by the admiration of their benevolence, and become attached to them from love to their amiable and generous spirit.   They are the friends who are drawn around them by the hope of sharing in the plunder—of getting something by it—profiting by their generosity and profusion—ever studious to please, and ever hinting, broadly or otherwise as circumstances may require.   They are friends, not of the *man*, but of his *table and of his purse*.   And if the rich man be a *miser*, his friends are his *hangers-on*, his *parasites*—persevering in attentions, fawning, flattering, accommodating, submitting to any indignity, patient of contradiction and insult, anticipating every wish, watching every look, running on every service; and all without one solitary feeling of real regard to aught else whatever but the *coffers and the lands*.

The spirit of the former of the verses is many a time very affectingly exemplified in the case of persons who have been reduced from affluence to poverty by sudden or gradual reverses.   How many, in these circumstances, prove, as good Matthew Henry calls them, "swallow-friends, that leave in winter."   They become shy of him to whom they had paid court.   They find out plausible excuses for avoiding his company, and withdrawing from his house.   They put the best face upon it they can, while every one sees the true cause. Poverty has stripped off all the former attractions.   There is no longer anything to be had.   Their friendship thus ceases at the very moment when it comes to be most needed.—Let not the blame of desertion, however, be put down, without exception, to this score.   It does sometimes happen, that persons who are reduced in their circumstances act in such a manner as to bring upon themselves the very desertion and neglect, of which they subsequently complain, and which they are fond to impute, with real or affected self-complacency, to the pride, and selfishness, and insensibility of others,—casting severe reflections on those by whom they are forsaken, when the fault lies entirely with themselves; when, by their unbecoming temper and behaviour, they have driven off those by whom they might otherwise have been befriended and succoured.

A *selfish* spirit, however, when that leads to the conduct described, is always a *sinful* spirit. "He that despiseth his neighbour"—his *poor* neighbour, "*sinneth*"—sinneth *against God.* There is sin against the arrangements of His providence. There is sin against the frequent and express commands of His word.* There is sin against the manifestations of His distinguishing love: for God has not only, in the strongest terms, avowed himself jealous for the poor, making their interests his own; but "to the poor the gospel is preached," and of those who become the subjects of God's grace, and heirs of glory, a large proportion belong to this class.† And, finally, there is sin in the contempt at once of God's threatened vengeance against all who treat the poor with neglect or cruelty, and of His promised special favour to all who treat them with kindness and generous sympathy.

"He that despiseth his (poor) neighbour *sinneth;*" and in *sin* there can be *no happiness.* Hence the force of the antithesis—"He who hath mercy on the poor, *happy is he.*" "Happy is he," for his conduct is *obedience* to God's command;—and in "the keeping of his commandments there is a great reward." "Happy is he," for he hears a voice saying—"Is not this the fast that I have chosen, to deal thy bread to the hungry, and that thou bring the poor that are cast out to thy house; when thou seest the naked, that thou cover him; and that thou hide not thyself from thine own flesh? Then shall thy light break forth as the morning, and thine health shall spring forth speedily: and thy righteousness shall go before thee; the glory of the Lord shall be thy rere-ward. Then shalt thou

---

* Comp. Deut. xv. 7—11; Luke xii. 33; xiv. 12—14.
† See James ii. 5—7.

call, and the Lord shall answer; thou shalt cry, and he shall say, Here I am. . . . The Lord shall guide thee continually, and satisfy thy soul in drought, and make fat thy bones: and thou shalt be like a watered garden, and like a spring of water, whose waters fail not." He is " happy " also because of the pleasure found in the gratification of the benevolent affections—God having so constituted our nature, that in proportion as it is delivered from the disturbing forces of corruption, and restored to its original rectitude, it derives enjoyment from the exercise of kindness. " Happy is he," in a word, for he is GOD-LIKE—like HIM whose bounty supplies the universe.

Verse 22. " Do they not err that devise evil? but mercy and truth shall be to them that devise good." This may still be applied to *the poor.** They who thus "*devise evil*" against the poor do egregiously err, if they expect to prosper. The hidden curse of God is upon them. But the verse may be understood *more generally*—of the " devising of evil," of whatever kind, and from whatever motive, whether of malice, resentment, envy, avarice, or ambition. To him who "*devises good*"—who lays himself out in planning and executing designs of benefit to others, there shall be " *mercy and truth.*" From his fellow-men he shall experience universal love and esteem. He shall find sympathy in his distresses and reverses, faithfulness in dealing (for if anything will secure a man from being cheated and defrauded, it will be a character for disinterested kindness, tenderness, and liberality) and the general exercise of practical gratitude. And the LORD will make him to experience His love, and will fulfil to him faithfully all His " precious promises."

Verse 23. " In all labour there is profit: but the talk of the lips tendeth only to penury." It must be obvious that by "*the talk of the lips*" is to be understood, not the legitimate use of the powers of speech in professional business. This, of course, comes under the description of the "labour in which *there is profit.*" The reference is to vain, idle,

---

* Comp. Isa. xxxii. 6—8.

empty talk—useless gossip. The character is that of the man whose tongue is ever in motion; who is uneasy till he gets some one on whom to inflict his prosings or his frothy tattle. He goes in quest of such. He gets them inveigled to hear him. He stands or sits idle with them. His work and his family are neglected. The great talker is seldom a great worker. A busy tongue makes idle hands. If the mouth *will* be heard, the noisy loom must stop; and he who prefers the sound of his tongue to that of his shuttle, had need, at the same time, to be a man who prefers talk to meat, hunger to fulness, starvation to plenty. The husband's words will neither make into food nor clothing. Back and belly must alike starve: such talk "*tendeth only to penury.*"

Verse 24. "The crown of the wise is their riches: but the foolishness of fools is folly." The meaning of the first clause is obvious. When a wise man has "*riches,*" it is a part of his wisdom to know the proper use of them: and by putting them to that use,—by doing with them all the good in his power, they become a *crown* to him. He thus frames for himself a diadem of beauty more truly glorious than if the most exquisite skill were expended in working up all his gold and jewels into one as rich and costly as ever adorned a monarch's brow. O what is the most gorgeous and dazzling earthly crown compared with a diadem of which the component parts are the blessings of the destitute relieved, the ignorant instructed, the vicious reclaimed, the afflicted comforted, the dying cheered with the hope of life, the perishing rescued from perdition and brought to God! This is a royal crown indeed!

"*The foolishness of fools is folly,*" is an expression which, taken by itself, might simply signify, that place a fool in any variety of circumstances, he will still identify himself; his "foolishness" will still be "folly"—never long-concealed: while it is folly, in regard to its ultimate product, to himself as well as to others. Of no benefit to his fellow-men, it leaves him in a fool's plight at last. Ah! surely that "foolishness is folly" indeed, of which this is the termination!

But it cannot fail to strike you, that there is no direct antithesis between the one clause of the verse and the other; there being no reference to "*riches*" in the latter, as there is in the former. To remove this defect, it has been conceived by some that in the latter part of the verse there is what critics call a *paronomasia;* the same assortment of letters having two significations, equally arising out of the primary meaning of the root—the one, *fulness* or *wealth,* and the other *grossness, stupidity,* or *folly.* It will then read—"but the *fulness* of fools, or the *wealth* of fools, is *folly;*"—and what may be called the play on the words has been successfully enough imitated in English—"but the *abundance* of fools is *abundant folly.*" The sentiment will thus be, that while, by the use of his riches, the wise man converts them into a crown of glory, the possession of riches by the fool only *augments his folly,* by giving him new and more varied means and opportunities of displaying it. His wealth puffs him up. His foolish and weak mind is inflated by it; and, in the littleness of his vanity, and the trifling, ostentatious, or absurd uses to which he applies his ill-bestowed abundance, he only renders himself the more a fool.

In conclusion, let Christians, rich and poor, seek grace so to regulate their whole course that they may put honour upon the Son of God, and that "the word of God and his doctrine be not blasphemed." Beautiful is it to see, in all situations, the happy influence of right principle—the faith of divine truth showing itself in appropriate conduct; and appropriate conduct avowing its originating and guiding principle in the faith of divine truth! This is "holding forth the word of life."

OTHER FINE VOLUMES AVAILABLE

1980-81

TITLES CURRENTLY AVAILABLE